DOLLAR APOCALYPSE

Survival Guide for the Next Great Depression

David Bates & Claude Davis

Published by GLOBAL BROTHER.

SORRY!
WE'RE OUT OF
GAS TODAY

TABLE OF CONTENTS

out of order

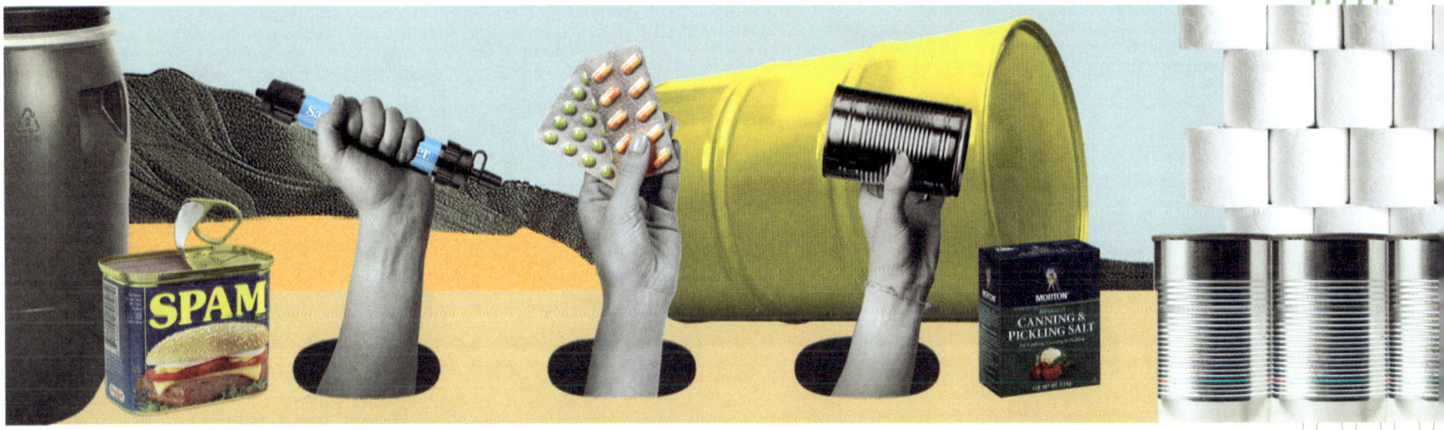

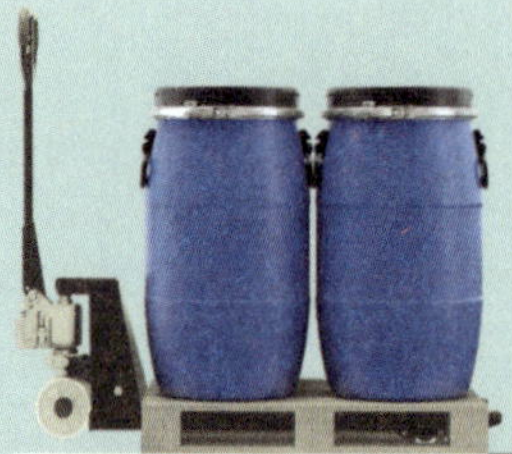

nomy Collapses

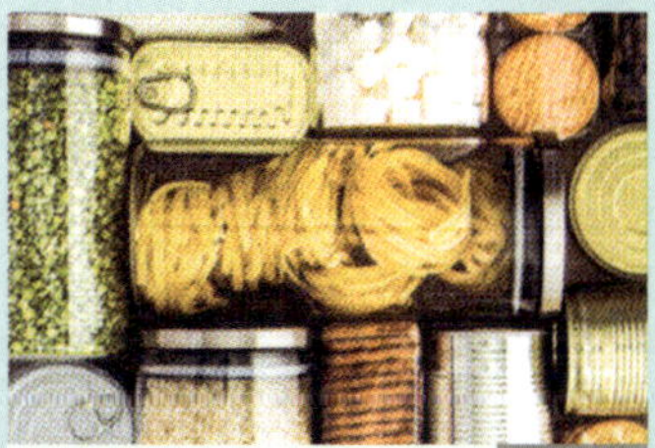

on the Day the Eco

DISCLAIMER

The information presented in this book, including but not limited to natural and medicinal remedies, food and prepping solutions, historical and social data, financial and economic information, and security details, is provided for general informational and educational purposes only. It is not intended as, nor should it be construed as, medical, financial, legal, or other professional advice.

This book has not been created to be specific to any individual's or organization's situation or needs. Every effort has been made to make this book as accurate as possible. However, there may be typographical and/or content errors. Therefore, this book should serve only as general guide and not as the ultimate source of subject information.

The authors and publishers of this book are not licensed medical practitioners, financial advisors, or legal professionals. Any health-related or medical information contained herein should not be used as a substitute for professional medical advice, diagnosis, or treatment. Always seek the advice of a qualified healthcare professional regarding any medical condition, and do not disregard professional medical advice or delay seeking it based on information provided in this book. Some products described in this book do not comply with FDA, USDA or FSIS regulations or local health codes. The instructions provided have not been reviewed, tested or approved by any official testing body or government agency.

Similarly, financial, legal, and security information included here should not be interpreted as advice tailored to your individual circumstances. You are encouraged to consult with licensed professionals in these areas before making decisions or taking any actions that could affect your financial security, personal safety, or legal standing.

While every effort has been made to ensure the accuracy and reliability of the information contained in this book, no representations or warranties are made, express or implied, about the completeness, accuracy, reliability, suitability, or availability of the information, products, services, or related graphics. Any reliance you place on such information is strictly at your own risk.

The authors and publishers disclaim any liability for any direct, indirect, incidental, consequential, or other damages arising from the use of this information. By using this book, you acknowledge that you are responsible for your own choices and actions. You hereby agree to be bound by this disclaimer, or you may return this book within the guaranteed time for a full refund.

ABOUT THE AUTHORS

David Bates

is an economist who doesn't blindly trust our government, or the lies spewing out of the FED. He knows there's always a story not being told. In late 2007, finding that story ahead of time saved his own family from financial ruin, and helped a lot of his friends and coworkers do the same. After his retirement from high finance, Mr. Bates has switched from analysing company balance sheets to dissecting the financial dealing of the federal government. And what he's uncovered deep inside the belly of the beast is not only disturbing, but also very dangerous for you and every other hardworking American. History has shown us time and time again that 'the little guy' always finds out about bad things after it's already too late, while the rich elites and government cronies always get advance warnings. With this book, David is trying to change that.

Claude Davis

is a survival expert and one of the leading historians of The Great Depression. He's dedicated his life to study the people and survival strategies of the lean 1930's, when a quarter of Americans were unemployed... when tens of millions had been displaced and were living homeless on the streets, or in shanty towns...and when poverty and misery gripped our nation for almost a decade. As he'll tell anyone who'll listen, many of the 'snowflakes' alive today would not make it if another crisis like that ever came along. Claude is one of the few, if not the only one person alive today who knows exactly what families did to survive back then, and that's why his knowledge, as it's saved in this book, will probably prove invaluable in the difficult days ahead.

PART ONE

INGENIOUS STRATEGIES *That* SAVED PEOPLE *During* ECONOMIC CRISES OF THE PAST

Chapter 1

Learn from the Past: Economic Crises That Changed the World

The United States has not always been an undeniable global force or an economic juggernaut. In fact, the nation was in debt before it even turned one year old. Well over a century after gaining its independence, the economic tides would change as European and global instability opened the door for the United States' emergence as a burgeoning superpower.

The events of World War I and its subsequent impact on nations like Britain and France required the assistance of an industrialized nation; far enough away for manufacturing facilities and farms to remain unscathed but close enough culturally and politically to make sense as a crediting nation.

The U.S. would continue to solidify its place as an economic power throughout the 1920s as its dollar continued to flow through Europe like refined fuel, and there would be no question as to which nation could (and would) bankroll much of the world following the Second World War.

The strength of the United States economy was only further solidified upon the U.S. Dollar becoming the world's official reserve currency, but the economic prosperity and notoriety the United States has enjoyed has not been unabated.

"The crisis you have to worry about most is the one you don't see coming."

Mike Mansfield

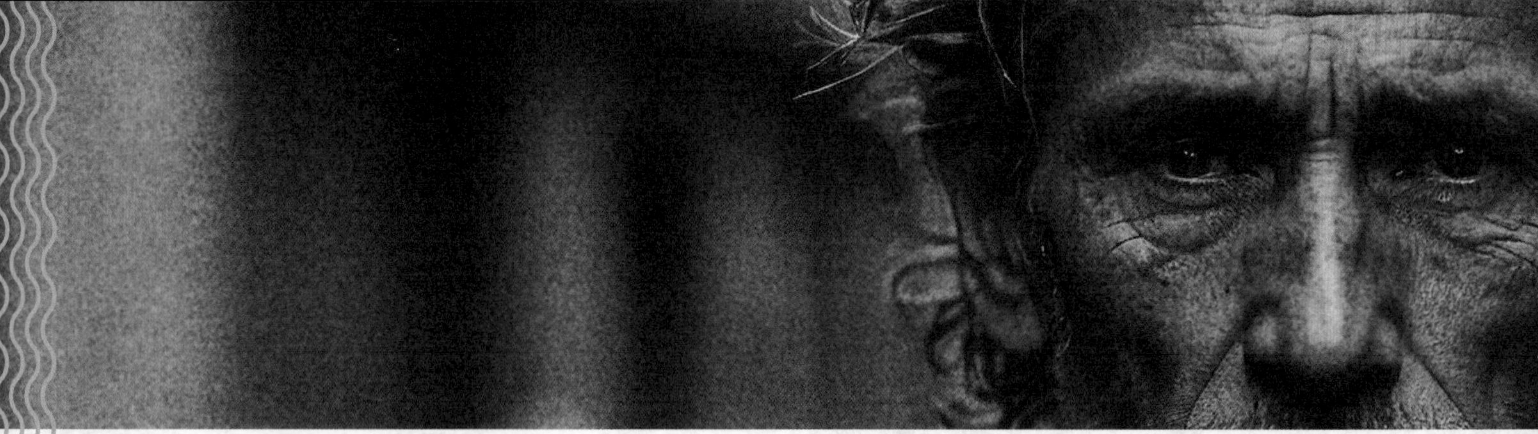

The Great Depression

Whether it be the Great Depression that blindsided much of the developed world, oil and energy crises throughout the 1970s and 1980s, or more recent economic hiccups, economic growth has not come without its growing pains and has left its share of victims in its wake. The economic crises that have impacted the United States and the world have varying origins that wrought widely differing effects on business, the people, and governments, many of which are still being felt or even yet to be fully realized.

The Great Depression officially began in 1929, following a decade largely marked by prosperity, confidence, and a sense that only good times were ahead. Numerous contributing factors created the Depression, with the most infamous and perhaps important being the collapse of the United States stock market. October 29, 1929, "Black Tuesday," signaled the end of economic optimism in the United States and several parts of the world. The 1920s had been fraught with speculation, which artificially elevated stock prices. Economic optimism only served to feed the bubble, which was doomed to burst on that fall Tuesday. Banks and individual investors were in the crosshairs as a massive financial panic led to bank runs and the liquidation of shares on a scale never seen before.

A subsequent consequence of this catastrophic market crash was the collapse of banks nationwide. Banks suffered massive losses as their investments failed and as investors and individuals defaulted on loans they could no longer pay. When panicked individuals rushed to their banks to withdraw their funds, most found that their money was simply gone.

Businesses were barely holding on as they cut back on spending, investing, and production. These factors contributed to a decrease in demand and supply and an increase in unemployment. A subsequent decrease in international trade, along with severe drought and the devastation of millions of acres of farmland in the Midwest, all made matters worse for the American people.

For the average American, the collapse of the stock market was catastrophic. Many of those who had invested their money had no real sense of what that even meant, but a collapse certainly could not be anything good. People raced to their banks to withdraw their money, with many being told that their money was simply gone.

Banks were as exposed to this financial collapse as any other, and there was no safety net or government insurance to make their clients whole again. Businesses shuttered, leading to a soaring unemployment rate, peaking at 25% at the height of the Depression. Workers who were fortunate enough to hold onto their positions often saw their wages cut or hours reduced. The standard of living decreased significantly for many Americans, especially those in cities. Minorities suffered disproportionately, too.

Lange, Dorothea, photographer. People living in miserable poverty, Elm Grove, Oklahoma County, Oklahoma. Oklahoma United States Oklahoma County Elm Grove, 1936. Aug. Photograph. https://www.loc.gov/item/2017763118/.

Already facing discrimination and a lack of opportunity, these people were usually the first to be laid off and then the last to be rehired if they even had a chance to get their jobs back. Racially motivated violence and tension also saw increases during this time period.

As jobs were lost, the ability to afford one's home was lost as well, leading to a wave of foreclosures. Families and individuals who had lost everything often moved from their cities to the outskirts, building makeshift homes out of scrap metal or cardboard, dubbing them "Hoovervilles," after President Herbert Hoover, who most (erroneously) blamed for their suffering. Women and children were frequently pressed into the work-

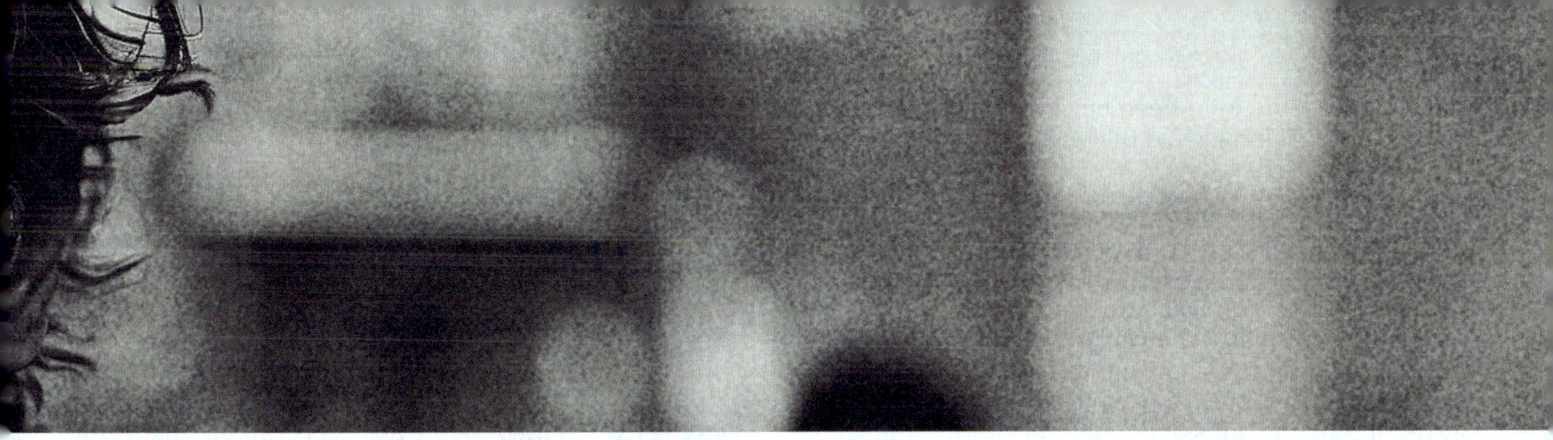

force to help support their families, which led to the breakdown of the traditional family dynamic and an increase in industrial and agricultural casualties as inexperience brought upon many costly incidents. Schools frequently closed as budgets were slashed and children withdrew to take jobs to help their families. This led to a decrease in literacy rates along with the quality of education for several years in the U.S.

It was not just investors or those in cities that were impacted by this Depression, either. Middle America was going through its worst drought in recorded history, further complicated by years of over-farming and irresponsible production strategies.

These conditions collectively created the Dust Bowl, which led to a massive wave of food shortages, poverty, and an exodus of Americans from the nation's breadbasket towards California. It would take several years for the bread of the nation to return to pre-Dust Bowl prosperity. Advances in farming techniques and new knowledge of crop rotation helped alleviate strain, in addition to the end of record drought conditions.

The United States government under Republican President Herbert Hoover took a laissez-faire approach to the Depression at its onset. Private charity was encouraged, and Hoover was sympathetic to the average American's plight, but he believed that one needed to pull themselves up by their bootstraps and embrace rugged individualism during tough times. This approach drew immense criticism, and Hoover's fate was sealed when he ordered military intervention when World War I veterans marched in the nation's capital demanding their bonuses for wartime service be paid early. It may not have been his fault, but what Hoover did was the common denominator for many who were suffering, and he simply needed to go in their eyes.

The government underwent a complete 180 when Democrat Franklin D. Roosevelt was elected in 1932. Roosevelt, or "FDR," as he is known, enacted sweeping legislation to restore confidence among the public. The New Deal was a package of laws all geared to provide relief, recovery, or reform, and ultimately designed to pull the nation out of its dire situation.

The Social Security Administration was established to help provide financial assistance for the elderly while programs like the Works Progress Administration put Americans back to work by creating government initiatives.

Several banking reforms were also created to ensure that Americans would no longer have to fear their money being lost by a bank ever again. A few New Deal initiatives still exist and have an impact in the United States to this day, signaling their significance.

United States Resettlement Administration, Lee, Russell, photographer. Corner of dormitory, homeless men's bureau, Sioux City, Iowa. Sioux City United States Iowa. 1936, Dec. Photograph. https://www.loc.gov/item/2017735332/.

While the New Deal had a pronounced effect on the morale of Americans, the single greatest factor in ending the Great Depression in the United States would be its involvement in World War II. Millions of Americans were called upon to contribute to the war effort as production skyrocketed and jobs were created to ensure victory.

The 1973 Energy Crisis

By the 1970s, the United States had become one of two indisputable economic and political powerhouses of the world, with the Soviet Union being the other. This did not make it impervious to the actions of other nations, though. The 1973 energy crisis and subsequent recession were brought on by the actions of a few nations that collectively make up what is known as the Organization of Arab Petroleum Exporting Countries, or OAPEC. The

United States had long been unwavering in its support for the nation of Israel, and that support would have consequences in 1973.

OAPEC placed an embargo on the United States and other nations who stood by Israel as it fought the Yom Kippur War against a coalition of Arab states. Egypt and Syria launched a surprise attack against the Israelis on October 6, 1973, which then led to the Saudi Arabian government leading the charge toward a full-scale oil embargo against nations supporting Israel. With the United States importing massive amounts of oil from these Middle Eastern nations, the effects were nothing short of catastrophic on the economy and society as oil supplies dwindled, creating a severe shortage.

The Organization of the Petroleum Exporting Countries, or OPEC, which had been founded in 1960, had consolidated power and controlled the world's oil market, allowing them to set prices at their own discretion while essentially holding the rest of the world hostage to their demands. The United States had failed for years to address its problematic and growing reliance on foreign oil to meet its energy demands.

There were few regulations in place domestically to govern public and corporate energy consumption, which only served to make the 1973 embargo a much greater economic disaster than it might have been otherwise. The United States also lacked the infrastructure and technology to feasibly turn up the dial on domestic oil production to help combat the effects of the OAPEC embargo.

These factors combined with the United States' economic policies to create a supply-side shock that only served to make matters worse.

The embargo had its intended effect in truncating the amount of oil flowing into the United States. There were several economic ramifications from this oil shortage and subsequent energy crisis, such as inflation, rising unemployment, and a decrease in consumer confidence, all of which impacted the American public.

Protests became more common as decreasing confidence in elected officials and political leaders became symptoms of the energy crisis. Discontent also resulted in changing cultural attitudes in the United States about conservation and sustainability at both the individual and corporate levels.

The recession that occurred was a direct result of these factors as businesses faced high operating costs, economic growth came to a screeching halt, unemployment surged, investments suffered, and production decreased dramatically. Increases in gasoline, heating oil, and other forms of fuel all created suffering for most Americans as difficult choices had to be made about where their money would be best allocated.

Many turned to public transportation, carpooling, or even riding bicycles to circumvent fuel shortages and save money. An unintended effect of these changes was a decline in larger, American-manufactured automobiles in favor of smaller imports that were more fuel-efficient.

National Archives and Records Administration, Falconer, David, photographer. Gas rationing system (odd-even plan) is announced in an afternoon newspaper being read at a service station with a sign in the background stating no gas is available, Portland, Oregon. Oregon, Portland, 1974. Jan. Photograph. https://catalog.archives.gov/id/555474?objectPage=3/.

On a day-to-day level, people lined up in abnormally long lines to fill their gas tanks, with many waiting hours only to find that these gas stations had run out of fuel. Fuel began to be rationed as Americans had to sacrifice on an individual level, all while paying higher prices. These increases in fuel prices led to an increase in goods and services across the board, placing further financial strains on families across the country.

Businesses in both manufacturing and transportation sectors were especially vulnerable to the energy crisis as they pivoted to find alternatives while attempting to salvage as much of their workforce as possible. Unfortunately, layoffs were inevitable, and unemployment peaked at 9% in 1975. On a positive note, the crisis led to a shift in awareness about the importance of energy security and the value of environmental protections, sustainability, and energy conservation.

Faced with myriad problems and few viable solutions, the U.S. government deployed numerous strategies in the hopes that a few would stick. One of the first initiatives born out of this energy crisis was dubbed "Project Independence," which President Richard Nixon introduced with the goal of making the nation energy independent by 1980. As part of this plan, the United States would invest in producing its own energy, create the Strategic Petroleum Reserve, and launch a series of domestic initiatives to conserve energy. The government would spend millions to research alternative energy sources and their viability, and even reduced speed limits to conserve fuel, and extended daylight savings time to reduce the amount of electricity being used.

Several other factors would also combine to help lift the nation out of its economic woes brought on by the 1973 oil embargo. The Energy Policy and Conservation Act was passed in 1975, which is often considered to be one of the most important pieces of energy legislation in U.S. history. This act mandated improvements to the overall fuel efficiency of automobiles and, when coupled with the creation of the SPR, helped lay the groundwork for a more energy-conscious society. The deregulation of oil prices during the decade allowed market conditions to dictate and encourage domestic oil production, helping to stabilize the energy market stateside. Aside from energy-centered approaches toward stabilizing the economy, the United States also looked towards fiscal measures to help create economic growth. Tax cuts were made, and an increase in public spending was viewed as a way to help encourage investment and restore consumer confidence. Several industries saw deregulatory measures taken to encourage competition and bring some level of efficiency to the economy. Overall, significant groundwork was laid that would continue to influence U.S. energy policy over the next several decades, while an improvement in diplomatic relationships with OAPEC nations ultimately pulled the country out of the crisis.

The 1973 energy crisis lasted just shy of two years but was felt immensely by businesses and people alike. With its end came a much-needed sigh of relief, but the other shoe was about to drop. 1979 was a calamitous year across the world, with economic, political, and societal upheaval seemingly occurring in every corner of the globe.

The United States once again found itself hostage to a dependency on Middle Eastern oil, this time for reasons they had not yet wrestled with. Shah Mohammad Reza Pahlavi had established a rather favorable relationship with the U.S. government, ensuring his pockets were lined and that the U.S. would always have a steady flow of oil.

The Iranian Revolution and subsequent overthrow of the Shah put an end to that sweetheart deal as a new Islamic Republic was established under Ayatollah Khomeini. Iran's new leadership was extremely skeptical of the West, which culminated in drastically cutting oil production and exports, having a reverberating effect worldwide as one of the world's largest oil producers suddenly made an about-face.

The sudden loss of one of the world's largest oil exporters created a supply shock that induced panic in the global oil markets.

The ensuing recession that began in the United States was linked with the shock felt by the global oil market as nations began to hoard oil in fear that Iran's new leadership would create an economic catastrophe.

Rising oil prices led to increasing production costs for virtually all other goods and services, increasing inflationary pressures. These issues led to a reduction in consumer spending and a decline in consumer confidence, which in turn contributed to pains in the business sector, which was already reeling due to increases in energy costs.

The Federal Reserve determined that interest rates needed to rise to help combat inflation, but this contributed directly to reductions in consumer spending and business investment, further contributing to the economic downturn.

The pain felt at the pump was once again crippling to most Americans. Gas prices more than doubled in some areas from 1978 to 1980, putting them at prices that had never been seen before. The long lines that were all too familiar in the early part of the decade were back once more, with wait times exceeding an hour being common and gas stations completely drying up before midday in some cases.

Americans were once again compelled to make sacrifices as the government enacted odd-even rationing, dictating what days one could even fill up their gas tanks based on license plate numbers.

The average American felt a deep sense of frustration and inconvenience due to these schemes, but the effects were not just mere annoyances. The economy at large once again seemed to be preying on the public, with stagflation marking the day.

The 1979 Energy Crisis

Stagflation is present when the economy is no longer growing, and inflation and unemployment are high. The price of goods soared while businesses felt the pressures brought on by increasing operating costs that could seemingly only be relieved through laying off their workforce and cutting corners in other areas.

There was significant psychological damage incurred by the American public due to the previous oil shock that occurred in 1973. With many Americans still shaking off the effects of that previous energy crisis and subsequent recession, this second oil crisis seemed to bring fears and panic back in an even more intense fashion.

Many Americans reacted harshly to rising oil prices and the disruptions that were occurring in everyday life. A panicked public turned to hoarding fuel and many other household products, which only served to make matters worse.

The United States government reacted rather slowly to this second energy crisis and subsequent recession. Due to the perceived lack of experience in responding, many Americans lost trust in their government, which was still damaged from the Watergate scandal and the resignation of President Nixon only a half-decade prior.

Albeit delayed and largely ineffective, President Jimmy Carter attempted to put an end to the energy crisis and subsequent recession in numerous ways, but it is important to note that nothing he did would salvage public perception that he was an ineffective executive.

Carter promoted the conservation of energy and implored Americans to reduce their own energy consumption through measures like turning down their thermostats in the winter. The Strategic Petroleum Reserve was increased under Carter to improve the U.S.'s ability to sustain its own energy needs down the road.

With this being the second energy crisis in less than a half-decade, the United States government renewed its efforts and investments in domestic energy sources, such as nuclear power and coal. A worldwide coalition was also created, known as the International Energy Agency, which promoted collaboration and exacted solutions to fortify the global energy supply.

The energy crisis and subsequent recession would have a profound impact on the future of America, as Democrat Jimmy Carter would be ousted in favor of Republican Ronald Reagan, ushering in an entirely new and transformative era of U.S. politics and economic policy.

The Reagan Administration implemented a series of tax cuts aimed at stimulating investment and boosting economic growth. Incentives were created to encourage businesses to invest in emerging technologies and equipment that would help usher in a new era for the energy, infrastructure, and manufacturing sectors, among others.

As several nations began to produce their own oil, OPEC's dominance over the world oil market weakened, helping reduce energy prices nationwide.

As is typical with the end of most recessions, consumer spending and confidence increased as inflationary pressures eased and interest rates decreased. By the middle of the 1980s, the United States economy was expanding, and the recession was in the rearview for Americans. The end of the second oil shock was brought about by a combination of factors that would see a stronger, more energy self-sufficient United States emerge.

The Great Recession

The United States enjoyed a degree of prosperity and prestige throughout the next two decades, with its greatest moment perhaps being its emergence as the lone world superpower after the collapse of the Soviet Union. While economic hiccups and minor recessions occurred in the 1990s and early 2000s, these paled in comparison to what was on the horizon. There had been murmurs for some time that the U.S. housing market was a bubble. By late 2007, these murmurs turned to roars as that bubble burst. So, how did things get to that point?

The 1990s saw banks and other lenders loaning out money rather indiscriminately, with very loose criteria being used to determine who was eligible and for what terms. Lenders issued subprime mortgages to borrowers with poor credit histories and other characteristics that would disqualify them from eligibility in most other eras of U.S. history. These mortgages were then bundled into securities that were sold to investors around the world. Essentially, investors, hedge funds, and banks were tied up in an extremely risky asset class that had the potential to make them a fortune, but also had the ability to bankrupt them. Unfortunately, the latter always had the higher probability of playing out, and it would. As is the case with any modern financial collapse, the contributing factors and subsequent effects were easy to spot after the fact, but very few actually imagined that a large recession was imminent.

Mortgages began to default as home prices dropped in 2006, which was a first sign that things were not alright in the housing sector. Banks and other financial institutions experienced massive losses because of nonpayment, and this was only made worse as massive investment banks began to go under as well. These factors, combined with few regulations and a lack of oversight, contributed to the worst economic downturn since the Great Depression. A severe lack of oversight stemming from regulation that occurred in the 1990s and early 2000s also fed the beast that would become the Great Recession. Commercial banks were allowed to act in a similar fashion to investment banks, which resulted in even greater risks being taken at the highest levels.

Several other factors contributed to the Great Recession ranging from monetary policy to psychological. The Federal Reserve had held interest rates low after the September 11th terrorist attack to help stimulate the economy, which made borrowing an easy venture for corporations, banks, and individuals. This simple fact invited interested parties to take on more "easy" debt, which in hindsight only exacerbated the situation. On a psychological level, many financial institutions erroneously believed that they were too big to fail and would have the federal government behind them to prop them up if they faced any type of failure due to their risky investment strategies. Financial institutions and lenders had been gambling and preying on the weak for quite some time,

Many young Americans would have to forgo purchasing their first home for several more years or would forgo attending college and opt to find a job to support themselves or their families during uncertain times. Several similarities exist between the Great Recession and the Great Depression, as is to be expected with a large fiscal crisis.

Americans became preoccupied with worries over their job and financial security, overly worried about their futures, and mental health crises popped up across the nation at alarming rates. Even after the recession wound down, wages remained stagnant or grew at slow rates, while people struggled to recoup lost wealth and were forced to deal with the financial and psychological ramifications of the recession for years.

but it would all finally come to a head.

Unfortunately, the effects of the Great Recession were not confined to the elite nor to massive financial conglomerates. As is the case with most financial recessions and depressions, the brunt of the damage is absorbed by the people.

As a result of the widespread effects of the housing and financial market collapses, numerous industries suffered and thousands of businesses nationwide either closed or were severely hindered in their operations. Unemployment would peak at 10% as tens of millions of Americans found themselves without jobs.

Millions more would lose their homes as banks foreclosed, something that many Americans actually had no idea could occur due to lenders having little obligation to inform them of what their mortgage terms really entailed. Homelessness rates increased nationwide and trillions of dollars in wealth were wiped away in a plummeting stock market. This was especially impactful for Americans whose retirement savings were tied up in the market or for Americans with a significant amount of their money contained in another investment portfolio.

Prices increased across the board, consumers cut back on spending, which severely hurt the hospitality industry and others that many Americans viewed as unnecessary expenditures.

The United States government scrambled to find solutions to this economic crisis as the nation was teetering between recession and depression. The Emergency Economic Stabilization Act of 2008 facilitated the purchase of $700 billion in toxic assets from banks and other institutions. This was one of many steps taken to help restore confidence in the imperiled financial system as well as encourage lending nationwide. The Federal Reserve would take steps never considered prior, such as lowering the federal funds rate to almost zero and purchasing government securities and mortgage-backed securities to help ease the economy. Most notably, the Obama Administration would enact various stimulus packages to help ensure various investment firms and banks would not fail and to provide relief to the American public. The Dodd-Frank Wall Street Reform and Consumer Protection Act would be passed in 2010, providing enhanced oversight of financial institutions along with enacting stricter regulations on various financial instruments.

It would be through these reforms and the stabilization of various financial markets and the housing industry that would ultimately pull the United States out of the recession by 2010, but the effects would continue to be felt for several years afterward, even as the economy significantly improved.

The COVID-19 Crisis

The nation continued to see economic expansion throughout the Obama administration and enjoyed a great deal of economic prosperity amidst Donald Trump's term in office. Although overshadowed by scandals, both real and imagined, the economy was prosperous during the Trump years.

Many referred to the economy during this period favorably, and for a time, it seemed as though nothing would derail the growth. However, along came a public health crisis known as the coronavirus pandemic, which led to the COVID-19 recession, or pandemic recession.

The COVID-19 recession was unique compared to other economic downturns in history as its primary causes stemmed from the outbreak of a virus and the measures implemented to contain its spread. Social distancing, restrictions on travel, and the shuttering of businesses,

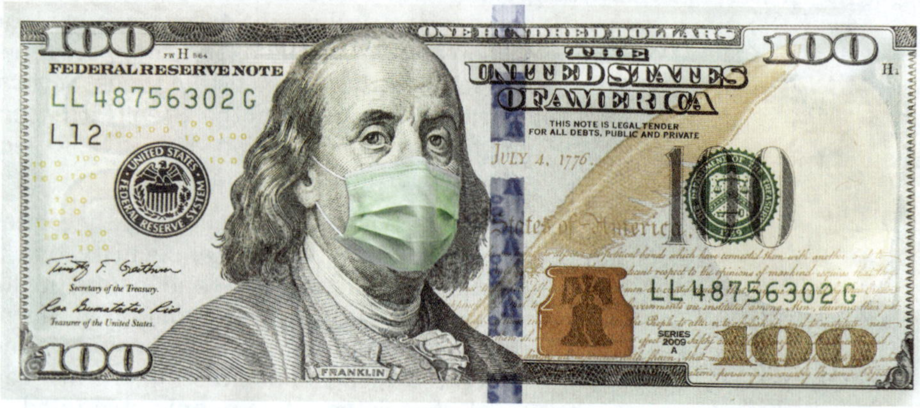

factories, and other manufacturing plants severely damaged the economy. With most industries being closed or severely restricted, consumer spending reached lows not seen in decades.

Across the country and world, factories closed or laid off workers to operate at a reduced capacity, leading to global supply chain issues. Investors, unsure of what lay ahead, reacted in real time to new developments, leading to severe volatility and instability in financial markets, with some of the largest industries experiencing financial challenges due to low demand. Even some of the largest corporations, like Boeing and Disney, experienced profit losses that could never have been predicted before the pandemic.

The pandemic blindsided the American public as it hit all corners of society, and the ensuing recession had a similar effect. There had never been a situation quite like this in a modern industrialized society where a public health epidemic had triggered such economic devastation. The impact felt by Americans was both sweeping and uneven. Many Americans lost their jobs either permanently or temporarily as businesses shut their doors. With this situation in the workforce, families saw their savings accounts quickly dwindling (if they had any to begin with) while struggling to pay their basic living expenses. Those fortunate enough to shift to remote work eventually did so, but for the vast majority who relied on physically going to work, options seemed scarce. Both renters and homeowners faced significant hurdles in affording their payments on time. Renters struggled as their jobs were either gone or severely at-risk, while many homeowners faced similar challenges. Landlords were not immune to their renters' plight as many relied on their tenants to pay rents to cover their mortgages.

The situation was calamitous, increasing the already intense psychological impact on mental health across the nation. Many individuals reported increased anxiety and general stress due to financial worries and other pandemic-related stresses. The changes that labor markets underwent to work around pandemic restrictions greatly impacted the public both at the time and into the present. Remote work became far more common, and several workplaces determined that this model, or something similar, would be how they conducted business in the future. Many employers realized that their workforce was just as, if not more, productive working remotely than commuting to work. Studies are still determining the overall effect of remote work on both employees and employers, but this trend has had staying power ever since.

Other effects of the COVID-19 recession and subsequent shutdowns were observable in virtually all areas of American society. Feelings of isolation and loneliness swept over many as a lack of physical interaction took its toll on mental well-being. Social interactions that still took place were often heavily restricted, such as dining out, which changed how family and friends connected. Vulnerable populations, such as those in lower socioeconomic brackets, disabled Americans, and minority populations, faced food insecurity, difficulties accessing childcare, healthcare, and overall economic instability disproportionately.

The United States government faced a unique set of circumstances and problems in their quest to combat the economic downturn resulting from lockdown measures. Collectively, these measures aimed to support businesses both large and small, provide public support, and stabilize the economy. Several relief packages were passed to help provide relief and stimulus to businesses and the public. The Coronavirus Aid, Relief, and Economic Security (CARES) Act was passed almost immediately after shutdowns began, providing over $2.2 trillion in direct payments to people, expanded unemployment benefits, loans to businesses, and funding for vital public services, such as hospitals. These efforts continued with subsequent packages, such as the American Rescue Plan, passed a year later.

The government strove to do all it could to help ailing businesses and individuals, but these efforts also had unintended consequences that further exacerbated the economic situation.

The Federal Reserve kept interest rates at or near 0% to encourage spending and investment. This had positive effects in the short term but resulted in a gradual raising of rates over several years, putting the country in danger of another economic recession. Not all efforts made were entirely a result of the COVID-19 recession but were catalyzed by the unforeseen circumstances that had swept the nation and world.

The Biden Administration quickly passed various infrastructure bills that would see billions, and even trillions, invested in clean energy and infrastructure, projected to add jobs to the economy and aid in expansion. Several bills were passed to aid in chip manufacturing and to further efforts to bring general technological manufacturing back to the United States to help it continue to compete with China.

Several hurdles still exist today stemming from government efforts to stimulate the economy, protect individuals and businesses, and prioritize public health. It seemed for a time that every effort, no matter how well-intentioned, had some negative externality associated with its creation that is still being dealt with today.

Future Implications

The United States has grappled with both severe and minor economic recessions and depressions throughout its history as an independent nation. Considered the world's greatest superpower, it faces unique challenges as challengers emerge to its global economic dominance.

Moving into the future and beyond the coronavirus pandemic and recession is still a chapter in its economic history that has yet to be completed, but several potential routes lie ahead for the United States.

Inflation and rising costs of living may continue to plague the public and businesses, eroding overall purchasing power and necessitating action from both the public and private sectors. At the same time, increased investments in emerging technologies and infrastructure could boost productivity, create new industries, generate more jobs, and spur economic growth.

Economic prosperity and growth do not guarantee indefinite increases in wealth and living standards. The capitalist economy, embedded within a network of interconnected global economics, inevitably experiences cycles of pain and recovery. The United States has felt the effects of economic downturns numerous times in less than a century and will need to adapt and evolve to address future downturns.

Efforts to combat societal and financial effects will need to be nuanced and precise as the world continues to grow and change. Reflecting on past experiences may offer the wisdom and guidance necessary to navigate future challenges and set a course for sustained progress.

"The history of money is, in many ways, the history of the rise and fall of empires."

Ray Dalio

Chapter 2

The Rise and Fall of World Reserve Currencies:

Precious Insights from People Who Lived Through Them That You Can Use When the Dollar Falls

Most people think the dollar is forever.

In some people's minds they've started seeing it as immune—too entrenched, too powerful, too essential to ever fail.

They treat it like gravity – always there, always holding everything together. But currencies don't live forever. And they don't die by accident. **They fall for the same reasons, every time.**

America didn't invent fiat currency.

This isn't about abstract theories. It's about what's already happening – and what comes next. **Because history's got a cycle.** And the same story has already played out for the Dutch guilder, the British pound, and a long list of once-untouchable currencies.

The Dutch guilder once anchored global trade. At its peak, Amsterdam led world finance and shipping. But wars, deficits, and overextension eroded trust. Confidence slipped. The guilder fell.

Their empire soon followed.

So, the question is not if the U.S. dollar will fall - it's when it will fail. And right now, we're standing on the edge of the abyss.

Why Paper Dies

Fiat currency has no intrinsic value.

Treasury Dept. Ofc. of Treasuer of U.S. view showing arrangment of coin and currency in reserve vault. , 1914. Photograph. https://www.loc.gov/item/2016852671/.

It isn't tied to any commodity, doesn't represent a claim on real assets, and isn't backed by productivity or output. It survives entirely on confidence—confidence in the issuing government, in its political stability, in its perceived economic strength, and in the assumption that others will continue to accept it in exchange for real goods. When that trust erodes, there is nothing underneath to catch it as it falls.

This wasn't always the model. For centuries, currencies were tethered to something tangible: gold, silver, grain, land, or measurable units of labor. These systems weren't perfect, but they imposed natural limits.

A king couldn't mint more silver than he had mined. A central bank couldn't expand the money supply without securing more gold.

With fiat, those limits vanish. Governments are free to issue currency in any amount at any time, regardless of what's been produced or earned. There's no restraint, no consideration for the people, and no honesty—only policy.

And those policies always follow the same path. Fiat systems begin out of necessity. The first round of printing is almost always justified: to fund a war, to survive a crisis, to jumpstart recovery from a depression or some other disaster. But once the mechanism is in place, and once the public tolerates it, printing becomes the standard response to every shortfall. Spending rises. Deficits expand. Voters are promised more than can be delivered through tax revenue alone.

The money printer fills the gap.

Inflation begins gradually. Purchasing power drops slowly at first, and most people adjust. The middle class tightens its belt. The poor absorb the worst of it. Meanwhile, governments, corporations, and those with access to capital are insulated, at least temporarily. They benefit from low interest rates and asset bubbles created by "easy money". But over time, the damage compounds in silence. As real wages stagnate and debt grows, the currency ceases to function as a store of value. It becomes something transactional— used because people have no alternative, not because they trust what it's worth.

Eventually, that changes too. **As inflation accelerates, people start moving their wealth out of the system. First slowly, then suddenly.** They buy hard assets. They shift to foreign currencies. They turn to barter, commodities, or black markets. Demand for the currency falls, and the government responds as it always does: by printing more. Printing becomes a weapon against collapse that hastens the very collapse it is trying to avert. What began as a tool to "manage a crisis" becomes the cause for the next currency apocalypse.

Fiat currency systems do not collapse because of bad luck. They collapse because their structure rewards short-term survival over long-term solvency. Every government with a reserve currency always abuses the power to print more. Every empire that controls that currency suffers the same consequences. And every fiat currency goes through the same stages: inflation, devaluation, panic, and replacement.

There are no exceptions, just different timelines.

How a Fiat Collapse Happens

Once a government gains the power to issue currency without restraint, that power becomes policy. It may begin with restraint, even good intentions, but the outcome is always the same. The temptation to solve complex problems with newly created money is never resisted for too long. Wars, recessions, political instability, overpromised entitlements—each becomes a justification to expand the money supply. And every time that expansion is allowed, it becomes harder to stop.

At first, it looks like a solution. Inflation is low. Markets are rising. Borrowing appears painless. But the consequences aren't immediately, they're distributed, quiet, and cumulative. Every round of new issuance chips away at the currency's value. What used to cost one unit now costs two. Wages lag. Savings erode. The middle class starts to hollow out.

The public rarely notices the shift as it's happening. That's the danger. The damage doesn't come all at once—it unfolds over years, sometimes decades.

We've seen it repeatedly.

As I mentioned, the Dutch guilder once served as the global standard for trade in the 17th century. Backed by a disciplined financial structure and an expansive maritime empire, it was the most trusted currency of its time.

The Dutch were early adopters of central banking, joint-stock corporations, and multinational trade. Amsterdam's stability, legal infrastructure, and merchant dominance made the guilder accepted and desired by all—It was trusted across borders before national currencies were even standardized.

But sustained warfare with Britain—costly, prolonged, and politically necessary—drove the Dutch government to print beyond its means. As debt mounted and trade deficits widened, the guilder lost all credibility. Inflation sets in. Capital fled. The currency declined, and the Dutch Empire collapsed.

The British pound sterling fell in the same way, only slower. It held world reserve status well into the 20th century. But after two world wars and the loss of its colonial leverage, Britain was burdened by debt, declining output, and massive reconstruction costs. The government relied on devaluation and printing to stay afloat. Confidence in the pound evaporated. By 1944, global finance abandoned it in favor of the U.S. dollar at Bretton Woods. The empire shrank in lockstep, with the following period being particularly dire for its citizens. As you know Great Britain has not recovered since.

In both cases, collapse wasn't caused by bad luck or one reckless policy. It was the result of repeated decisions made under pressure—always choosing immediate reward over long-term gain, convenience over control. Once a government crosses the line into habitual printing, every future crisis becomes a reason to accelerate the printing machines.

There is no turning back from that point without pain. And most nations would rather delay pain until it's too late to avoid a collapse, than fix the cause.

Reserve Currency Never Holds Up

A reserve currency is not just the most traded or widely held. It is the one currency the world defaults to when conducting business across borders. It's the unit of account for global trade, the basis of foreign reserves, and the benchmark for most commodities. For the country that issues it, the benefits are enormous: lower borrowing costs, persistent demand for its debt, and the ability to fund domestic priorities with money that other nations are willing to hold. But those benefits come with structural consequences that no country has ever outrun.

In order to maintain global liquidity, the issuer of a reserve currency must consistently provide more currency to the world than its domestic economy requires. That means running huge trade deficits becomes a feature, not a flaw. In the case of the United States, this has created a feedback loop: the world needs dollars, so the U.S. runs deficits to supply them. To fund those deficits, the government issues debt. That debt is purchased in dollars, completing the cycle. But each round expands the money supply and raises long-term obligations. The U.S. must borrow more, spend more, and issue more, simply to maintain its role at the center of the system.

Politicians lean on debt because it postpones hard choices. Wars don't need to be financed with sacrifice. Domestic programs don't require a corresponding increase in taxation. P**olicy becomes centered on maintaining liquidity rather than solvency, and every crisis becomes an opportunity to print, borrow, or bail out.**

This is how reserve status mutates from privilege to dependency. The economy begins to revolve around issuing more and more debt. Politicians no longer ask what the country can afford, they ask how much more the system can tolerate.

This structural flaw is in no way unique to the US dollar. The pound sterling was supported by a vast empire, a dominant navy, and industrial superiority. But running an empire is expensive. The costs of defending and administering global colonies, combined with the devastation of two world wars, pushed Britain into a state of chronic borrowing and monetary erosion. Sterling remained dominant far longer than it should have because there was no immediate alternative. But once the U.S. emerged from World War II as the creditor to the world—and once confidence in British solvency broke—sterling collapsed quickly.

Every reserve currency in modern history has collapsed, not due to invasion or sudden destruction, but because the weight of maintaining global liquidity eventually exceeds the fiscal discipline required to support it. Reserve status allows excess to flourish unnoticed—until it can no longer be sustained. By the time confidence begins to fade, the internal system is already too compromised to reform without triggering an economic collapse.

Bretton Woods

In the summer of 1944, the global financial system was reengineered at Bretton Woods, New Hampshire. The United States, having emerged from the Second World War militarily victorious and economically untouched, assumed a role previously held by the British Empire. The dollar would now serve as the world's primary reserve currency, pegged to gold at $35 per ounce. Every other major currency would peg to the dollar. It was a hierarchical system built on tangible value, backed by real reserves, designed to stabilize global trade and discourage reckless monetary expansion.

But by design, it relied on trust—and on discipline from the very nation entrusted to lead it.

For a time, it worked. The U.S. enjoyed unparalleled growth, and the dollar's strength was unquestioned.

Yet behind that dominance, pressures were building. By the 1960s, American foreign and domestic policy had become unsustainably ambitious. The Vietnam War, along with the massive welfare spending under the Great Society, pushed federal expenditures far beyond what could be justified by gold reserves or tax revenue. International confidence began to waver. Foreign governments, led by France, began redeeming dollars for gold, calling America's bluff.

Faced with a binary choice—economic contraction or monetary independence—President Nixon chose the latter. In August 1971, **the United States unilaterally ended the dollar's convertibility to gold, destroying the final restraint on monetary creation. From that moment forward, the world's reserve currency became a fiat instrument—no longer backed by anything but the perceived credibility of the issuing government.**

This is not new; the world has seen it before. In the 3rd century AD, the Roman Empire faced a similar crisis. Military expansion, internal instability, and rising bureaucratic costs led to the systematic debasement of their currency, the denarius which as you can imagine was the world's reserve currency at the time. Silver content fell steadily as emperors attempted to fund the state without raising taxes or cutting spending. Public confidence collapsed. Prices rose uncontrollably. By the time Emperor Diocletian attempted to impose price controls and force stability through law, **the economy had already disintegrated beneath the surface.** The coins still circulated—but they no longer meant what they once had. Trade suffered. Military loyalty faltered and a total collapse soon followed—extinguishing the light that was Rome and ushering in the Dark Ages.

The same pattern is unfolding in the United States today...

Once freed from gold, the U.S. dollar became a tool of policy rather than value. Inflation surged in the 1970s, leading to wage stagnation and public disillusionment. By the time it was brought under control through interest rate hikes in the early 1980s, the stage had already been set for a new paradigm: **government spending without consequence, supported by central bank liquidity.**

In 2008, the collapse of the housing market and the exposure of systemic risk in financial institutions triggered an unprecedented intervention. The Federal Reserve created trillions of dollars digitally, initiating "quantitative easing" to buy toxic assets and Treasury bonds. It was framed as a temporary fix.

It became the new normal.

Twelve years later, in response to COVID-19, the money printer roared back to life. Trillions more were created to finance direct stimulus checks, corporate bailouts, and state-level support. For the first time, a significant portion of the American public experienced **direct monetary benefit** from central bank activity—blurring the line between fiscal and monetary policy entirely.

Fast forward to today and the consequences are unavoidable. **National debt surpassed $36 trillion. Interest payments on that debt exceeded defense spending. Inflation surged beyond official targets.** The government's response? More spending. More issuance.

Debt ceilings have become political theater—suspended or raised repeatedly with no plan for long-term balance.

The very idea of financial restraint has become a joke.

Meanwhile, global institutions took note. Central banks began stockpiling gold. New Trade blocs formed to bypass the dollar. Energy deals, once locked to petrodollars, shifted to yuan and rubles.

For the first time in generations, there were signs that the dollar's **role as the global reserve currency is no longer safe.**

The fall of the gold standard did not cause collapse overnight. It caused a **slow rewiring of the economy,** reshaping incentives, encouraging addiction to debt, and normalizing perpetual deficits.

And like every fiat regime before it—from Rome to the Weimar Republic to post-war Britain—**the decay began the moment value was cut off from discipline.**

The Warning Signs Are Here

A full collapse of the U.S. dollar hasn't happened yet—but the **global response shows that confidence in its future is quickly eroding.**

Foreign central banks are increasing their gold reserves at the fastest pace in decades. China has been accumulating steadily for years, and Russia has already reduced its dollar exposure to near zero. These indicate a long-term shift away from the current global system and toward hard, sovereign-held assets.

At the same time, BRICS nations are actively working to undermine the dollar's dominance. Trade between these states is increasingly settled in national currencies, bypassing the dollar entirely. Long-term plans include the creation of a new settlement system, possibly backed by commodities, to replace reliance on SWIFT and the U.S. financial network.

The petrodollar system, once untouchable, is being sidelined. **Saudi Arabia has already signed oil agreements outside the dollar, including deals priced in yuan. Russia is already settling energy trade in rubles and gold. As more nations adopt alternative mechanisms for key exports, the dollar's centrality to global markets continues to slip.** This doesn't cause collapse directly—it just removes the stabilizers that once prevented it.

April 2010, new yorkers going against the banks. John Ferry, creative commons.

The world has seen this before. Once global trust fades, all bets are off. Foreign governments reduce exposure. Alternative payment systems form. Political instability takes center stage. Growth slows and Inflation becomes entrenched.

The End: What Collapse Looks Like

Inflation is usually the first symptom. Enough to make saving pointless and debt attractive. Enough to force every household to adjust its expectations downward. It eats wages, eliminates fixed incomes, and hollows out the middle-class while being dismissed as transitory.

Once trust fades, the capital flees. Investors redirect their holdings into commodities, hard assets, and currencies backed by stronger fundamentals or more reliable regimes. At the sovereign level, this means a reduction in dollar-denominated reserves, followed by the development of trade alternatives. At the individual level, it means exiting the system while the exits still work.

Eventually, the dollar loses its privilege.

And once the dollar becomes just another currency—no longer the default, no longer protected by necessity—then the real crisis begins.

No major reserve currency has recovered from that phase. Not the guilder. Not the pound. Not the dollar once trust is gone.

The Final Illusion

The United States is not immune. No reserve currency lasts forever.

Every empire believed it had more time. Every reserve currency was once believed untouchable. And every one of them collapsed under the weight of bad financial decisions—chronic deficits, political indulgence, and abuse of monetary power.

The dollar entered its last dance decades ago. We are now in the final stages, just before the music stops.

Those who still clinging to the illusion that "it can't happen here" are the ones who will have their lives up ended once the inevitable does happen.

Use this book to prepare before it's too late, you are one of the few who will know how.

Chapter 3

What People in Venezuela Would Tell You to Do Right Now

"How did you go bankrupt? Two ways. Gradually, then suddenly."

Ernest Hemingway

They didn't notice the collapse until they were already living inside it.

Most Venezuelans will tell you this plainly.

No single day marked the end. No alarms. No orders. Just the slow vanishing of normal things. First aspirin. Then bread. Then gasoline. Then trust.

Forewarning from the Ruins

When bread and aspirin disappeared, word-of-mouth networks took over. Families passed news along the apartment blocks—if a bakery had flour, a cousin would call before dawn, and neighbors would wake each other to get in line early. Street WhatsApp groups exploded in size. Maria José Quintero, a mother in Valencia, described how she checked her phone every morning for "secret" alerts: "You'd only know where to go if you were in the group." This was how people avoided wasted trips and found what little was left.

You should set up encrypted group chats with neighbors or family now, using Signal or WhatsApp, to share critical information about supplies. Train your group to avoid posting in public; in Venezuela, police sometimes shut down informal markets if word spread too wide.

Beyond being stable and somewhat safe, Venezuela had once been the richest country in Latin America. Oil revenues flowed, cities grew, and in 2001, the average Venezuelan earned more than citizens of Poland or Croatia.

Streets were clean. Shelves were stocked. Democracy, though flawed, seemed eternal.

At its peak in 2012, Venezuela's GDP per capita reached over $14,000 in purchasing power parity, placing it ahead of Colombia and Peru, and on par with Poland and Croatia at the time.

Oil exports accounted for more than 95 percent of total export revenue, creating the illusion of prosperity without resilience. Caracas had one of the highest urban living standards in the Southern Hemisphere.

But this isn't about Venezuela. It's about America, and what we can learn before it's too late.

In Venezuela the first fracture was economic. It had tied everything to oil. When global prices crashed in 2014, over 80 percent of their exports vanished. The currency lost weight. Hyperinflation surged. Four years later, prices were doubling every nineteen days. Salaries couldn't buy bread.

A group of Venezuelans eating garbage on the streets of Caracas in May 2018 By NoonIcarus - Own work, CC BY-SA 4.0, https://commons.wikimedia.org/w/index.php?curid=68862308

And it got worse.

Under Hugo Chávez, and even more under Nicolás Maduro, courts bent to the presidency. Elections blurred into theater. Journalists died or submitted. Military loyalty replaced competence. Corruption became policy.

Key legislative changes like the 1999 Constitutional Assembly and the 2004 Supreme Tribunal restructuring removed checks and balances, consolidating executive control.

And when almost no independent institution remains, democracy dies.

The government's food distribution network, CLAP, turned groceries into political ransom. Medicine became contraband. Religion withered behind exhaustion. Neighbors fell silent. More than six million citizens fled, the largest exodus in the Western Hemisphere. According to a 2019 Human Rights Watch report, CLAP food boxes were regularly delayed or denied in opposition strongholds, weaponizing hunger.

Psychological survival was as important as food. In Maturín, a group of neighbors met weekly not just to trade, but to share stories and check on each other's mental health. "If we stopped talking, the silence ate us alive," said Jorge Silva, a baker who lost his shop but kept his community intact.

What an Economic Collapse Looks Like from the Inside

In Venezuela, the value of money collapsed faster than the public could react. Prices rose faster than wages, and by the time the government finally acknowledged it, the currency was already next to useless. Banknotes were printed with more zeroes, then replaced entirely.

Salaries that once paid for monthly essentials could no longer cover a single day's worth of food. Cash transactions became impractical. Supermarkets began weighing currency instead of counting it. People bartered with cigarettes, gasoline, or powdered milk.

The families who kept eating did it by dividing roles: one person hunted down rumors about shipments, another ran point on barter trades, another cooked bulk staples to stretch food further, and everyone kept a stash hidden. Side hustles, like fixing shoes, selling homegrown greens, or running errands for the elderly, became the norm.

Every skill was put to use, and nothing was traded in the open until trust was proven over time.

In Puerto Ordaz, former office worker José Manuel González started a barter chain, he traded homemade arepas for gasoline, which he then exchanged with a taxi driver for cartons of eggs. "Everything was three or four steps," he told BBC Mundo.

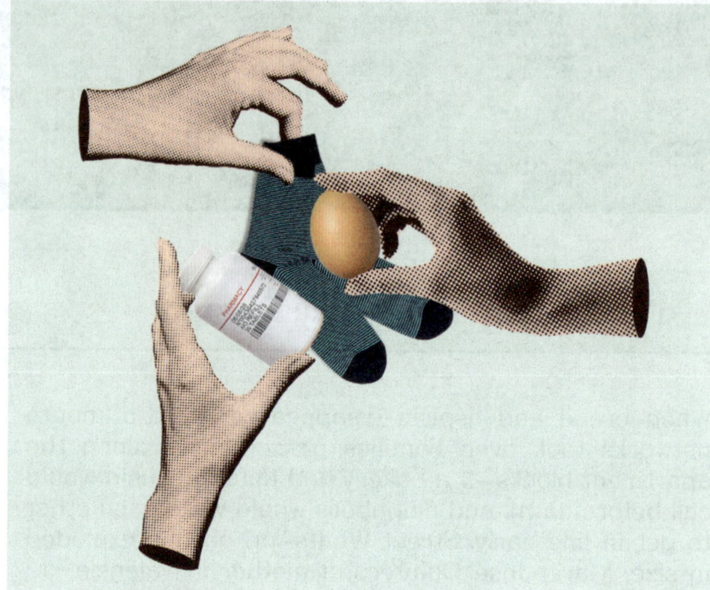

Most successful barters happened at small, trusted meetups. Large markets became targets for theft, so people arranged swaps through friends and only brought what they could afford to lose.

In Caracas, food shoppers like Rosa Colmenares would ask friends working as supermarket clerks to call if a delivery truck arrived, so they could form a line before word spread. "We slept in shifts just for bread," Rosa, commenting to El Nacional. The fastest learned to bring small change or barter items; the slowest often left empty-handed. If you're preparing, build relationships with store staff, couriers, and anyone connected to supply. Information is as valuable as currency during a crisis.

The one who made it through did not wait for official guidance, they learned to act early, trust quietly, and protect their supply lines. When prices changed by the hour, those who bought essentials in bulk, like beans, oil, and soap, before the chaos, are the ones that kept trading power the longest.

You should start bartering small, essential items locally. Start now, before you need to. Write down a hard-copy list of trusted contacts. Never trust the first deal, never risk your whole supply, and never meet in the same place twice. In Venezuela, the difference between feeding your family and losing it all often came down to a single decision: bring only what you can afford to lose, and keep the rest hidden.

At one point it cost 200,000 bolívars to buy a single egg. A teacher's monthly salary, once the pride of the middle class, could barely buy a loaf of bread. Families bartered soap for rice, aspirin for bus fare. Children were pulled from school to stand in food lines that sometimes ended with empty shelves.

In the fishing town of Rio Chico, Mileidy Lovera carried a bucket of fresh snapper along the roadside, offering a trade to anyone with cornmeal or baby formula. "Cash is worthless here," she told Reuters, "I have to trade fish for flour so I can feed my son." By 2017, she and her neighbors ran their own micro-market, swapping each morning on the beach. What kept her family alive was not luck, but the habit of bartering daily and building trust with five other mothers who could be counted on for honest exchange.

In 2018, Reuters reported that pharmacies in Caracas sold diapers behind locked glass and antibiotics via WhatsApp, all secure like contraband. Venezuela's inflation rate had reached 130,060% by that time. The bolívar had lost so much credibility that some store owners refused currency altogether, accepting only dollars (USD) or goods in kind.

In any collapse, building a barter circle with neighbors (committed, specific, and small) was the key. Americans should prepare by knowing what trade goods hold value (soap, medicine, fuel, canned goods, items for infants like diapers) and learning to build these networks before money fails.

Shortages followed in the once-rich South American country. The state-imposed control over food and medicine, but couldn't maintain supply. Basic goods disappeared from shelves. Flour, sugar, rice, and oil first became scarce, then inaccessible. Medical imports ceased almost entirely. Pharmacies stocked vitamins, bandages, and little else. Antibiotics vanished. Insulin became contraband. Families hoarded what they could and traded the rest through private networks.

After her child's asthma attack, Maria Gutierrez of Valencia went pharmacy to pharmacy, only to find the shelves empty. "I started growing eucalyptus in pots," she told NPR. She learned to boil the leaves to clear her son's lungs when inhalers ran out, trading jars of homemade salve for neighbor's antibiotics. Maria's WhatsApp group included four nurses and three mothers who exchanged home remedies, smuggled antibiotics, and warnings about fake medicine in the market.

You need to know basic herbal remedies, grow adaptable plants, and form trusted health exchange groups. Venezuelans survived by sharing remedies and vetting supplies in private circles, not relying on official channels.

Identify border towns, import sources, and plant-based remedies before shortages hit. Build local knowledge networks, and document safe, proven home treatments.

Those with relatives abroad survived on remittances. In Maracaibo, Alfredo Salazar, a retired engineer, survived entirely on $60 his daughter wired from Panama each month. He told The Guardian that the first thing he did when the blackout hit in 2019 was to text her: "Please send dollars, not bolívars." Alfredo's apartment complex pooled money to buy water from a delivery truck, each tenant contributing part of their remittance—without dollars, the truck would drive past.

Successful families kept children and elders useful and safe—never sending them out alone, and always pairing them with someone who knew the neighborhood. Some ran errands at dawn to avoid crowds and risk. In the city of San Fernando, several women organized block rotations, sending two from each family to wait in line while others stayed home to cook or guard supplies. Rotating jobs and protecting the vulnerable meant nobody was left exposed too long.

In their financial crisis, USD became king. Venezuelans who had set up remittance accounts and kept a working phone always had an edge. Americans should maintain access to stable currency, keep backup ways to receive and store money, and consider family pooling for essentials.

But what does an American fall back on? There is no easy access to a strong foreign currency like the pound or Euro. Silver and gold are the way to go to hedge against hyperinflation of the dollar and a collapse of the systems relying on it.

Power outages also became regular occurrences in Venezuela. Clean water became a daily concern. The state blamed foreign interference. The public knew better, but most said nothing.

The middle class disintegrated quietly, in full view of a population trained not to notice. There were no headlines, no statistics, no formal declaration. Professionals lost access to the goods and services that once defined their status. Engineers became delivery drivers. Accountants left to clean houses in Colombia. Teachers took second jobs as street vendors. The outward appearance of civility remained for a time — pressed shirts, polished shoes — but beneath the surface, families were pawning wedding rings and skipping meals.

As the legal economy decayed, the black market took over. Controlled food supplies were diverted. Hospital medications were stolen before they reached patients. Gasoline was smuggled through border routes and sold at ten times the official price. Shady deals were done in alleyways and on encrypted apps.

Everyone participated. There was no alternative.

WhatsApp became a shadow economy platform. Barter groups used the app to coordinate private trades in real-time, antibiotics for fuel, rice for baby formula. Sellers operated in USD when possible, particularly in urban zones. Outside Caracas, gasoline smuggling became the most reliable income for entire towns. Some local police not only tolerated it but were themselves part of the operations.

By 2023, over 7.7 million Venezuelans had fled their country, more than those who fled Syria at the height of its civil war - hungry, disillusioned families crossing borders in silence hoping their cousins in Peru or Colombia still had spare room on the floor and some food.

Security disintegrated quietly. The police remained visible, but trust in them disappeared. Some officers turned to extortion. Others looked away. Armed robberies became common. Kidnappings surged. Gangs operated openly in certain districts, filling the void left by the state. The military still marched in parades, but in the neighborhoods, protection came from neighbors with shotguns and reinforced gates.

True survivors protected their streets by rotating sentries (guards and watchmen), one or two at a time, never announcing the schedule, and always changing routes. They agreed on low-tech signals (a flashlight blink, a curtain drawn a certain way) to signal trouble or let neighbors know when it was safe. Every new face was quietly vetted, and anyone who couldn't answer a simple question about a local event was kept at a distance. Americans should agree on signals and roles with neighbors now, even if it's just a check-in text or a spare key exchange.

The Lies They Believed

Now here's where it gets interesting. Most Venezuelans did not believe they were witnessing a collapse. Not at first anyway. The early signs were framed as temporary, the result of bad weather, foreign interference, or momentary mismanagement. State media repeated phrases like "temporary adjustment" and "economic recalibration." Officials gave speeches in clean suits, using optimistic graphs to explain away empty shelves.

I expect something similar will happen here.

The population wanted to believe it. The calm voices on TV were saying this has happened before and everything turned out fine. Supermarkets were restocked — briefly. Fuel returned — in some districts. The worst was always just behind them. That lie lasted for years.

Normalcy bias is not unique to Venezuela. It is present in every population that has grown used to stability. People assume the systems around them are permanent.

They believe that because the lights came on yesterday, they will come on again tomorrow. That salaries will be paid. That law will be enforced. In Venezuela, it was common to hear phrases like "This is just a rough patch," even as the currency lost 90 percent of its value in a single year.

The government controlled the narrative. State broadcasters showed full shelves, foreign conspiracies, and official parades. There was always an enemy to blame: foreign governments, capitalists, smugglers, internal traitors. Policies that caused the crisis were defended as solutions. When price controls created shortages, the government doubled down. When capital fled the country, restrictions increased.

Criticism became treason. Dissent was treated as sabotage. And free speech died.

In Venezuela, late-night comedians mocked the opposition instead of the government that was to blame for everything. The not so free press rebranded inflation as a "global phenomenon." Government ads showed smiling families waving food boxes. In America, too, the clown masks are smiling. The same outlets that hid bailouts and pharmaceutical lies now brand meat, gas, and independence as threats to the planet. When all the news points one way, the truth is usually found in the opposite direction.

The signs were visible in Venezuela just as they are here, but they were easy to ignore. Inflation was explained as "transitory." Shortages were rebranded as "redistribution." Economic contraction became "a necessary correction." These were not exclusive to Venezuela. Americans have heard their own versions: "This is the cost of progress." "We're building back better." The slogans change. The mechanism doesn't.

Government messaging under Maduro adopted phrases like "Plan de la Patria," "Economic War," and "Anti-Imperialist Sovereignty." These replaced measurable policy with ideological theater. Hugo Chávez once declared on national television: "Socialism or death — we say socialism and we are going to build it." Today, American media repeat their own versions: "This is the cost of transition." "It's transitory." "We're building back better."

When U.S. Fed Chair Jerome Powell called inflation 'transitory' in 2021, it echoed the same euphemisms Venezuelans heard in 2014.

Two countries worlds apart and yet the same tricks played out on its population.

By the time the public stopped believing the official story, the alternative was harder to face. The collapse meant their savings were gone. Their institutions were corrupted. Their nation had been lost. It was easier to keep waiting than to accept that no one was coming to fix it.

Parallels with the U.S. Right Now

What happened in Venezuela is not isolated. It is not a regional anomaly or a cautionary tale for failed states. The same architecture is now being built in the United States.

In the U.S., it's not food yet. But dependence is shifting. Federal incentives now dictate what energy you can afford, what appliances you may own, and soon, how your digital wallet is monitored. Scarcity becomes a lever. Rationing is called sustainability. And "loyalty," in time, is called compliance.

Inflation is no longer debated, it is simply renamed. Official metrics exclude housing, fuel, and food volatility, even as all three surge. A twenty-dollar bill no longer buys what it did last year, but the public is told to blame the weather, foreign wars, or temporary logistics. Prices rise; purchasing power drops.

As reported by the Bureau of Labor Statistics, real wages in the U.S. fell by over 3 percent for working-class sectors between 2022 and 2023. Food prices rose by 11.4 percent in 2022 alone, the sharpest increase since 1979. Meanwhile, the Federal Reserve added over $4 trillion to the monetary base from 2020 to 2022, more than the previous century of U.S. history combined.

Meanwhile, government spending continues at historic levels, and the national debt climbs past thresholds once considered dangerous.

Scarcity has been normalized. Basic goods are delayed, backordered, or suddenly unavailable. Some shelves are half-stocked. Others are rearranged to appear full. Shortages are explained away as transitional; the cost of progress, or symptoms of "post-pandemic realignment." These excuses have become routine. They are delivered with professional calm, but they are masking erosion.

Institutional trust is collapsing, not in theory but in practice. Federal agencies are now openly partisan. Intelligence services, law enforcement, and even regulatory bodies are increasingly leveraged along political lines. The IRS monitors transactions once considered private. The Department of Justice prosecutes unevenly. Corporate tech platforms act as censorship arms, deplatforming users, throttling dissent, and algorithmically suppressing narratives that challenge approved doctrine.

Surveillance is embedded in daily life. Phones track location. Banks report behavioral anomalies. Social media captures opinions and aligns them with risk profiles. Every transaction, message, and movement feeds a system that no longer hides its hunger for compliance. The state does not need to knock on your door. It already lives in your pocket.

Internal files released through Twitter in 2022 confirmed direct coordination between federal agencies, including the FBI and Department of Homeland Security, and social media companies to suppress narratives deemed politically disruptive. This was not theoretical censorship. It was institutional, traceable, and executed without transparency.

Wealth inequality is widening. Home ownership, once the foundation of the American middle class, is now out of reach for millions. Rent consumes half of household income in many cities. Food costs have outpaced wages. Credit cards bridge the gap — briefly. Meanwhile, corporate profits set records and political donors expand their influence.

These are not isolated issues. They are linked. Venezuela showed the world what this process looks like in fast motion. America is moving more slowly, but the shape is familiar.

What Venezuelans Wish They Had Understood Sooner

Venezuelans now speak openly about what they missed, and when. Most say the same thing: the window to act felt optional, right up until it wasn't.

The collapse started with comfort. Gas was still flowing. Schools were open. The power came back, eventually. So, people stayed. They waited for a change. They trusted institutions that had already been compromised. And by the time they realized the floor was gone, they were already in free fall.

The first lesson is that reform becomes impossible long before collapse becomes visible. Once courts are corrupted, once the press is subservient, once elections are rigged behind the theater of ballots, you do not vote your way out. You do not organize. You do not reverse course. You endure, or you leave.

The second lesson is that inflation is theft. Not metaphorically — directly. It robs savers, punishes earners, and rewards debt. It makes planning impossible. It ends trust in contracts and prices. Venezuelans who held currency lost everything. Those who held assets or left early kept something. The rest became poor, regardless of profession, education, or loyalty.

The third lesson is that control over goods means control over people. Food distribution became a political weapon. Compliance meant calories. Opposition meant hunger. It did not take armed patrols or mass arrests. Just paperwork, identification, and silence.

A study by Datanálisis showed that recipients of the CLAP food program were overwhelmingly from pro-government districts. In opposition zones, rations arrived late or not at all. Complaints could get a family removed from the list entirely. Hunger became a vote.

Many say they believed things would get better. That the institutions would self-correct. That the military would intervene. That the world would not let it happen.

They were wrong.

And the ones who left early, when it felt dramatic, even cowardly, are now the ones supporting entire families from abroad.

No one who stayed too long thought they were staying too long at the time. That is how it always happens.

The ones who did stay, and survived, followed a strict set of rules:

- ✓ Never meet for a trade in the same place twice.
- ✓ Always bring a friend or family member; never go alone.
- ✓ Use decoys, wrap your real barter items in plain newspaper, and carry an empty bag to throw off thieves.
- ✓ If trading medicine, check labels and seals. Counterfeits killed.
- ✓ Never display a full stash. Bring only what you can afford to lose.
- ✓ Trust was currency. Trade only within vetted circles; new faces were watched, not welcomed.

If you're American, practice this now: go to a local flea market and barter for a tool or a staple, no cash. Note who tries to talk you up, who seems desperate, and how you build trust or suspicion. It's not about the money—it's about watching human nature shift under stress.

Cultural Decay and Demoralization

Before Venezuela collapsed economically, it broke culturally.

The first cracks appeared in trust. Neighbors stopped speaking openly. Friends became cautious. People whispered instead of asking questions. In public, everyone repeated the right slogans. In private, they said nothing. The boundaries of speech shifted, not by law, but by fear. A wrong phrase could cost you your job, your ration card, or your child's spot in school.

The state formalized media control through the 2004 Ley Resorte, a law used to punish broadcasters for airing content considered "contrary to national interests." Over time, this gave the government legal cover to dismantle nearly every major independent news outlet. Self-censorship became survival.

The next fracture was in religion and tradition. Churches remained open, but attendance dropped. Faith was replaced by frustration. National holidays became politicized events. Flags still flew, but fewer people saluted them. Weddings were postponed. Family gatherings disappeared. A culture that once celebrated life through music, meals, and community shifted toward isolation and suspicion.

Morality became fluid. Theft, once condemned, became tolerated. Eventually it became necessary. Families praised relatives who found ways to "get things done," regardless of legality. Bribes were normalized. Smuggling was expected. Selling expired medicine or stolen gas was treated as survival, not crime.

The social contract rewrote itself around desperation.

Authority collapsed in stages. Police were feared more than criminals. Teachers were no longer paid on time, then not at all. Judges enforced what they were told, or nothing. No one trusted institutions, but no one replaced them either. Gangs filled the vacuum. Informants became common. Children learned not to speak freely at home.

It wasn't always soldiers with guns. Sometimes it was neighbors. People whispered less because the state had ears, but also because betrayal became instinct. A woman might report a colleague to gain favor. A store clerk might call authorities just to secure extra rice. When trust dies, tyranny no longer needs to knock.

It walks in with your permission.

Over time, people stopped making long-term plans. They stopped investing in their homes, their work, their future. The concept of progress, the assumption that life would improve with time, was gone. All that remained was the present. What could be secured today. What could be hidden. What could be traded.

Once that shift happens, collapse becomes irreversible.

The View from the End

You think it will be obvious when your country falls apart. You think it will look like war, or invasion, or fire in the streets. It won't.

It will look like everything is going the same as always.

You'll go to work. You'll stop for gas. You'll scroll past headlines about shortages, protests, corruption – but you'll keep scrolling. You'll hear about new laws, new rules, new limitations. You'll adapt. You'll tell yourself things have been worse. That it will level out. That it's just a cycle. You'll keep saying that until it stops being true, and by then, you won't be allowed to say anything at all.

Do you really want to be saying one day:

"I was a professional. I owned a home. I had a family. I paid taxes, voted, and followed the rules. I watched my bank account evaporate. I watched groceries disappear, not all at once, but shelf by shelf.

I watched my children shrink while the government told us we were lucky. I stayed too long because I believed the system would fix itself. It didn't."

Stop thinking this can't happen where you live. It can. It is. You're just not calling it by the right name yet. Inflation is not a fluke. Shortages are not logistics. Censorship is not safety. And when your middle class disappears, it will not come back.

No one will save you. Not the party you vote for. Not the media. Not the courts. Not the military. Not the billionaires. You have to save yourself.

Prepare while you still have choices.

In the U.S., the language is softer: "diversity," "misinformation teams," "decolonization." But the effect is identical. The institutions that were once brakes now serve as accelerators. Bureaucrats now rewrite definitions, not just laws.

Stock food. Secure water. Build cash reserves in hard currency. Know where you would go, and how, if you had to leave.

What You Should Do Now: A Survival Blueprint

Know Your People

Survival starts with faces, not fences. If you walk your block and can't name who lives behind each door, you are already alone. In Venezuela, neighbors became the first and last line of defense. Trust brought warnings, food, and safety. Anonymity bred suspicion or made you a target.

Begin where you live, not in theory, but on the ground. Walk your street. Learn who lives behind every door within a hundred yards.

If you don't know your neighbors now, start today. Knock. Make a reason if you have to, borrow a tool, offer a cup of coffee, bring over a newspaper clipping. You must recognize every face, every child, every dog that belongs, and who or what does not. Draw a map if you need to. Record names, skills, and special resources by hand. When the internet is down, when a phone battery dies, paper and memory are all that stand between you and becoming invisible, or worse, prey.

Harden Your Network

Don't wait for a crisis to build alliances. Find at least three neighbors you trust and make a quiet pact. Information is your most valuable currency, but it is only as good as the circle in which you share it. Agree to check on each other, to trade news about shortages, strange vehicles, or rumors of local trouble. Practice together.

Stage a trade day in your neighborhood, not because you need to, but because the first time should never be under pressure. Trade a can of food, a flashlight, or an hour's work. You will learn whose handshake means something and who hedges or lies. If you're the one holding back, change. Familiarity, not cash, is what lets a neighborhood lock its doors when the sirens fade.

Rehearse Disaster

Don't just imagine disaster—rehearse it. Set aside a weekend to go without electricity and running water. Tell your family the reason: "This is not a game. We're going to find our weak spots before reality exposes them." Note where your plan fails: spoiled food, medicine that must be refrigerated, toilets that don't flush, the impulse to check a dead phone.

Try living without a smartphone for forty-eight hours. Force yourself to use printed contact lists. You'll discover quickly how fragile digital habits are. The Venezuelans who made it through weren't improvising during blackout—they had already rehearsed the darkness, the silence, the boredom, and the cold.

Secure Real Value

Money, in a collapse, becomes a trickster. The currency you trust today can become worthless overnight, as it did in Venezuela. The smart ones diversified while they could. Keep cash in small bills—enough to buy food, not enough to tempt a thief. If you can, collect old U.S. silver coins or fractional silver rounds; they carry value across borders and crises. Hide your reserves in at least two different places. If you're robbed, flooded, or forced to flee, your backup stash will buy you time. Don't tell anyone, not even family, where every hiding place is.

Value is what you protect before anyone else thinks it matters.

Master the Art of the Barter

Barter is not simply a substitute for cash; it is a test of trust and judgment. In Venezuela, the ones who survived longest knew what truly held value: soap, canned food, medicine, batteries, clean water, diapers, and fuel.

If you don't know what's prized in your community, or in general, you're already behind. It's time to learn.

Start now: try trading something small with a neighbor or at a local market. Observe the negotiation, the hesitation, the subtle calculations. Record what is worth more than its price on a good day. Write out a guide to barter values and keep it with your emergency supplies. In a crisis, your ability to trade wisely will mean the difference between eating and hunger, between trust and betrayal.

Build and Guard Information

Knowledge is a force multiplier. Print out guides for first aid, edible wild plants, water purification, and emergency repairs. Laminate them if possible. Put copies in your home and your vehicle. Join or create an encrypted group chat for emergencies, but also have a fallback for when cell service is lost.

Simple codes, paper notes, or even prearranged light signals can serve when nothing else will. In Venezuela, those with information survived, those without depended on rumors and hope—both in short supply and deadly.

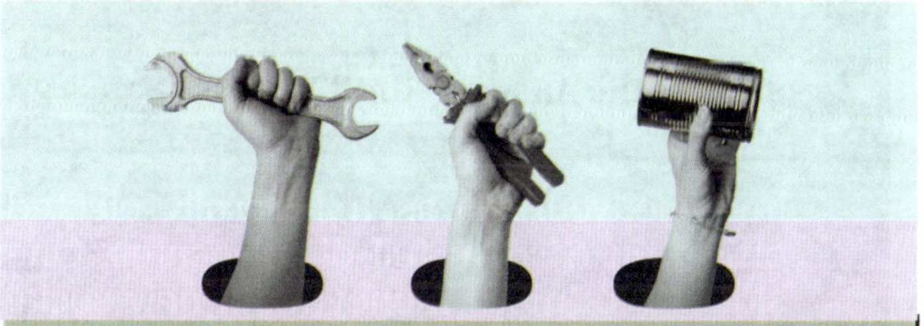

Test and Maintain Your Supplies

Preparedness is a living process, not a box checked once. Each month, go through your supplies. Rotate food and medicine so nothing spoils. Test your water filter and run your generator until you know every sound and smell. Check batteries and flashlights, fix what breaks, and restock what's missing.

Teach every member of your household how to use these tools, don't assume they'll "figure it out." In Venezuela, hospitals were empty, but homes that had a basic first aid kit, a sewing kit, and someone with steady hands saved lives.

Protect the Vulnerable

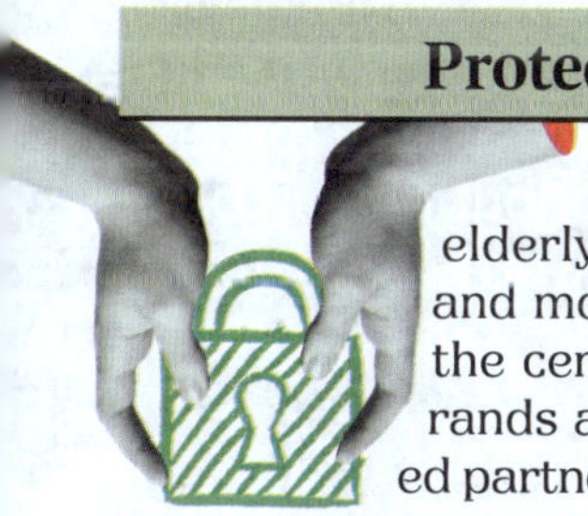

In every collapse, it's the children, the elderly, and the disabled who suffer first and most. Build your routines with them at the center. Never let the vulnerable run errands alone or stand in line without a trusted partner.

Create a rotation for food or water collection that keeps everyone safe and shares the risk. If someone in your home has special needs, double your preparation for them—extra medication, specialized food, mobility aids. In Venezuela, families that organized and protected their weakest members made it through together. Those who left them unplanned were often separated, sometimes forever.

Secure Your Home and Street

Physical security is more than guns and locks. In Venezuela, the best defense was layers: reinforced doors, window bars, dogs that barked at strangers, and well-lit entryways. But the most effective system was human: neighbors who agreed on signals, like a curtain pulled a certain way or a flashlight blink after dark and stuck to them. Make sure your neighbors know what to look for and what to do if trouble comes. Decide in advance how to respond. When everyone knows the drill, you are harder to target and harder to break.

Harden Your Mind and Spirit

Finally, prepare your mind. Accept, fully, that no government, no party, and no outside force will ride in to save you when systems fail. Survival is not a fantasy for doomsday preppers. It is the last discipline of ordinary people who refuse to be victims. Talk with your family about these realities. Share real stories of survival, and the lessons bought by pain and loss.

Teach your children, your parents, and your friends that the world they know can vanish, and that resilience is a habit learned before it is needed. In Venezuela, those who kept faith with each other, who remembered joy and held fast to hope, endured what others could not.

You need to master these rules now, or you will have to invent them in a panic, one loss at a time.

In an American suburb, it might be a flashlight passed over a fence at midnight during a blackout, or a neighbor's voice on the other side of a storm door asking, quietly, "Do you need anything?" The first act of survival is always the same. It is making yourself known. It is letting someone else see you, and seeing them, before you need them. That's where it begins. That's how you make the collapse survivable.

Chapter 4

How the US Went Broke and the Coming Crisis. Forgotten Lessons from the Great Depression You Will Need Soon

"When the people find that they can vote themselves money, that will herald the end of the republic." Benjamin Franklin

Debt Is the Answer - Until It Isn't

Imagine yourself as a federally elected official in a room full of advocates. One side wants more money for a new social program aimed at supporting single mothers. The other side wants tax relief for the hardworking American citizens. Let's assume there's only $3 trillion in revenue available, all of which is committed, but both sides in front of you want $500 billion towards their causes.

Is there a way to make both sides happy? Well, yes, there is. As a politician, you can say yes to both. How? The answer is simple. You can simply tell the U.S. Treasury to issue another $1 trillion in debt. Both sides get the $500 billion they're asking for, and you won't have to worry about paying back the debt because that won't need to be paid back for many years – perhaps never. It's not your problem.

This is, in a nutshell, exactly what has happened in the U.S. over the past 60 years. Debt has been and continues to be the answer. Unfortunately, the scheme can't go on forever. Americans are fast approaching the point where debt is no longer the answer – and it's frightening.

Taking a Trip Down Memory Lane to the 1960s

Let's take a trip down memory lane to the groovy 1960s. For most of American budget history, presidents, Congress, and their advisors thought that it was in the best interest of the country to balance the budget.

This common-sense view of spending and revenue began to change in the 1950s, and took a real turn with, at the time, a "momentous" change in policy, summarized by President Kennedy's statement:

Kennedy speaks at Rice University on September 12, 1962.

"It is not a question of whether taxes should be reduced. Any such hesitation would ignore the plain fact that the economy is not producing at full capacity. The real question is when tax reduction should take place. The right time, I am convinced, is the nearest possible date.

This does not mean that a budget deficit is necessarily a cause for concern. Our practical choice is not between a tax-cut deficit and a budget that is continuously in balance. We have presently built into our revenue system a substantial, long-term, inescapable deficit—just as we have built into it a substantial, long term, inescapable expansion of our economy."

What is so bold about this statement? The was a bold at the time – because it countered the prevailing belief that tax cuts should only happen when the budget was balanced. Kennedy argued that economic growth itself would eventually reduce the deficit by increasing government revenue. Over the past 60 years, Kennedy's view has won the day.

Some Background on the Debt Picture

Before delving future into the starting ground for the U.S. entering the edge of bankruptcy, here's a look at where debt has been.

In the first quarter of 1966, U.S. public debt stood at $321 billion. Large in terms of dollars, but fairly small when looked at from the perspective of the current federal government debt picture. In early 2025, federal government debt is about $36 trillion, an 11,115% increase over almost 60 years. If only we could get that type of return on our money!

Public Debt in Trillions of Dollars

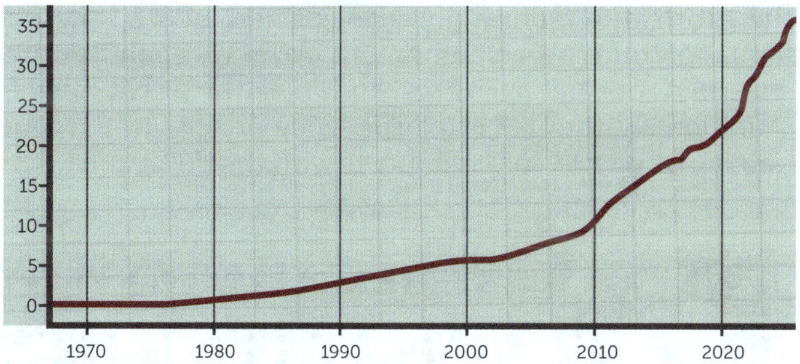

source: U.S. Department of the Treasury. Created by Econometric Studios, LLC

Economists often refer to the debt issue in relative terms, in this case as a percentage of Gross Domestic Product (GDP). By this measure, public debt floated around 40% of GDP in 1966. Fast forward to 2025, and debt is now above 120%. This picture is the very definition of the edge of bankruptcy.

Public Debt as Percentage of GDP

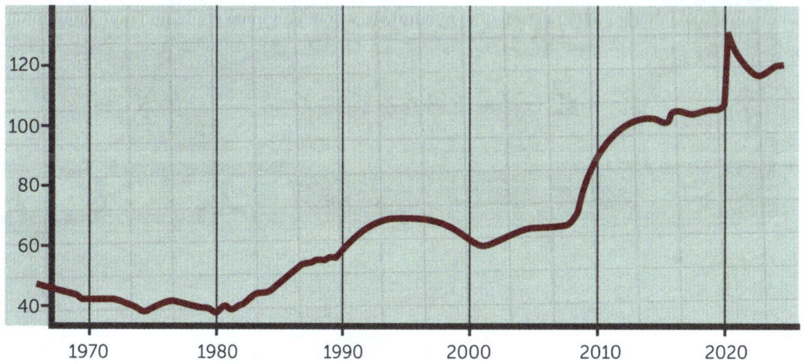

source: U.S. Department of the Treasury. Created by Econometric Studios, LLC

The 1970s – The Decade That Changed Everything

The American government has always been in some form of debt. For instance, in an effort to survive the military onslaught from the British, the federal government borrowed $75 million from France and other private investors to fund the Revolutionary War. That is not what we're talking about today. No wars or other threats to the survival of the American government exist. Indeed, throughout most of its history, the federal government has lived mostly within its means, aiming to balance the books and gradually repay its modest financial obligations. That is no longer the story line.

What we saw in the 1960s turned into the beginning of something that would restructure the financial world in the 1970s.

On the Edge of Default

Let's go back to 1971 and the administration of President Richard Nixon. In the early 1970s, the U.S. was struggling with the ability of foreign governments to convert the U.S. dollar to gold at $35 per ounce. With many other currencies pegged to the U.S. dollar, the $35 per ounce was an international commitment. This was why the dollar was once known to be "as good as gold". The problem with the commitment, though, was that the dollar was under pressure to depreciate, meaning gold was becoming more valuable than $35 per ounce. Why? Because in the 1960s, the federal government had inflated the dollar supply due to its commitment to the Vietnam War and several domestic programs, known as the Great Society . Additionally, the U.S. ran large trade deficits at the time, and it was paying for its imports with the dollar.

As one might expect, investors and other countries questioned whether the American spending picture was backed by real gold. Some countries, including France and Switzerland, started redeeming their dollars for gold to find out, and what they found out wasn't in America's best interest. America's gold reserves were beginning to dwindle.

With rumours accelerating that the gold convertibility window was about to be closed, countries rushed to drain U.S. gold. By 1971, the U.S. was down to $300 million in gold reserves, resulting in a dramatic decline of the dollar. Thus, the Nixon Administration was forced to suspend the Bretton-Woods system and do away with the Gold Standard. It was a change for the ages.

For the first time on a broad scale, the world moved to what is known as a fiat monetary system. It is the system we have today. A fiat monetary system is one in which paper currency isn't backed by a tangible asset like gold. Previously, the amount of gold constricted a government's ability to spend, but now the gloves were off.

Interestingly, the change occurred during the Stagflation era, spurred by OPEC suspending oil exports to the U.S., resulting in oil prices quadrupling. In 1973, inflation reached 8.8%, and by 1980, the Great Inflation Era reached its high watermark of 14.6%. In short, the 1970s was marked by high inflation, high interest rates, little economic activity, and elevated unemployment levels. Although stagflation would give way to an economic boom in the early 1980s, the echoes of the Nixon Administration's decision remain today, helping to lay the groundwork for a currency without substance. **Let's say that again – a currency without substance.**

The Fiat Money System Didn't Immediately Lead to the Debt Edge

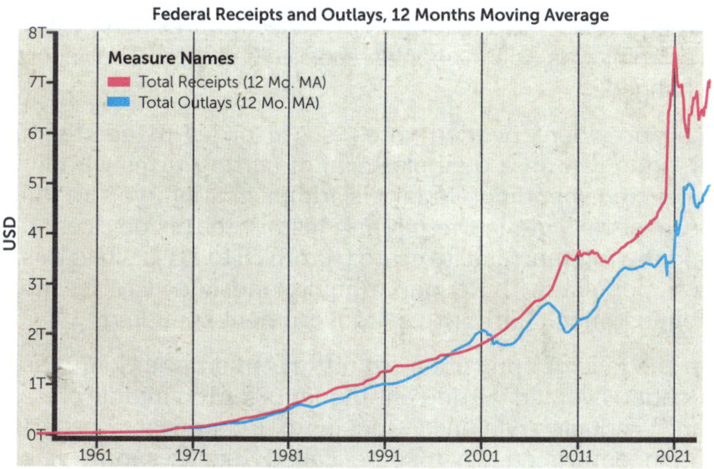

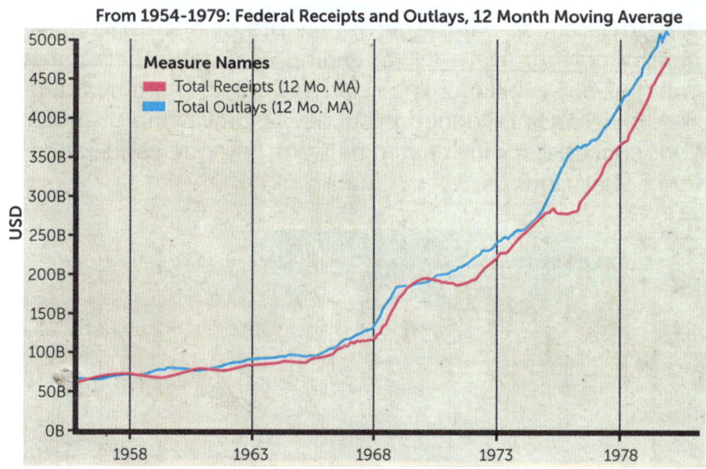

Although Nixon ushered in a new era of fiat currency, the idea was not new. Current historical research suggests that the Chinese were the first to "invent" fiat currency. I In the seventh Century during the Tang Dynasty, people used to receive promissory notes from their agents in exchange for metal coins. Tvhen, for making transactions, people would use the promissory notes . Known as "flying cash", wealthy merchants would park their heavy string of coins in depository institutions in exchange for the fiat currency. Fiat currencies came to Europe in 1660 when Johan Palmstruch of Sweden issued the first European banknotes. Perhaps unsurprisingly, the first notes were backed by bank deposits, but eventually demand exceeded the bank's reserves and the notes became a form of fiat currency. Fiat currency first came to the U.S. in 1690 when the Massachusetts Bay Colony faced a coin shortage and turned to paper money to pay soldiers returning from a failed expedition against Quebec.

During the 1960s, although President Kennedy had pushed for a budget policy that pushed aside a commitment to a balanced budget, federal finances, when measured by revenue and expenditure, were still relatively in alignment – at least by today's standards (first figure that follows). The fiat era blew through the moderate suggestions by President Kennedy, with the hole between federal revenue and expenditure expanding significantly (see second figure that follows).

The Reaganomics Era and a New Era of Spending

The 1970s ended with federal receipts at $481 billion (12 month moving average). Spending, on the other hand, ended at $509 billion . The relatively small, continous deficit of the 1970s balooned in the 1980s (following graphic). What caused the wide chasm between revenue Vand expenditure? Let's look.

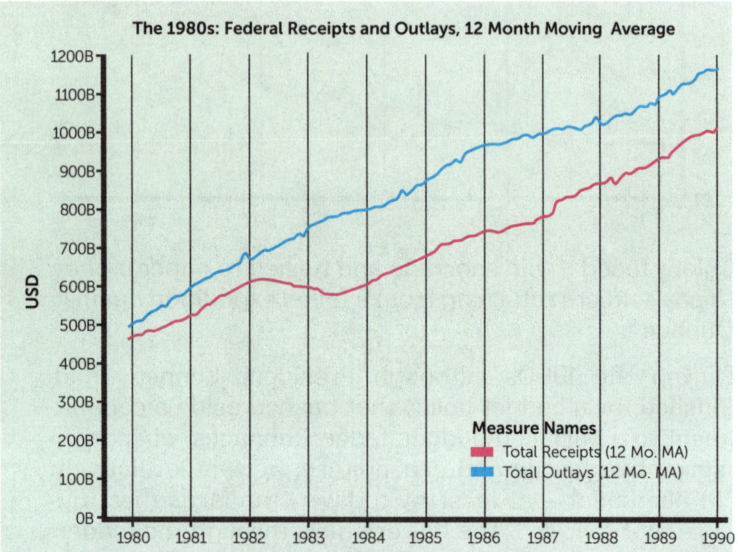

The 1970s ended with inflation higher than Americans had ever seen. This continued into the 1980s. Inflation was only bested – at least the high inflation of the President Carter years – when Federal Reserve Chairman Paul Volcker, nominated in 1979 by President Jimmy Carter – put the breakes on economic growth. The Federal Reserve achieved its goal of getting inflation below 4% in the summer of 1982.

When President Reagan was first elected president, fiscal restraint was still a popular economic motion. That soon changed.

The president needed votes, so, in order to get them, Reagan ran on a dual platform of cutting taxes without reducing spending. Under his administration, we saw the largest tax cuts in the nation's history to this day, reducing the top marginal tax rate from 70% to 28%. While this was popular, with Reagan winning landslide victories, he found it much harder to cut government spending.

In the face of opposition from the Democratic Congress, Reagan avoided cutting entitlements for the middle class and reducing defence spending. Economist Herbert Stein embraced what some called "punk" supply-side economic theory, claiming that higher overall tax revenues from economic growth would balance reductions to tax revenues from tax cuts. Although there is still considerable debate about the effects of the Reagan tax cuts, most economists appear to agree that the tax cuts had the intended effect of boosting economic growth while also acknowledging that the boosted economic growth was not enough to cover the reduced tax revenue – at least in the short term.

The budget deficit that followed the tax cuts created a problem for President Reagan. Concerned about how the debt markets would respond to continued deficit spending, President Reagan performed a 180 with the biggest tax increase in history. When netting the tax cuts with the tax increases, President Reagan's moves still put much more money in people's hands had no tax cuts or tax increases occurred, but there was one loser in the fiscal moves – an increasing fiscal deficit – at least in the short term.

Deficit Spending and the Countdown to Meltdown

What started in the 1960s, expanded in the 1970s, and ballooned in the 1980s, exploded in the aftermath of the 2008 financial crisis. For a brief period in the early 2000s, the federal government actually took a break from the deficit spending, experiencing a "peak" surplus at $278 billion in April 2001. The surplus didn't last long, as a recession, the Bush tax cuts, and lack of discipline to reduce spending led to more debt-financed spending. The budget picture really deteriorated in response to the 2008 financial crisis and the Covid-era pandemic response.

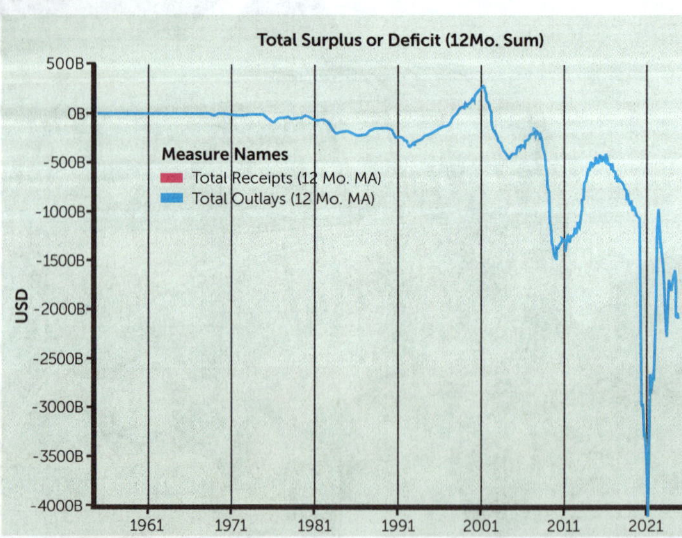

Writing philosophically, deficit spending is a powerful tool. Intelligent investor Know how to use debt to their advantage. Indeed, debt-financed growth can lead to a better budget picture than would otherwise be the case. That's not what we've seen from the federal government, though. Deficit spending only works over time when it finances successful investments. When a government fails to understand investing "rules", eventually deficit spending reduces what a government can invest in and changes expectations – often for the worse.

In the federal government's case, the government has ran deficits in 48 of the past 52 years. On the surface, it must seem amazing to lay observers how presidents, Congress, and economists thought this wouldn't lead to a pending meltdown if no changes are made.

Normalizing Bad Behaviour Is the Problem

In reality, the countdown to meltdown really stems from normalizing bad behaviour. The "normalization" of deficit spending over a half-century has driven the country to debt levels few countries have seen before. Part of the spending side of the equation stems from large-scale entitlement programs, which have resulted in over $100 trillion in accrued liability . Some scholars have suggested that the inception of Medicare and Medicaid were the initial drivers of normalizing bad financial behaviour .

What does this all mean? Well, the reality for American citizens is that **their government is addicted to spending, and spending has grown to such an extent that the only course of action that is politically feasible is more debt.** It is for this reason that now, more than ever, smart citizens should prepare themselves for the day when either taxes rise by an unpalatable amount and/or entitlements and other socialized costs become more reasonable in size.

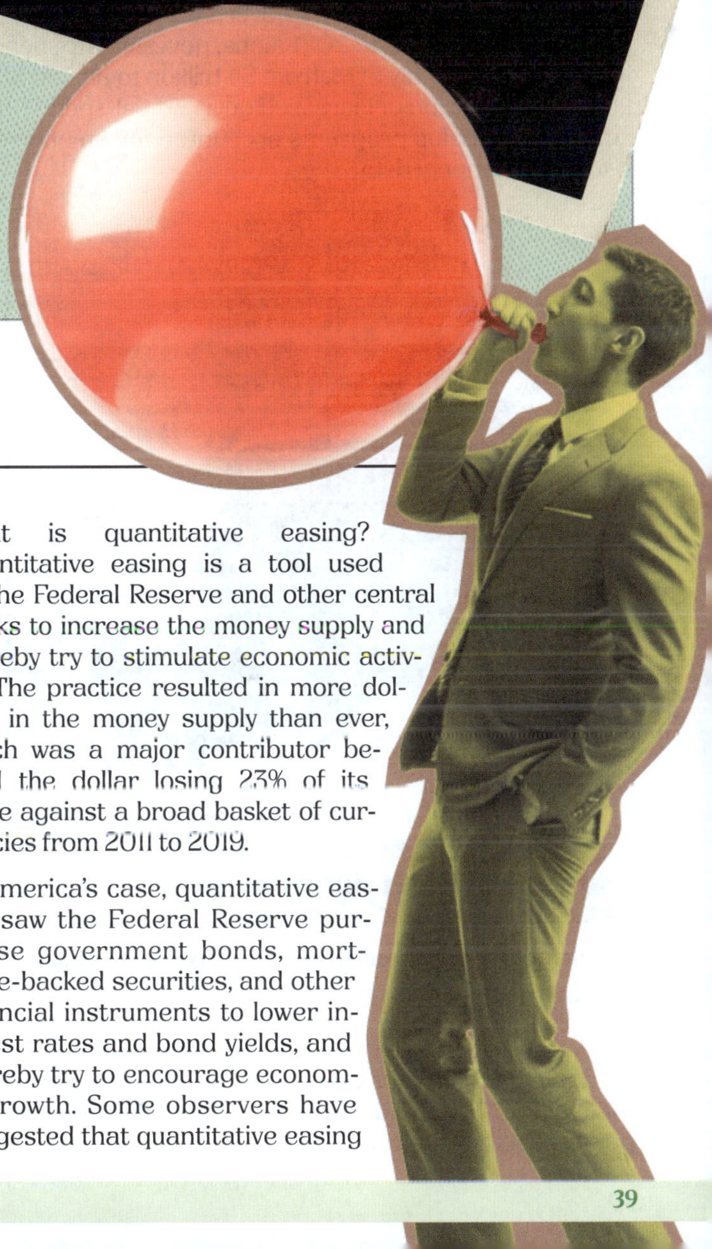

The Introduction of Quantitative Easing

There is perhaps no more inside baseball term than "quantitative easing". What does it mean and how is it connected to the federal government sliding closer to the edge of bankruptcy? The answer to that question lies in how the federal government responded to the 2008 subprime mortgage crisis. When housing prices began to decline, more and more homes went underwater, meaning that the mortgage on the home was more than the value of the home. During what became known as the Great Recession, more than four million Americans saw their homes foreclosed upon. Companies like Wall Street giant Lehman Brothers and Bear Stearns either closed their doors or were sold for pennies on the dollar. It was the deepest financial crisis since the Great Depression.

The collapse of Wall Street titans and the difficulty of families losing their homes led to a Federal Reserve practice that changed the American and global financial world, perhaps forever. It was perhaps the most significant response the global financial crisis – the introduction of the quantitative easing era.

What is quantitative easing? Quantitative easing is a tool used by the Federal Reserve and other central banks to increase the money supply and thereby try to stimulate economic activity. The practice resulted in more dollars in the money supply than ever, which was a major contributor behind the dollar losing 23% of its value against a broad basket of currencies from 2011 to 2019.

In America's case, quantitative easing saw the Federal Reserve purchase government bonds, mortgage-backed securities, and other financial instruments to lower interest rates and bond yields, and thereby try to encourage economic growth. Some observers have suggested that quantitative easing helped the U.S. avoid another Great Recession, while others suggest that rising inflation by putting more dollars into the system failed to produce any tangible results and certainly failed to spur healthy growth.

Overall, the Great Recession saw quantitative easing in action from 2009 to 2014, increasing the Federal Reserve's balance sheet and leading to bank reserves growing to over $4 trillion. Disappointingly for the Federal Reserve, banks were reluctant to lend their reserves to stimulate growth. Instead, over $2.8 trillion in reserves were held in bank vaults generating interest income, never reaching the businesses as intended.

Aside from failing to achieve its intended effects, the larger Federal Reserve balance sheet also resulted in national debt levels growing even more because it enabled the federal government to do something on a broader scale that it had become accustomed to – extra borrowing. As with prior spending and revenue decisions since the 1960s, the quantitative easing "experiment" brought America closer to a financial meltdown.

COVID-19 Spending Spree

Perhaps one of the most "traumatic" events of our lifetimes, the COVID-19 pandemic resulted in economic shutdowns worldwide. In response to the shutdowns, the federal government under the administrations of President Trump and President Biden "intervened" to mitigate a potential steep economic downturn . The responses, though, came at an incredible cost to the national debt and deficit.

If one measures the federal government response to the pandemic from 2019 to 2021 alone, government spending increased by roughly 50%, from $4 trillion to almost $8 trillion. A combination of increased government spending, tax cuts, and stimulus programs accounted for an enormous rise in the national debt.

It's understandable that governments around the world allocated some deficit-financed funding to the potential economic harm from the pandemic. The response, though, was likely too much – way too much. Generations to come will be dealing with the financial problems created by the overreaction to the pandemic.

In reality, the COVID-19 spending has been so substantial that the U.S. may never recover that lost ground. Even in 2024, the full economic impact of government spending during the pandemic continues to be evaluated. Perhaps the lesson individuals can take from the pandemic response is that citizens should prepare for crises by maintaining their own cash reserves and other preparations.

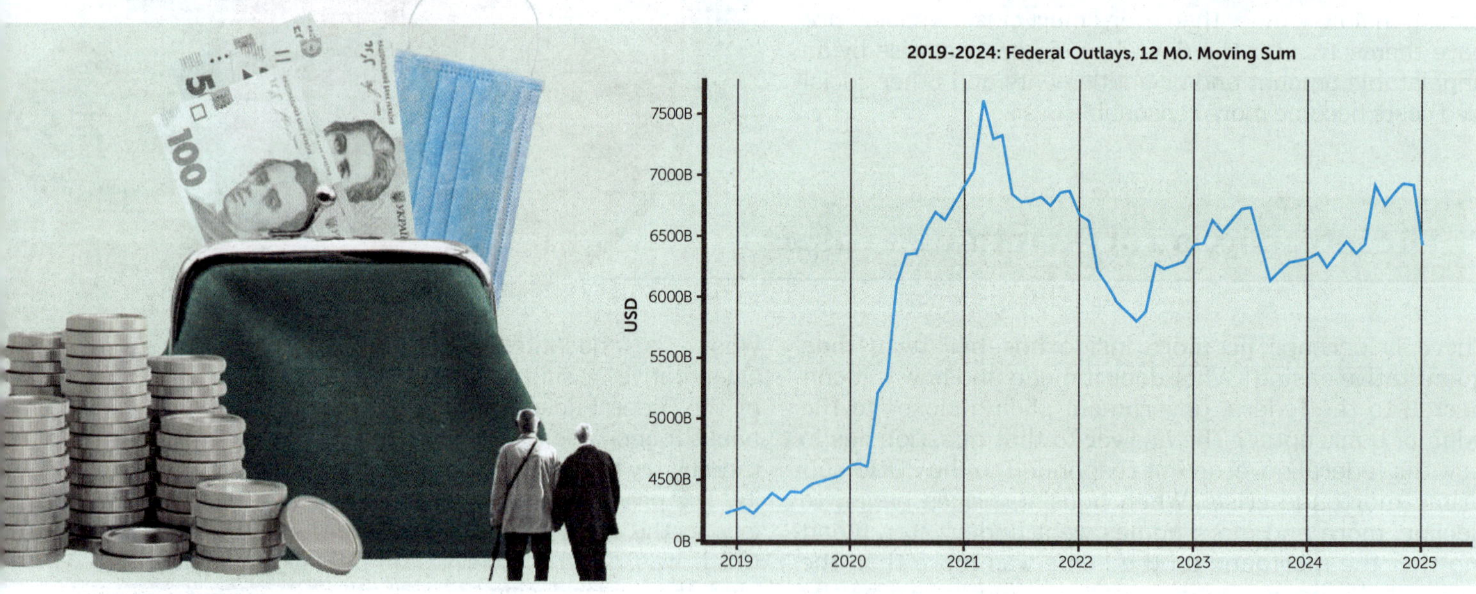

Behavioural Economics

Thinking Deeper About Human Nature and the Causes Behind the Debt

There is, of course, something deeper going on here – human nature. Remember, decisions that led us to where we are now were made humans – some elected, some appointed, some unelected and unappointed – all of whom have deep seeded feelings about the American individual and about what they'd like the future to look like. The system we have is largely based on popularity contests, and with popularity contests, a politician doesn't win votes by saying no. Humans – whether politicians or non-politicians – generally know that to get ahead, they must make others happy. And making others happy rarely involves saying no. Human nature operating within the current American political system is, by and large, the main driver behind the American slide towards the edge of bankruptcy.

Looming Debt Crisis and What It Means for You

Although there's still time to right the ship, the edge of bankruptcy is fast approaching. Unless there is a concerted effort and pressure from the voting American public, the debt spiral will eventually lead to defaulting on the federal debt. It could happen soon – perhaps in the next few years – and it will happen sooner if the dollar loses its reserve currency status. Should the U.S to default, the effects will be felt around the world, potentially leading to a global economic collapse far worse than any that came before. Such a scenario, even if it seems far off, would result in the end of the economic system as the world knows it. One study, conducted by economic research firm Moody's Analytics , found that a single default would wipe out 1.5 million jobs within one week. Longer defaults would sink 7.8 million jobs, spike borrowing rates, and potentially erase $10 trillion in household wealth.

The fact is the federal government has found itself in a situation whereby it must continue to print dollars and expand the money supply to meet its debt obligations should, at the very least, make Americans a little nervous. As the interest on the national debt grows, every dollar in Americans' bank accounts gradually become less valuable. As case in point, the dollar has lost 90% of its value since 1971, and although it's not inevitable, unless action is taken to right the course, the situation will continue worsen towards the edge of bankruptcy.

How do we actually know that the U.S. is heading in this direction? Well, one answer is past experience.

As an exemple, let's go back to the early 1920s when eight German marks were worth one U.S. dollar. At the time, the problem in Germany was that the country was broke. Since the end of World War One, Germany had amassed a massive debt t stemming from the Treaty of Versailles. With no other option, the Weimar government printed more money to pay off its debt, lowering the value of the mark. In just two years, the value of the mark dropped from 8:1 (mark to U.S. dollar) to 7,350:1. Eventually, the currency became worthless, and Germany returned to the gold standard when the mark collapsed to 4.2 trillion marks to the dollar.

In an eerily similar position, the U.S. is heading down the same path. Unless the smart men and women running the federal government find a way to convince the American public that more prudent financial practices are needed, the national debt will become unsustainable, and the government will either have to default or debase the dollar further. Naturally, should the federal government fail to reverse course, citizens can expect their paper currency to become worthless, the markets to crash, and inflation to spike. This potentiality suggests that smart investors and citizens avoid holding paper currency, which is why tangible assets may become more valuable.

Not Everyone Was a Loser in 1920s Germany

Looking back at 1920s Germany, not everyone was wiped out. The rich who held gold and real estate largely weathered the storm. In some cases, they even grew their wealth while much of the population struggled to buy bread. History doesn't always repeat itself, but it does rhyme. Without a course correction, that rhythm is eerily similar.

No individual can solve the debt crisis or avert disaster. However, what citizens can do is prepare for the worst, meaning preparing for everything from supply shortages, social unrest, and the potential collapse in the value of the U.S. dollar.

For those paying attention, the signs are flashing red.

Government spending continues unchecked, central banks resort to increasingly desperate measures, and inflation quietly erodes the purchasing power of ordinary people.

This isn't fearmongering. It's pattern recognition.

When institutions strain under pressure, it's often individual preparation and community-level action that carries people through. The time to think, plan, and reposition isn't after confidence collapses. It's now, when quiet warning signs still flicker beneath a facade of stability.

PART TWO

WHAT TO DO *and* HAVE READY *before* THE NEXT GREAT DEPRESSION

Chapter 5

Family Economy - How to Preserve Your Assets While Most People Will Lose Everything but the Shirts on Their Back

"The only real security that a man can have in this world is a reserve of knowledge, experience, and ability."

Henry Ford

There's No Turning Back

An economic collapse is not a news event. It is a structural implosion that moves downward, starting in markets, moving through institutions, and ending in the household, where its damage becomes permanent. While governments debate stimulus, while headlines call it "instability," and while central banks reposition interest rates, middle-class families lose access to everything they believed was theirs: income, liquidity, assets, and purchasing power. A collapse begins long before a family realizes it. And by the time the symptoms are undeniable, most of the wealth is already gone.

Prices accelerate upward, but paychecks do not. Equities remain on paper, but become inaccessible or unsellable without catastrophic loss. Savings lose function in real-time. Every item of value becomes harder to exchange. Families that once had $10,000 in a bank account or a stock portfolio discover that it no longer equates to food, fuel, rent, or medicine. Wealth still exists, but it has shifted elsewhere.

Weimar Germany, 1923:

The Weimar example remains the clearest demonstration of how an economic collapse destroys the concept of savings altogether. **A loaf of bread cost 160 marks in late 1922. By November of 1923, it cost 200 billion marks.** The monthly wage had to be paid in daily installments, and workers raced to spend it before prices doubled within the hour. Families who had saved responsibly for retirement, education, or property were ruined. The government attempted to revalue savings accounts, but the process was arbitrary and unequal. The vast majority were simply erased. Even families that held property saw its value collapse in real terms, since renters could no longer pay, and maintenance costs outpaced any theoretical return. **The only families who preserved their wealth were those who had diversified into foreign currencies, gold coinage, or physical trade goods before the peak devaluation. Everyone else was financially extinguished.**

Argentina, 2001:

At the start of the crisis, Argentina had a 1:1 peg between the peso and the U.S. dollar. This illusion of parity gave households false confidence in the peso as a store of value. When the government lost the ability to defend the peg, capital flight began. Foreign reserves collapsed, and the government initiated the corralito, freezing bank accounts and limiting withdrawals to 250 pesos per week, equivalent to about $75 USD at the time. **In one month, the peso devalued to nearly 4:1. Families with life savings in the bank lost over 70 percent of their purchasing power.** Real estate contracts collapsed, wages stagnated, and imported goods disappeared from shelves. Overnight, the middle class had no liquid assets and no access to credit. **Those who sold early (before the freeze) were able to reposition capital into hard assets. Those who waited, or who assumed the government would stabilize the situation, were wiped out.**

Venezuela, 2016:

This collapse followed a different mechanism. Rather than a discrete currency revaluation, **Venezuela entered hyperinflation through unrestrained monetary expansion and forced price controls. Monthly inflation hit 50 percent by late 2016 and peaked at 65,000 percent by 2018.** Families still technically "owned" homes, vehicles, and savings—but none of those assets could be exchanged for food, fuel, or medicine. Currency devaluation became so extreme that a kilogram of rice cost more than a week's wage. **The bolívar became so worthless it was used as scrap paper.** Most financial institutions collapsed into dysfunction, while **barter, gold fragments, and fuel vouchers replaced money.** Households that had previously been stable were forced into subsistence living, often relying on black market access or remittances from relatives abroad.

Across all three cases, the sequence was consistent:

Asset values appeared stable, but liquidity evaporated.	**Access to capital was denied** through withdrawal limits, freezes, or currency failure.	**Prices surged,** but incomes did not adjust.	**Government intervention** either failed or actively worsened the collapse.	**Households that waited lost control** over their ability to convert or preserve any wealth.

A collapse doesn't always start with war, or looting, or even an announcement. Often, it starts with a transaction that doesn't go through. A fuel station that only accepts cash. A transfer that gets "flagged for review." An employer who delays payroll "until next week."

Most families will stay locked in place. They will hold onto losing assets, waiting for recovery that never arrives. They will check retirement accounts every morning while the real economy collapses outside their front door. They will believe themselves "secure" because their home value remains unchanged on paper, or their stocks are "only down 20 percent." They will not sell until it is too late to get out. They will not convert until no one is buying. And when they realize the money is gone, they will also realize that they cannot buy food, they cannot withdraw cash, and they cannot move.

Several foreign nations including China, Japan, and Saudi Arabia started to sell off their holdings of U.S. long-term Treasury bonds by 2024. BRICS nations are developing a commodity-based trading system to displace the petrodollar. The end of global dollar demand could trigger collapse rather than an internal failure.

Grocery shrinkflation, rising deductibles, unfilled job postings despite unemployment, small business closures despite record corporate earnings—all are signs that the macro economy has already decoupled from the family economy.

If your household's financial reality depends on the continuation of normal institutions (banking, fiat currency, digital systems, capital markets, municipal services) you are not truly prepared for collapse.

There is no turning back because the collapse has already begun. The only question is whether you convert before the trap is sealed, or become another case study in what happens to those who waited.

Cut Your Losses: Liquidate the Money-Pits

What to sell now, while the markets still allow you to

Preserving wealth requires cutting loose the assets that will betray you. Families are often destroyed financially not by what they fail to buy, but by what they refuse to sell. Sentiment, ego, and inertia keep people holding stocks, currencies, and luxuries long after the signals are obvious. Value isn't what the asset used to be worth, value is what someone will give you for it today, in real time.

Tech equities are among the first casualties in a collapsing market. Companies like Tesla, Meta, Nvidia, and others in the speculative growth sector are valued not on what they make today, but on theoretical future returns. When credit tightens and consumers stop spending, these forecasts implode. Even if the companies survive, the price correction is brutal. Amazon lost ninety-five percent of its value after the dot-com bust and took nearly a decade to recover. Facebook shed a quarter trillion dollars in market cap in one quarter alone. If you're still holding these, you are exposed to a drawdown that could occur overnight. Retail investors will always be the last out the door. Sell now, while the price still reflects anything close to optimism. These stocks do not hold during contraction, they disintegrate.

Cryptocurrency does not behave like a hedge. It is not digital gold. It is a speculative vehicle with terminal counterparty risk and no guaranteed exit. Platforms collapse, wallets are frozen, and exchanges vanish with user funds. In 2022 alone, FTX, Voyager, and Celsius collapsed and locked out their clients. Users had assets on paper, none of them could sell. In real-world collapse zones like Lebanon or Venezuela, crypto was not used as a replacement currency. It was useless without stable power, mobile data, and access to trusted brokers. You do not own anything if you cannot convert it in the moment you need to. Sell it now, while the networks function. The next system failure may be permanent.

Exotic forex pairs such as Turkish lira, South African rand, Argentine peso, or even the Hong Kong dollar, are nonfunctional during global or regional collapse.

These currencies are thinly traded, often under capital controls, and are prone to violent repricing when the dollar slips or reserve flows shift. If you are holding these instruments on the assumption that you will arbitrage out of dollar collapse, you are betting against reality. Even in professional markets, liquidity dries up fast. On the civilian level, you won't be able to convert anything. They will become numbers on a screen with no bridge back to food or fuel.

Luxury assets, including boats, high-end vehicles, designer watches, and collectibles, are dead weight in a collapse. These items carry high maintenance cost, steep devaluation curves, and near-zero liquidity when the market contracts. Boats require fuel, docking fees, repairs, and insurance even when idle.

In 2008, luxury watercraft dropped more than fifty percent in value within a year, with some unsold for seasons at a time. High-end vehicles like BMW, Audi, and Porsche carry inflated resale prices that collapse the moment financing vanishes. Without credit-fueled buyers, those markets collapse into salvage.

Designer goods and collectibles may hold personal value, but unless you have a direct buyer today, you are holding a vault full of metal and leather that no one will want once collapse takes hold. Sell them now. Get hard currency, tools, or tradeable assets before the market disappears.

Urban real estate is another slow trap. While it may feel safe to own property, that ownership becomes meaningless once municipal functions collapse. During Argentina's economic failure, real estate in Buenos Aires became unsellable for over a year. In parts of Venezuela, Caracas landlords could neither collect rent nor evict tenants. In 2008,

U.S. property owners in cities like Las Vegas and Miami lost forty percent of property value, not because homes were worthless, but because buyers had vanished and banks wouldn't lend. If you're holding real estate in a city that depends on police, water, electricity, and centralized commerce, you are holding a liability that cannot be carried into a hard reset. Sell it while you can. Convert into land you can live on, not land someone might want later.

You must also close the cash drains. Recurring subscriptions, software licenses, media platforms, fitness services, unnecessary insurance policies, and any other auto-drafted service must be cut now. These systems will either shut down or offer no utility when the grid fails. Every dollar wasted on unused digital access is a dollar that could go toward medicine, tools, or fuel. Recurring expenses are death by paper cut. You cannot afford to carry burn-rate overhead into collapse. Cancel everything you do not use, and then cancel half of what remains.

The markets will give you one last window.

There is always a lag between when the system breaks and when the public accepts it. During that lag, prices still exist. Buyers are still available. Conversions are still possible. Once that window closes, value evaporates—not slowly, not over time, but all at once. You cannot exit a collapsing market on your terms. You can only exit now. The longer you wait, the more someone else sets your price.

You are not giving up these assets. You are escaping them!

Depression-Proof Investment Classes

Most stocks are speculative abstractions. In a collapse, only a small class of equities survives—the ones tied to infrastructure, energy, food, and logistics. These are not "forever stocks" or long-term growth plays. They are operational companies embedded in national continuity. Their products are either regulated, rationed, or subsidized when markets break. They are the last to be liquidated and the first to be propped up, not because they're beloved, but because the system can't function without them.

Look at the 2000 to 2003 dot-com collapse. While speculative tech lost over 80 percent of its value, companies with real infrastructure and supply chains survived. Apple was not a growth stock in 2002. It was a distressed hardware manufacturer with collapsing margins and a hostile PC market. Yet it had retained manufacturing capacity, cash on hand, and control of its physical product pipeline. From a bottom around $7 (split-adjusted), Apple stabilized and survived not because of narrative, but because it still made and delivered tangible goods. Amazon followed a similar trajectory. After losing 95 percent of its share value post-bubble, it emerged not through hype, but by becoming an irreplaceable logistics backbone for digital retail. It shed illusions and retained function.

Ford and GE during World War II serve as the classic case study. Civilian markets were frozen. Consumer goods were banned. But both companies survived and scaled because their factories were repurposed for military output. Ford manufactured bombers. GE built engines and electrical systems for government and war contracts. Their existence became tied to state survival. In economic terms, they were not stocks, they were wartime utilities. These companies endured because what they made could not be allowed to disappear. They received contracts, subsidies, and materials access even when private industry was collapsing.

In the stagflationary period of the 1970s, few companies retained value, but those tied to food, fuel, and infrastructure did. Archer Daniels Midland was not glamorous, but it processed wheat, corn, and soy at national scale. Its margins were volatile, but its relevance was not. ExxonMobil, despite price volatility, remained profitable across oil shocks because it controlled upstream assets—refining, transport, and reserve access. It wasn't just selling fuel. It was extracting, moving, and converting a commodity the world could not operate without. Even when margins compressed, volume and necessity kept it solvent. Companies like Burlington Northern (now under Berkshire Hathaway) survived because rail cannot be replaced, even during contraction. Shipping collapses, air travel shrinks, but freight rail remains essential for bulk grain, chemicals, and industrial parts. Rail companies with secure right-of-way and low debt service retain value when everything else gets delisted.

If you must hold equities into a collapse window, they must meet these minimums:

They control or move essential goods: food, energy, water, transport

They generate cash flow under price regulation

They have hard assets: land, fleets, mineral rights, storage infrastructure

They operate within systems too critical to fully shut down

They have historic or current ties to government contracts, subsidies, or resource allocations

This includes:

ADM (agriculture and food processing)

XOM (energy extraction and downstream)

CNI or UNP (rail freight)

LMT or NOC (defense manufacturing)

PWR or CEG (grid energy and infrastructure)

DHR or MDT (medical and diagnostics equipment)

Avoid consumer brands, financials, SaaS, entertainment, or speculative pharma. These entities collapse fast under credit crunch and disappear completely under wage-loss cycles. When households stop spending, Disney stock is dead. But fuel still gets burned. Grain still gets milled. Electricity still flows. Ammunition still gets manufactured.

These stocks are not a guarantee. They are a hedge against being exposed to air. If your capital must stay in the market for legal or logistical reasons, rotate now. These are the companies that survive not because they're the best—but because they are the last ones left standing.

Millions of families have wealth trapped in employer-sponsored retirement accounts. If those assets remain in high-volatility funds, they will be decimated. Reallocation inside the plan to inflation-resistant sectors is better than waiting for liquidity that may never return.

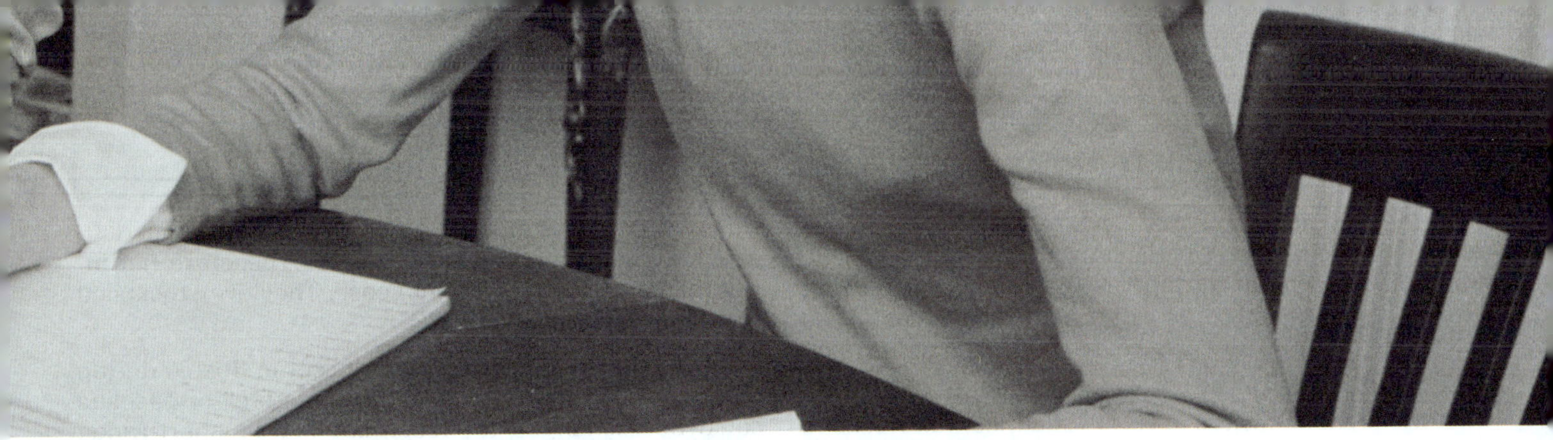

The 4 Golden Assets

Historical monetary collapses reveal four asset classes which consistently maintain their value across different times and regions. These are not trends. These assets serve as functional anchors maintaining purchasing power in situations where money becomes ineffective. These assets maintain their value independently of investor trust and digital or banking systems. They operate when everything else stops.

1. Precious Metals: Gold, Silver, and Barter-Grade Denominations

Gold and silver are not investment vehicles in collapse. They are currency replacements. When fiat fails, hard metals reassert their utility—not because people love them, but because they are universally recognized, cannot be debased, and do not require digital systems to exchange.

In Germany (1923), Yugoslavia (1992), and Zimbabwe (2008), gold remained convertible for food, fuel, clothing, and escape. During Argentina's 2001 collapse, silver jewelry and gold coins were often traded in informal markets for rice, flour, propane, and antibiotics. The metals held value even when banks froze, and official exchange rates collapsed.

Functionality requires form. One-ounce coins are valuable but impractical for daily trade. What mattered during hyperinflation were small, divisible units: 1/10 oz gold coins, pre-1965 U.S. silver quarters and dimes (90% silver), or local equivalents with known composition. These pieces are not for investing—they are for exchange. You cannot make change with a gold bar. But a silver quarter can buy a meal.

If acquiring metals, prioritize:

- U.S. silver coins (dimes, quarters, half-dollars dated 1964 or earlier)
- 1/10 oz or 1/4 oz gold coins (American Eagle, Maple Leaf, Krugerrand)
- Sovereign-minted bullion over private bars
- Secure, offline, non-bank storage

Avoid speculative numismatics or large bars. If you cannot trade it hand to hand, or if its value depends on collector premium, it will be ignored when collapse hits the ground.

2. Farmland – Yield, Shelter, and Access Control

Farmland is not about real estate appreciation. It is about continuity of production, sovereignty of movement, and secure location during resource denial. Land that produces calories, stores water, and allows controlled access is a high-order asset that functions across collapses and generations.

Historically, landowners in rural Argentina, Ukraine, and Poland retained wealth through inflation, invasion, and regime change. In the U.S. Dust Bowl of the 1930s, families that held usable land—even marginal—were able to grow, trade, or stabilize, while displaced urban populations collapsed under unemployment and food line dependency. In Venezuela's ongoing collapse, many of the only functioning food sources come from remote private holdings that are policed by armed families or co-ops, not the state.

Collapse reduces the value of trophy property but elevates producing acreage. The key is functionality. You want:

- **Soil fertility (measured or observable)**
- **Water access (well, creek, or catchment)**
- **Space for growing staple crops and legumes**
- **Physical defensibility (distance from highways, single road entry)**
- **Legal clarity of title (especially in contested or shifting jurisdictions)**

Farmland holds because it produces. Whether you farm it yourself or lease it under fair terms, the land becomes a currency-generating system. It is one of the few assets that function under barter, state rationing, or cash collapse.

3. Hard Commodities – Fuel, Fertilizer, Medicine, and Seeds

Hard commodities are non-currency items with functional value under conditions of scarcity. These are not investments in the traditional sense. They are stockpiled tools for survival and trade.

Fuel was the most critical barter asset in Bosnia during the siege of Sarajevo, where even one liter of gasoline could be exchanged for food, clothing, or short-range mobility. In Argentina, propane and diesel became parallel currencies during the winter of 2002. Antibiotics and antiseptics were used as storehouses of value in Eastern Europe throughout the 1990s.

Key hard commodities that hold or appreciate value during collapse include:

- **Gasoline (stabilized, rotated, stored in metal cans)**
- **Propane (20 lb tanks and adapters)**
- **NPK fertilizer (bagged, sealed, low moisture exposure)**
- **Over-the-counter medicine (ibuprofen, loperamide, antiseptic wipes, first aid)**
- **Antibiotics (azithromycin, amoxicillin, etc., where legal and safe)**
- **Seeds (heirloom, non-GMO, stored with desiccants in mylar)**

These assets become value anchors when markets break. You are not stockpiling these to use. You are stockpiling them to trade, leverage, or preserve optionality.

Storage must be quiet, secure, and rotated. These items lose value if spoiled or discovered by desperate neighbors. You are operating a micro-infrastructure node, not a storefront.

Urban families can store barter goods in stairwell closets, garage overhead bins, under-floor compartments, or off-site lockers. Vacuum-sealed food, boxed OTC meds, and fuel tabs can be concealed in ordinary containers.

4. Stable Non-Western Currencies – Swiss Franc, Norwegian Krone, Singapore Dollar

When the U.S. dollar, euro, or pound suffer collapse-level devaluation, currency repositioning can preserve substantial purchasing power, but only if done early and into specific sovereigns with low debt, export-driven economies, and fiscal discipline.

Historically, the Swiss franc (CHF) has retained stability due to the Swiss National Bank's conservative monetary policy and high reserve ratios. During periods of global uncertainty, capital inflows into the CHF surge—not due to growth, but to safety. Switzerland's banking privacy laws and neutrality add to its resilience.

The Norwegian krone (NOK) is resource-backed by oil exports, low national debt, and a sovereign wealth fund that buffers against external shocks. The Singapore dollar (SGD) is similar, rigidly managed, tied to trade volume, and supported by one of the most stable banking systems in Asia.

These are not currencies you use daily. These are capital shelters. You convert fiat into them before your local currency erodes, and then hold in physical or offshore accounts until stability returns. Physical banknotes in CHF or NOK are ideal but hard to obtain in volume. Multi-currency accounts in offshore jurisdictions are another method, but must be vetted thoroughly.

What does not qualify as a stable refuge:

Chinese yuan (CCP capital controls)

Japanese yen (massive debt overhang)

Any Latin American, Middle Eastern, or African currency not backed by commodity surplus

Once functional markets return, you must rotate some back into high-liquidity assets. The best wealth preservers become traps when they are held beyond their strategic window.

"We're all just nine meals away from anarchy and one antibiotic away from death."
Michael Osterholm

Chapter 6

Vital Medicines You Need to Acquire Before Pharmacies Run Dry

In a crisis where pharmacies run dry, having a well-stocked home medicine cabinet is essential. This chapter outlines the vital medicines and first aid items to stockpile before an emergency hits. I'm talking about everything from everyday over-the-counter pills to crucial prescription medications and first aid supplies – all chosen for their broad usefulness in a survival situation like the economic collapse coming our way.

By preparing these medicines in advance, you give yourself the best chance to treat common injuries and illnesses, manage chronic conditions, and handle medical emergencies when help is not on the way. Let's dive into the must-have categories: general medicines, antibiotics, meds for pre-existing conditions, and first aid essentials.

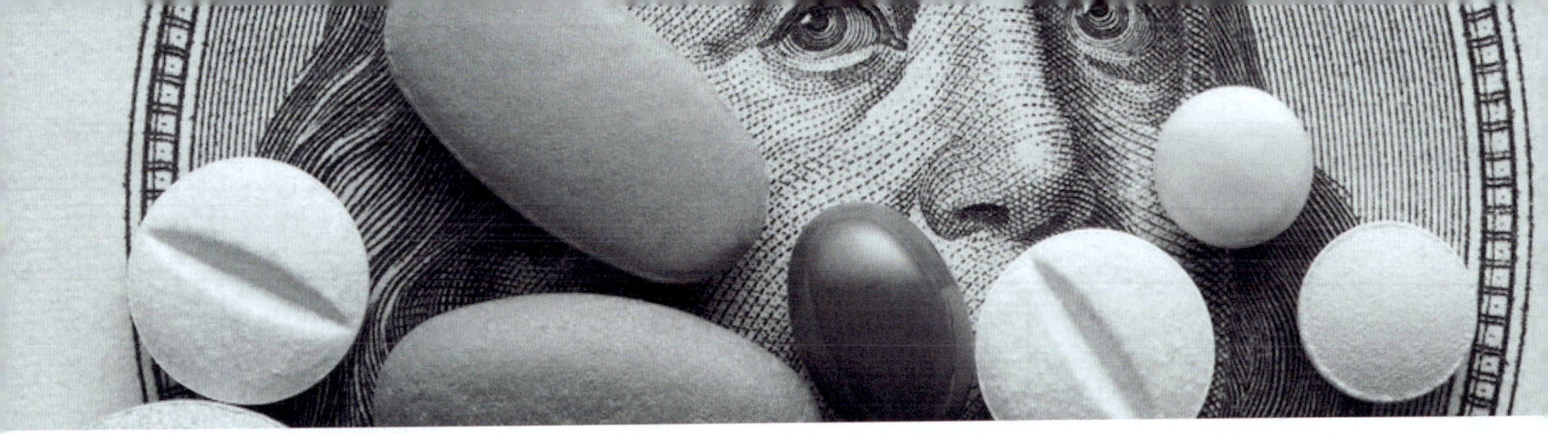

General Medicine

When pharmacies are closed or looted, you'll lean on a core stash of over-the-counter (OTC) medicines for day-to-day problems. These include pain relievers, fever reducers, stomach and digestive aids, and allergy medications. In normal times, we take a quick trip to the drugstore for these; in the next crisis, you'll need to have them on hand. Each item below is inexpensive now and widely available in the U.S. at stores like Walgreens, CVS, Walmart, or online retailers.

Luted Pharmacy during New York Protests, June 1st 2020

OTC Painkillers and Anti-Inflammatories

Stock up on two main types of OTC painkillers: acetaminophen and NSAIDs (nonsteroidal anti-inflammatory drugs). Both help reduce pain and can bring down a fever.

Acetaminophen (Tylenol, Mapap, generics)

Used for pain relief and fever reduction. Generally safe but can cause severe liver damage if taken in excess. Avoid mixing with alcohol or other acetaminophen-containing products.

Standard dosage: 325 mg or 500 mg every 4-6 hours as needed (max 4,000 mg/day).

While acetaminophen is one of the most common pain relievers, its primary advantage in a survival situation is that it doesn't cause stomach irritation like NSAIDs, making it safer for individuals with ulcers, gastritis, or blood clotting disorders. It is also the preferred option for children, as well as pregnant or breastfeeding women. However, in extreme heat or high-exertion situations, dehydration increases the risk of liver toxicity, making proper hydration critical. Acetaminophen poisoning is a major risk if combined with alcohol or taken in excessive doses over multiple days. Symptoms of overdose (which may not appear immediately) include nausea, jaundice, confusion, and abdominal pain. **If an emergency overdose occurs, activated charcoal can help absorb some of the drug if taken within one hour.** Otherwise, the only effective treatment is **N-acetylcysteine (NAC), which should be stocked if possible.**

Acetaminophen works centrally in the brain, blocking pain signals without the stomach irritating effects of NSAIDs. This makes it ideal for people with ulcers or those prone to stomach sensitivity. However, its effectiveness is lower for inflammatory pain (such as arthritis), where NSAIDs are superior. It has a synergistic effect when combined with caffeine (as seen in Excedrin), which can enhance pain relief for migraines. While expiration dates for acetaminophen are conservative, studies indicate it remains effective for years if stored properly.

Price Range: $4 to $12 for 100 tablets of 500 mg strength.

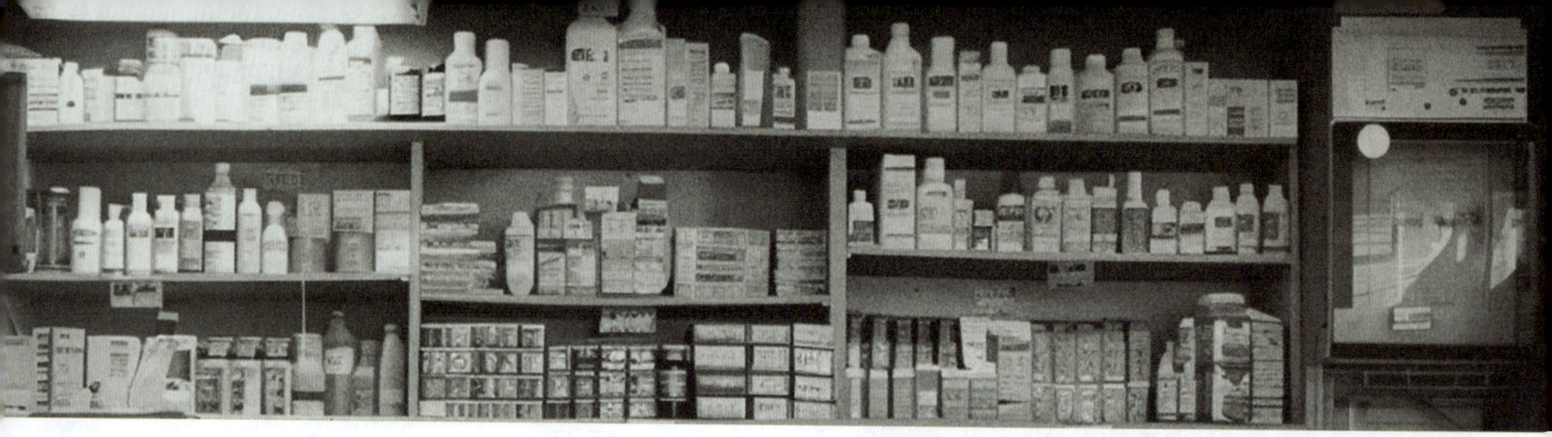

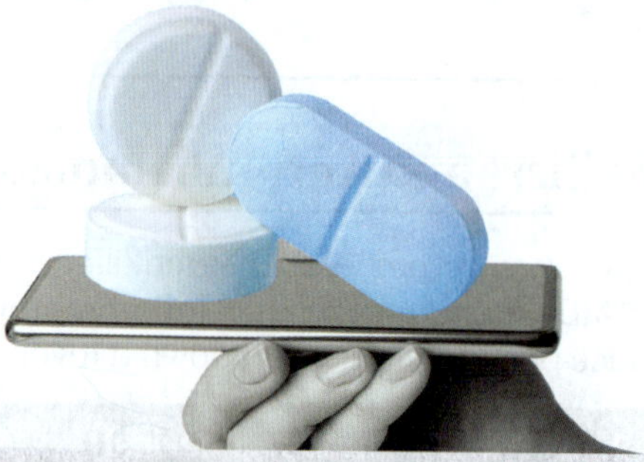

Ibuprofen (Advil, Motrin, generics)

An NSAID effective for pain, fever, and inflammation. Can cause stomach irritation and should be taken with food.

Dosage: 200-400 mg every 4-6 hours (max 1,200 mg/day OTC).

Ibuprofen is one of the most effective and versatile NSAIDs available, particularly for **reducing inflammation, swelling, and pain from injuries.** In a survival scenario, it can help manage **joint pain, sprains, and post-injury swelling** when mobility is essential. Additionally, it is sometimes used to **prevent high-altitude sickness** by reducing inflammation in the brain's blood vessels. However, ibuprofen carries a **high risk of kidney damage if taken without sufficient water,** so staying hydrated is critical. Unlike acetaminophen, **ibuprofen also thins the blood slightly,** which can be problematic for treating wounds or injuries where clotting is necessary. It should also be avoided in cases of **severe dehydration, gastrointestinal ulcers, or pre-existing kidney conditions,** as it can worsen these issues quickly.

It is also used in high doses (prescription strength) for conditions like tendonitis, menstrual pain, and migraines. In long-term emergency scenarios, ibuprofen can be used to reduce fever in infections or help with post-injury swelling. However, it can raise blood pressure and reduce kidney function if taken continuously, especially without adequate hydration. Those with a **history of cardiovascular disease should use it cautiously,** as NSAIDs can slightly increase the risk of heart attack and stroke.

Price Range: $5 to $15 for 100 tablets of 200 mg strength.

Naproxen (Aleve, generics)

A longer-lasting NSAID that reduces the number of doses needed per day.

Dosage: 220 mg every 8-12 hours (max 660 mg/day).

The primary benefit of naproxen over ibuprofen is its **longer half-life,** meaning it provides sustained relief **without needing multiple doses per day**—a huge advantage if medication supply is limited. It is commonly used by individuals with **arthritis, chronic pain, and recurrent migraines.** However, in a survival situation, naproxen can also **help manage swelling after surgery or wounds,** making it a useful **post-trauma medication.** Despite its effectiveness, it shares many of ibuprofen's risks: **stomach bleeding, kidney stress, and blood thinning effects.** Since it lasts longer in the bloodstream, it should be used **cautiously in elderly individuals or those prone to internal bleeding.**

Price Range: $8 to $20 for 100 tablets of 220 mg strength.

Aspirin (Bayer, Ecotrin, generics)

Used for pain relief, inflammation, and as a blood thinner for heart attack prevention. Not recommended for children due to the risk of Reye's syndrome.

Dosage: 325-650 mg every 4-6 hours (max 4,000 mg/day).

Unlike other pain relievers, aspirin has **unique anti-clotting properties, making it indispensable for anyone at risk of heart attacks or strokes.** In a survival situation, a person experiencing chest pain should immediately **chew and swallow 325 mg of aspirin,** as this can help break up small clots in the arteries. Aspirin is also useful for **reducing inflammation** in arthritis or muscle injuries, though it has a much higher risk of **causing stomach bleeding than ibuprofen or naproxen.** Due to its **permanent blood-thinning effect,** aspirin should be avoided before surgeries or in cases of **trauma with heavy bleeding.** It is also dangerous for children with viral infections, as it can trigger **Reye's syndrome,** a rare but fatal condition. Additionally, aspirin **can be used to treat fever in severe infections,** making it one of the most multi-purpose painkillers to stockpile.

Price Range: $2 to $10 for 100 tablets of 325 mg strength.

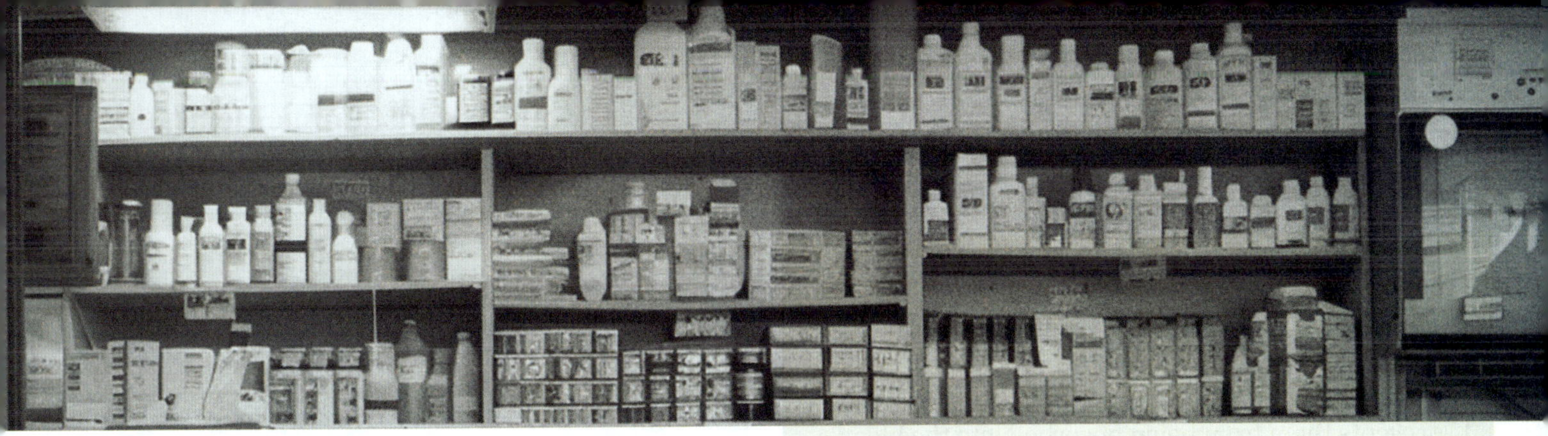

Gastrointestinal Relief

Digestive troubles can hit hard in survival situations, especially if food or water quality is compromised. Keep these on hand:

Loperamide (Imodium A-D, generics)

Treats diarrhea and prevents dehydration.

Dosage: 2 mg after first loose stool, then 1 mg after each subsequent stool (max 8 mg/day OTC).

Diarrhea is one of the **leading causes of death in a crisis,** as it rapidly depletes the body's fluids and electrolytes, leading to fatal dehydration. Loperamide slows gut motility, reducing stool frequency and allowing more fluid absorption. However, **it does not cure infections,** so if diarrhea is caused by bacterial contamination or parasites, loperamide can actually **worsen the illness by preventing the body from expelling harmful toxins.** In cases of **food poisoning or dysentery,** an antibiotic or activated charcoal should be used first. **Overuse of loperamide can lead to severe constipation, toxic colon syndrome, or even heart arrhythmias at very high doses,** so it should be used cautiously and **never for more than two consecutive days** unless under medical guidance.

Price Range: $7 to $15 for 24 caplets of 2 mg strength.

Bismuth Subsalicylate (Pepto-Bismol, Kaopectate, generics)

Relieves diarrhea, nausea, and indigestion.

Dosage: 30 ml or 2 tablets every 30-60 minutes as needed (max 8 doses/day).

More than just a simple stomach remedy, bismuth subsalicylate is a **mild antibacterial agent,** meaning it can help reduce gut infections causing traveler's diarrhea or food poisoning. Unlike loperamide, it **doesn't slow gut motility,** so it can be safely used for diarrhea that involves foodborne pathogens. Additionally, it **reduces nausea, coats the stomach lining, and relieves heartburn,** making it extremely useful in cases of **acid reflux, mild ulcers, and general stomach distress.** However, it can cause **black stools and tongue discoloration,** which are harmless but alarming if unexpected. Since it contains salicylates, it should not be given to children recovering from viral illnesses, as it carries the same Reye's syndrome risk as aspirin.

Beyond treating diarrhea, bismuth subsalicylate has antibacterial properties and can help fight traveler's diarrhea by reducing harmful bacteria in the gut. It also coats the stomach lining, providing relief from nausea, indigestion, and mild food poisoning. Because it contains salicylates (like aspirin), it should not be taken with other blood thinners or given to children recovering from viral infections. In long-term storage, Pepto-Bismol tablets are preferable over liquid, as they last longer and are easier to transport.

Price Range: $5 to $10 for an 8 oz bottle.

Digestive Enzymes (Lactaid, Enzymedica, generics)

Useful for those with food intolerances or to help adjust to an unusual diet.

Activated Charcoal (multiple brands)

Used for poisoning treatment and can help with gas or diarrhea.

Dosage: Typically, 1 g/kg body weight in poisoning cases.

Activated charcoal is a **lifesaving treatment for certain poisonings, drug overdoses, and toxin ingestion,** as it binds harmful substances in the stomach and prevents them from being absorbed into the bloodstream. This makes it essential for survival scenarios where **accidental food poisoning, toxic plant ingestion, or medication overdose might occur.** It can also reduce gas and bloating, though this is a secondary use. However, **charcoal should not be used if caustic chemicals (acids, alkalis) were swallowed,** as it won't neutralize them and could worsen esophageal damage. Additionally, it interferes with many medications, **so it should not be taken at the same time as prescribed drugs** unless treating an overdose.

Oral Rehydration Salts (ORS)

Essential for treating dehydration due to diarrhea or heat exhaustion. Drinks like Gatorade or similar products can be an aid to reverse dehydration.

As mentioned, dehydration kills more people in survival settings than any other condition, and Oral Rehydration Salts (ORS) are the most effective way to **rapidly restore fluids and electrolytes** lost through vomiting, diarrhea, or extreme exertion. Unlike sugary sports drinks, **ORS contains a precise balance of sodium, glucose, and potassium** to maximize water absorption. They should be stockpiled in individual packets for emergency use. If unavailable, a homemade ORS can be made using **6 teaspoons of sugar, ½ teaspoon of salt, and 1 liter of clean water.** However, improper ratios can be dangerous—too much salt can worsen dehydration, while too little won't help.

Antispasmodic Medication (Dicyclomine, Hyoscyamine, or OTC Peppermint Oil Capsules)

For severe stomach cramps.

Antiallergic and Antihistaminic Medications

Allergies don't take a break just because all hell is breaking loose outside. Here are the anti-allergy medications to stock-up on:

Diphenhydramine (Benadryl, generics)

Fast-acting for allergic reactions and also a sleep aid.

Dosage: 25-50 mg every 4-6 hours as needed.

Diphenhydramine is not only an antihistamine for allergies but **also a mild sedative** and sleep aid. It can be useful in stressful survival situations where sleep is difficult to achieve. It also works as an emergency anti-nausea drug and can be used to counteract motion sickness. However, diphenhydramine can cause drowsiness and **slows reaction times,** so it should be avoided when alertness is necessary, such as operating machinery or defending a perimeter in a survival scenario.

Price Range: $4 to $12 for 100 tablets of 25 mg strength.

Cetirizine (Zyrtec), Loratadine (Claritin), Fexofenadine (Allegra)

Non-drowsy options for daily allergy management.

Dosage: 10 mg once daily.

These **second-generation antihistamines** are preferred for long-term allergy control because they do not cause drowsiness like diphenhydramine. **Cetirizine** is stronger for hives and rashes, while **loratadine** is the most "truly" non-drowsy option. **Fexofenadine** is the best choice for those needing allergy relief while performing physically demanding tasks since it causes the least drowsiness. These medications are ideal for **outdoor survival,** where exposure to pollen, dust, or insect bites can trigger allergic reactions.

Price Range: $10 to $25 for 30 tablets of 10 mg strength.

Epinephrine Auto-Injector (EpiPen, Auvi-Q, generics)

Life-saving for anaphylaxis.

Use an EpiPen immediately at the first sign of a severe allergic reaction (anaphylaxis)—such as swelling of the throat, difficulty breathing, rapid heartbeat, or sudden hives—especially after exposure to a known allergen like peanuts, bee stings, or certain medications. Inject the EpiPen firmly into the outer thigh, through clothing if necessary, and hold it in place for about 3 seconds.

Hydrocortisone Cream 1%

Treats skin rashes and itching.

Antibiotics (Broad-Spectrum)

I don't have to tell you that antibiotics are crucial for treating infections that, if left untreated, could become fatal. In a crisis, you won't be able to get them anymore, and the worst part is that before a crisis they require a prescription. But there is a way around that – fish antibiotics which are almost identical to human antibiotics. Here's what you should get and how to take them:

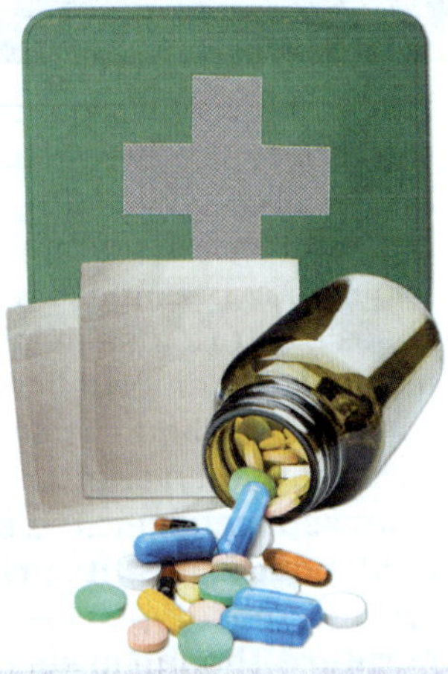

Amoxicillin (Fish Mox, generics)

Treats respiratory infections, strep throat, and some urinary infections.

Dosage: 500 mg every 8 hours.

Amoxicillin is one of the **most widely used broad-spectrum antibiotics,** effective against **respiratory infections, sinusitis, strep throat, urinary tract infections, and some skin infections.** It is usually **well tolerated,** though allergic **reactions are common in those with penicillin allergies**. In a survival situation, amoxicillin should be **reserved for moderate to severe bacterial infections,** as improper use can lead to **antibiotic resistance.** If treating a wound infection, **mark the borders of redness with a pen to track its spread,** and only continue the antibiotic if symptoms persist or worsen.

Price Range: $10 to $30 for 30 capsules of 500 mg strength.

Doxycycline (Fish Doxy, generics)

Effective against respiratory infections, Lyme disease, malaria prevention, and some skin infections.

Dosage: 100 mg twice daily.

Doxycycline is a **powerful antibiotic that covers a range of infections, including pneumonia, Lyme disease, Rocky Mountain spotted fever, and even bioterror threats like anthrax or plague.** Unlike penicillins, it also **covers some antibiotic-resistant bacteria.** It should be used as a **first-line option for tick-borne diseases or lung infections.** However, **doxycycline makes the skin highly sun-sensitive,** so those taking it should avoid prolonged sun exposure to prevent **severe burns.**

Price Range: $15 to $50 for 30 capsules of 100 mg strength.

Cephalexin (Keflex, Fish Flex, generics)

Good for skin and soft tissue infections.

Dosage: 500 mg four times daily.

Typically prescribed for 7 to 14 days depending on infection severity. Do not exceed 14 days without expert oversight. Can cause nausea, diarrhea, or allergic reactions in penicillin-sensitive individuals. **Prolonged or repeated use may lead to secondary infections like yeast overgrowth.**

Price Range: $12 to $35 for 30 capsules of 500 mg strength.

Sulfamethoxazole-Trimethoprim (Bactrim, Bird Sulfa, generics)

Used for urinary tract infections and some MRSA infections.

Dosage: 800/160 mg twice daily.

Standard course is 7–10 days for most infections; some MRSA treatments may require 14 days. **Avoid use in patients with sulfa allergies. Stay hydrated to prevent kidney issues.** Watch for signs of rash or allergic reaction. D**o not exceed 14 days without medical advice due to increased risk of side effects like hyperkalemia or blood disorders.**

Ciprofloxacin (Fish Flox, generics)

Broad-spectrum for gastrointestinal infections, UTIs, and more serious bacterial threats.

Dosage: 500 mg twice daily.

3 to 14 days depending on the condition—shorter for UTIs (3–5 days), longer for more serious infections. **Avoid use in children or during pregnancy.** May cause tendon inflammation or rupture—especially in older adults. **Do not take with calcium, iron, or antacids within 2 hours of dose.** Prolonged use increases risk of antibiotic resistance. **Do not exceed 14 days** without clinical reassessment.

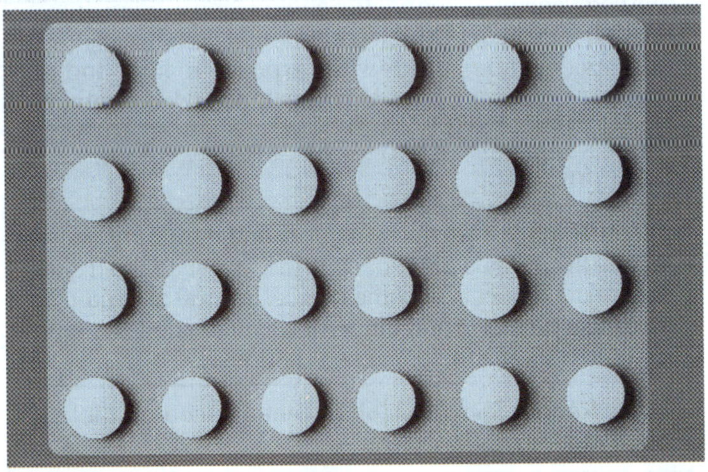

Medications for Pre-Existing Conditions

If you or your family members rely on prescription medications, it is critical to stockpile them whenever possible. Key categories:

Asthma Inhalers

Albuterol inhalers are essential. Primatene Mist is an OTC alternative.

Albuterol (Ventolin, ProAir, Proventil): A life-saving bronchodilator for asthma attacks, COPD, and other respiratory distress situations. Each inhaler contains **200 doses**, but during emergencies, using a **spacer device** can make each dose more effective and stretch supply. They are typically only available through prescription.

Price Range: $22 to $60 for one inhaler containing 200 doses of 90 mcg strength.

Primatene Mist: The only FDA-approved **OTC inhaler,** Primatene Mist contains epinephrine instead of albuterol. It is a **temporary solution** for mild asthma but not as effective as prescription inhalers. Since epinephrine can raise heart rate and blood pressure, **it should not be used excessively.**

Price Range: $30 to $38 for one inhaler containing 160 metered sprays of 0.125 mg strength.

Heart Medications

Blood pressure meds, nitroglycerin, and blood thinners should be stocked.

Blood Pressure Medications: Stockpiling **ACE inhibitors (lisinopril, enalapril) and beta-blockers (metoprolol, propranolol)** is crucial for managing hypertension. In emergencies, **hibiscus tea and garlic supplements** have mild blood pressure-lowering effects if pharmaceuticals run out.

Price Range: $4 to $20 for 30 tablets of 10 mg strength.

Nitroglycerin: Essential for angina (chest pain) and **emergency heart attack treatment.** Nitroglycerin tablets degrade quickly when exposed to light and air, so they must be stored in **sealed, dark containers.**

Price Range: $15 to $25 for 25 tablets of 0.3 mg strength.

Blood Thinners: Warfarin, aspirin, and newer anticoagulants like Eliquis prevent clots that can lead to strokes. If pharmaceuticals become scarce, **natural alternatives like turmeric and ginger** have mild blood-thinning properties but should be used cautiously.

Price Range: $5 to $10 for 120 enteric-coated tablets of 81 mg strength.

Diabetes Medications

Insulin (Regular and NPH) is available over-the-counter at Walmart. Stock up on metformin and other Type 2 diabetes medications.

These are the only **types of insulin available OTC in the U.S.,** typically sold at Walmart. Regular insulin acts quickly, while **NPH is intermediate-acting,** making it better for sustained blood sugar control. If refrigeration becomes an issue, consider **Frio cooling cases** or store insulin in a **well-insulated cooler with ice packs.** In emergency settings, insulin expiration can be stretched—while its effectiveness decreases, it may still be better than nothing. **Unopened insulin kept refrigerated can often remain usable for 6–12 months past its printed expiration date. Once opened, most types last about 28 days at room temperature,** though in survival scenarios they may still work up to 45 days, though less predictably. **Heat above 86°F can ruin insulin quickly, so storage matters.** Watch for signs it's gone bad—cloudiness, clumps, or no blood sugar response. Even weakened insulin is often safer than none at all.

Price Range: $24 to $26 for a 10mL vial (1000 units).

A staple for Type 2 diabetics, metformin is one of the most widely prescribed and safest oral medications. **Extended-release versions** last longer, making them preferable for rationing in a survival setting. Metformin is also being researched for **anti-aging and endurance benefits,** meaning it could have additional uses outside of diabetes.

Price Range: $4 to $12 for 60 tablets of 500 mg strength.

Thyroid Medications

Levothyroxine is essential for those with hypothyroidism.

Levothyroxine (Synthroid): This synthetic T4 hormone is critical for hypothyroid patients. In a crisis, some may be able to reduce dosage if **iodine-rich foods** (such as seaweed) are available to support thyroid function. Levothyroxine has a **long shelf life** if kept in dry, cool conditions.

Price Range: $4 to $10 for 30 tablets of 50 mcg strength.

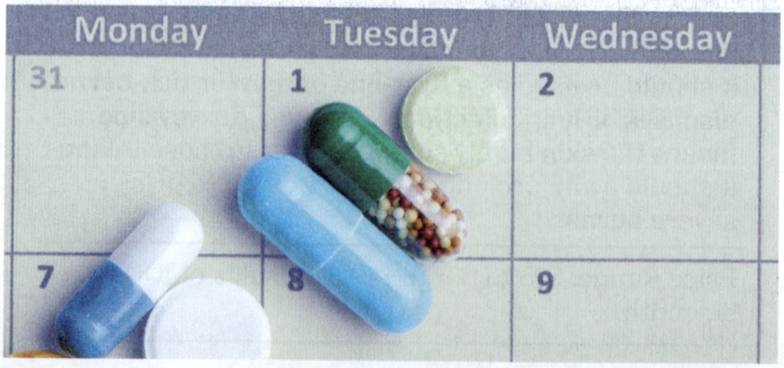

Mental Health Medications

Ensure a stock of antidepressants, anti-anxiety, and anti-seizure medications to avoid withdrawal issues.

Antidepressants (Fluoxetine, Sertraline, Bupropion): Abruptly stopping SSRIs or SNRIs can cause **severe withdrawal, mood swings, and suicidal thoughts. Bupropion (Wellbutrin)** is often easier to stockpile as it is also used for **smoking cessation** and has fewer withdrawal effects.

For Sertraline, **Price Range:** $4 to $15 for 30 tablets of 50 mg strength.

Anti-Anxiety Medications (Benzodiazepines – Xanax, Ativan, Valium): These are **controlled substances,** making stockpiling difficult. However, in a survival situation, even a small backup supply can be crucial for those with severe anxiety or panic disorders. If unavailable, **L-theanine, valerian root, and magnesium** can provide mild calming effects.

Price Range: $10 to $50 for 30 tablets of 0.5 mg strength.

Anti-Seizure Medications (Gabapentin, Lamotrigine, Keppra): Seizure control is life-or-death, so keeping a 3–6 month supply is ideal. Gabapentin is often easier to obtain and also doubles as a nerve pain treatment.

First Aid Essentials

A well-stocked first aid kit is essential, as you can imagine, especially in a world where the risk of getting shot or stabbed goes up. It should include:

Bandages and Dressings

Adhesive bandages, gauze pads, trauma dressings, and hemostatic agents like QuickClot.

Adhesive Bandages (Band-Aid, Nexcare): Stock **various sizes,** including **butterfly closures** for deep cuts.

Gauze Pads & Rolls: Essential for **wound packing and covering large injuries.** Sterile gauze is best, but in a pinch, **boiling clean fabric** can create an emergency alternative.

Trauma Dressings (Israeli Bandage, OLAES Bandage): Designed for **severe bleeding,** these dressings **apply direct pressure** and can be used **with or without a tourniquet.**

Hemostatic Agents (QuickClot, Celox): These contain **kaolin or chitosan,** which help blood clot faster. **Essential for gunshot wounds or deep lacerations** in survival scenarios.

Wound Cleaning and Antiseptics

Alcohol wipes, hydrogen peroxide, povidone-iodine, and antibiotic ointments.

Alcohol Wipes & Hydrogen Peroxide: Used for **sterilizing skin before injections or cleaning minor cuts.** Hydrogen peroxide can also be used as a **disinfectant for surfaces** but should not be used long-term on wounds as it can **slow healing.**

Povidone-Iodine (Betadine): Best for deep wounds and water purification in extreme situations. Povidone-iodine is effective against **bacteria, viruses, and fungi,** making it superior to alcohol in many cases.

Antibiotic Ointments (Neosporin, Bacitracin): Helps prevent infection in **minor cuts and burns. Bacitracin is a good alternative for those allergic to neomycin (found in Neosporin).**

Fracture and Sprain Supplies

SAM Splints, elastic bandages, and slings.

SAM Splints: Lightweight, moldable splints that can stabilize broken bones and sprains. They are compact and **should be in every emergency kit.**

Elastic Bandages (Ace Wraps): Ideal for **sprains, swelling, and compression bandaging.** They also work for **securing splints in place.**

Slings & Triangle Bandages: Multi-purpose and can be used for **shoulder injuries, arm immobilization, or securing bandages.**

Medical Tools

Gloves, scissors, tweezers, thermometers, and blood pressure cuffs.

Gloves (Nitrile or Latex-Free): Prevent contamination during wound care. Nitrile gloves are preferred as they are more resistant to **chemical exposure.**

Trauma Shears: Designed to **cut through clothing, seat belts, and thick materials** in an emergency. Unlike regular scissors, **they are designed to be safe against skin.**

Tweezers: Essential for **removing splinters, ticks, and debris from wounds. Fine-tipped tweezers** work best for precision.

Thermometers: Fever detection is critical for **identifying infections or heat-related illness. Digital thermometers are ideal, but glass mercury thermometers last longer** without batteries.

Blood Pressure Cuffs: Useful for monitoring **hypertension, shock, or dehydration levels.** Manual cuffs are more reliable in long-term crises than digital versions, which require batteries.

CPR Masks and Eye Wash

Essential for emergency scenarios.

CPR Pocket Masks: Provide a **safer way to give mouth-to-mouth resuscitation,** reducing disease transmission risk. Many models come with **oxygen inlets** for advanced first aid.

Sterile Eye Wash (Saline Solution): Flushes out debris, chemicals, or infections from the eyes. In **dusty or smoke-filled environments,** having multiple bottles is crucial for eye health.

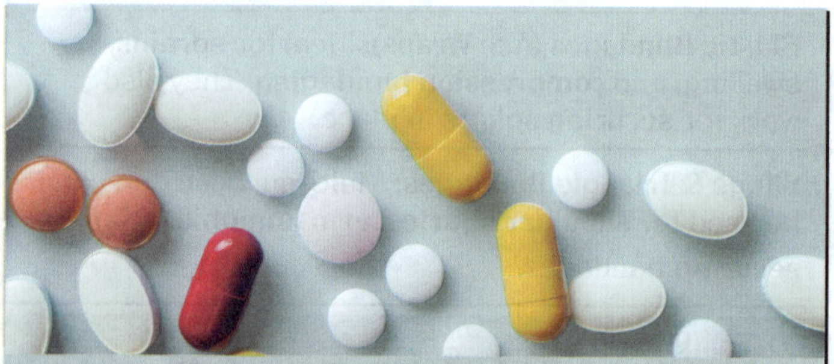

5. Where and How to Obtain Essential Medicines and First Aid Supplies

In normal times, acquiring medication is as simple as visiting a pharmacy or placing an order online. However, for those preparing for a crisis scenario where pharmacies may be inaccessible, knowing where to source these essential drugs and medical supplies in advance is critical.

1. Retail Pharmacy Chains and Big-Box Stores

Walgreens, CVS, Rite Aid, Walmart – Most over-the-counter (OTC) medicines, first aid kits, and even some emergency prescription medications (e.g., insulin) can be purchased at these nationwide chains.

Costco and Sam's Club – These warehouse stores often sell bulk quantities of OTC pain relievers, allergy medications, and first aid supplies at a lower per-unit price.

Grocery Chains (Kroger, Publix, Albertsons, Safeway, etc.) – Most major grocery stores have in-house pharmacies that carry the same drugs as retail pharmacies.

2. Online Pharmacies and Medical Supply Retailers

Amazon, Walgreens.com, CVS.com, Walmart.com – Most common medications and first aid supplies are available online for direct delivery.

GoodRx and Mark Cuban's Cost Plus Drug Company – Prescription medications can be acquired at a discount through online platforms that negotiate lower prices with manufacturers.

Survival and Prepper Supply Websites (BePrepared.com, MyMedic.com, Rescue-Essentials.com) – These sites cater specifically to preppers and survivalists, selling specialized medical kits, trauma gear, and first aid essentials.

3. Fish Antibiotics and Veterinary Sources

Many preppers have turned to fish and bird antibiotics as a legal workaround to stockpile medications without a prescription. Brands like Fish Mox (Amoxicillin), Fish Flox (Ciprofloxacin), and Fish Doxy (Doxycycline) contain the same active ingredients as human versions.

Available from: Pet supply stores like Chewy.com, Tractor Supply Co., and veterinary supply websites.

Verification: Ensure that the product lists only the antibiotic ingredient without additional additives.

Storage: Keep in a cool, dry place; rotate stock to maintain potency.

4. Prescription Medication Stockpiling Strategies

For essential prescription medications, consider these methods:

90-day supplies – Many insurance plans and doctors allow extended supplies of maintenance medications.

Asking for travel prescriptions – Some doctors will prescribe an additional supply if you mention long-term travel or emergency preparedness.

Patient Assistance Programs – Some pharmaceutical companies offer assistance for those who need bulk access to essential medications.

Compounding Pharmacies – In some cases, compounding pharmacies can prepare custom doses of essential medications, particularly for unique health conditions.

5. International and Alternative Sources

In some cases, preppers have obtained medications from international pharmacies where laws differ on prescription requirements.

Reliable international pharmacies: Canadian pharmacy networks, Mexico border pharmacies, and online retailers that adhere to international standards.

Warnings: Counterfeit drugs are rampant in online marketplaces—always verify sources through user reviews and independent verification tools like PharmacyChecker.com.

The Role of Organized Crime in Medicine Supply Chains

In times of economic collapse, organized crime groups often step in to fill the void left by legitimate pharmaceutical supply chains. One of the most concerning groups in this regard is **Tren de Aragua**, a Venezuelan criminal network known for smuggling drugs, weapons, and illicit pharmaceuticals across South and Central America into the U.S.

Impact on Medicine Access: During supply chain breakdowns, black market operations often control access to critical drugs, including antibiotics and painkillers.

Risks of Counterfeit Medications: Criminal syndicates frequently produce counterfeit drugs that contain little to no active ingredients, making them not only ineffective but potentially dangerous.

Security Concerns: Those seeking black market medications must be aware of potential scams, violence, and legal ramifications associated with illicit purchases.

In times of crisis, access to essential medications can mean the difference between life and death. By proactively building a stockpile of vital drugs through reputable and legal sources, you protect yourself and your loved ones from the uncertainties of disrupted supply chains. Prioritize long-term planning by purchasing in bulk when feasible, ensuring proper storage conditions, and staying informed about expiration dates and safe usage guidelines.

Equally important is vigilance aca prevalent during shortages or emergencies. Always verity the authenticity of medicines and avoid risky sources that may exploit desperate situations. Investing in quality supplies now ensures that you're prepared to manage common ailments, chronic conditions, and unforeseen medical emergencies when professional care is out of reach.

By taking these steps today, you empower yourself to face tomorrow's challenges with confidence and peace of mind.

"When you have food on the table, you have many problems. When you don't have food on the table, you have only one." Milton Friedman

Chapter 7

20 Long-Lasting Foods You Need to Stockpile Before They Become Unaffordable

You may not feel it yet. The stores are still open, your fridge still hums, and the tap still runs. But the cracks are already forming beneath your feet. Food prices are rising quietly. Package sizes are shrinking silently. A few empty shelves here. A missing item there. It doesn't look like collapse—yet.

But that's how it starts.

The question is no longer if disruption is coming. It's when. And more importantly—will you be ready when it does?

Why Stockpiling Food Is No Longer Optional

It's easy to take the abundance of the modern food supply for granted. For most people, grocery stores stocked floor-to-ceiling with food and goods seem as reliable as running water or electricity. But history—and recent events—tell a vastly different story. In the blink of an eye, economic instability, supply chain disruptions, and global crises can empty supermarket shelves and send prices soaring out of control.

The last several years have demonstrated precisely how fragile our supply chains truly are. In 2020, the COVID-19 pandemic exposed deep vulnerabilities, causing widespread shortages of everyday items like flour, yeast, canned foods, and even toilet paper. The subsequent inflationary spiral pushed prices to record levels, pricing staples out of reach for millions.

Yet even now, many families remain unprepared, assuming the system will always correct itself. This assumption is dangerously flawed. When disruptions occur, they hit swiftly and without warning, leaving only the prepared able to weather the storm comfortably.

Inventat un tag June 1st 2020

Why Long-Lasting Foods Are the Cornerstone of Emergency Preparedness

In a short-term emergency, you can probably get by with what's already in your kitchen. A snowstorm, a temporary power outage, or a brief supply chain hiccup? Most pantries can handle that. But in the face of something deeper—a prolonged economic collapse, civil unrest, a natural disaster that wipes out infrastructure, or a geopolitical event that fractures global trade—your strategy needs to go far beyond a few days.

Long-lasting foods are the workhorses of true preparedness. . While your fridge and freezer become liabilities in a blackout or grid-down scenario, your stockpile of durable foods becomes a fortress.

Long-lasting foods are reliable. They provide consistent nutritional value even when resupply is impossible. In crisis, you don't want to be calculating spoilage dates or hoping the power comes back before your meat thaws.

Equally important is the psychological edge these foods offer. Instead of worrying where the next meal will come from, you can focus on higher-level survival: protecting your home, filtering water, managing security, or helping neighbours in need.

In truth, every crisis has two phases: the shock, and the aftermath. And it's the aftermath—the long, grinding uncertainty—that usually breaks people.

So whether you're preparing for inflation, blackouts, conflict, or systemic failure, your first layer of defense isn't at the door—it's in the pantry. And the time to build that defense is not after the headlines turn red. It's now.

Practical Criteria for Selecting Long-Lasting Foods

To build an effective food reserve, consider these five practical criteria:

1. Shelf-Life

When you're selecting foods for long-term storage, shelf-life should be one of your top priorities. Foods that last for years, or even decades, allow you to rotate your stockpile less frequently, saving both time and money. Aim for items with shelf lives measured in years rather than months. Properly stored canned goods, dehydrated products, freeze-dried meals, and grains can last anywhere from five to thirty years—sometimes even longer.

2. Nutritional Value

In a crisis, calories alone aren't sufficient. Your body needs balanced nutrition—proteins, healthy fats, vitamins, and minerals—to maintain physical strength and mental clarity under pressure. Prioritize nutrient-dense, calorie-efficient foods that provide sustained energy. Good options include dried beans, lentils, nuts, seeds, powdered eggs, dehydrated vegetables, and fortified emergency food packs.

3. Ease of Storage

Foods that require minimal space and no refrigeration or special handling are invaluable. Look for lightweight, stackable items in sturdy packaging that can withstand long-term storage conditions—dry, cool, and dark spaces—without deteriorating. Compact foods such as dried beans, rice, powdered meals, and vacuum-sealed meats are ideal for maximizing limited storage areas.

4. Affordability

Choose foods you can accumulate gradually, without creating financial hardship. Bulk buying, seasonal sales, and off-brand alternatives can help stretch your budget without sacrificing quality or nutritional standards. Affordable staples like rice, beans, pasta, and canned vegetables form the backbone of most effective stockpiles.

5. Versatility

Your emergency food should be adaptable enough to create varied, nutritious meals. Versatile ingredients—like rice, pasta, canned meats, and dried spices—can be combined in numerous ways to prevent menu fatigue. Variety in your diet is not only more enjoyable but also psychologically essential, helping maintain morale during difficult times. Include foods you can mix-and-match easily to create balanced meals from limited ingredients.

A Blueprint for Food Stockpiling

We've identified **twenty of the most essential long-lasting foods** that every prepared household should stockpile—not someday, but now, before inflation, supply shocks, or political disruption send prices skyrocketing and availability plummeting.

Each food in this chapter has been selected with precision, based on the five critical criteria we've just listed. These foods are staples that have proven their worth across generations, wars, famines, and modern-day crises.

But we'll go deeper than just saying what to buy. For each item, you'll find:

- **Why it matters in a survival context**
- **How long it truly lasts (and how to extend that shelf life)**
- **Best storage methods for real-world conditions**
- **Ideas for preparation and usage, even in resource-limited environments**
- **Helpful tips to help you stretch your food investment further without sacrificing nutrition or morale**

Whether you're brand new to preparedness or well into building your long-term pantry, this resource is designed to help you think smarter, store better, and act faster. You're not just stockpiling calories—you're building a lifeline for your family that will hold up when all systems fail.

Use this advice and your family will still eat well, stay healthy, and keep moving forward—while others will be forced to ration, scavenge, or go hungry.

Now let's begin—because when the world shifts, it's the prepared who will rise.

The 20 Must-Have Survival Foods to Stockpile Today

This list is by no means an end-all be all, but it's a very good start and it will get you thinking in the right direction. So by all means if you can stockpile other long-lasting foods do so, but you might want to start with these:

1. Canned Foods

When it comes to reliable, ready-to-eat provisions, **canned foods** are unmatched. They cover a wide spectrum: vegetables **like corn, beans, and tomatoes;** fruits preserved in **syrup or juice**; protein sources such as **tuna, chicken, spam, and corned beef;** full meals like **soups, stews, and canned pasta** dishes including **ravioli or spaghetti.**

Properly stored, canned foods can last **three to five years,** often even longer if kept in a cool, dry place with stable temperatures and no exposure to light or humidity. What makes them exceptional is that most of them require **no cooking at all.** In a power outage, a grid-down scenario, or any situation where fuel is limited and smoke and fire might draw unwanted attention, opening a can might be the most nourishing thing you can do.

What's more, canned goods retain a surprising amount of their **nutritional value**—especially canned legumes and meats, which are high in protein and essential minerals. Their **versatility** is spectacular: use them straight from the can, warm them over a flame, or combine them with dry staples like rice or pasta to stretch a meal further. They are as much about **security** as they are about **sustenance.**

2. Powdered and Dehydrated Foods

Powdered and dehydrated foods are another essential. These **include items such as instant mashed potatoes, powdered eggs, non-fat dry milk, pancake and baking mixes, and even powdered cheese.** Each of these brings something critical to your food reserve: long shelf life, concentrated nutrition, and minimal time for preparation.

Many powdered products, if sealed correctly, can last up to **ten years or more.** Whether you're using **vacuum-sealed mylar bags, oxygen absorbers, or airtight buckets,** these foods resist spoilage and require very little to become edible again—usually just water. The advantage here isn't just storage—it's **efficiency.** You're getting foods that pack a caloric punch and are easy to use in austere conditions.

For instance, powdered milk offers essential **calcium and protein,** making it especially valuable for children. Powdered eggs are versatile and can be used in baking, scrambled on their own, or mixed with vegetables and dried meats. These aren't just backup ingredients—they're functional staples that allow you to **replicate normalcy** in a very abnormal time.

3. Beef Jerky and Dried Meats

Dried meats such as **beef jerky, turkey jerky, dried sausage,** and traditional survival food like pemmican are compact, nutrient-dense, and protein-rich. They were used by soldiers, hunters, and nomads for centuries to sustain energy without refrigeration or fire.

Unopened jerky products typically last **one to three years, but pemmican**—a mix of dried meat, fat, and sometimes berries—can last **five years or more** if stored in a vacuum-sealed container. The sheer protein density of these items makes them an ideal food for hard physical labor or periods of high stress. Just a few bites can curb hunger and replenish strength.

In emergencies, every calorie matters, and dried meats deliver **long-lasting satiety.** They're **ready to eat,** require **no prep,** and occupy very little space in your backpack or supply bin. They can also be added to soups, stews, or rehydrated with broth or water to stretch their utility even further. These aren't snacks—they're survival tools.

4. Pickled Foods

While often overlooked, **pickled foods** deserve serious attention. Items like, **sauerkraut,** and **pickled vegetables** such as **beets, onions, and peppers** not only last a long time—usually a **minimum of one to two years**—but offer an additional benefit: they're a **natural probiotic.**

Pickled items help replenish **gut flora,** support **digestion,** and maintain **immune health,** which becomes especially important when fresh produce and varied meals become scarce. Pickles also provide **salt and acidity,** two valuable components in a crisis diet where flavor fatigue can become a real problem. Having food that not only nourishes but stimulates the appetite is more important than it sounds.

Stored in glass jars or food-safe plastic containers, these foods can often outlast their labeled expiration dates by months or years if kept cool and out of direct sunlight. And once opened, they still keep for weeks in the fridge—or outside it, depending on your setup. In a world of MREs and powdered mixes, the snap of a crisp pickle could offer more than flavor—it could offer **comfort.**

5. Fermented Foods

Beyond the pickled classics, **fermented foods** deserve a spotlight of their own. Staples like **kimchi, fermented cabbage, miso, and tempeh** are not just long-lasting—they're **biologically active,** meaning they evolve over time while enhancing their nutritional profile. These foods offer a rare combination in the world of prepping: longevity and **gut-level health benefits.**

Stored properly—typically **refrigerated,** vacuum-sealed, or in fermentation crocks—many of these foods can last **several months to a few years,** sometimes even longer depending on the acidity and salt content. Fermented foods help maintain **digestive function,** especially when fiber and fresh produce become scarce.

When food variety shrinks and caloric efficiency becomes the priority, the digestive system can slow or become imbalanced. That's where fermented foods shine—they support **intestinal flora,** boost **immune health,** and can enhance **nutrient absorption** across your entire diet (which is absolutely vital in a crisis). In times of stress, when hygiene may be compromised and your immune system strained, a few spoonfuls of fermented cabbage or a bowl of miso will help your body out a great deal.

6. MREs (Meals Ready to Eat)

If there's a food category designed specifically for a catastrophe, it's the **MRE—Meals Ready to Eat.** Originally developed for the military, these self-contained rations have become a **cornerstone of emergency preparedness.** They are compact, **calorie-dense,** and built for scenarios where cooking is not an option.

Modern MREs contain everything from **hearty entrees** like chili mac or beef stew, to **side dishes, snacks, desserts, electrolyte drink mixes,** and even **heaters** that require no flame. A well-made MRE provides up to **1,200 calories** or more in a single pack and includes vital **macronutrients and micronutrients** to sustain physical energy and cognitive clarity under pressure.

Their shelf life ranges from **five to seven years,** and in some cases even longer if stored in cool, dry conditions. The key benefit is **total readiness.** In a grid-down situation or during evacuation, MREs require no water, no utensils, and no power. They're **morale-boosting, portable,** and designed to **withstand extreme environments.** Whether you're bugging out or hunkering down, having a few boxes of MREs is like having insurance you can eat.

The biggest downside of MRE's is that they're not really designed to be eaten for a long time and being ultra-processed they wreak havoc on your gut. But that's where the probiotic staples we told you about come in. So, if you're eating MRE's make sure you add some fermented or pickled foods to your diet.

7. Food Buckets

While MREs are built for mobility, **emergency food buckets** are optimized for **long-term storage and feeding multiple people.** These multi-serving kits, sold by companies like **Augason Farms, Wise Company, or Mountain House,** contain pre-packaged meals that can be rehydrated with water and typically offer **hundreds of servings per bucket.**

The shelf life is impressive—**10 to 25 years,** depending on the packaging and the manufacturer. These buckets are usually filled with a wide range of freeze-dried or dehydrated meals: **pasta alfredo, rice and beans, scrambled eggs, creamy soups, and even desserts.** They're designed to be **stackable, sealed against oxygen and moisture, and easy to transport** if needed.

While they require water to prepare, they're remarkably **cost-efficient per calorie,** especially when purchased in bulk. If you're building out a **deep pantry or a long-term bunker stash,** this is one of the most strategic investments you can make. They offer **variety,** which helps fight food fatigue, and **portability,** which makes them viable even during relocation or crisis migration. They're not gourmet—but when the shelves are bare and the power is out, they'll feel like it.

8. Instant and Powdered Drinks

One of the most overlooked categories in food stockpiling is **instant and powdered drinks,** but their importance becomes clear the moment fresh milk, juice, or coffee is no longer accessible. **Powdered milk, instant coffee, electrolyte mixes, and juice powders** like orange or berry drink crystals provide both **hydration** and a much-needed **mental lift** during stressful times.

These mixes are light, compact, and highly efficient. They can last up to **ten years or more** when kept sealed in dry conditions, often outlasting even canned beverages in functionality. **Powdered milk,** for instance, offers critical **calcium, protein, and vitamin D,** and can be used in baking or as a direct milk substitute. **Electrolyte powders** are key in situations where water is limited or sweat loss is high, helping replace lost **sodium, potassium, and magnesium.**

Beyond the physiological, these drinks provide **psychological comfort.** A cup of coffee can **stabilize mood, increase alertness,** and offer a small but vital sense of **normalcy.** Juice mixes—especially those fortified with **vitamin C**—can serve as immune support and as a treat for kids in the household. These aren't luxury items—they're multipliers of both **health and morale.**

9. Rice and Pasta

If you had to choose just one staple to stockpile for sheer **versatility, shelf life, and caloric efficiency,** it would be hard to beat **rice and pasta.** These foundational carbohydrates are the backbone of survival diets around the world—and for good reason.

White rice, when stored in airtight, oxygen-free containers, can last **20 to 30 years** or more. It's incredibly compact, **easy to cook,** and compatible with virtually any other food—from canned vegetables to powdered sauces. Pasta, especially **dried semolina varieties,** shares many of the same advantages. With a shelf life of around **10 to 15 years** when properly packaged, it's both **durable and universally comforting.**

The appeal of these foods goes beyond survival. They allow for meal variation even when ingredients are limited. Rice can be made into stir-fries, soups, casseroles, or eaten plain. Pasta can be transformed with sauces, herbs, oils, or just a bit of canned meat. In a long-term crisis scenario, **caloric density and flexibility** become non-negotiable, and rice and pasta deliver both in abundance.

They're also **cost-effective,** easy to portion, and **kid-friendly**—making them a must-have for any household prepping for instability.

10. Protein and Granola Bars

Compact, calorie-rich, and **ready to eat right out of the wrapper,** they're the ultimate grab-and-go energy source—whether you're bugging out, rationing supplies, or just trying to get through the day.

Most protein bars come with a blend of **macronutrients**—typically 10–20 grams of **protein,** moderate **carbohydrates,** and a modest amount of **healthy fat.** They're designed for fast energy and satiety, and the better ones also contain added **vitamins and minerals.** Granola bars, while often lower in protein, provide **fiber, complex carbs,** and are ideal for quick snacking or adding to a larger meal.

With a shelf life of **1 to 3 years** when unopened, and potentially longer if vacuum-sealed, they're also a great way to **stretch your food reserves.** Keep a box or two in your vehicle, go-bag, or emergency kit. In moments of stress, fatigue, or displacement, they can keep you sharp—and even bring a bit of morale with their sweet, chewy consistency.

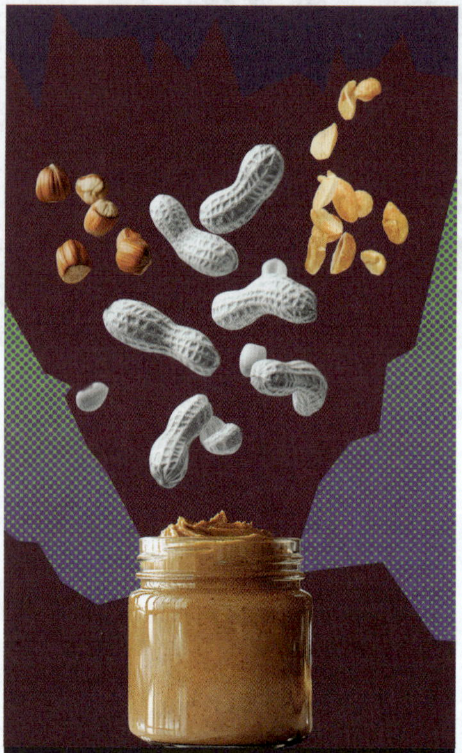

11. Nuts and Nut Butters

When food gets scarce, **calories matter,** and few foods pack as much energy per ounce as **nuts and nut butters.** A spoonful of **peanut butter** delivers over **90 calories,** much of it from **healthy fats and proteins** that can sustain energy and preserve muscle mass.

Stockpile options include jars of **peanut butter, almond butter, cashew spread,** as well as bags of **shelled nuts, trail mix, and roasted seeds.** Properly sealed and kept in a cool environment, many nut butters can last **2 to 3 years** unopened—and even longer if refrigerated or vacuum-sealed. Raw or dry-roasted nuts, particularly **almonds, pecans, and walnuts,** can last **2 to 5 years** when kept in oxygen-free containers.

Nut butters are a lifesaver in high-stress scenarios: they require no prep, take up minimal space, and can be eaten straight, spread on crackers, mixed into oatmeal, or used to add fat to rice and grain dishes. Plus, they're **kid-approved,** which makes them doubly valuable in family prepping scenarios. Just make sure you rotate your stock and check for rancidity over time, especially with higher-fat nut varieties.

12. Cooking Oils and Fats

It's easy to forget that **fats are essential nutrients**—not just for flavor or calories, but for **hormonal balance, brain health, and the absorption of fat-soluble vitamins.** Without them, even the most carbohydrate-rich prepper pantry becomes nutritionally incomplete. That's why having a strategic stockpile of **cooking oils and traditional fats** is non-negotiable.

Top long-lasting options include **olive oil, coconut oil, ghee, lard, and beef tallow.** Each has unique strengths. **Olive oil,** especially in dark glass or metal tins, can last up to **2 years** and is excellent for dressings and light cooking. **Coconut oil** has a naturally long shelf life—up to **5 years**—due to its saturated fat content and antimicrobial properties.

Ghee, or clarified butter, is shelf-stable. It can last **years unrefrigerated** and provides that creamy richness missing from many survival foods. Meanwhile, **tallow and lard**—once staples in traditional kitchens—are making a comeback. Properly rendered and stored in cool, airtight containers, these animal fats can remain usable for **up to 5 years** or more.

Beyond cooking, these fats can even be used for **emergency candles, barter, or caloric supplementation** in a survival ration.

13. Bouillon Cubes and Broth Concentrates

Sometimes, it's not just about what you eat—it's about how it **tastes.** In a long-term crisis, **morale matters,** and so is the ability to transform bland rice, pasta, or dried beans into something truly comforting.

Compact and potent, these concentrated flavor bombs are one of the most **underrated additions** to any pantry. Whether you go with classic **chicken, beef, or vegetable bouillon,** or modern **bone broth powders** rich in minerals and collagen, you'll be amazed at how far a single cube or scoop can go.

Properly stored, bouillon cubes can last **well over 5 years,** especially when vacuum-sealed or kept in airtight glass jars. Bone broth powders, depending on the formulation, can also exceed **4 to 7 years** if kept cool and dry.

Beyond flavor, these cubes are rich in **electrolytes and minerals,** offering a **hydrating, replenishing, and gut-soothing** addition to any meal or standalone hot drink. When you're cold, tired, or emotionally worn out, a warm mug of broth can be the **difference between despair and resilience.**

14. Dried Fruits and Fruit Snacks

While many focus on starches, proteins, and fats, **fruit** is often the first thing to disappear in a crisis—and one of the hardest to replace. That's why **dried fruits and fruit leathers** deserve a place of honor in any long-term stockpile.

From **raisins and dates to apricots, prunes, and apples,** dried fruits are nature's original survival candy. They're packed with **natural sugars, fiber, and essential vitamins** like potassium, magnesium, and antioxidants—especially if unsulfured and minimally processed. Shelf life can range from **2 to 5 years** when vacuum-sealed and stored in a cool, dark place. Freeze-dried options can stretch that life even further.

Fruit leathers and pure fruit bars are **mess-free snacks** that bring variety to otherwise repetitive meals. And in a world where fresh produce is scarce or non-existent, these snacks provide a **taste of normalcy.**

They're also **compact and lightweight,** making them ideal for go-bags and mobile scenarios. Whether eaten plain, mixed into oatmeal, or rehydrated for stews and sauces, dried fruit keeps you going with both **energy and hope.**

15. Chocolate and Cocoa

If there's one item that consistently shows up in **wartime rations, polar expeditions,** and underground bunkers, it's **chocolate.** And not just because it tastes good—though that certainly helps. **Dark chocolate and cocoa powder** provide a rare trifecta in survival food: **calories, antioxidants, and psychological uplift.**

Let's start with shelf life. **Dark chocolate,** with a high cocoa content and minimal dairy, can last **2 to 5 years,** especially when stored in cool, dry, low-humidity conditions. Cocoa powder, if kept sealed and moisture-free, can last **indefinitely**—and still deliver rich flavor, healthy fats, and deep satiety.

From a nutritional standpoint, chocolate contains **flavanols,** natural compounds that improve **circulation, mood, and cognitive function.** It's also energy-dense, making it an excellent quick-calorie source during periods of high physical output or low morale.

But its greatest asset may be emotional. When you're facing a dark night in a cold cabin, or watching your food reserves shrink, a piece of chocolate or a hot mug of cocoa can **reignite your mental strength.**

16. Hardtack and Historical Survival Foods

When we talk about **food that lasts,** it's impossible not to mention **hardtack**—a food that helped feed armies, sailors, and explorers for **centuries.** Often dubbed "survival bread," hardtack is little more than flour, water, and salt, baked into rock-hard biscuits that can **last decades** when kept dry.

Hardtack may not win culinary awards, but what it lacks in taste, it makes up for in **durability and practicality.** Properly stored in tins or vacuum-sealed containers, hardtack can literally **outlive its maker.** All it needs is a good soak—in soup, broth, or water—to be made edible again.

Alongside hardtack, consider **pemmican,** another historical marvel. Invented by Indigenous peoples and later adopted by Arctic explorers, pemmican is a dense blend of **dried meat, rendered fat, and sometimes berries.** It's ultra-light, ultra-caloric, and can last **years without refrigeration.**

You can buy pemmican commercially from specialty survival food brands or learn to make it yourself with a dehydrator and some beef. The same goes for hardtack—it's easy to bake in bulk and stash away as an emergency fallback.

17. Protein Powders and Supplements

When food becomes scarce, maintaining your **muscle mass, energy, and immune resilience** is critical—and that's exactly where protein powders earn their keep. Whether you're surviving off bulk carbs or rotating through canned goods, protein can often become the most **difficult macronutrient** to source consistently.

Whey, plant-based blends, and egg white protein powders offer compact, nutrient-dense solutions that can **last 2 to 5 years** when stored in sealed, dry containers. They're shelf-stable, lightweight, and easily mix into water or milk substitutes—even without a blender.

In a collapse scenario, where physical exertion increases and access to fresh meat is uncertain, having a steady supply of protein powder can **make all the difference.** It supports **muscle repair, immune function, and energy metabolism**—all while requiring **no refrigeration and minimal space.**

Even a single scoop can provide **20 to 30 grams of high-quality protein,** which is critical if you're relying on rice, pasta, or starches for most of your calories. It's also a smart option for those managing **medical conditions or older adults** who need protein density without heavy meals.

18. Seeds (Chia, Flax, Hemp)

Tiny but mighty, **chia, flax, and hemp seeds** are some of the most **nutrient-dense foods on the planet,** and they store far better than most people realize. Properly sealed in mylar or airtight containers, they can last **2 to 4 years,** and even longer in oxygen-free environments.

These seeds are **fiber-rich,** packed with **plant-based protein,** and loaded with essential fatty acids—especially **omega-3s,** which are crucial for brain function, inflammation control, and cardiovascular health.

Chia seeds in particular can **absorb 10 times their weight in water,** making them ideal for hydration strategies and **quick, no-cook meals** like chia puddings or survival gels. Flaxseeds can be ground for baking or added to cereals and soups. Hemp seeds are excellent over rice, mixed into yogurt alternatives, or eaten straight for an energy punch.

They take up almost no space, require no cooking, and are **incredibly versatile**—from thickening stews to powering your morning with superfood oats. They also double as a source of **emergency plant-based nutrition** in vegan or low-meat scenarios.

In short: seeds are survival fuel in concentrated form.

19. Instant Meals and Meal Kits

Sometimes the most valuable resource in a crisis isn't food—**it's time.** When stress is high, fuel is low, and energy is fading, having a few **no-brainer, one-step meals** can be a lifesaver. That's where **boxed macaroni and cheese, instant noodles, and shelf-stable pasta or rice kits** prove their worth.

They're **cheap, calorically dense, and incredibly easy to prepare.** Add water, maybe a dash of oil or powdered cheese, and you're set. Many of these meals are fortified with **vitamins and minerals,** and the shelf life ranges from **2 to 5 years,** depending on packaging.

Pro tip: store these meals with **flavor boosters** like bouillon cubes, oil packets, or spice blends to **elevate the taste** and prevent meal fatigue over time. It's a small prep, but it pays off big.

20. Specialty Nutritional Foods (Powdered Butter, Dehydrated Cheese, Tahini)

To round out your long-term pantry, don't overlook **specialty foods** that may not be obvious staples—but dramatically increase your **meal flexibility, caloric density, and nutritional value.** These include shelf-stable items like **powdered butter, dehydrated cheese, and tahini (sesame paste).**

Powdered butter gives you all the fat and flavor of traditional butter, without the refrigeration or spoilage issues. It works perfectly in baking mixes, sautéing, or mashed potatoes—and can last over **5 years** when sealed. The same goes for **dehydrated cheese powder,** which adds flavor, protein, and fat to pasta, rice, or emergency casseroles. Think mac & cheese or nacho-style rice bowls, even in a blackout.

Tahini, meanwhile, is a **nutritional powerhouse.** Made from sesame seeds, it's rich in **healthy fats, iron, calcium, and protein.** It's excellent on its own, as a spread, or added to sauces, dips, and flatbreads. Plus, it stores well for **2 to 5 years** unopened, especially in glass jars or vacuum-sealed tins.

Survival Food Comparison: Choosing What's Right for You

After reviewing the 20 essential long-lasting foods, you might be asking: Which of these should I prioritize? The truth is every item on this list serves a specific role—and the most effective preparedness strategy includes a good mix of them. But when budget, space, or urgency are tight, making smart comparisons helps you stock more effectively.

Calories vs. Nutrients

High-calorie foods like rice, pasta, oils, and nut butters give you raw energy—critical in survival scenarios with heavy labor or cold weather.

Nutrient-dense foods like seeds, dried fruits, fermented products, and protein powders help maintain immune health and muscle mass over time.

Balance is key: combine energy-dense staples with nutrient-rich supplements for sustained health.

Shelf Life: Longest Lasting Champions

Hardtack, white rice, and food buckets can last 20–30 years.

Powdered and dehydrated items often hold 5–15 years when sealed properly.

Canned goods and MREs average 5–7 years, but many last longer than their "best by" dates.

If you're planning for deep preps or bunker storage, lean toward hardtack, rice, and sealed buckets.

Prep Time & Convenience

Grab-and-go options like granola bars, jerky, or MREs require zero prep—ideal for bug-out bags or emergencies on the move.

Simple-prep meals like instant noodles, boxed mac & cheese, or powdered mixes offer fast calories with minimal fuel or water.

Every pantry should include a mix of instant-use and basic-prep options for flexibility.

Affordability Breakdown

Budget-friendly staples: rice, pasta, bouillon cubes, peanut butter, dried beans.

Mid-range: canned meats, powdered eggs, protein bars, powdered drinks.

Higher-cost but high-value: food buckets, MREs, **freeze-dried specialty items.**

Start with low-cost basics and scale up with premium items as budget allows.

Versatility in Meal Planning

Highly versatile: rice, pasta, canned vegetables, sauces, seeds, oils.

Moderately versatile: dried meats, powdered eggs, chocolate, broth powders.

Specialized but powerful: MREs, tahini, powdered butter. Focus on foods that can be used in multiple recipes to prevent boredom and menu fatigue.

Quick-Reference Comparison Table

Food Type	Shelf Life	Prep Required	Calories Dense	Nutrient Dense	Cost Efficiency	Ideal Use Case
Canned Goods	3–7 years	No	Moderate	Moderate	High	Core pantry, low-prep meals
Powdered/ Dehydrated	5–15+ years	Minimal	High	High	High	Compact storage, cooking base
Jerky & Dried Meats	1–3 years	No	High	High	Moderate	Protein punch, bug-out bags
MREs	5–10 years	None	High	Balanced	Low/High	Evacuations, instant-use scenarios
Food Buckets	10–25+ years	Yes (add water)	High	Moderate	Moderate	Long-term reserves
Seeds & Nuts	2–5 years	Minimal	High	High	Moderate	Daily supplements, high fats
Instant Meals & Kits	2–5 years	Minimal	High	Low/Moderate	High	Stress-free hot meals
Chocolate & Cocoa	2–5 years	None	High	Moderate	Low/Moderate	Morale booster, energy snack
Bouillon/Broth Powders	5+ years	Minimal	Low	Moderate	High	Flavor, electrolyte support
Hardtack/ Pemmican	10–30+ years	Some (rehydrate)	High	Moderate	Very High	Endurance rations, historical fallback

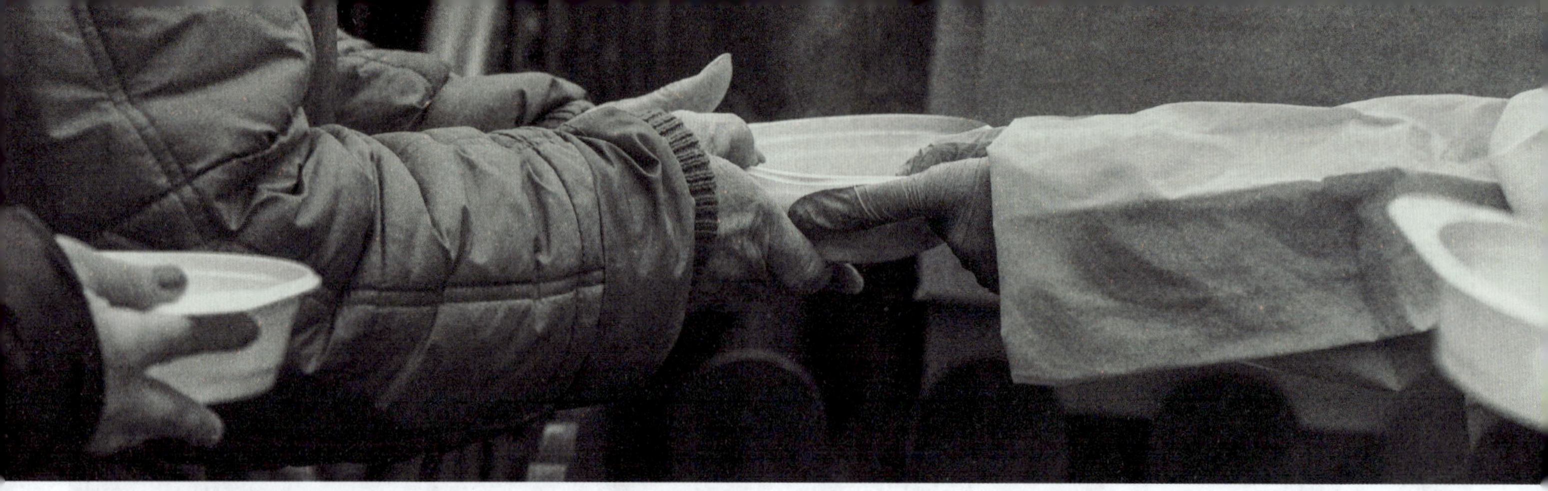

Final Strategy Tip: Diversify to Fortify

The smartest stockpile is a **balanced mix** across categories. Build your foundation with grains, canned goods, and protein bars. Then fill the gaps with specialty items like fermented foods, broth, or powdered cheese to create variety and nutritional depth.

Practical Storage Tips: How to Make Your Food Last for Years (or Decades)

Building a long-term food supply is one part strategy, one part logistics—and that second half can make or break your preps. **It's not just what you store, but how you store it** that determines whether your supplies will still be edible when you need them most. Improper storage shortens shelf life, invites spoilage, and turns hard-earned food security into wasted effort.

But when done correctly?

It can preserve your investment for decades. Here's how to get it right.

Optimal Storage Conditions: Cool, Dry, and Dark

These three words are the golden rule of food storage: cool, dry, and dark. Heat speeds up chemical reactions that cause food to spoil. Moisture leads to mold, rust, and bacterial growth. Light—especially UV light—can degrade fats and vitamins and break down packaging. That's why your long-term food stash should never be in the kitchen pantry or above the garage.

Instead, aim for **basements, root cellars, under-bed bins, interior closets,** or any place that stays **below 70°F (21°C)** year-round. If you live in a hot climate or have limited space, **insulated storage totes, mylar bags with oxygen absorbers, or DIY underground coolers** can create micro-environments that dramatically extend food life. The darker and drier the space, the better. If it feels like a place you'd store wine or family heirlooms, it's likely good for food, too.

Shelf-Life Maximization Techniques: Rotation, Labeling, and Tracking

Even foods with ultra-long shelf lives can degrade if you neglect them. That's why every serious prepper lives by one core principle: **"Store what you eat, and eat what you store."** This is the philosophy behind the **FIFO method**—First In, First Out. When you bring in new supplies, place them at the back of the shelf or stack, and rotate older items to the front so they get used first.

Don't rely on memory or "eyeballing it" when managing a stockpile. **Label everything clearly with the purchase or expiration date,** and if you repackage items from their original containers into mylar, jars, or buckets, be sure to note what's inside and when it was sealed. Consider keeping a **master inventory list** (digital or physical) with quantities, locations, and ideal use-by dates. This way, you're not guessing during a high-stress situation or mid-crisis.

For advanced preppers, using **color-coded bins, QR labels, or laminated checklists** can help you streamline inspections and reduce the risk of forgotten goods going bad in a corner. If you have multiple storage locations (like a bug-out cabin or a second pantry), tracking contents across spaces is even more important.

Finally, **don't be afraid to rotate into daily use.** Open that bucket of pasta, try that powdered cheese, eat a can of soup on a rainy evening—not just to avoid waste, but to familiarize yourself and your family with the flavors, cooking times, and texture of your food reserves. The middle of a crisis is the worst time to discover your powdered milk tastes awful or your kids won't touch your "emergency chili."

Action Steps: Buy Now, or Pay Later

Whether it's runaway inflation, global supply chain breakdowns, social unrest, or simply empty shelves at your local store, food becomes the first pressure point in any crisis. And once the panic begins, it's already too late.

That's why now—not tomorrow, not "someday"—is the best time to act.

The Window Is Closing

Prices are rising, packaging is shrinking, and certain items are disappearing from store shelves with alarming regularity. Whether you're seeing it in the cost of your weekly groceries or the "out of stock" tags on staples like rice, flour, or powdered milk, the writing is already on the wall. **What you can buy today for $50 may cost $100 next year—or may not be available at all.** That's not fearmongering. That's basic math in a time of economic contraction.

If that system falters, even temporarily, the consequences for the unprepared are immediate and brutal.

How to Build Your Stockpile Strategically

If you feel overwhelmed by the idea of building a deep pantry, don't aim for a year of food overnight. Start small. One week. Then two. Then a month. Build from there.

Each time you go to the store, add a few extra shelf-stable items to your cart. Focus on foods you and your family already eat, and then branch into long-term additions like MREs, food buckets, and specialty preps. You don't need to buy everything at once. But you do need a plan.

Here's a simple formula:

Buy what lasts: Prioritize items with a shelf life of 3 years or more.

Buy what you eat: Rotate regularly to prevent waste and keep your diet familiar.

Buy what fills you: High-calorie, nutrient-dense foods should be the backbone of your storage.

Buy what's missing: Identify gaps—are you light on protein, fats, or hydration? Fill them.

Store it smart. Track it clearly. Rotate it intentionally.

Don't Wait for a Crisis to Get Started

The biggest mistake most people make is waiting. Waiting for a "better deal." Waiting for a "confirmed crisis." Waiting until they "have more space" or "figure it all out." But a collapse doesn't care about any of that.

And when it arrives, those who stocked up early won't just have food—they'll have leverage. Peace of mind. Options. Meanwhile, everyone else will be lining up outside empty stores, or waiting in soup line, wondering how things could've changed so fast.

So, let this be your wake-up call.

If you've read this far, you already know what needs to be done. Now it's just a matter of doing it. **One list. One item. One week of food.**

If you start today, you're already ahead of 95% of the population. If you wait? You'll be one of the 95% chasing crumbs when it's too late to act.

Throughout history, the systems we trust – supply chains, currencies, governments – have often appeared strongest right before the fall.

You don't need to predict the exact day food shelves go bare, or the precise hour the banks freeze withdrawals. You just need to act before those things happen.

So start today. Build your long-lasting stockpile, one meal at a time. Stock what matters. Do it now while everything still feels normal.

And when that's no longer the case you won't be begging. You'll be leading.

Chapter 8

37 Items You Need to Get Before They Vanish from the Shelves

"In a crisis, we don't rise to the level of our expectations, we fall to the level of our training"
Archilochus (paraphrased by Navy SEALs)

In an unpredictable world plagued by supply chain disruptions and economic volatility, stockpiling food and other essentials is no longer optional—it's essential.

Whether facing a temporary power outage or a prolonged collapse of infrastructure, the difference between struggling and thriving during hard times often comes down to what you have on hand.

From calorie-rich staples to non-food essentials, these items address the basic needs for survival, maintaining a level of self-sufficiency and comfort, for when modern conveniences fail.

Stocking these items ahead of time provides a buffer against the unknown, possibly getting you out of a jam when it matters most.

1. Uncooked White Rice (25 lb or more)

White rice is a survival staple with a decades-long shelf life when stored correctly. It provides over 1,800 calories per pound and requires only water and heat to prepare. A single 25 lb bag yields more than 40,000 calories, enough to sustain an adult for nearly three weeks. It stores compactly in mylar bags with oxygen absorbers, then sealed inside food-grade buckets. Rice is one of the first items to disappear during supply chain disruptions, bulk buying waves, or rationing events. Keep a minimum of 75 lbs per adult for long-term emergencies. Purchase from restaurant supply stores, warehouse chains, or ethnic grocers.

Average cost is $15 to $22 per 25 lb bag. Properly stored in a cool, dry place, it lasts up to 30 years. High utility and long shelf life make it both a foundational food and a valuable barter item.

2. Dehydrated Potato Flakes

Instant potato flakes are a lightweight, fast-prep carbohydrate source that rehydrate with only hot water and can be mixed cold if necessary. They require no soaking, cutting, or fuel-intensive cooking, making them ideal in grid-down scenarios. One #10 can provide dozens of servings, takes minimal space, and resists spoilage for over a decade if stored sealed. These are among the first shelf-stable carbohydrates to sell out during food shortages and transportation shutdowns. Keep at least two #10 cans per person.

Pricing ranges from $13 to $20 per can. Available from preparedness food distributors, LDS canneries, and some wholesale food vendors. Store in dry cabinets or sealed totes away from heat. When access to fresh potatoes ends, this item fills the gap for both calories and comfort. Barter value increases rapidly in environments with limited cooking capacity.

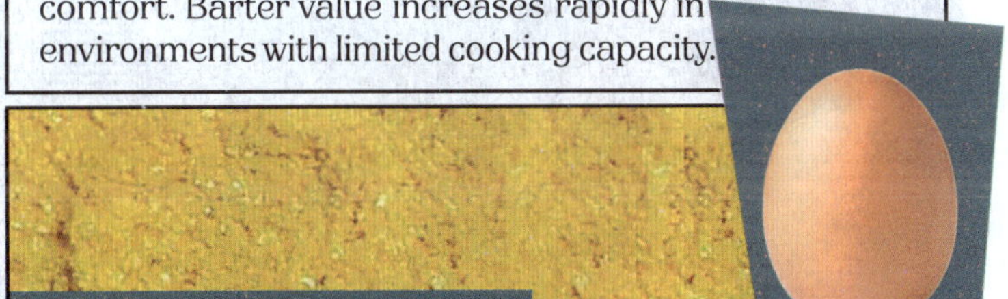

3. #10 Can of Powdered Eggs

Powdered eggs replace the need for refrigeration while providing protein, fat, and versatility for cooking and baking. One #10 can of whole powdered eggs contains the equivalent of 70–80 eggs and can be scrambled, baked into bread, or stirred into stews. They are actual eggs in dehydrated form. Powdered eggs are heavily in demand during any prolonged food distribution breakdown and are regularly out of stock during times of instability. Shelf life exceeds five years when stored airtight and cool.

The average cost is $25 to $45 per can. Purchase from trusted survival food vendors such as Augason Farms, Rainy Day Foods, or preparedness co-ops. Store unopened cans in climate-controlled spaces. Their nutritional value, compact form, and role in meals requiring fat or protein make them one of the highest-value food items in a long-term emergency.

4. Powdered Milk (3.5 lb Canisters)

Powdered milk provides shelf-stable nutrition when refrigeration becomes unreliable or unavailable. One 3.5 lb canister typically yields about 20 quarts of milk once reconstituted and contains essential fats, calcium, and protein that are otherwise difficult to replace in a collapsed food system. It is especially important for children, pregnant women, and the elderly, and plays a key role in baking and rehydrating other dry mixes. Powdered milk has a shelf life of 10 to 20 years when stored in a cool, dry space. During previous periods of rationing or market collapse, it consistently ranked among the most sought-after staples. Purchase sealed canisters from LDS food storage centers, baking supply wholesalers, or preparedness distributors.

Expect to pay $15 to $25 per canister. Store unopened in sealed containers with desiccants. Once opened, use within 3 months. Has high barter value where dairy access is limited.

5. Canned Pinto Beans (12-Pack, 15 oz Cans)

A standard case of canned pinto beans provides a complete plant protein, fiber, iron, and essential calories with no cooking required. Each 15 oz can is ready to eat, making it ideal for situations where fuel, time, or water are limited. A single can delivers roughly 350–400 calories. Unlike dry beans, these require no prep and are safe for immediate consumption. Shelf life averages 3–5 years and extends longer when stored in stable, cool temperatures. Pinto beans are among the first items to disappear during natural disasters and panic-buying events. One full case provides around 4,500 calories total and serves as an emergency protein reserve or trading commodity. Buy from discount grocers, warehouse clubs, or wholesale supply outlets.

Price per case averages $12–$18. Store in totes or stacked boxes in dry, pest-resistant areas. High-value item during prolonged outages or food inflation.

6. Canned Spam (12 oz Cans)

Spam is a fully cooked, shelf-stable pork product with high protein and fat content, making it one of the most compact and energy-dense meats suitable for long-term storage. It can be eaten cold or heated with minimal fuel, and it mixes well with grains or pasta. One can contains around 1,000 calories, including hard-to-replace fats that are often lacking in collapse diets. Spam has an average shelf life of 3–5 years but often remains edible much longer if stored properly. In historical crises, including wartime rations, island blockades, and civil unrest, Spam became a prime target for looters and black marketeers. Stock 10 to 20 cans per adult depending on dietary needs. Purchase from grocery chains, military surplus channels, or long-term food retailers.

Expect to pay $2.50–$4.00 per can. Store in cool, dark locations and rotate every 2–3 years. Reliable trade item in protein-deprived environments.

7. Beef Jerky (10 oz Vacuum-Sealed Bags)

Beef jerky is one of the most portable and shelf-stable protein sources available. A single 10 oz vacuum-sealed bag provides 700–900 calories of lean, low-moisture meat that does not require refrigeration or cooking. It is ideal for evacuation kits, mobile operations, or fuel-scarce scenarios. Properly sealed jerky can last 1 to 2 years without degradation and longer when stored in mylar with oxygen absorbers. It disappears quickly in crises due to its portability, taste, and barter value. Choose high-salt, low-moisture varieties for maximum longevity. Avoid "gourmet" versions with added sugars or artificial flavoring that spoil faster.

Expect to pay $10 to $16 per bag depending on quality and brand. Buy from hiking outfitters, warehouse clubs, or direct meat processors. Keep 3 to 5 bags per adult in rotation. During shortages of fresh or canned meat, jerky trades at a premium.

8. Military MRE Meal Pouch (Single Unit)

A Military MRE (Meal, Ready-to-Eat) is a self-contained, waterproof ration pack designed for complete sustenance under field conditions. Each pouch includes an entrée, side dish, dessert, drink mix, utensils, and a flameless chemical heater. With approximately 1,200–1,300 calories per unit, a single MRE can sustain an adult for a full day if rationed properly. Shelf life ranges from 5 to 10 years depending on storage temperature. MREs have been the default survival ration in war zones, refugee corridors, and natural disaster zones where no cooking, water, or power is available. Once shortages begin, these vanish from military surplus stores and preparedness suppliers rapidly.

These are on average $10 to $15 per pouch when bought in quantity, or $100–$130 per case (12 units). Store unopened in climate-controlled conditions. Ideal for bugout bags, vehicle kits, or fallback locations. MREs have strong barter value in short-term emergencies where mobility or time is constrained.

9. Heirloom Survival Seed Vault (Sealed Multi-Pouch Box)

A seed vault contains sealed packs of non-GMO, open-pollinated seeds capable of being regrown and saved year after year. Unlike hybrid or treated grocery-store seeds, heirloom seeds ensure self-sustaining food production after supply chains collapse. A quality seed vault will include staples like corn, beans, squash, tomatoes, leafy greens, and root vegetables, each packaged for multi-year shelf life. In long-duration collapses, seeds become untradeable (or extremely high value) assets, few people have them, and those who do, don't part with them. Purchase from trusted seed banks or off-grid agricultural suppliers.

Prices range from $35 to $90 depending on contents and packaging. Store sealed in mylar or vacuum-packed boxes in a dry, cool, dark environment. Do not freeze unless vacuum-sealed. One vault per household is the minimum; larger homesteads should keep multiples. During past famines and embargoes, seeds were worth more than currency. This is not an optional item.

10. Morton Canning and Pickling Salt (4 lb Box)

Canning salt is pure sodium chloride without additives, anti-caking agents, or iodine. This makes it the only suitable type for preserving meats, fermenting vegetables, and preparing long-storage food without chemical contamination. A single 4 lb box is enough to cure dozens of pounds of meat or produce. Unlike table salt, canning salt doesn't cloud brines or affect fermentation. During blackouts and energy crises, when freezers fail, salt is the fallback preservation method—and one of the first things to vanish from supply chains. Available at grocery chains, hardware stores, or preservation supply vendors.

Costs $2 to $5 per box. Store in airtight containers in a dry environment to prevent clumping or contamination. Keep at least 3 to 5 boxes per household. Also essential for electrolyte replacement in hot or labor-intensive conditions. High barter value when refrigeration systems collapse.

11. Iodine Water Purification Tablets (Bottle of 50)

Each iodine tablet disinfects one quart of untreated water, neutralizing bacteria, viruses, and protozoa within 30 to 45 minutes. In disaster zones or during municipal water failure, these tablets are a frontline defense against waterborne illness. One bottle purifies up to 12.5 gallons—enough to keep one person hydrated for over a week. Shelf life is typically 4 to 5 years; store in a cool, dry place and replace periodically. During Katrina, Haiti, and similar events, bottled water was stripped out within hours, leaving purification tabs as the only safe option.

Expect to pay $8 to $12 per bottle. Buy from outdoor supply stores, tactical gear outlets, or long-term survival vendors. These tablets are light, compact, and essential in mobile kits, bugout packs, and cache points. In barter, they hold value equal to antibiotics in regions with unsafe water.

12. Aqua-Tainer Water Container (7-Gallon, BPA-Free, With Spigot)

A 7-gallon Aqua-Tainer is one of the most reliable and affordable ways to store clean water for emergencies. Made from BPA-free food-grade plastic, it includes a threaded spigot and molded handle for controlled dispensing. Each full container supplies one person with drinking and sanitation water for three to four days at minimum survival usage. These containers are in high demand during boil notices, power outages, and natural disasters. They are typically sold out within hours of a water advisory announcement. Purchase from hardware chains like Lowe's or Home Depot, sporting goods stores, or emergency supply retailers.

Expect to pay $18 to $30 per unit. Store elevated and out of direct sunlight to prevent plastic degradation and algae growth. Keep multiple containers per household and rotate stored water every six months. In water-scarce conditions, a filled container becomes a direct substitute for bottled water and has barter value accordingly.

13. Manual Hand Pump for Water Wells

A manual hand pump is a permanently installed non-electric pumping system that draws water directly from an existing well. It is a critical fail-safe when electric pumps stop working during grid failure. Compatible with both shallow and deep wells, these systems allow year-round water access using human power alone. Homes with these systems maintained full water supply while others relied on melted snow. Pumps are not interchangeable; purchase models matched to your well's depth and casing from deep-well specialists or rural water supply companies.

Cost ranges from $300 to $1,200 depending on depth and materials. Installation requires planning and often retrofitting. Install before a crisis if possible. Once shortages begin, stock vanishes nationwide. No water supply system is complete without manual backup.

14. Sawyer Mini Water Filter Kit

The Sawyer Mini is a pocket-sized, field-rated water filtration system capable of treating up to 100,000 gallons. It removes 99.99999% of bacteria and 99.9999% of protozoa using a hollow fiber membrane. Requiring no electricity, heat, or chemicals, it operates through gravity, squeezing, or straw-suction methods. Ideal for bugout bags, vehicle kits, and low-weight mobile survival setups. In countries with failed infrastructure filters like this replaced bottled water and saved lives.

Available at outdoor retailers, survival gear stores, and large online suppliers. Price ranges from $18 to $30. Store with a pre-filter screen or coffee filter to prolong lifespan and prevent clogging. Always keep multiple units per household. In barter scenarios where water is plentiful but unsafe, these filters become both currency and life insurance.

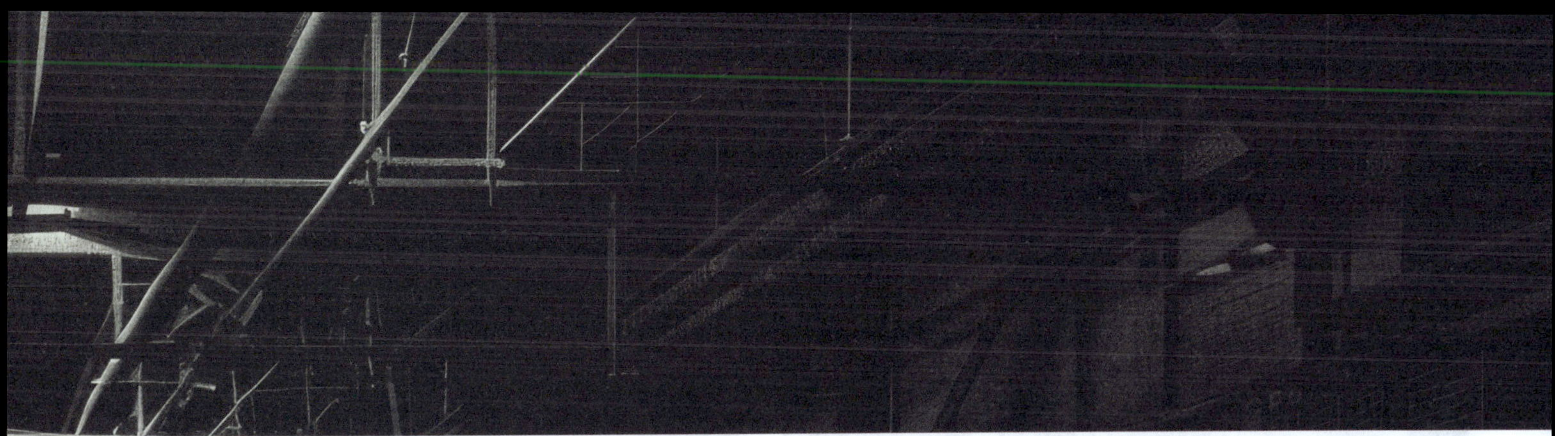

15. 55-Gallon Rain Barrel With Gutter Diverter Kit

A sealed 55-gallon rain barrel, when paired with a downspout diverter, allows you to harvest and store dozens of gallons per rainfall. Made from food-grade plastic, these barrels include overflow ports, spigots, and mesh screens to prevent mosquito breeding. In a long-term grid failure or drought, rainwater catchment becomes the only sustainable source for flushing, gardening, or filtration into drinking water. Rain barrels have been legally restricted or taxed in some drought-prone states, more evidence of their strategic value. Install on a back gutter and keep out of street view. Clean the roof and flush the first rainfall to reduce contaminants. Purchase from water catchment suppliers, homestead retailers, or farm supply chains.

Expect to pay $60 to $120 per system. Store dry between seasons and screen all openings. Rainwater becomes an emergency buffer that outlasts stored jugs and is immune to transportation failures.

16. Wool Survival Blankets (100% Wool, 66x90 Inches)

A full-size wool survival blanket is essential for non-electric thermal protection. Wool retains up to 80% of its insulating power even when wet and does not melt or ignite easily near open flame, making it suitable for use next to campfires or wood stoves. Each blanket of this size can fully wrap an adult or cover a sleeping area. During freezing blackouts these blankets preserved body heat when indoor temperatures dropped below safe levels. One is not enough, stock two per person for full coverage and redundancy.

These are $25 to $60 depending on weight and weave. Purchase from military surplus dealers, wool mills, or preparedness retailers. Store folded in airtight plastic bins or vacuum-sealed bags to prevent moth damage or mold. In barter, a clean, unused wool blanket is considered high-value during any cold-weather disaster.

17. Battery-Powered Emergency Fan (10-Inch, D-Cell Operated)

A 10-inch battery-powered fan is a life-saving tool in heat emergencies, especially when trapped indoors during blackouts. These fans reduce the risk of heat exhaustion, dehydration, and sleep disruption in sealed buildings with no airflow. Models powered by D-cell batteries are ideal for compatibility with basic storage systems and can run 30–70 hours per battery set. During coastal blackouts and summer outages, these units are consistently sold out within the first two days.

Price ranges from $15 to $35. Purchase from hardware stores, camping gear outlets, or disaster readiness distributors. Store with two complete battery sets per fan and a solar or crank charger if available. Include in go-bags, elderly care plans, and vehicle kits. Lack of airflow in high heat is one of the most underestimated threats in a power-down environment.

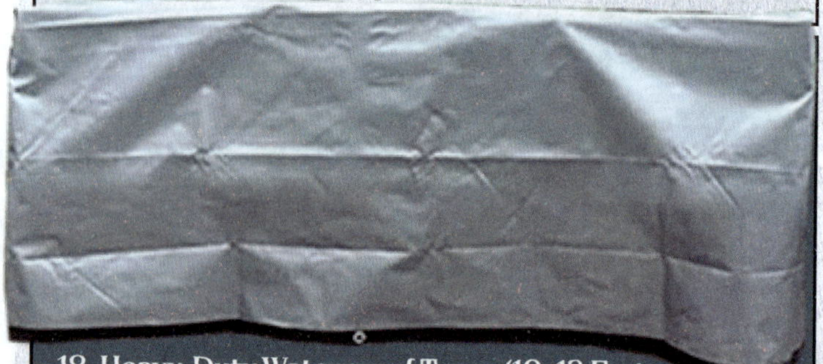

18. Heavy-Duty Waterproof Tarps (10x12 Feet, Reinforced)

A single 10x12 foot polyethylene tarp becomes a shelter, water catchment system, windbreak, or protective cover during any infrastructure failure. Unlike lightweight consumer tarps, heavy-duty models resist UV damage, wind shredding, and abrasion. Reinforced grommets allow for strong tie-downs in improvised structures or to secure loose materials. During post-disaster recovery, tarps vanish immediately from stores and become black-market items.

Expect to pay $12 to $30 depending on weight and brand. Buy from industrial supply outlets, farm co-ops, or construction-grade hardware retailers. Store rolled and dry to prevent microcracks or mold. Stock 2–3 tarps per household minimum. Their sheer number of uses makes them a tactical necessity, not an accessory.

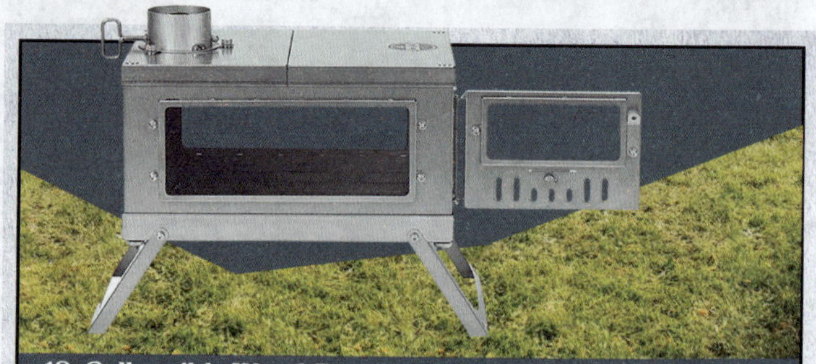

19. Collapsible Wood-Burning Stove (Portable, Solid Fuel Capable)

A collapsible wood stove allows you to cook, boil water, and generate passive heat using sticks, twigs, or biomass without needing fuel canisters. These stoves pack flat for storage or travel and provide an off-grid cooking solution during gas shortages, blackouts, or grid collapse. Models with secondary combustion chambers offer low-smoke output and higher efficiency. In locations where bottled gas disappears within hours, such as earthquake zones or in supply chain shutdowns, these stoves allow continuous food prep.

Expect to pay $40 to $90 depending on construction. Available through survival retailers, bushcraft outfitters, or online prepper suppliers. Test thoroughly before an emergency to learn heat control and placement. Store with fire starter kits, gloves, and spare grates. Strong barter item during cold-weather fuel scarcities.

20. Wool Socks (Midweight, Adult Size, 1 Pair)

One pair of midweight wool socks is a critical component of body temperature regulation, mobility, and foot health. Wool naturally wicks moisture, insulates even when wet, and resists odor buildup. Unlike cotton or polyester, it prevents blistering and frostbite under extreme conditions. A single quality pair can be worn for multiple days if dried properly. Military and refugee records show that untreated foot injuries are among the most common causes of evacuation failure and hospitalization.

Price ranges from $10 to $25 per pair. Buy from outdoor retailers, cold-weather surplus outlets, or reputable sock manufacturers (not fashion brands). Store sealed in dry containers, ideally with desiccant packets. Keep a minimum of five pairs per adult. Extremely valuable in barter once footwear or laundry access is compromised.

21. Diesel Generator (Portable, 2000W–3000W Range)

A compact diesel generator in the 2000 to 3000-watt range provides critical off-grid electricity for refrigeration, lighting, tool use, and medical equipment. Diesel is more stable than gasoline, stores longer, and ignites at a higher temperature, making it safer and more practical for long-term storage. During major crises, generators have sold out within a day. Quiet models with fuel-efficient engines are preferable for security.

Expect to pay $600–$1,500 depending on output and features. Purchase from farm supply dealers, heavy equipment rental outlets, or industrial hardware stores. Store indoors, chained or caged, with periodic testing under load. Maintain a 20–30 gallon diesel reserve with proper stabilizer (see Item 24). Generators without fuel or cables are targets for theft and useless after failure. Always secure with locking cables and sound-muffling shields.

22. Folding Solar Panel Kit (100-Watt, With Controller)

A 100-watt folding solar panel kit is a portable, renewable energy solution for keeping small electronics operational during extended outages. Paired with a charge controller, it can recharge phones, radios, lanterns, flashlights, and power banks daily. Unlike fuel-based systems, solar operates silently, draws no attention, and does not degrade with use.

Expect to pay $130–$250 for a complete kit with controller and cables. Buy from off-grid energy retailers, emergency expos, or online prep stores. Store in a dry area protected from dust and moisture. Test output monthly with real-world devices to confirm function. Critical for long-term survival, especially where refueling or generator concealment is impractical.

23. Rechargeable USB Power Bank (20,000mAh Capacity)

A high-capacity USB power bank (20,000mAh) provides multiple recharges for smartphones, headlamps, radios, or USB lanterns. A single unit can deliver three to five full phone charges and retain usable power for months in storage. Choose rugged, water-resistant models with dual ports and visible charge indicators. Pair with a solar panel kit for continuous recharging.

Price ranges from $25–$60 depending on brand and features. Purchase from electronics chains, emergency suppliers, or camping outfitters. Store charged and test quarterly. In barter, power banks become essential tools for communication, lighting, and morale, especially in urban areas.

24. Diesel Fuel Can (5-Gallon, With Stabilizer)

A sealed 5-gallon diesel fuel can is the cornerstone of generator, heater, or off-road equipment operation in collapse scenarios. Diesel remains usable for up to 12 months untreated, and up to 3 years when properly stabilized. Metal or HDPE fuel cans with vented caps are best. Store in shaded, elevated areas to prevent moisture or rust infiltration. During gas station outages and panic buying events, fuel containers and stabilizers are among the first items to disappear.

Expect to pay $20–$40 for a compliant fuel can and $10–$15 for stabilizer concentrate. Buy from farm co-ops, auto supply chains, or tool stores. Label and rotate every 6–12 months. Never store indoors or near flame.

25. Kerosene Lamp (With Spare Wick and Fuel Reserve)

A kerosene lamp provides reliable room lighting without electricity or batteries. Fueled by paraffin or clear lamp oil, it burns for 10–12 hours per fill and can be adjusted for brightness. Unlike candles, kerosene lamps produce more light and last longer per unit of fuel. This lighting method remained in use in rural areas worldwide well into the 20th century, and remains common in blackouts where batteries fail. During the 1973 energy crisis and modern grid failures, lamps and oil disappeared from hardware stores within days.

Price per lamp: $15–$35. Purchase from Amish hardware stores, preparedness suppliers, or general hardware retailers. Keep two to three replacement wicks and a quart of sealed lamp oil per lamp. Store lamp oil in a cool place, tightly capped, away from heat. Provides stable indoor lighting, trades well in electricity-deprived regions, and supports morale through long winter nights.

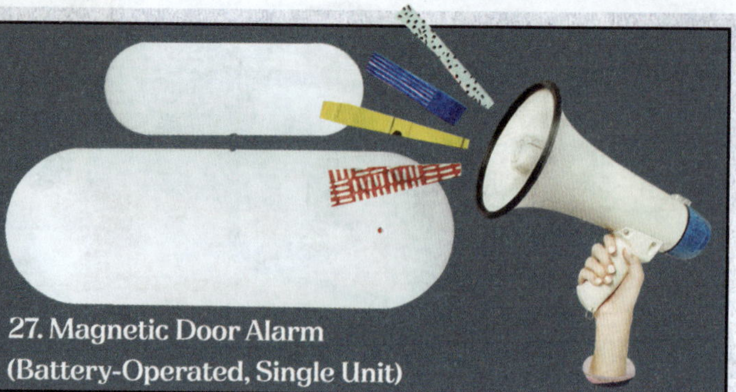

27. Magnetic Door Alarm (Battery-Operated, Single Unit)

A battery-powered magnetic door alarm provides a loud siren when a door or window is opened, offering immediate intrusion detection without wiring or network dependency. These devices are crucial for nighttime defense, sleep security, or monitoring vulnerable entry points. In the early hours of civil unrest or post-disaster looting, shelves clear of basic alarm systems.

Each unit costs $10–$20. Mounts with adhesive or screws in seconds. Use in homes, sheds, or mobile shelters. Found at home security aisles, general hardware stores, or military surplus outlets. Operates on standard AAA or button-cell batteries, use rechargeable versions for long-term setups. Include in early warning networks when cameras or power are unavailable. These alarms are small, cheap, and often overlooked until it's too late.

26. Motion-Triggered Security Camera (MicroSD-Based, Standalone Recording)

A weatherproof motion-triggered security camera with local MicroSD storage operates independently of Wi-Fi or cloud services. These units detect movement, record video to onboard memory, and operate on DC power or solar input. In grid-down or communications blackout scenarios, they provide critical surveillance when power and internet-based systems fail. Widely used in rural security and during the 2020 unrest, these cameras sold out across multiple regions. Look for models with infrared night vision, motion sensitivity adjustment, and MicroSD card slots (not reliant on monthly cloud subscriptions).

Expect to pay $40–$90. Available at hardware chains, surveillance suppliers, or online electronics wholesalers. Mount at entry points and conceal cabling. Power with battery banks or solar panels. Store additional memory cards and test regularly. Effective for compound perimeter monitoring, especially when manpower is limited.

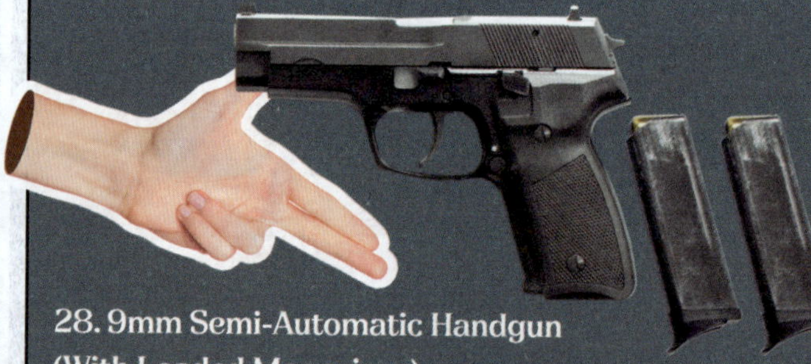

28. 9mm Semi-Automatic Handgun (With Loaded Magazines)

A 9mm semi-automatic handgun is the standard civilian defensive weapon for mobility, concealment, and deterrence. It is easy to train with, widely available, and chambered in the most globally common caliber. A full magazine offers effective defense from both threats and opportunistic criminals during breakdowns in civil order. In every major historical collapse firearms and ammunition became unpurchasable within days. Purchase legally from a licensed dealer and ensure you have at least two to four loaded magazines per firearm. Train weekly in safety, malfunction clearing, and draw technique. Store in a secured, hidden location with quick access.

Average cost: $300–$700. Use steel-cased or brass ammo as available, but remember steel isn't reloadable. In barter conditions, a reliable sidearm or spare ammo carries immense defensive and transactional value. Never trade without absolute need.

29. Over-the-Door Security Bar
(Telescoping, Floor-Braced)

This adjustable tension bar installs under a standard doorknob and braces against the floor, making it nearly impossible to kick in the door from outside. It requires no drilling or structural modification and can be moved between locations. During high-crime periods or riot conditions, home entry points are tested first, and unsecured doors are the first failures. These security bars are one of the fastest-selling items after any urban panic.

Priced between $20 and $40, they're available at big-box stores, locksmith vendors, or online safety retailers. Ideal for apartments, rentals, or temporary shelters. Store with instructions clearly labeled and test for fit before deployment. Affordable, effective, and completely silent, they harden your perimeter without escalating your visible posture.

30. Lockable Steel Filing Cabinet
(4-Drawer, Vertical)

A four-drawer, lockable steel filing cabinet is the backbone of physical information control during collapse. This cabinet protects property deeds, family records, passports, insurance policies, medical documentation, and emergency contact files, each of which may be the only proof you have of identity or ownership after systems fail. A proper filing cabinet deters theft, organizes critical data, and allows fast evacuation of essential documents.

Expect to pay $80–$200. Purchase from office suppliers, surplus auctions, or corporate liquidation sales. Bolt it to wall studs or floor anchors to prevent removal. Use waterproof folders and fire-resistant sleeves where possible. In emergencies, paper speaks louder than memory.

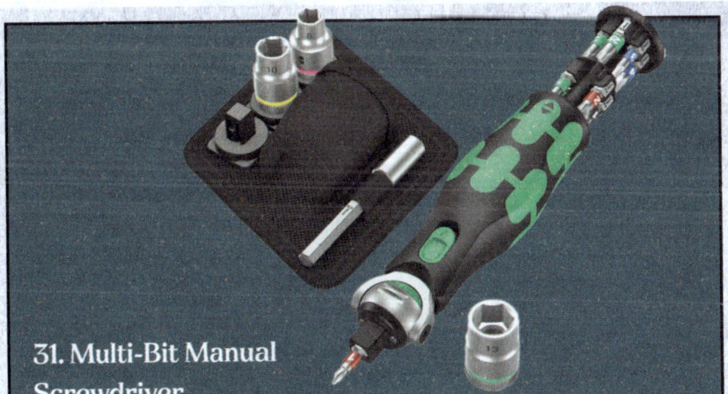

31. Multi-Bit Manual Screwdriver
(Interchangeable Heads, Hand Tool)

A multi-bit manual screwdriver replaces an entire drawer of electric tools and specialized drivers when power fails. With a single shaft and a magnetic tip, it accommodates Phillips, flathead, Torx, and square-drive bits, all stored in the handle or pouch. In blackout conditions or when battery tools fail, this simple hand tool allows you to open appliances, tighten hinges, maintain locks, dismantle electronics, or repair furniture. During prolonged supply chain disruptions, broken gear cannot be replaced, it must be fixed. These screwdrivers sell out rapidly in crises, especially among renters or displaced families trying to maintain essential equipment.

Cost: $8 to $20. Purchase from hardware chains, tool trucks, or used tool dealers. Store in your daily-use drawer, not buried in long-term storage. One of the most quietly essential tools in post-collapse life.

32. Gorilla Tape Roll
(Black, 35 Yards)

Gorilla Tape is a heavy-duty, reinforced adhesive tape far stronger than standard duct tape. It bonds to rough surfaces, stays stuck in wet and cold environments, and withstands abuse. It's used for sealing tent rips, holding broken gear together, repairing tarps, waterproofing seams, and even patching footwear or clothing in the field.

Price: $9 to $12 per roll. Buy from hardware chains, outdoor outfitters, or prepper suppliers. Store in sealed containers in dry, temperature-stable conditions. Rotate rolls every 2–3 years to avoid glue breakdown. In barter, it's a compact, high-value asset with hundreds of uses.

33. Unscented Household Bleach (Quart, 6% Sodium Hypochlorite)

One quart of unscented blevach can purify hundreds of gallons of water, sterilize surfaces, eliminate mold, and prevent microbial outbreaks in shared spaces. Use 8 drops per gallon to make untreated water safe to drink. During infrastructure collapse, where sewage, water, and garbage systems fail, bleach becomes a frontline health defense. Only plain bleach (no scents, thickeners, or detergents) is safe for purification.

Price: $2 to $4 per quart. Buy from grocery or hardware stores. Store sealed in dark, cool environments away from metal tools. Replace every 12 months, as potency drops after opening. Essential for household sanitation, wound cleanup, and water potability in all environments.

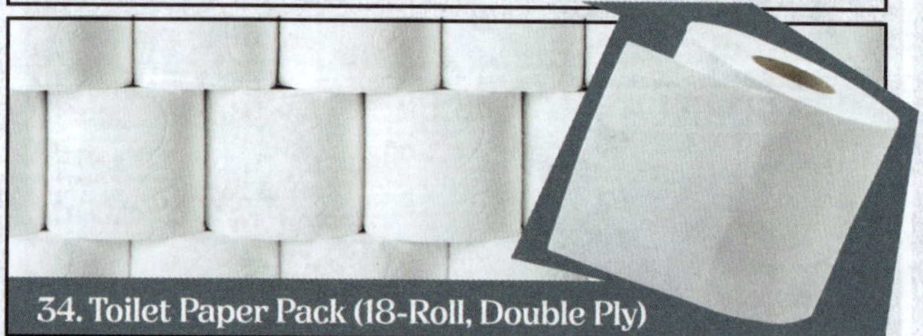

34. Toilet Paper Pack (18-Roll, Double Ply)

An 18-roll pack of double-ply toilet paper offers over a month of sanitation for a family of four under rationed use. While often mocked, TP is hard to improvise. Leaves, rags, or paper substitutes carry risk of infection or plumbing damage. During the COVID-19 lockdown, it became a national panic item for good reason. In deeper economic collapse, paper goods vanish due to factory slowdowns, shipping interruptions, or panic hoarding.

Expect to pay $12 to $20 depending on brand and region. Buy from warehouse clubs or wholesale supply chains. Store sealed in totes or plastic bags to protect against humidity, rodents, and insects. In prolonged emergencies, toilet paper is a high-morale barter item, particularly for families or groups with children and elders. Stock it before the shelves empty again.

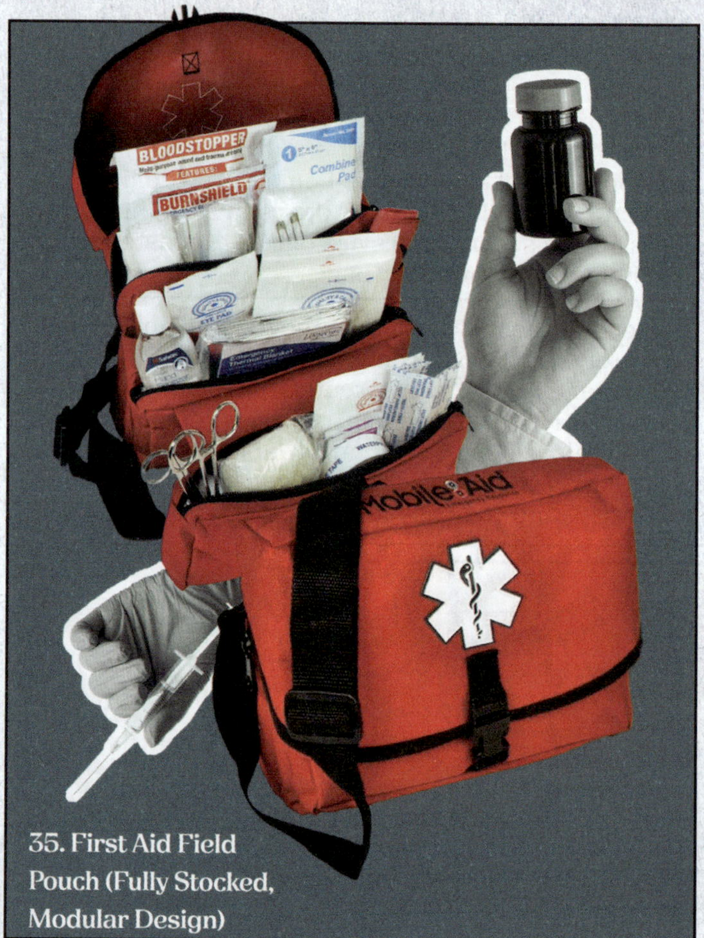

35. First Aid Field Pouch (Fully Stocked, Modular Design)

A fully stocked first aid field pouch includes trauma bandages, gauze rolls, antiseptic wipes, latex-free gloves, pain relievers (ibuprofen or acetaminophen), tweezers, burn gel, electrolyte packets, and wound closure strips. In collapse scenarios, basic medical access vanishes within days. Pharmacies are looted or closed, and black-market prices for over-the-counter meds soar. Build a pouch that fits on your belt, pack, or vehicle visor.

Price: $40–$90 depending on contents. Buy from tactical medical outlets, hunting stores, or EMT supply vendors. Customize the layout for your needs: bleeding control, burn treatment, mobility injuries, or basic illness. Store duplicate kits in every major location like your home, car, and bugout bag. This pouch is not a backup. It's your frontline defense against injuries that no one else will treat.

36. Box of Bic Lighters (50 Count, Standard Flint)

A 50-count box of Bic lighters is a fire-starting goldmine. Each lighter provides up to 3,000 ignitions, making it exponentially more efficient than matches or ferro rods for daily use. In fuel-scarce scenarios—especially after hurricanes, grid failures, or urban riots, lighters become a top-tier barter item, used to ignite stoves, lanterns, candles, or fires for warmth and water boiling. They are prized by smokers, preppers, and anyone cut off from electricity.

Cost per box: $30–$40 wholesale. Purchase from overstock liquidation suppliers, dollar stores, or prep wholesalers. Store in cool, dry containers. Distribute among all kits, bags, and caches. Trade value is extremely high once matches are used up and open flame becomes essential.

37. Encrypted USB Drive (32GB Minimum, AES-256 Encryption)

A rugged USB flash drive with at least 32GB capacity and AES-256 encryption lets you store copies of everything that proves who you are: birth certificates, ID scans, land titles, financial data, medical histories, contact lists, prescriptions, family records. When digital systems crash, you may still need to prove ownership, access resources, or rebuild identity. This drive becomes your digital skeleton key, but you must also print those files and laminate the copies, storing them in a secure, fire-resistant folder.

Buy quality encrypted drives from electronics retailers, not novelty sticks or unbranded models. Store one on your person, and the other in a secure offsite location. Without verified identity, property or freedom becomes negotiable. This drive ensures your proof survives even if the system doesn't.

Chapter 9

How to Build a Year-Long Fresh Water Stockpile

This chapter shows you how to build a yearlong freshwater stockpile using:

1. Rain
2. Wells
3. Filters
4. Pumps
5. Barrels

"We never know the worth of water until the well runs dry."
Thomas Fuller

Water Storage: Containers & Placement

You need about 365 gallons minimum per person for basic survival (1 gal/day), but much more for luxuries like bathing if not near surface water. Add extra for cooking or livestock.

Before you start collecting your water reserves, you need to know how to safely and properly store it.

Best Long-Term Containers

When storing water long-term, the container you choose matters as much as the water itself. The wrong materials can spoil the supply over time—leaching chemicals, growing bacteria, or degrading in sunlight. The right ones, by contrast, can keep water safe and drinkable for a year or more with minimal maintenance.

The 55-gallon blue plastic drum.

The most widely used and affordable option is the standard 55-gallon blue plastic drum. Made from food-grade high-density polyethylene (HDPE), these barrels are built to resist UV light, prevent chemical breakdown, and withstand both heat and cold. They should be stored in shaded or indoor spaces whenever possible, and always sealed with airtight lids to keep out pests and airborne contaminants. A single drum holds nearly two months' worth of drinking water for one person and can be rotated in pairs or series for easier use.

275-gallon IBC totes

For higher capacity storage, 275-gallon IBC totes provide industrial-grade volume in a single footprint. These square tanks are framed in metal cages for stacking and transport and often include built-in spigots for easy draining. They're ideal for rural properties, group storage plans, or preppers with more space to work with. As with any plastic container, make sure the tote is food-grade and was never used to store chemicals or non-consumable liquids.

5-7 gallon jugs

Smaller containers still have a place in the system. Five-gallon jugs are easy to carry, simple to rotate, and convenient for moving water from main storage to where it's needed. They're also perfect for storing treated water in grab-and-go kits or bug-out vehicles. For slightly more volume and better handling, seven-gallon Reliance Aqua-Tainers are a common prepper staple. These rigid containers have integrated spouts, molded handles, and stack well when empty or full.

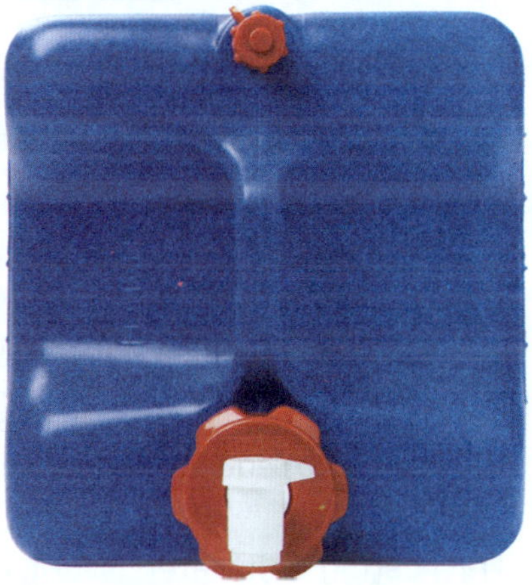

Avoid storing water in anything not specifically marked food-safe. Thin plastic containers may degrade, crack, or leach contaminants into the water over time. Never use barrels that once held oils, fuels, or chemicals—even if they've been rinsed. Metal containers should also be avoided unless they're lined and designed for potable storage. Over time, rust and corrosion can spoil even clean water, especially if stored outdoors or exposed to temperature swings.

Proper containers are the backbone of a long-term stockpile. Once filled, they need to be treated, labeled, and rotated—

but it all starts with choosing the right vessel. Everything else builds on that.

Storage Tips

Even clean, treated water can degrade over time if left in the wrong conditions. Heat, light, and exposure to air are the primary threats, and all of them are avoidable with basic planning.

Store water in cool, dark places where temperature remains stable year-round. Basements, interior closets, root cellars, or underground shelters are ideal. Avoid areas exposed to direct sunlight, heat from appliances, or freezing temperatures that could crack containers or expand seals. If outdoor storage is necessary, insulate and cover the barrels or totes with UV-resistant tarps and position them against shaded walls.

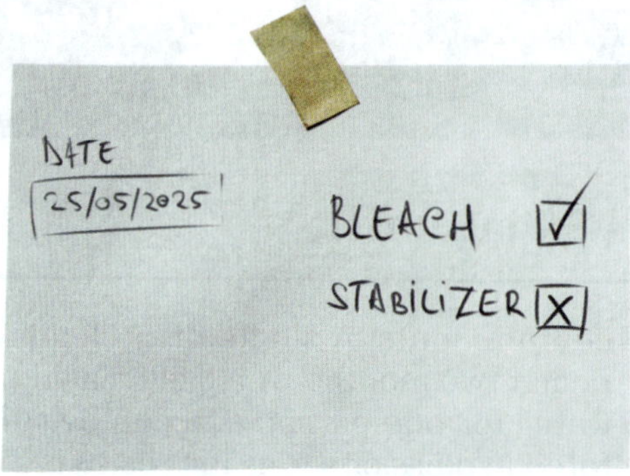

Every container should be labeled clearly with the date it was filled and what treatment method was used—bleach, stabilizer, or none. This makes it easy to track rotation and verify safety before use. Water doesn't expire, but it can pick up taste, sediment, or biological growth if neglected. Marking each barrel allows you to rotate intelligently and with confidence.

As a rule of thumb, stored water should be rotated every six to twelve months, depending on conditions. If your space and resources allow it, stagger your rotation so you're always refreshing a portion of your supply without draining the entire system at once.

For longer-term storage, **commercial water stabilizers** are available and widely used. These products extend shelf life by suppressing microbial growth and maintaining clarity over time. Most are added at the time of storage and last several years when kept sealed in proper conditions. They don't eliminate the need for treatment before use, but they reduce the risk of spoilage and extend rotation cycles significantly.

Rainwater Harvesting Systems

Rain is one of the few water sources that doesn't require digging, travel, or fuel to access. It arrives freely and frequently in much of the United States, and when captured properly, it can serve as the foundation of a long-term water reserve. Whether you're living in a rural homestead or an urban neighborhood, collecting rainwater is one of the and most reliable ways to reduce dependence on fragile infrastructure.

Harvesting rainwater is not limited to rooftops. From complete barrel-and-gutter systems to improvised tarp setups in the open, the principle remains the same: catch the rain where it falls, channel it where you want it, and store it safely until it's needed.

The two most accessible methods are roof-based gutter systems and ground-level catchment rigs. One uses existing structures to maximize collection; the other can be built from scratch with little more than cordage, plastic sheeting, and gravity. Both are worth understanding—and building—before the next major crisis arrives.

Gutter to Barrel Setup

To start collecting rainwater, begin by inspecting your roof and gutter system. The surface area of your roof determines how much water you can collect. **For reference, a 1,000-square-foot roof will yield approximately 600 gallons of water for every inch of rainfall.** The goal is to channel that runoff into secure storage without contamination.

Install gutter diverters where the downspouts meet the vertical drop. These are simple attachments that reroute rainwater from your existing gutter system into a holding container. They can be found at most hardware stores or ordered online. **For best results, add a first-flush filter just below the diverter. This device allows the initial runoff—typically containing dust, bird feces, pollen, and debris—to bypass the storage barrel entirely. Once the first few gallons have been discarded, cleaner water is allowed through.**

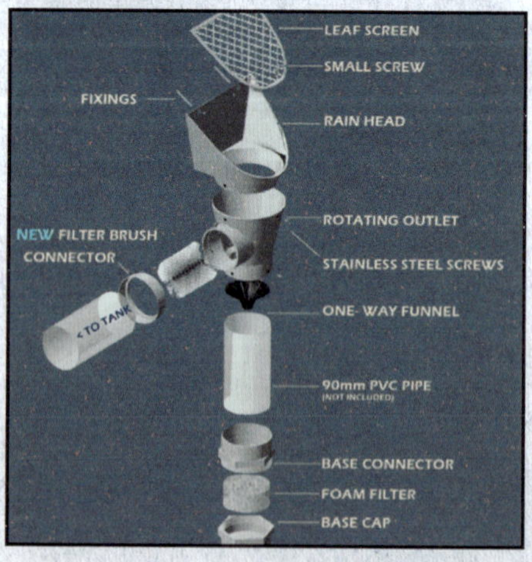

At the entrance to each barrel, affix a fine mesh screen to keep out any insects and organic debris that might have gone through. Standard mosquito netting or even a repurposed screen door mesh works well, as long as it's stretched tight and sealed around the edges.

For containers, use only food-grade options. Blue HDPE plastic barrels (usually 55 gallons) or the larger totes, as previously mentioned, are widely available and overall easy to transport.

Once your barrels or totes are in place, elevate them using cinder blocks, bricks, or a sturdy wooden platform. Elevation allows gravity to assist with water flow, especially if you're siphoning into smaller containers or routing water into the house. Keep your tanks shaded or covered to prevent algae growth. If full shading isn't possible, wrap the barrels in black UV-resistant plastic sheeting or paint them with non-toxic black exterior paint to block light.

After filling, treat the water with a measured amount of unscented household bleach if you're storing it long term. This step can be delayed if you're planning to filter or boil the water later, but treating in advance helps suppress biological growth during storage.

With a properly built gutter-to-barrel system, you can capture and hold hundreds of gallons with every rainfall, building a renewable reserve that doesn't rely on electricity, fuel, or municipal infrastructure.

Tarp-Based Rain Collection

When no gutters exist—or when you're on the move—a simple tarp setup can provide the surface area you need to catch rainwater. The method is low-tech, fast to assemble, and highly effective in areas with moderate to heavy rainfall.

Start with a clean tarp, ideally at least 6 by 8 feet in size. Larger tarps increase collection volume but require more space and support. Suspend the tarp using trees, poles, or even scavenged furniture, forming a shallow basin with a slight low point at the center or one edge. The angle should be steep enough to shed water but gentle enough to hold it briefly before guiding it toward your container.

At the lowest point of the tarp, create a controlled outlet. This can be done by slightly cutting or folding a corner to direct water into a funnel or tube, or by allowing it to flow directly into the mouth of a storage container placed below. Secure the tarp tightly to prevent flapping, and position the container so the water drops cleanly in without spilling down the sides.

Use a filter cloth, bandana, or mesh at the drainage point to catch leaves, insects, or airborne debris. The collected water will still need purification before drinking, but this simple barrier prevents larger contaminants from entering your supply.

If you're working with limited gear, you can improvise containers using clean plastic bins, lined buckets, or even trash bags placed inside stable frames to hold their shape. For longer-term setups, pair the tarp system with food-safe drums or IBC totes, just like you would in a rooftop system.

Tarp-based harvesting is especially useful for mobile camps, bug-out locations, or backyards without gutter access. It's also an ideal secondary method during long storms—once barrels fill from the roof, you can set up tarps to keep collecting while it lasts. With enough surface area, a tarp setup can yield dozens of gallons per day during rainfall, and it requires no permanent infrastructure to do so.

Groundwater Extraction

While rain can be seasonal or unpredictable, groundwater remains one of the most stable and renewable water sources available—if you know how to reach it. Whether accessed by a hand-dug well, a driven sandpoint, or a converted deep well with a manual pump, groundwater gives you the ability to draw clean, cold water from beneath your feet even when every surface source has dried up.

Most groundwater systems require upfront labor or installation, but once built, they can produce water for years with little maintenance. In rural or off-grid settings, shallow wells and manual pumps are often the only dependable long-term source available. Even city folk can benefit by learning the techniques and tools needed to tap aquifers without relying on the grid.

This section breaks down the core methods of groundwater extraction, focusing on systems that can be built or maintained without electricity.

Digging a Shallow Survival Well

In areas with a high-water table, a shallow well can easily supply fresh groundwater. If you're living off-grid or in rural land with soft soil, a hand-dug or driven well offers a dependable, low-tech way to access water. It requires some elbow grease, and patience,—but once completed, a shallow well can serve you for years.

The process begins with selecting a site. Look for low ground where vegetation is green and moisture is present year-round—especially after dry spells. Avoid placing your well near septic systems, livestock pens, or fuel storage, as runoff can contaminate the groundwater. If you're working in a clay-heavy area, wait until the ground is saturated from recent rain. This softens the soil, making it easier to dig, while still leaving the water table low enough to avoid a flooded shaft.

To begin digging, use a post-hole auger or shovel to open the shaft. A well-point system can also be driven directly into the soil using a sledgehammer or slide hammer, depending on the terrain. Once you've reached moist, sandy soil—usually 15 to 30 feet down—install a six-inch PVC casing to keep the walls from collapsing. At the base of the casing, a sandpoint with stainless steel mesh will allow water to enter while blocking sediment.

Fill the area around the sandpoint with clean gravel to act as a basic filtration bed. This reduces fine particulates and prevents clogging. At the top of the casing, cap it with a secure cover or vented seal to keep out insects, animals, and surface runoff.

Once the well is stable, install a manual pump. Commercial options like the Simple Pump or Bison Pump can be mounted directly onto the casing and drawn by hand. For a more budget-conscious build, a PVC piston-style pump can be assembled using off-the-shelf hardware parts and mounted with a simple lever system. In colder climates, insulate the housing or drain the pump between uses to prevent freezing.

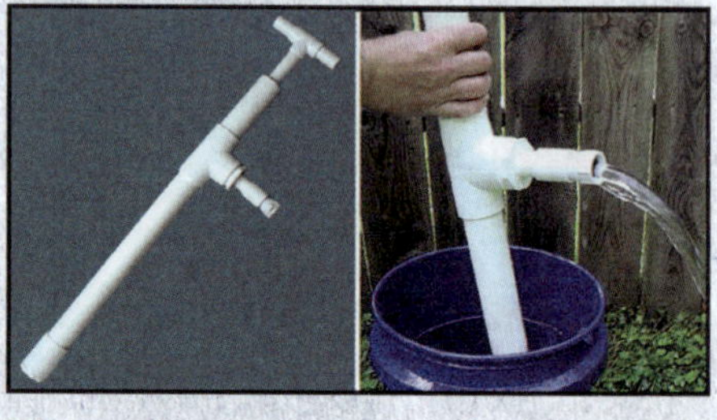

Water drawn from a shallow well should still be run through a proper filtration system before drinking. While groundwater is generally safer than surface sources, it can still contain bacteria or minerals depending on the depth and soil composition. Pump the water into sealed tanks or directly into your purification setup as part of your regular routine.

Done correctly, a shallow well becomes one of the most resilient water sources available—unseen, protected fromv surface contamination, and fully independent of weather cycles.

Accessing a Deep Well Without Power

Many properties already have deep wells installed, often reaching depths between 100 and 400 feet. These wells are typically accessed using submersible electric pumps, which work well—until the power goes out. In a blackout scenario, this type of well becomes inaccessible unless it's been adapted for off-grid draw.

Converting a deep well for manual use involves adding a secondary draw system alongside the existing electric pump. Most modern well casings are large enough to accommodate both. With the right setup, a manual pump can be installed without removing or interfering with the electric system, giving you a backup in case the power goes out.

The most straightforward solution is to install a deep-well-capable manual pump such as the Simple Pump. This system uses a narrow piston and lift rod assembly that fits inside a 4-inch casing and can pull water from depths up to 325 feet, depending on the configuration. It's designed specifically for side-by-side installation with submersibles, and it allows you to draw water during outages without tearing out the original setup.

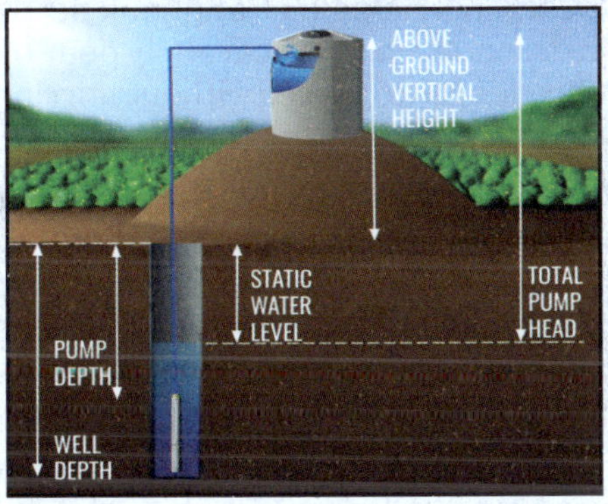

If installing from scratch, verify the static water level before choosing equipment. Static level refers to the height water naturally rests at in the well when not being pumped. It's different from total depth and it determines the specifications your handpump must meet. You'll need a water depth gauge or a weighted string to get an accurate reading. If the water is deeper than 25 feet, a suction-style pump won't work—you'll need a lift-style piston pump capable of operating below the static line.

Installing any deep-well conversion involves lowering a draw pipe and lift rod through the casing. The pump handle is mounted at the surface, either directly to the casing or via a support bracket. Make sure all joints are sealed, threaded tight, and supported by a proper cap or flange. Use food-safe pipe materials, and avoid galvanized steel unless the water is being filtered after collection—zinc can leach under certain conditions.

While installation can be done independently with mechanical skill, it often helps to consult a local well driller for a one-time assist—especially to verify casing diameter, depth, and safety. Once installed, test regularly and keep spare rods, seals, and pump heads on hand. In a true grid-down situation, you'll want to know the system works before you're relying on it.

A properly adapted deep well is one of the most reliable water sources you can have. It taps an isolated, protected supply far beneath the surface—insulated from drought, contamination, and most natural disasters. With the right manual access, it can provide for your household indefinitely, without ever needing a generator or fuel.

Installing a Manual Hand Pump

When the power fails, so does anything connected to a well pump. Without a manual backup, even a deep, reliable well becomes useless. Installing a hand pump ensures access to groundwater when the grid is down, the generator runs dry, or mechanical systems fail. It's one of the most critical upgrades you can make to a survival water system.

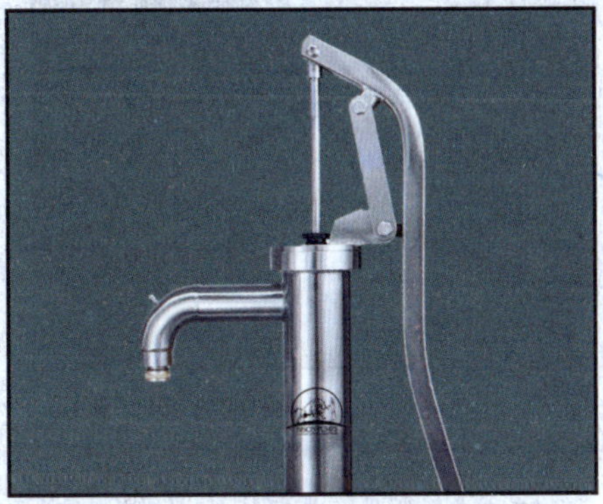

The most reliable manual pumps are built from stainless steel or high-grade polymer and are designed to operate without electricity. Modern designs can be installed alongside an existing electric pump, allowing both systems to draw from the same well casing. This dual setup means the hand pump can be used immediately when needed, without disconnecting or removing the primary pump.

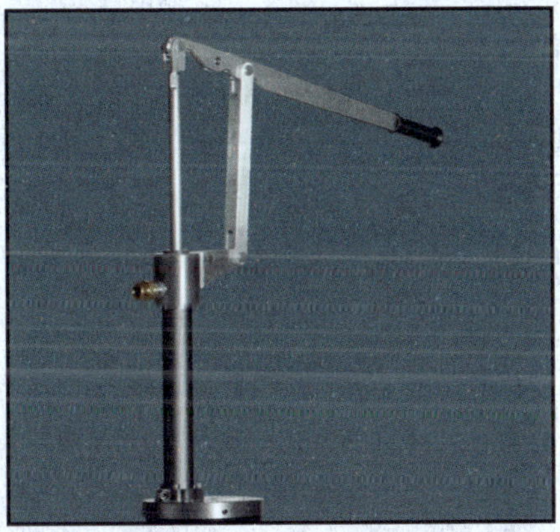

Two of the most proven options on the market are the Bison Pump and the Simple Pump. The Bison is constructed from stainless steel and designed for long-term durability in harsh conditions. It bolts directly onto the well casing and includes a freeze-proof design when properly installed. The Simple Pump is modular, lightweight, and compatible with deep wells—drawing from depths over 200 feet in some configurations. Both systems can deliver water to pressure tanks or uphill storage with the addition of check valves.

For those on a tighter budget, the EZ Water Well Hand Pump is made from PVC and performs reliably in shallow wells up to 25 feet deep. It's lighter and easier to install but lacks the longevity of metal-based systems. A fully DIY option can be built using off-the-shelf PVC parts, a piston seal, and a basic lever assembly. These homemade pumps are ideal for shallow setups, backup installations, or learning the mechanics before investing in a full system.

Whatever model you choose, installation requires attention to seals, fittings, and freezing protection. Every pump system should include at least one check valve to prevent backflow and keep the line primed. Always stock spare gaskets, O-rings, and lubrication for ongoing maintenance. In freezing climates, either install the pump below the frost line with a sealed sleeve or drain the pipe after each use to prevent cracks and damage.

A manual pump turns a passive water source into an active one. With a few strokes, clean groundwater is in your hands—no power, no noise, no fuel, and no outside help required.

River and Lake Water

In a crisis, water you can see—rivers, lakes, ponds, even creeks—might seem like an easy win. But open water can carry serious risks if you're not careful. Pollution, animal waste, and bacteria can all make you sick. Still, if handled the right way, these sources can keep you going when other options dry up.

This section will show you how to find the safest surface water, how to avoid trouble, and how to make it safe to use.

Identifying Safe Surface Water Sources

Fast-moving creeks, cold rivers, or lakes fed by springs are your best bet. The water is cleaner, less likely to be full of bugs or bacteria, and usually smells better too. Skip anything that's stagnant, muddy, or covered in algae. If it smells bad or looks off—cloudy, oily, or slimy—move on.

Stay away from spots near farms, factories, or towns. If you can, follow the water upstream. If you see dead animals, trash dumps, or pipes draining into it, find another source. Try not to collect water right at the shoreline—use a clean container tied to a rope or stick to dip deeper out.

Drawing, Settling, and Pre-Filtration

Once you collect the water, let it sit still for a few hours—overnight is best. This helps dirt and junk settle to the bottom. Then carefully pour off the clearer top layer without stirring up the muck.

If the water's really dirty, pour it through a clean cloth, bandana, or a homemade filter using sand and charcoal before you treat it. This doesn't clean it fully, but it helps your gear last longer and makes real treatment more effective.

Once prepped, the water must still be treated—boiled, chemically disinfected, or run through a high-grade filter capable of removing bacteria, protozoa, and viruses if possible. These steps are covered in full in the upcoming **Water Filtration & Purification** section, but for river and lake water, **never skip them.**

Water Filtration & Purification

All the stockpiling in the world doesn't matter if your water is unsafe. Contaminated water kills more people after disasters than starvation ever has.

Identifying Contaminated Water

Don't let clear water fool you—it can still be full of things that'll wreck your health. Bacteria, parasites, and chemicals don't always look dirty. You won't have a lab kit in a survival situation, but your senses—especially sight and smell—can help you steer clear of danger.

Start by checking the look of it. If it's cloudy, murky, or full of stuff floating around, you'll definitely need to filter it. Even if it looks better after settling, any leftover haze or odd color might still be a warning sign.

Color matters too. Reddish or brown usually means clay or iron—mostly harmless. But green or blue tints, especially in still water, often mean algae or cyanobacteria. These can be toxic and aren't always removed by boiling. If you see green slime, surface scum, or oily patches—skip it.

Smell is a big red flag. Clean water shouldn't smell like anything. Rotten egg smells? Probably bacteria. Musty or sewage-like? Could be from feces. Chemical or metallic stink? Walk away.

Look around the area. Even a flowing creek can be risky if there's farmland, houses, or roads nearby—runoff can carry waste and poison. In the wild, signs of animals—like droppings or dead wildlife near the water—can mean it's contaminated with parasites like Giardia.

Also watch for bugs. Mosquitoes or larvae usually mean stagnant water that's low in oxygen and high in bacteria. Cold, fast-flowing water is safer, but never guaranteed safe.

When in doubt: filter it, treat it, or find better. Appearances alone won't protect you.

Parasites and Microbes to Watch For

Untreated water may look clean, but it often carries invisible threats that can shut down a survival plan in days. Even a single sip of contaminated water can introduce parasites or bacteria that trigger dehydration, illness, or worse—especially when medical help isn't coming. Understanding what you're up against is the first step toward purifying water correctly.

Giardia is one of the most common waterborne parasites. Found in streams, ponds, and even melted snow near animal traffic, it causes sudden and severe gastrointestinal distress—diarrhea, cramping, gas, and vomiting. Symptoms can begin within days and may last for weeks if untreated, leading to dangerous fluid loss. It spreads through fecal contamination and is especially common in wilderness areas with beaver or livestock presence.

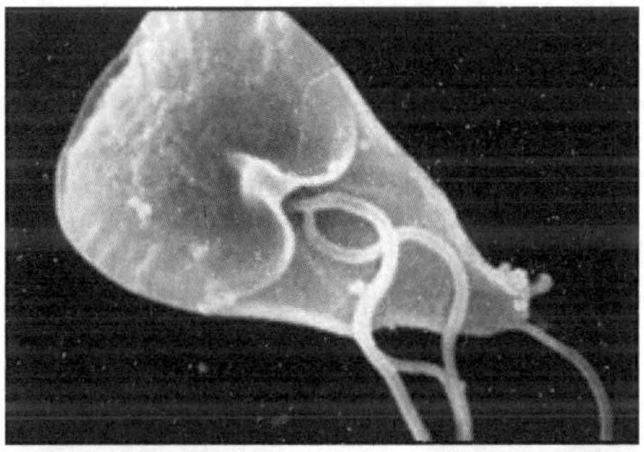

Cryptosporidium is a microscopic parasite that resists standard chlorine treatment and thrives in stagnant water or runoff zones. It's transmitted through animal waste, particularly from cattle or wildlife near open water. Like Giardia, it attacks the digestive tract, but it's more difficult to eliminate and harder to filter due to its small size. Boiling is the most reliable way to kill it.

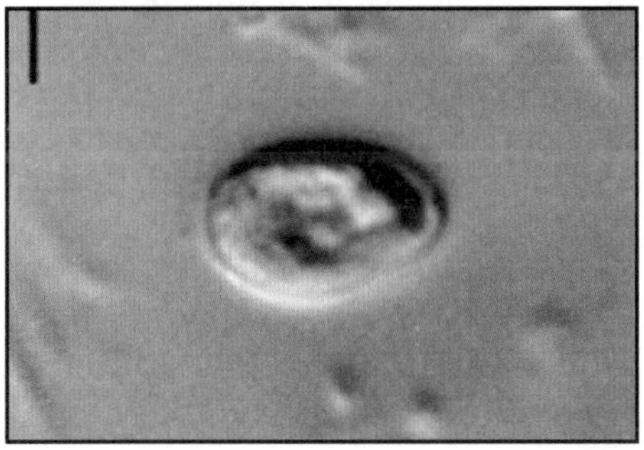

E. coli is a bacteria group linked to human and animal feces. Not all strains are harmful, but some cause bloody diarrhea, severe abdominal pain, and kidney complications. It enters water through sewage leaks, agricultural runoff, or direct contamination by animals. Surface water in urban areas is particularly susceptible.

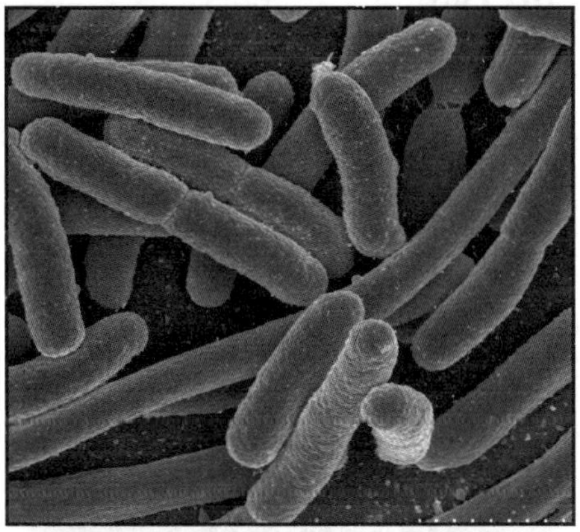

Leptospirosis is less common but highly dangerous. Spread through the urine of infected animals—especially rats—it enters the body through mucous membranes or small skin cuts when wading through or drinking from contaminated water. It can cause high fever, muscle aches, vomiting, and, in severe cases, organ failure. Unlike many other pathogens, leptospirosis can survive in both fresh and brackish water.

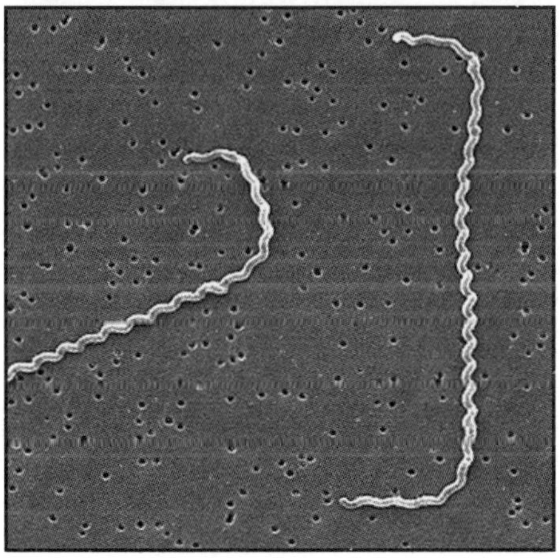

Each of these threats reinforces a single truth: no untreated water is safe. Whether it's clear as glass or drawn from a pristine stream, purification is mandatory—every time.

DIY Filtration Systems

For filtering water in the field or at home, there are three tiers of -accessible systems: home-built slow filters, modular gravity towers, and portable field tools. Each serves a different scale of need, and a smart prepper has at least one in place before it's needed.

The bio-sand filter is one of the most effective homemade systems for processing large quantities of water at a stationary location. It works by passing water slowly through a vertical column of gravel, coarse sand, and fine sand layered precisely. The top layer collects organic matter and bacteria, which are gradually broken down by a living layer called the biological zone. Below that, the fine sand catches remaining particles, and the gravel base supports drainage. A cloth or screen over the top keeps insects and debris from falling in. These systems can process gallons per day, but they require patience to build and at least a few weeks to mature before they become fully effective. Once active, they can run maintenance-free for months at a time.

For those able to stock supplies ahead of time, **Berkey-style gravity filters offer a modular solution using stackable buckets and high-efficiency ceramic or carbon filters.** The most popular are Black Berkey elements, which remove bacteria, protozoa, and even some viruses. By drilling a hole in the bottom of a food-grade bucket and installing the filter element, you can stack that bucket over a second clean container to create a two-tier system. Water slowly drips through, removing contaminants as it moves. These systems are ideal for daily use in a fixed location and can be scaled to family size by adding more filters or larger buckets. Because they operate passively, they require no electricity or pressure.

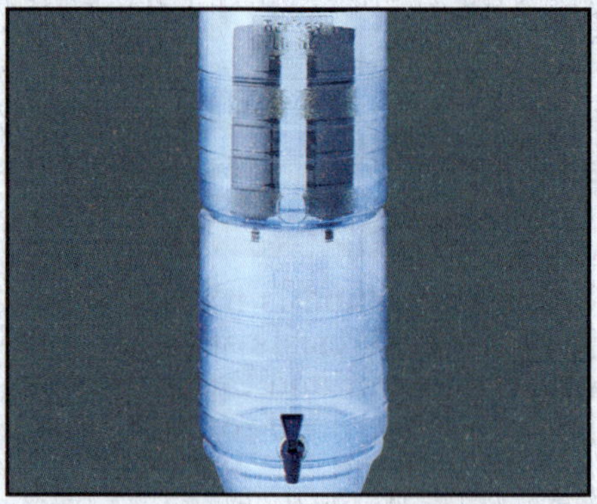

For mobility or bug-out scenarios, **the Sawyer Squeeze is one of the most reliable compact filters available. It screws directly onto soft water pouches or bottles and allows clean water to be squeezed out on demand.** It's effective against bacteria and protozoa, though not viruses, and requires occasional backflushing to maintain flow rate. Lightweight and rugged, it's suited for pack use, resupply runs, or travel between more permanent collection points. While it won't replace a base camp filter, it's the kind of tool you always want with you.

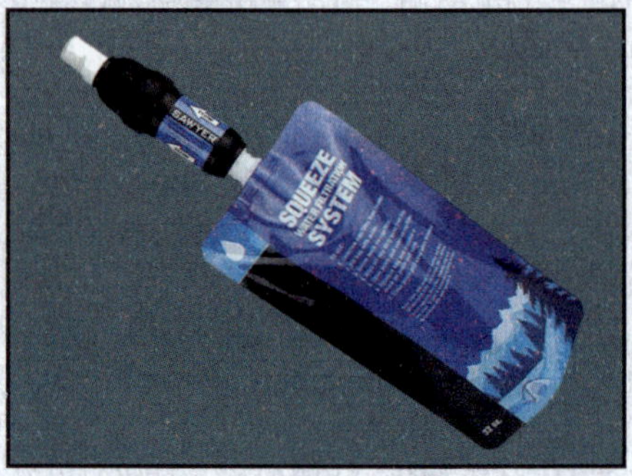

Having one filtration method is good. Having all three—stationary, modular, and mobile—means you're prepared no matter where the water comes from or how far you have to go to get it.

Disinfection Methods

Filtering removes visible particles and many harmful organisms, but disinfection is what makes water truly safe to drink. Once water is physically clean, it still needs to be chemically or thermally treated to kill bacteria, viruses, and microscopic parasites that filters may miss. In survival conditions, several proven methods can be used depending on your situation, resources, and time.

Bleach remains one of the most reliable and accessible disinfection tools. Unscented household bleach with 6% to 8.25% sodium hypochlorite can be added directly to clear water at a rate of eight drops—about one-eighth of a teaspoon—per gallon. For cloudy water, the dose should be doubled. After adding bleach, stir the water thoroughly, then let it sit uncovered for at least thirty minutes. If it still smells slightly of chlorine afterward, it's safe to drink. If not, repeat the dose and wait another thirty minutes. Always check the label—avoid splashless or scented varieties, which may contain additives not safe for consumption.

Boiling is one of the most effective ways to kill all pathogens, including viruses and chlorine-resistant parasites like Cryptosporidium. Bring water to a full, rolling boil and maintain it for at least one full minute. At higher elevations above 6,500 feet, extend that time to three minutes. Boiling doesn't remove chemical contaminants or improve taste, but it guarantees microbial safety when done correctly. Use a clean pot with a lid to reduce water loss, and allow the water to cool naturally with the lid on to avoid re-contamination.

If fuel is limited, small rocket stoves or solar water heaters can provide consistent boiling capacity using scrap wood or sunlight. They're slow, but reliable—especially at base camps.

For portable or fast-use disinfection, water purification tablets are compact, lightweight, and effective. Brands like Potable Aqua, Katadyn, and Aquatabs are widely available and made for emergency kits or bug-out bags. Most use iodine or chlorine dioxide to neutralize biological threats. Follow the manufacturer's instructions carefully—most tablets require a wait time of 30 minutes to 4 hours depending on the water temperature and clarity. Tablets can alter taste, but in an emergency, safety comes first

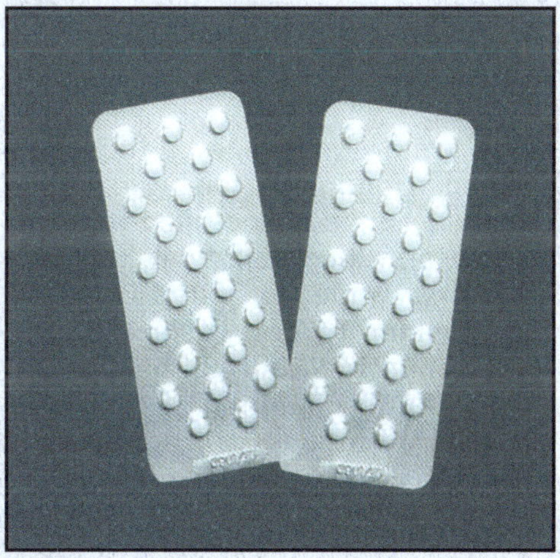

In sunny climates with limited gear, solar disinfection—known as SODIS—offers a last-resort method. This process uses ultraviolet light from the sun to kill microorganisms. Fill clear plastic PET bottles with water, shake to oxygenate, and lay them flat in direct sunlight for at least six hours. In overcast weather, double the time. This method works best in equatorial or summer conditions and requires full sun exposure. While it's not as reliable as chemical or thermal methods, it can be life-saving when no other option exists.

Each of these methods has its place. The key is matching the method to the environment—and never skipping disinfection, no matter how clean the water appears. In **a grid-down world, water is life**—but only if it's safe.

Method	Removes	Limitations	Best Use Case
Boiling	Bacteria, viruses, protozoa	Requires fuel and time; no chemical removal	Stationary base, cold environments
Bleach	Bacteria, viruses (not Cryptosporidium)	Doesn't remove sediment or chemicals; taste alteration	Rapid disinfection of clear water
Filtration	Sediment, bacteria, protozoa	May not remove viruses unless specified	Daily drinking water prep
Purification Tablets	Bacteria, viruses, some protozoa	Long wait times; taste changes	Bug-out bags, short-term travel
SODIS (Solar)	Bacteria, viruses (under ideal conditions)	Requires sunlight, PET bottles, and long exposure	Emergency fallback, sunny climates
Bio-Sand Filter	Sediment, bacteria, protozoa	Needs maturation time; bulky	Off-grid homestead, long-term use
Berkey-style Filter	Bacteria, protozoa, some viruses and chemicals	Slow flow rate, initial cost	Home use, high-volume filtration

Storing Faucet Water Before It's Needed

When disaster is approaching but the taps are still flowing, time becomes your most valuable asset. The hours before a major event—whether it's a storm, power grid failure, or civil disruption—offer a final window to capture clean, pressurized water straight from your home plumbing. Once that pressure drops or contamination enters the system, the opportunity is gone. Knowing how to quickly store large volumes of potable water from your faucet is one of the simplest and most effective ways to secure immediate reserves before the crisis locks in.

Water BOB – Short-Term Bathtub Reserve

The Water BOB is a collapsible plastic liner designed to fit inside a standard bathtub and store up to 100 gallons of clean water. It's one of the fastest and most efficient ways to create a sealed, sanitary reserve using the pressurized water already flowing through your home. When a collapse is imminent—whether it's a natural disaster or a loss of public utilities—the Water BOB should be filled immediately. Don't wait for confirmation of outage. Once the water slows or becomes contaminated, the opportunity is gone.

To use it, unroll the liner into a clean bathtub and connect the included fill hose to the faucet. Turn on the cold tap and let the liner fill completely, then seal the top. The system includes a built-in siphon or gravity-fed spout, allowing you to draw water later without opening the whole container or exposing the contents to contamination. Stored properly, the water inside will remain potable for weeks, especially if pre-treated with bleach or stabilizer at the time of filling.

Every household should have at least two Water BOBs—one for immediate use, one as backup. They fold flat for storage, require no tools to deploy, and turn a fixture most people overlook into one of the most valuable short-term assets in the home.

When a collapse gives you just hours to act, this is the kind of tool that converts minutes into gallons.

The Last Hour Water Capture Plan

In addition to the Water BOB, other parts of your home can be turned into temporary reservoirs if you act fast. **Every sink, container, and vessel you have should be considered fair game the moment you know the system might fail.** Start by filling every available food-safe container—pots, pitchers, large cooking bowls, and jugs. Don't forget the washing machine basin; if it's clean, it can hold several gallons. Toilet tanks can be flushed and filled with clean water too, as long as they're free of chemical tablets or residual disinfectants.

Plastic storage bins, even those not intended for liquids, can be lined with clean trash bags and filled with tap water for hygiene use. While this isn't drinking-grade storage, it will serve for flushing toilets, washing hands, or cleaning gear during the first few days of a disruption. Double-lining helps prevent leaks and adds redundancy in case of puncture.

Faucet-mounted hose bibs can also be used to fill outdoor barrels or garden tanks quickly. If you have rain barrels or IBC totes already installed, top them off while the municipal pressure still works. Many of these containers are gravity-fed and can serve as both primary and backup sources once the flow stops.

You can also fill every drinking container in the house—water bottles, thermoses, hydration packs, and travel mugs. These will be the first things you reach for, and they take only seconds to prepare. Label containers if necessary to keep drinking water separate from hygiene or cleaning reserves.

In the final minutes before the grid drops, prioritize speed over perfection. Clean the containers as best you can, use what you have, and capture everything you can. Potable water in a collapse isn't just for drinking—it's for cooking, sanitation, bartering, and staying operational under pressure. The faucet is still the cleanest source you'll have. Use it while you can.

Graywater Recovery – Pushing Every Drop

When fresh water runs low, every gallon counts. Graywater reuse keeps you cleaned off, hydrated, and operational for much longer.

Graywater Sources

In a long-term crisis, fresh water must be prioritized for drinking, cooking, and essential hygiene. But that doesn't mean every other use has to draw from the same reserve. Graywater—used but relatively clean water—can be captured and reused for tasks that don't require potability. Knowing where it comes from, and how to handle it safely, allows you to stretch your fresh supply much further.

The most common graywater source is sink runoff, especially after handwashing or rinsing dishes. As long as it doesn't contain harsh chemicals, bleach, or food scraps, it can be used for cleaning tools, flushing toilets, or even pre-washing clothes. Shower runoff is another valuable stream. Collecting water at your feet as you bathe—especially with biodegradable soap—gives you gallons of graywater per use, suitable for mopping, rinsing gear, or irrigating non-edible plants.

Washing machines, especially older top-loading models, discharge large volumes of relatively low-contaminant water. If your system allows it, this can be routed into barrels or directly into outdoor holding tanks. Just ensure the detergent is low-phosphate and biodegradable if you plan to use the water around plants.

Even water used for rinsing fruits, vegetables, or grains can be saved. Instead of pouring it down the drain, route it into a bucket under the sink. This lightly-used water is ideal for pre-washing surfaces, soaking tools, or watering landscape plants where food crops aren't involved.

These graywater sources won't replace your drinking supply—but they reduce how often you have to tap into it. Every gallon you save for non-critical uses is one more gallon available for drinking.

How to Reuse It Safely

Graywater is useful, but only when handled correctly. Once water has been used, even lightly, it begins to degrade quickly. Bacteria multiply fast in warm, nutrient-rich conditions, and graywater can become a health risk if left standing too long. Never store it for more than twenty-four hours. After that, it becomes a breeding ground for microbes you don't want near your skin or gear.

If you're reusing graywater for irrigation, especially around ornamental plants or trees, make sure all soaps or cleaners used are biodegradable and phosphate-free. Regular dish soap, bleach, and antibacterial products can damage soil, harm roots, or create chemical buildup over time. There are many biodegradable options available, and switching to them now, before a crisis, sets you up for safer reuse later.

When reusing graywater for flushing toilets or irrigating tough landscaping, it's best to run it through a simple filter. A layered bucket filled with charcoal, gravel, and cloth will remove larger debris and cut down on odor. It won't purify the water, but it makes it safer to handle and less likely to clog systems or leave residue.

For limited hygiene use—like washing hands, feet, or performing sponge baths—you can build a finer filter using a container filled with cloth, fine sand, and activated charcoal. This setup won't make the water drinkable, but it will reduce skin irritation and visible grime. Always wash off filtered graywater with a quick rinse of clean water afterward when possible.

Never drink graywater unless you've built a full multi-stage filtration system that includes charcoal, sediment barriers, chemical treatment, and UV sterilization. Even then, it should be considered a last resort. **Graywater is meant for extending your fresh supply, not replacing it.** Its strength is in what it frees up, not what it substitutes. Used wisely, it turns waste into resource.

Redundancy = Survival

The average American uses 50+ gallons of water per day (from dishes, showers, drinking, and cooking). In a crisis, you'll survive on 1–2, or less even. A full-year stockpile isn't about comfort—it's about control. Use your clean water sparingly, for necessary things.

Use every strategy
in this chapter.
Build your layers:

Rain catchment
Stored reserves
Filtration systems
Wells or hand pumps
Water BOBs
Graywater recovery

When the faucets stop flowing and trucks stop hauling water bottles, the only water you'll have is the water you planned for, or that you worked for.

And the people who didn't?
They'll give anything for a sip.

Stored water doesn't just keep you alive—it gives you a lot of leverage. In a barter economy, clean water becomes a tradeable currency. The more you have, the more stuff you can get for it. But be careful you don't want anyone to know you've stashed a lot of it or they might pay you a visit. Only trade it in small quantities far ay from home. And make sure they don't follow you back.

Chapter 10

Ingenious Ways to Save Money for Darker Days

In times of instability—rising inflation, economic uncertainty, and looming supply chain disruptions—saving money isn't just a good idea. It's a survival MUST. But forget stock advice and finance apps. This is about real-world tactics you can use right now to stretch every dollar, cut unnecessary expenses, and find new ways to generate income with the tools, time, and skills you already have.

This chapter shows you how to build long-term resilience with practical, often overlooked methods that work even when systems fail. Whether you're preparing for the next collapse or just trying to stay afloat, these strategies are for anyone who wants to stop leaking cash and start building lasting security.

"Too many people spend money they haven't earned, to buy things they don't want, to impress people they don't like."
Will Rogers

Start Saving Now

Saving money isn't about getting rich—it's about getting serious. You don't need a perfect plan, just a real one. Start by shifting your mindset: every dollar you don't waste is a dollar you keep in your pocket. Adopt the "pay yourself first" rule—put something aside the moment your money comes in, no matter how small. Then track the leaks. Cancel what you don't use. Cut what you don't need. **Saving is a habit, not a windfall,** and the longer you wait, the harder it gets. Do it for your future when you might not be able to earn any longer. Do it for your family.

Stop Paying for Credit

If you're carrying credit card debt, it's time to eliminate it. High interest builds fast and eventually will trap you. Try to pay off the balance and stop using the cards. Cut them up if you have to. If you're stuck with high-interest car loans, shop around for refinancing options. Every percent you drop in interest is money back in your pocket.

And don't trust banks too much. In a real financial collapse, digital access to your savings may vanish overnight. Keep some emergency cash at home, and think about converting savings into tangible assets—silver coins, durable goods, land, and items that can be used or traded when systems fail. Even the best modern insurance can become useless overnight in the worst of circumstances.

Saving First, Spending Later

The single most important habit you can build to protect yourself financially—especially in uncertain times—is this: **pay yourself first.**

That means every time you get paid, you immediately take a set amount and move it out of reach before you do anything else. Not after the bills. Not once you've bought groceries or grabbed lunch. **First.**

It doesn't have to be a huge chunk to start. Even 5% of your paycheck adds up. If you can do 10%, great. The key is consistency, not perfection. Think of it like this: when you pay rent, you don't ask if you feel like it—you just do it.

Start treating **your own savings with that same seriousness.** Make it automatic if you can. Many banks let you set up an automatic transfer into a separate savings account. If you're paid in cash, physically pull it aside and store it somewhere safe.

This is absolutely not some money for you to dip into for a new phone or going to a concert. This is your lifeboat—your backup power when things get tight or unpredictable. And in a dark and uncertain situation, digital accounts may not even be accessible. That's why it's smart to diversify what you're saving into. Some should be in cash, so you can get to it quickly without an ATM. Some could be converted into precious metals like silver or gold coins. Some could be stored value—long-lasting food, medical supplies, even batteries or tools you can barter if needed, and especially clean water.

Start small if you have to, but start now. Don't wait for a "better time" or a perfect paycheck. If you can train yourself to pay yourself first when money is tight, you'll be ahead of 90% of the world when things get worse.

Letting Go of Nonessentials

Before you can start saving in a serious way, you have to stop the leaks. That means **being honest about your spending.** Go through your bank statements and look for anything you're paying for that isn't essential—especially subscriptions. Streaming services, fitness apps, random upgrades, premium versions you don't really use—those little charges add up fast.

Free services like **Pluto, Tubi, and Crackle** give you plenty to watch without the monthly fees of other streaming apps. You can get access to thousands of shows and movies at no cost—and skip the $60–100 monthly cable bill entirely.

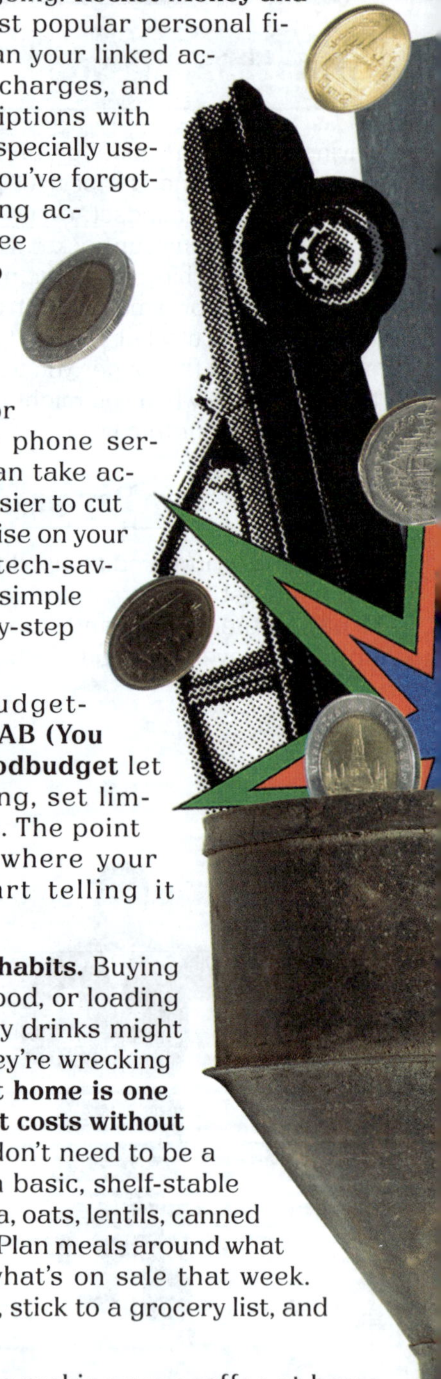

Use tools designed to help you get control of where your money is actually going. **Rocket Money and Trim** are two of the most popular personal finance apps that can scan your linked accounts, flag recurring charges, and help you cancel subscriptions with just a few taps. They're especially useful for spotting things you've forgotten about—old streaming accounts, fitness apps, free trials that turned into paid plans, and so on.

Other options on these apps can also help you negotiate lower bills for things like internet or phone service. Also, these apps can take action for you, making it easier to cut down the background noise on your finances. If you're not tech-savvy, many of them offer simple dashboards and step-by-step support.

Even more basic budgeting apps like **Mint, YNAB (You Need a Budget), or Goodbudget** let you categorize spending, set limits, and visualize waste. The point is to stop wondering where your money went—and start telling it where to go.

Next, look at your food habits. Buying takeout, grabbing fast food, or loading up on snacks and energy drinks might seem convenient, but they're wrecking your budget. **Cooking at home is one of the fastest ways to cut costs without sacrificing quality.** You don't need to be a gourmet chef. Start with basic, shelf-stable staples: rice, beans, pasta, oats, lentils, canned vegetables, frozen meat. Plan meals around what you already have and what's on sale that week. Build a simple meal plan, stick to a grocery list, and avoid impulse buys.

Even small changes—like making your coffee at home instead of hitting Starbucks—can make a noticeable difference over time. Replacing convenience with intention is one of the smartest money-saving shifts you can make.

Slash Transportation Costs

For most families, transportation is the second-highest monthly expense after housing—and often the most quietly draining. Between gas, car payments, insurance, repairs, and depreciation, a single car can cost you well over **$700 a month**, according to AAA estimates. That's nearly **$8,500 per year.** Multiply that by two cars, and you've got a leak that could sink your whole budget in the next crisis.

One of the most effective ways to cut this is by reducing how often you drive—or eliminating the need for a second vehicle altogether.

Public transit might not be luxurious, but it is drastically cheaper. A monthly **subway or bus pass** in most U.S. cities ranges from **$60 to $130.** Even if you still drive occasionally, replacing your daily commute with transit can cut your fuel bill by half and delay oil changes and maintenance. That alone can save **$150 to $300** a month. Fewer miles also means lower wear and tear and can even drop your insurance premiums if you report reduced mileage to your provider.

Cities with commuter rail or regional trains make it even easier if you live farther out. Park once, ride in, save money. Some employers even offer commuter benefits that cover part of the fare—free money on top of the savings.

If you're in a two-car household, ask the hard question: do you actually need both? Selling one vehicle can bring in thousands up front and eliminate **$100 to $300/month** in insurance alone, not to mention gas and maintenance.

Don't want to sell your **extra vehicle**? Let it pay for itself.

With apps like Turo or Getaround, you can list your car for short-term rentals. Whether it's an old sedan, a commuter hybrid, or a weekend-ready SUV, likely there's someone nearby who needs it. Rentals can earn you anywhere from **$25 to $100 (or even a lot more) a day,** depending on the vehicle and market.

When you drive yourself, fuel costs add up fast, especially with fluctuating prices. Use the **GasBuddy app** to find the cheapest gas near you. In cities or along major highways, price differences can be **30 to 60 cents per gallon**—which adds up if you're filling up weekly.

Finally, if you're still paying off your car at a high interest rate, check your options for **refinancing.** Many credit unions and online lenders offer much better rates than the dealership gave you. Even a **2–3% lower APR** can save you **hundreds per year,** and it only takes a few minutes to check.

Cut Utility and Living Expenses

Monthly bills can bleed your wallet dry without you noticing—but with a few smart changes, you can plug those leaks fast.

Start with electricity. Even when your devices are off, they still sip power. It's called phantom energy use, and it adds up. Plug devices into **smart plugs or basic power strips,** and turn them off when not in use. It's an easy habit with real savings. Swap out old light bulbs for LEDs—they last longer and use a fraction of the energy.

Next, take a look at your windows. Heat escapes fast in winter and seeps in during summer. **Thermal curtains** or clear **plastic insulation film** kits cost less than dinner out and can cut heating and cooling losses dramatically. They're simple to install and work in both hot and cold climates.

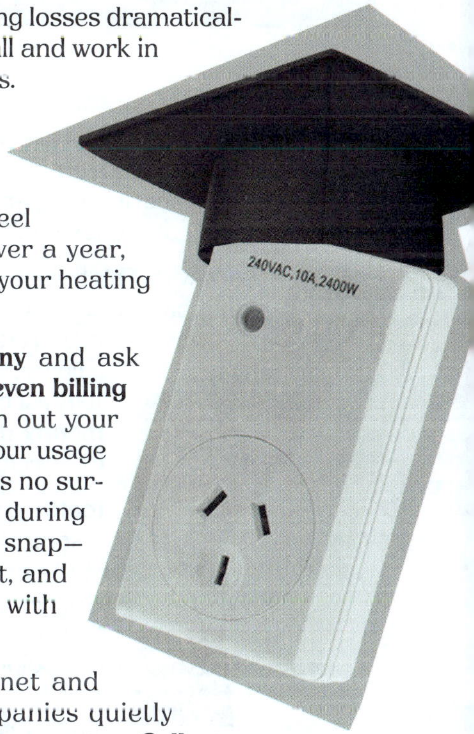

Adjust your **thermostat by just 2–3 degrees** down in the winter, up in the summer. It may feel like a small shift, but over a year, it can knock **10–15% off** your heating and cooling bills.

Call your **utility company** and ask about **budget billing or even billing** programs. These smooth out your payments by averaging your usage over the year. That means no surprise $300 power bills during a heatwave or freezing snap—you know what to expect, and that predictability helps with monthly budgeting.

Now look at your internet and phone bills. These companies quietly raise your rates after a year or two. **Call once a year** and ask for a better rate or current **promotional pricing.** They'd rather keep you at a lower rate than lose you to a competitor. It's an easy win that can save **$20–60/month.**

Don't stop there. Every **6 to 12 months, shop around for insurance quotes**—auto, renters, even life insurance. Loyalty doesn't get rewarded in these industries—shopping does. A few minutes of comparison can shave hundreds off your annual premiums, especially if your credit has improved or your car is aging.

Small changes add up fast when you're willing to adjust your habits. Energy, insurance, subscriptions, and utilities are all areas where companies profit from your inattention. Pay attention, act once or twice a year, and you'll save more than you thought possible.

Look for Deals, Buy in Bulk

Grocery spending is one of the easiest places to make fast savings—if you know where and how to shop. Discount stores like **Aldi, Grocery Outlet, and Walmart** consistently beat regular supermarkets on price for pantry staples, canned goods, and basic household items. Don't go in with a blind list. Instead, scan the week's deals, shop off-brand when possible, and compare price-per-ounce on the shelf tags. That's where real savings hide.

Planning meals around what's cheap, what's on hand, or what's on sale is the difference between spending $600 a month on food versus $300–$400. Stick to bulk-friendly staples like **rice, beans, pasta, oats, and frozen vegetables**—they stretch far, store well, and cost less per serving.

For even deeper savings, consider joining a warehouse club like **Costco or Sam's Club**. The membership pays for itself fast if you buy smart. Load up on toilet paper, dried beans, canned meat, flour, cooking oil, and long-shelf-life snacks. Can't store it all, or don't want the upfront cost alone? **Split bulk purchases with a friend or neighbor.** Two families can cut costs in half without wasting anything.

Example: A 50-pound bag of rice at Costco might cost $18—that's less than 40 cents a pound, compared to $1.20+ for smaller bags at the grocery store. If that's too much for one household, split it, re-bag it, and you both win.

Finally, don't forget rebate and reward apps. Tools like **Ibotta, Fetch, and Upside** give you cash-back or points for scanning receipts or buying certain items—things you might be picking up anyway. Used consistently, they can return **$10–50/month** with almost no extra effort.

Stacking strategies—discount stores, bulk buying, planning around deals, and rebate apps—turn your grocery routine into a money-saving engine. All it takes is paying attention.

Get Money Back on What You Do Spend

Rebates

Rebate and cash-back apps are some of the easiest ways to earn passive savings from everyday purchases. You're already buying groceries, gas, and household items—why not get some of that money back?

Start with **Fetch:** just scan your receipts after shopping. You earn points for nearly anything, which can be redeemed for gift cards to major retailers. On average, regular users can pull in **$5–15 per month**, more if they stack bonuses or referral codes.

Ibotta goes deeper. It gives you cash back on specific items, from brand-name snacks to cleaning supplies. You browse offers, add them to your account, and upload a receipt—or connect your store loyalty card. Ibotta users often earn **$20–50 per month** just for scanning and checking in on what's available.

Upside focuses on gas, groceries, and restaurants. You check the map for participating locations, claim an offer, and pay as usual. The app automatically credits your account with real money back, often **10–25 cents per gallon of fuel, or 5–15% back on groceries or meals.**

There are others, too:

- **Rakuten** (formerly Ebates) offers online cash-back at hundreds of retailers.
- **Receipt Hog** rewards you for uploading any receipts, not just groceries.
- **Capital One Shopping and Honey** find discounts and track price drops for online purchases.

Used together, these tools can quietly add **$30–$100+** per month to your budget, depending on how often you shop. It's not about gimmicks—it's about getting paid for what you already do. And in a crunch, those little returns could fund a tank of gas or your next grocery run.

Make it a habit: check offers before you shop, scan receipts right after, and let the savings grow in the background. It takes a few extra seconds, but over a year, it can return **hundreds.**

Food as an Investment with Returns

Food doesn't just feed you—it can fund you. When bought smart and used wisely, food becomes a financial asset with real return on investment. You can turn cheap ingredients into value-added goods, preserve long-lasting meals for future use, or trade surplus when cash runs dry.

You can make baked goods, jarred sauces, or even simple meal kits that sell for far more than their parts. Homemade breads, cookies, or spice blends—sold locally or online—often turn a few dollars of ingredients into $15–$30 worth of product.

If you're not selling, think of **canning and preservation.** Making your own jams, broths, soups, or pickled vegetables not only gives you healthier, shelf-stable food, but it also lets you build an emergency reserve that can later be used, sold, or traded. A well-stocked pantry is more than security—it's a silent savings account.

For side income, cottage food laws in many states let you legally sell certain home-cooked foods at markets or direct-to-consumer. That means your extra loaf of sourdough or six-pack of muffins can become income without a full commercial kitchen.

And even if you don't sell a single item, turning ingredients into ready-to-use meals saves time and money down the line. Food you prepare now avoids price hikes later—and gives you a backup plan when inflation or supply chain issues hit.

DIY Alternatives for Home and Self-Care

One of the fastest ways to plug the holes in your budget is to stop outsourcing things you can do yourself. From basic grooming to simple home and car maintenance, a little effort and a few tools can save hundreds, sometimes thousands, every year.

Cutting your own hair might sound risky, but it's easier than ever with YouTube tutorials for every style imaginable. A decent pair of clippers pays for itself in just one use. Even trimming your own beard, bangs, or kid's hair between salon visits stretches your dollars further. Nail care, skincare, and basic hygiene routines are all easy to manage at home with minimal investment.

Cutting your own hair or your kids' at home can save around **$20 to $60 per person** per visit, depending on the salon. Do that monthly, and you're looking at **$240 to $720 a year per person.** A quality clipper set runs $30 to $50—it pays for itself almost immediately. DIY nail care saves an additional **$20–$50 per session**, and even basic skincare or shaving routines done at home can save **hundreds annually** over store services or spa treatments.

For **home repairs,** don't rush to call a professional for every leaky faucet or hole in the drywall. Most minor fixes can be done with a few basic tools and a video guide. Sites like YouTube and DIY forums walk you through everything step by step. Replacing weather stripping, patching holes, fixing a running toilet—these are all beginner-friendly repairs that cost more in labor than materials if you hire out.

Fixing a leaky faucet yourself costs about **$5–$15** in parts. Hiring a plumber? That's easily **$150–$300** per visit. Patching drywall holes or sealing windows costs under **$30** in supplies, but over **$100** if done professionally. Replace weather stripping or fix a running toilet yourself, and you're saving **$100+** each time. Even doing 4–5 small repairs a year can save you **$500 or more.**

Then there's your **vehicle.**

Oil changes, replacing wiper blades, swapping out air filters, and even changing brake pads are within reach for most people with a little guidance. Auto forums, tutorial channels, and step-by-step guides are everywhere online. If you've got a jack, a wrench, and some time, you can avoid shop fees and upsells.

A shop oil change costs between **$50–$100.** Doing it yourself? About **$20–$30.** Air filters are $10 online but cost you $40–$60 installed. Brake pad replacement at a shop can be **$300–$600,** but DIY with decent tools and parts might only run **$80–$150.** Maintaining your own vehicle conservatively saves **$400–$1,000+ per year,** depending on how much you take on.

Making Extra Income

You don't need a degree, a business plan, or a big investment to bring in extra cash—you just need to use what you've got. That might be your time, your skills, your stuff, or even your space. Whether it's app-based gig work, selling secondhand finds, or offering small services in your neighborhood, there are more ways than ever to turn the gaps in your schedule into real income. What matters is consistency, effort, and knowing where to start.

Gig Work Nearby

You don't need a new career to start making money—you need to look around. Most people have overlooked income sitting right in front of them: **simple, low-barrier jobs** that pay cash, require no fancy credentials, and fit around any schedule.

Start with **app-based gig work. Instacart** pays you to shop for groceries. **DoorDash and Uber Eats** let you deliver food from local restaurants with just a car or bike and a smartphone. **Rover** connects pet lovers with people needing dog walks or in-home pet sitting. TaskRabbit is perfect if you've got tools, a strong back, or just some patience—people pay to have shelves mounted, boxes moved, furniture built, and leaky faucets fixed.

But the real gold is often **local microservices.** Babysitting, yard cleanup, snow shoveling, basic handyman help, house-sitting, or running errands for older neighbors—all of it pays, and all of it builds trust. These aren't high-skill jobs, but they're **high-trust.** People would rather hire someone nearby, someone they can text or call directly. That can be you.

To find work, advertise where your neighbors are already looking: **Craigslist, Facebook Marketplace, or local Facebook** groups. **Nextdoor** is especially useful—it's built for community members helping each other. A single post offering to do **$25 yard cleanups or $40 snow clearing** can land you regular weekend income.

None of these require a license, resume, or startup cash. Just **reliability.** Show up, do what you say, and do it well. Before long, you won't be hunting for work—**people will be messaging you first.**

Gig Work from Home

Not everyone wants to go door-to-door or haul bags of mulch. If you'd rather earn from the couch, there's more opportunity now than ever before.

Start with **UserTesting**—they pay you to test websites and apps, giving feedback as a regular user. It takes no special training, and each test usually pays $10 or more for 15–20 minutes of your time. Want higher payouts? Try Respondent.io, which offers online surveys, interviews, and feedback sessions. Depending on the topic, you might earn anywhere from **$20 to $100** for a half hour of honest input.

If you're even halfway decent with a keyboard, you can earn on Fiverr or Upwork. You don't need to be a graphic designer or programmer. There's steady demand for **data entry, typing, transcription, basic writing, and even editing resumes or proofreading documents.** These platforms let you build a profile around what you can already do, then grow from there.

The key is to start simple. Most clients aren't looking for perfection—they're looking for someone reliable, communicative, and able to follow directions. Even if you only make $50 your first week, that's $50 you didn't have—and it scales. Build reviews, gain momentum, and pretty soon, it's a serious side hustle.

Working from home means no commute, no gas, no dress code. Just a laptop, an internet connection, and a little focus.

Sell Off Your Clutter

You don't need to invent a product to start making money—you just need to look around your home. Closets, garages, and junk drawers are often full of items that still hold value. That old power tool, pair of boots, vintage toy, or electronics you haven't touched in years? Someone out there wants it.

Take a weekend and dig through your storage. If you haven't used it in a year, it's probably safe to sell. Start small—list on platforms like **eBay, Facebook Marketplace, OfferUp, or Mercari.** Snap a few clear photos, write an honest description, and price it to move. You'd be surprised how quickly things can sell when priced right.

You're converting junk into grocery money, fuel savings, or even an emergency fund.

Flip & Sell for Fast Cash

If you're willing to research a little, flipping items for profit is one of the fastest ways to bring in side income—and you don't need a storefront or startup capital to get started. You just need a good eye and multiple courses for buying and selling.

Start at Goodwill, garage sales, estate sales, or even the clearance racks of retail stores. These places are full of underpriced items that still hold resale value. Look for quality over quantity. What you're after is undervalued inventory—things people are practically giving away, that someone else would gladly pay for.

The trick is to pick **a niche** and get sharp in it.

Don't try to flip everything. Choose something you either already know a little about—or are willing to learn. Popular and consistent winners include **vintage toys, retro video games, power tools, rare books, kitchen gadgets, designer shoes, and small electronics** like cameras or smartwatches. Once you understand what to look for—brand names, model numbers, condition—you'll get faster and more profitable.

Use apps like **eBay, Mercari, Facebook Marketplace, and OfferUp** to list your finds. Search those platforms while you're shopping to see what things are actually selling for, not just listed. That's the key to knowing a real deal when you see one. Use the completed listings feature on eBay to check past sale prices, or scan barcodes right in the store using the app.

Don't forget the presentation. Clean up the item, take clear photos, and write an honest but appealing description. Speed and trust are what sell online. Make it easy for buyers to say yes.

This can become a full second income if you treat it seriously. **One $5 item flipped for $40 is all it takes to prove the model works.**

Turn Space Into Cash

If you've got space, you've got opportunity. Most people overlook what's already under their roof—or sitting in their driveway. But unused rooms, storage areas, or vehicles can all be turned into passive income with almost no overhead.

Start with your home. Got a **spare bedroom,** basement, or even just a private corner with a bed and door? That's an Airbnb listing waiting to happen. Even in small towns or rural areas, there's demand—especially from road-trippers, traveling nurses, or people relocating. You can rent by the night or by the week, and even long-term if you'd rather not have guests coming and going. Set your availability, establish house rules, and start earning.

If you're not comfortable with guests, look into **storage rental.** Sites like Neighbor.com let you rent out your **garage, shed, closet,** or any clean, secure space as personal storage for others. People need affordable places to store boxes, furniture, seasonal gear, or business supplies—especially in urban areas where commercial storage is overpriced. You stay in control, and it's passive income once you have a renter.

Not sure what you've got to offer? Do a walk-through of your home and yard. That corner of the attic? Those unused shelves in the garage? That covered carport that's just collecting leaves? All of it can become a source of side income if you package it right and list it in the right place.

The key is this: you don't need to buy anything new to start earning. What you already own might be exactly what someone else needs. List it, rent it, and let your space work for you.

Barter & Tangible Value

Store Your Wealth Where It Can't Disappear

In good times, banks and stock accounts seem safe. In bad times, they're just lines on a screen. If there's a bank run or digital systems crash, your savings might become unreachable. Keep some cash hidden at home for emergencies. Convert part of your savings into precious metals—silver coins are especially handy. Store useful goods too: propane, water filters, hand tools, even extra hygiene products. These things hold real value, even when the dollar doesn't.

Barter Is Always the Fallback

When money fails—and it has, time and again throughout history—value doesn't disappear. It just shifts. In a true economic collapse, it's not paper currency or digital bank balances that will matter. It's what you have, what others need, and what you can trade.

That's why bartering isn't just some old-time novelty—it's your last line of defense. The more self-reliant you are, the more leverage you'll have when systems falter. Start by thinking like a trader: what do you have in surplus? Canned goods, bulk rice, salt, batteries, tools, clean water, even hygiene items like soap and toothpaste—all of these become currency when shelves go empty, and banks close their doors.

If your last shopping trip resulted in more than you need, don't let it gather dust. **Trade the excess.** Swapping extra food for fuel, batteries for coffee, or labor for goods keeps communities alive when money no longer works. And barter doesn't have to wait for disaster. You can begin now—build local trust networks, swap with neighbors, and pay attention to what items stay in demand year-round.

Then there's the question of **savings.** If your emergency fund is sitting entirely in a bank account, it's exposed. In a serious crisis, banks may limit withdrawals, or if the grid collapses, they can go dark altogether. You'll want part of your savings in tangible assets—**precious metals** like silver or gold, fuel, quality tools, or shelf-stable supplies. These hold real value when plastic cards don't swipe and apps go offline.

Think of these items not as "expenses," but as **security assets**—a hedge against instability. You're not hoarding. You're preparing. You're building a reserve that can feed your family, help your neighbors, or secure the missing piece in your next trade.

Barter is the fallback, yes—but it's also a mindset. When you stop measuring value only in dollars and start seeing it in **usefulness, resilience, and exchange,** you take a step toward real independence. That's how you outlast the crash—by being ready to trade what matters, when it matters most.

Chapter 11

The Next Big Short: How to Invest Before the Collapse

History doesn't just punish the unprepared. It rewards those who are early, even when it feels uncomfortable to be. Because in a world where markets can be manipulated, narratives distorted, and headlines delayed, the edge goes not to the loudest—but to the quiet, disciplined few who had the courage to act before others even saw it coming.

"The late 2020s will be remembered as a time when the blind led the blind." Michael Burry

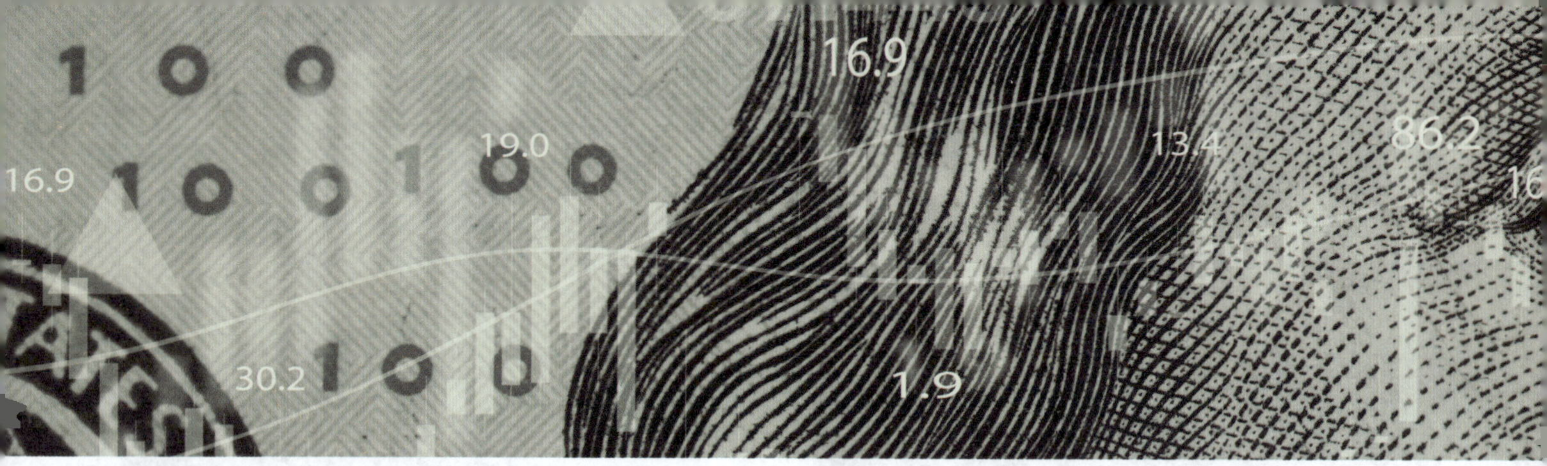

What If You Could See It Coming?

Every crisis has a warning.

The problem isn't that the signs aren't there—it's that most people are too distracted, too comfortable, or too confident to ever notice them. In 2008, while the media applauded the unstoppable rise of housing prices and Wall Street celebrated financial "innovation," a few people noticed something was off. I was one of those people. We were outsiders—independent thinkers with the humility to question what others accepted as cold hard truth. What separated us from the masses wasn't access to secret data or privileged information. It was our refusal to assume that the system always knew what it was doing.

Michael Burry, a former neurologist turned hedge fund manager, didn't come from a typical finance background. But he had a forensic eye for numbers and the patience to dig where others wouldn't. When he examined the structure of mortgage-backed securities—the very foundation of the financial boom—he found chaos hiding in plain sight. Loans were being issued to borrowers with no proof of income or assets, adjustable-rate mortgages were designed to spike payments beyond what people could afford, and entire bond tranches were constructed with the expectation that no one would ever default. Yet these toxic instruments were rated AAA and sold globally as safe investments.

Burry read the fine print.

And what he saw wasn't just flawed—it was catastrophic.

He wasn't alone. **Steve Eisman,** another iconoclast known for his blunt honesty and sharp skepticism, reached similar conclusions. As others praised the stability of the housing market and cheered its ongoing growth, Eisman began shorting it. He wasn't emotional. He wasn't hopeful. He simply looked at the numbers and didn't like what he saw. A few more names joined the ranks—people like **Greg Lippmann, Jamie Mai, and Charlie Ledley.** They placed massive bets, not because they were sure they'd win, but because they were sure something was wrong. And when the system finally collapsed under the weight of its own delusion, these few walked away with staggering profits.

They weren't just lucky.

They were ready.

You probably know this story, especially if you've seen The Big Short or read the Michael Lewis book. It's become a kind of economic mythology—a tale of eccentric geniuses beating the market at its own game. But there's a danger in treating it as leg-

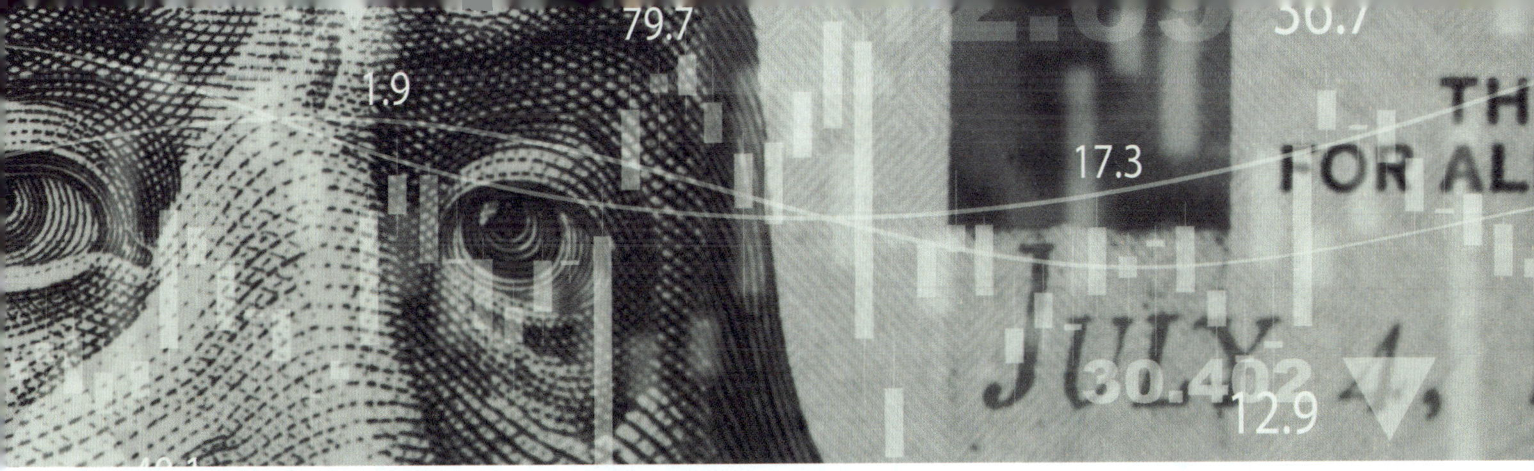

end. Because the more we convince ourselves that it was a one-time event, the less prepared we are for its sequel. The housing bubble may not repeat itself in exactly the same way, but the forces behind it—greed, complacency, denial—never left.

They've just shifted form.

As of 2025, the signs are back. The specifics have changed, but the story feels eerily familiar. We see frothy tech valuations that defy logic, consumer debt and credit card balances pushing new records, zombie companies kept alive by cheap credit, and central banks struggling to manage the consequences of years of artificial monetary expansion. Supply chains are fragile. Inflation remains volatile. The U.S. dollar, long considered untouchable, is under pressure both at home and abroad and lately does not act like the safe asset it was for generations. Same with T-bills. And yet, on the surface, optimism prevails. The market is still ok. The economy is still "resilient."

Headlines continue to suggest everything is fine.

Until it isn't.

This chapter isn't written for insiders with Bloomberg terminals or hedge fund playbooks. It's written for the people who understand that survival—and opportunity—comes not from reacting, but from preparing. It's for those who realize that when a collapse comes, it doesn't arrive with a warning bell or a flashing red light.

It arrives disguised as stability. It begins with confidence and "buying the dip" a true and tested methodology that will ruin so many lives in the next depression. And by the time the panic sets in, the most obvious trades have already disappeared.

That's why now is the time to think like Burry, like Eisman, and like all those who placed their bets before the crowd even saw the problem, let alone the outcome. Because while most people are still clinging to what worked yesterday, the few who are looking ahead will be the ones ready for tomorrow. They'll be in position not just to weather the downturn—but to make wealth off it.

Flashback: The Original Big Short (2008)

The 2008 financial crisis was one of the most devastating economic events in modern history. It wiped out trillions in global wealth, triggered mass foreclosures, and left governments scrambling to stabilize collapsing financial institutions. To most people—investors, bankers, politicians—it came as a shock. But not to everyone.

A small group of unconventional thinkers not only predicted the collapse—they profited massively from it. They weren't Wall Street celebrities or media darlings. In fact, many of them were laughed at, ignored, or even vilified at the time. They were outsiders: data-obsessed, skeptical, and profoundly contrarian. And when the world dismissed the danger, they placed the most audacious financial bets of the decade.

At the center of this group was **Dr. Michael Burry,** a reclusive hedge fund manager and former neurologist. He was brilliant, awkward, and obsessive about the details most people overlooked. Burry had a habit of reading the actual prospectuses behind mortgage-backed securities—those bundles of home loans sold as ultra-safe investments. What he found stunned him. Many of the underlying loans were time bombs: subprime mortgages given to people with poor credit, no income verification, zero money down, and adjustable interest rates that would explode after a few years.

So Burry did what almost no one else dared to do: he went short. Specifically, he used **credit default swaps (CDS)** to bet against the mortgage market. In simple terms, he paid a premium—like buying insurance—on the assumption that these securities would default. If the loans collapsed, the swaps would pay off big. If not, he would lose millions. At the time, the move looked insane. Housing prices had never fallen across the entire U.S. at once. His investors questioned him. Banks pushed back. Executives scoffed. Yet Burry trusted the data. He didn't just believe he was right—he knew it.

He's famous for saying: "Well, we pay roughly 80 to 90 million each year, which is high but I was the first to do this trade. Watch, it will pay. I may have been early, but I'm not wrong."

He wasn't alone for long. **Steve Eisman,** a blunt and brilliant fund manager at FrontPoint Partners, had also grown deeply skeptical of the mortgage boom. Eisman had an instinct for sniffing out fraud and delusion, and as he dug into the mortgage lending ecosystem, what he found was grotesque: loan officers boasting about pushing mortgages on people who didn't even understand the terms; banks repackaging risky debt with the confidence of seasoned gamblers. He too began shorting mortgage-backed securities. Another key player was **Greg Lippmann,** a Deutsche Bank trader who helped popularize CDS contracts as a vehicle for shorting the housing market. He wasn't a purist like Burry or an iconoclast like Eisman—he was a salesman, but he knew the market was rotten and used that knowledge to convince hedge funds to bet big against it.

These few—along with others like Cornwall Capital's Jamie Mai and Charlie Ledley—formed what would later be mythologized in Michael Lewis's bestselling book The Big Short, and in the Hollywood film of the same name. But their story isn't just entertainment. It's a blueprint. These were individuals who didn't follow the herd. They questioned consensus. They went deep into the data, past the headlines, past the "expert" forecasts. They challenged institutions and conventional wisdom, and they had the courage to take unpopular positions. In doing so, they turned millions into billions.

Yet the real lesson here isn't just about betting big. It's about **conviction over consensus.** These men didn't wait for a news headline to confirm their suspicions. They acted early, and they were willing to be wrong for a long time if it meant being right in the end.

And perhaps most importantly, they understood something few did at the time: **you don't need to be inside the system to beat it. You just have to see what others aren't willing to.**

In the years since 2008, Wall Street has tried to paint the crisis as a one-off—an aberration caused by a few bad actors and poor oversight.

But history tells us otherwise.

Crises are not a one time affair.

They are the product of human behavior old as time: greed, complacency, groupthink, and overconfidence. Which is why understanding what Burry, Eisman, and what others like them did in 2008 is more than just a lesson in finance. It's a mindset for surviving what's coming to America and getting your money in good on thenext big short.

Shorting 101: What It Really Means

For most people, investing is a simple narrative: buy something today, wait patiently, and sell it for a higher price in the future. It's the classic "buy low, sell high" philosophy that underpins almost every piece of conventional financial wisdom. From blue-chip stocks to real estate and crypto, the goal is always upward movement.

Profit, we're told, comes from growth.

But what if that story was only half the truth?

There's a parallel playbook that few talk about—and even fewer truly understand. One that doesn't rely on markets rising, optimism soaring, or economies expanding. It's the world of short selling.

Turning the Investment World Upside Down.

Short selling flips the script. It's a strategy designed to profit when prices fall—not rise. To many, that sounds counterintuitive. Why would you bet on failure? But failure, in financial markets, is just another form of movement.

And movement, in any direction, creates opportunity.

This model is powerful not just because it allows you to make money in falling markets—but because it reflects a deeper mindset. The short seller isn't blindly optimistic. They're skeptical. They search for cracks in the narrative, flaws in fundamentals, and bubbles hidden beneath the surface. They look for what everyone else is missing.

Here's how it works in the simplest terms:

1. You borrow shares of a stock from a broker at today's price—say $100.

2. You sell those borrowed shares on the market, pocketing $100.

3. You wait, hoping the stock price drops. It falls to $60.

4. You buy the shares back at $60 and return them to your broker.

5. The difference—$40—is your profit.

You never owned the stock. You never needed it to go up. You profited entirely from the gap between perception and reality.

Short Selling Process: Profit from Public Decline

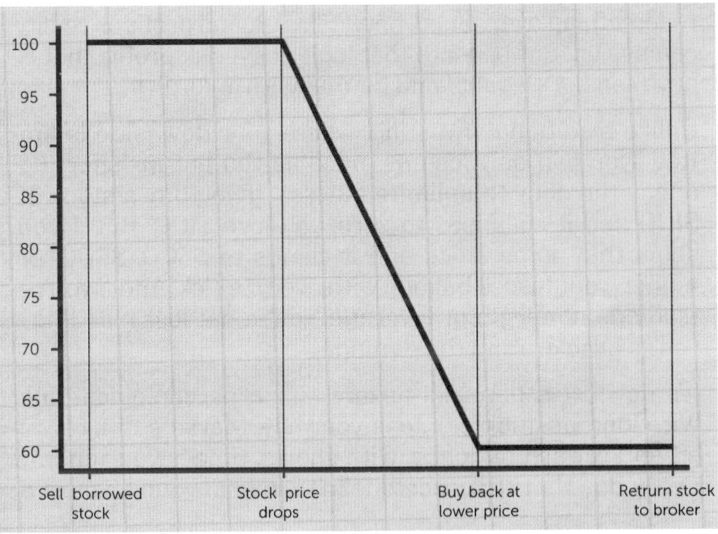

Today's Tools: Easier Access, Greater Risk

Back in 2008, shorting the market was reserved to a relatively small group of hedge fund managers and institutional players with the knowledge, capital, and access to complex financial instruments.

If you were a retail investor—someone managing their own money—you couldn't just hop on your computer and bet against the housing market. You needed a prime broker, you needed to understand credit default swaps, and you needed the guts to hold your position against a rising tide of public optimism.

Fast forward to today, and the landscape has changed dramatically. The democratization of finance has put powerful tools in the hands of everyday investors. Apps like Robinhood, Interactive Brokers, eToro, and Trading212 now offer features that were once the domain of Wall Street: shorting individual stocks, shorting entire sectors, or even speculating against the performance of global markets.

Inverse ETFs, for example, have become a popular gateway to shorting. These funds are designed to move in the opposite direction of a particular index or asset class. If the Nasdaq drops 2%, a 1x inverse Nasdaq ETF should rise roughly 2%. There are also leveraged versions—2x or 3x inverse ETFs—that amplify those movements. These tools allow investors to speculate on downturns without directly shorting a stock, and they're often easier to trade, with less margin complexity.

Beyond stocks, retail investors can also short **currencies, commodities,** and even cryptocurrencies. Platforms like Binance or Kraken allow margin trading on digital assets, while forex brokers let users trade pairs like USD/JPY or EUR/USD with the tap of a finger. **That means a person can bet against the dollar,—without needing to be a licensed financial professional.**

But there's a catch. Or rather, several.

Access isn't the same as mastery. Just because a tool is easy to use doesn't mean it's easy to use well. In fact, the simplicity of modern trading apps can often lure investors into taking on more risk than they understand. Flashy user interfaces, gamified experiences, and the illusion of control make shorting feel straightforward. But the underlying mechanics—and the risk—remain as dangerous as ever.

The Hidden Dangers of Shorting

Short selling may seem like a sharp, elegant move: identify something overvalued, bet against it, and profit as reality catches up. But beneath that logic lies a risk profile that is anything but elegant—and for many, it's unforgiving.

Unlike traditional investing, where your **downside is limited**—you can only lose as much as you put in—shorting opens the door to **unlimited losses.** If you buy a stock at $100 and it collapses to zero, you lose $100. But if you short that same stock and it climbs to $300, $500, or higher, your losses balloon with every uptick. And if you're trading on **margin or leverage,** you're not just bleeding—you're accelerating the damage.

It's not just a financial hazard—it's a psychological one. With long positions, time is your ally. Markets dip, recover, and reward patience. With shorts, time is your enemy. Every day that the price doesn't move in your favor is a day of rising pressure: from your broker, from your capital limits, and from your own mental state. **The longer you're early, the closer you are to being wrong in practice—regardless of whether you're right in theory.**

This is what makes shorting particularly dangerous in irrational markets. You can be absolutely correct in your analysis—a company may be overleveraged, unprofitable, even fraudulent—but if the market is still in love with the story, if momentum or hype or speculative frenzy keeps pushing the price up, **you're still losing.**

The market doesn't reward truth; it rewards timing.

As the economist John Maynard Keynes famously warned, **"The market can stay irrational longer than you can stay solvent."** Those who short must not only be correct—they must be correct **at the right time,** with enough discipline and capital to withstand being early.

Shorting requires more than conviction. It demands caution, resilience, and a plan for the moments when you're not just out of the money—but deep in a loss you didn't expect. It's a strategy best approached not with excitement, but with respect. Because while the rewards can be enormous, the cost of a misstep is rarely just theoretical. It's real, it's fast, and it's painful.

When the Crowd Turns Against You

If you want to understand just how quickly short selling can go from calculated to catastrophic, look no further than the now-legendary **GameStop short squeeze of early 2021.** What began as a niche conversation on a Reddit forum became one of the most chaotic market disruptions in recent history—and a cautionary tale for anyone betting against the crowd.

At the center of the storm was **r/WallStreetBets,** a forum filled with irreverent retail traders who, united by memes, frustration, and a sharp sense of irony, turned their attention toward heavily shorted stocks. GameStop—a struggling brick-and-mortar video game retailer—became the symbol of their uprising. Hedge funds had piled into short positions, convinced the company was dying. On paper, they weren't wrong. But markets don't just run on fundamentals—they run on emotion, momentum, and in this case, **collective outrage.**

Retail traders began **coordinating a buying frenzy,** not only purchasing shares but aggressively buying out-of-the-money call options, which forced market makers to hedge by purchasing even more stock. This created a **feedback loop** known as a gamma squeeze—amplifying the price with each upward tick. In just days, GameStop's stock price shot up from below $20 to nearly $500. Billions in short positions were obliterated.

Melvin Capital, one of the largest and most exposed hedge funds, lost more than 50% of its value within weeks and required an emergency capital injection from

By Mike Mozart from Funny YouTube, USA - GameStop, CC BY 2.0, https://commons.wikimedia.org/w/index.php?curid=89854717

other firms to stay afloat. Other funds weren't so lucky—they simply folded. The headlines painted it as a modern-day **David versus Goliath** moment: a group of everyday investors taking down the giants of Wall Street. And in some ways, it was. But beneath the populist narrative lay a far more enduring truth.

Shorting Works—Until It Doesn't

This episode wasn't about fundamentals. It wasn't about earnings, debt ratios, or business viability. It was about psychology, leverage, and momentum spiraling out of control. In markets driven by algorithms, social media, and 24-hour speculation, **the narrative can change faster than any analysis can keep up.** And if you're caught on the wrong side, data won't save you—only risk management will.

That's why e**very short position must be built on more than just conviction.** It requires structure: **stop-loss orders,** position limits, exit plans. Betting against the market is never just a trade—it's a test of discipline. You're stepping into the path of potential mania, and when the crowd turns against you, it doesn't just move fast—it crushes.

The GameStop saga reminded the world that financial markets are no longer ruled solely by hedge funds and institutional analysts. They are shaped, at least in part, by the collective will of online communities, meme culture, and viral momentum. And for short sellers, that's not just noise—**it's an existential risk.**

If you're going to step into this arena, do it with your eyes wide open. Because **in the age of social-driven trading, being right isn't always enough.** Sometimes, survival is the real victory.

Why Shorting Still Matters

With all of these risks, you might wonder: why short at all?

Because when used wisely, **short selling is one of the few tools that rewards clarity over hype.** It's the counterweight to a market built on speculation, cheap credit, and inflated expectations. It challenges fraudulent business models. It deflates bubbles before they grow too big. And in many of the most spectacular financial collapses—from Enron to Wirecard to the 2008 housing crash—it was the short sellers who sounded the alarm first.

Shorting isn't about rooting for failure. In a world where valuations can become divorced from reality, where AI-driven news cycles amplify market noise, and where central banks distort price signals with endless liquidity, short selling is often the only mechanism left for enforcing sanity.

And for investors who believe that another collapse is coming—whether triggered by debt, war, inflation, or geopolitics—shorting becomes more than just a tactic. It becomes a defensive play. A strategic hedge. A bet not just against assets, but against illusions.

Let's explore how you can use this strategy not just to survive the next depression in America—but to position yourself before it happens.

Because the NEXT BIG SHORT won't come with a warning. It won't feel like panic—at least not at first. It will feel like euphoria. Like "a buying opportunity."

Like nothing is wrong.

Until everything is.

The Tools Today: How You Can Short the Market

Understanding how short selling works conceptually is one thing—but knowing how to actually execute it in today's financial landscape is what really matters. With just a few taps on a smartphone, it's now possible to short stocks, indexes, currencies, commodities, and even entire economies. This kind of access was unthinkable in 2008. But as with any powerful tool, increased access comes with increased responsibility—and higher risk.

One of the most versatile and widely used instruments today is the **Contract for Difference, or CFD.** A CFD is a financial derivative that allows you to speculate on the price movement of an asset without actually owning the asset itself. You're not buying Apple stock—you're betting on whether Apple stock will go up or down. If you think the price will drop, you open a short CFD position. If you're right, you pocket the difference between the entry and exit price. If you're wrong, you pay the difference.

Now, here's the important caveat—**CFDs are banned for retail investors in the United States.** Regulatory bodies like the SEC and CFTC prohibit brokers from offering these instruments to U.S.-based retail traders due to their complexity and risk profile. That doesn't mean you can't short stocks in the U.S.—you just have to do it the traditional way: by borrowing shares from a broker, selling them on the open market, and later buying them back at (hopefully) a lower price.

This method still works, but it's more cumbersome. It involves meeting **margin requirements, paying interest on borrowed shares,** and dealing with **slower execution and higher costs.** For experienced traders, this may not be an issue—but for someone looking to react quickly to market shifts, it's a limitation.

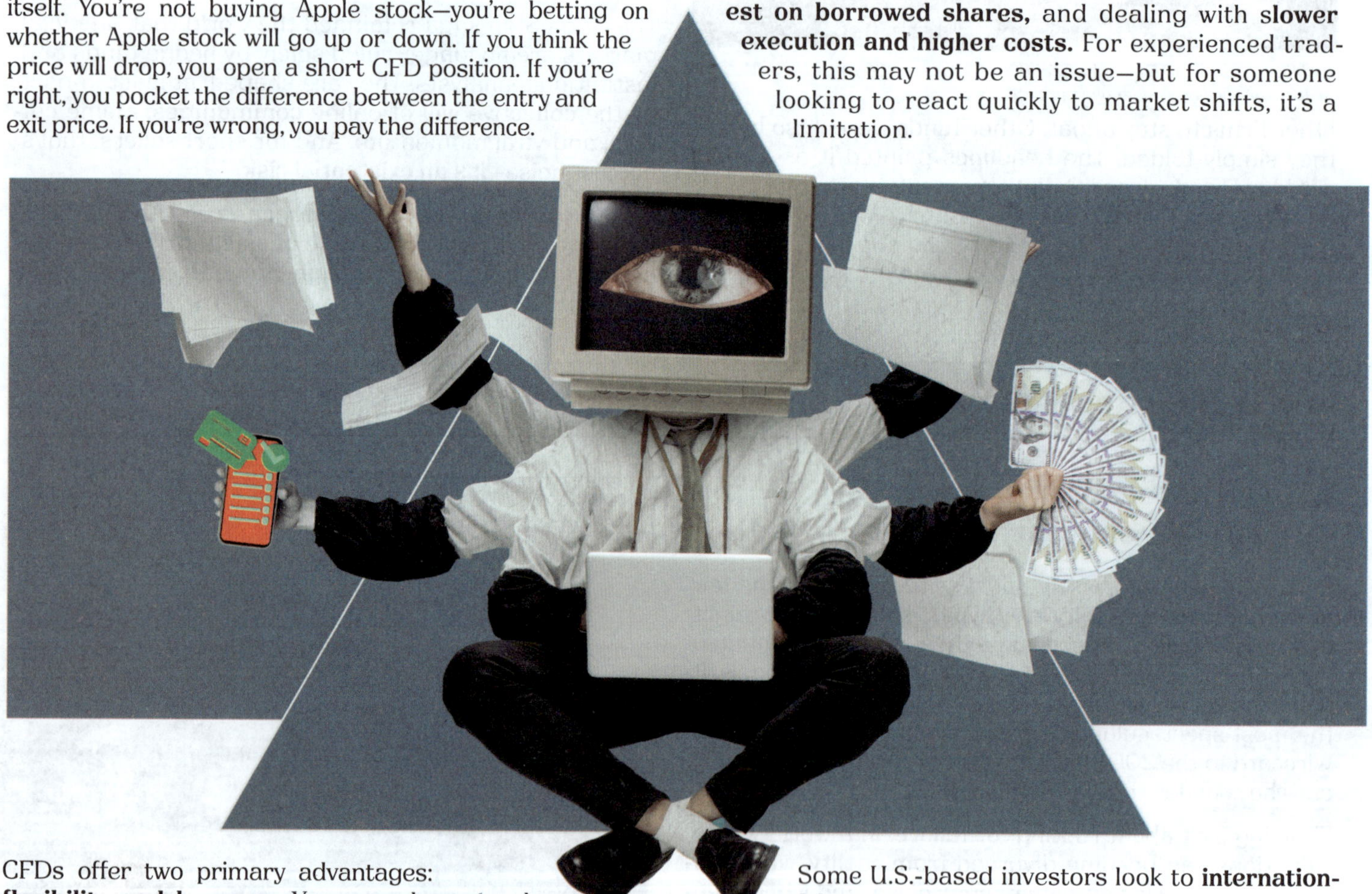

CFDs offer two primary advantages: **flexibility and leverage.** You can short nearly any market in the world, from equities and ETFs to commodities, crypto, and forex pairs. And because most brokers only require a fraction of the trade value to open a position—often 5% to 20%—your capital can be amplified significantly.

But that leverage is a double-edged sword. Just as it multiplies your gains, it also multiplies your losses. A 5% move against you could wipe out your entire position. And if your broker allows negative balances, you could end up owing more than you initially invested. It's not an exaggeration to say that CFDs, when used irresponsibly, can be financially devastating. **The same speed that makes them powerful also makes them dangerous.**

Some U.S.-based investors look to **international brokers** to access CFDs anyway. Platforms like **IG, eToro, or CMC Markets,** regulated in places like the UK, EU, or Australia, often accept non-domestic clients and offer full CFD access. But it's crucial to do your homework. Not every offshore broker is trustworthy. Look for **regulatory licenses,** transparent fees, clear terms, and a reputation for fair dealing. And be aware that some brokers may still restrict access for U.S. citizens, regardless of where the account is opened.

For non-U.S. residents, the playing field is much simpler. CFDs and inverse ETFs are readily available on most trading platforms. You can short entire sectors with a click. Want to bet against the Nasdaq, or against the Chinese yuan? It's never been easier.

But that simplicity is deceptive. Just because something is easy to do doesn't mean it's safe to do. With leverage, even small miscalculations can turn into major losses. That's why, before entering any short trade—especially one involving leveraged products like CFDs—you must have a strategy. **Know** when you'll enter the position, what **price levels** will trigger your exit, and how much you're willing to lose before pulling the plug. Always **use stop-loss orders.** Never risk money you can't afford to lose.

And never let a trade run on emotion or ego.

Shorting Is Not About Being Bold—It's About Being Precise

Short selling is often portrayed as an aggressive act—an all-or-nothing bet against the system. But that image is misleading. The best short sellers aren't reckless contrarians or theatrical market antagonists. They're surgical. Their strength lies not in audacity, but in **discipline, restraint, and clarity.**

When executed with skill, shorting is a tool for cutting through illusion.

But that same precision is what makes the strategy so dangerous when applied carelessly. **Shorting without structure is not strategy—it's self-destruction.** It's like stepping into a war zone wearing nothing but conviction. You may be right about the fundamentals, but if the market doesn't agree when you expect it to, your capital might not survive long enough to prove you right.

The financial landscape is full of stories about traders who saw the crash coming—**but still lost everything.** They had the insight, they saw the bubble, but they didn't manage their exposure, didn't hedge, or didn't know when to step aside. Because in short selling, being early feels exactly like being wrong. And if your timing is off in a market that moves by the second, insight alone won't protect you.

This is why the best short sellers are rarely gamblers.

In today's environment—where markets are driven by momentum, social sentiment, and algorithmic volatility—**clarity has become a rare and powerful currency.** While the crowd chases headlines and hype, the disciplined short seller steps back. They observe the herd—and walk the other way.

Sectors on the Brink:

Every collapse begins the same way: with clear signals that most people choose to ignore. The numbers shift. The headlines change tone. Layoffs begin to spike. Earnings stall. But because on the surface still seems calm—or even euphoric—few take action.

That's the trap.

To position yourself before the crash, you need to start by knowing where to look.

Right now, a number of sectors are flashing early warning signs. Some resemble the pre-crisis patterns of 2000 and 2008. Others are playing out on completely new terrain, driven by low interest rates, easy credit, and a public that has grown addicted to speculative hype. Below are the sectors most likely to unravel—and the data points you should be watching.

Real Estate: A Familiar Bubble

Housing markets across major cities are again showing signs of unsustainable price growth. In places like Toronto, San Francisco, Sydney, and even smaller metros in the U.S., median home prices have decoupled from local income levels entirely. In some areas, it would now take 10 to 15 years of median salary just to afford a modest home—with debt ratios climbing year after year.

Look for:

- Sharp increases in mortgage delinquency rates, especially subprime.
- Sudden drops in transaction volume (a leading indicator of price stagnation).
- Homebuilders issuing profit warnings or delaying projects.
- Rising vacancy rates in rental markets, especially in cities that saw overbuilding during the post-COVID boom.

Real estate bubbles tend to crack slowly, then all at once. The smart money pulls out early—before inventory piles up and price cuts begin to snowball.

Fintech & Buy Now, Pay Later: Easy Credit Cracks

The past few years have seen explosive growth in "Buy Now, Pay Later" platforms and alternative lending fintechs. These companies boomed by offering quick loans with slick user interfaces, often to people who couldn't get traditional credit. But the model only works when consumers repay—and when credit is cheap.

Now, with interest rates rising and consumer debt hitting all-time highs, cracks are beginning to form. Defaults are quietly climbing, and regulators are circling like vultures.

Watch for:

- Charge-off and default rates in quarterly earnings reports.
- Layoffs or cost-cutting at major fintechs like Affirm, Klarna, or Block.
- New regulatory probes from the CFPB or other financial watchdogs.
- Downward guidance or missed earnings estimates.

The same companies that sold financial convenience may become the first dominoes to fall once the lending cycle reverses.

Overinflated Tech: The "Growth at Any Cost" Hangover

Certain tech stocks—especially unprofitable ones—are still trading at valuations divorced from reality. Fueled by cheap money in the 2010s and pandemic-era investor enthusiasm, many of these firms scaled fast without ever proving a viable business model. They chased user growth, burned cash, and sold a dream.

Now reality is catching up. With capital tightening and profitability in focus, the weakest players are starting to fall.

Warning signs:

- Sky-high price-to-earnings (P/E) ratios with slowing revenue growth.
- High insider selling with little or no institutional buying.
- Dependence on stock-based compensation, which dilutes shareholders.
- Repeated rounds of layoffs or "strategic pivots" masking distress.

History repeats: Pets.com in 2000, WeWork in the late 2010s, and now a new crop of venture-backed darlings standing on shaky ground.

Zombie Companies: The Walking Dead of Capitalism

Zombie companies are those that generate just enough revenue to service their debt—but not enough to actually grow or turn a real profit. They survive purely because of low interest rates and a forgiving credit market. But in a tightening environment, that oxygen starts to run out.

As of this writing, it's estimated that nearly **15–20% of publicly listed companies in developed economies fall into this category.**

Spot the undead:

- Repeated refinancing of debt, especially with shorter maturities.
- Years of negative free cash flow, propped up by debt issuance.
- Debt-to-equity ratios spiraling upward.
- Bond downgrades and increasing short interest.

These companies may not make headlines when things go well—but they often lead the crash when funding dries up.

What History Teaches Us

In every major downturn—from the dot-com bust to the 2008 housing collapse—the sectors that imploded had a few things in common: unsustainable growth, overreliance on debt, and blind optimism. But none of them collapsed without leaving a trail. The signs were always there.

This time will be no different. If you're willing to read the data, stay skeptical of hype, and look where others aren't, you won't just survive the next downturn—you might be positioned to profit from it.

Case Study: Tariff-Induced Market Volatility in March-April 2025

In early 2025, global markets were rattled by a wave of sudden tariff policies from the U.S. administration—offering a real-time case study of how fragile modern markets can be in the face of geopolitical shocks.

On April 2, President Trump proclaimed "Liberation Day," unveiling a sweeping 10% tariff on all imports into the United States, alongside a much steeper 125% tariff on goods from China. The announcement hit markets like a sledgehammer. Within 48 hours, the S&P 500 dropped over 12%, while the Nasdaq slid by 14%, wiping out trillions in market value.

Investors scrambled. Retail traders dumped positions. Volatility spiked. Headlines warned of "Black April." Institutional analysts began forecasting a potential global recession, with fears that China or the EU might retaliate.

But then—on April 9—came an abrupt reversal. The White House announced a 90-day suspension of most new tariffs (with the exception of those targeting China), citing the need for "further evaluation." The news triggered one of the strongest single-day rallies in U.S. market history: the S&P 500 surged by 9.5%, the Dow jumped nearly 8%, and the Nasdaq rocketed back 12.2%.

Date	Event	S&P 500 Change	Dow Jones Change	Nasdaq Change
April 2	Tariffs Announced ("Liberation Day")	-12%	-10%	-14%
April 9	Tariff Pause Announced (excluding China)	+9.5%	+7.9%	+12.2%

Source: Market indices data from April 2025.

The sequence revealed two essential truths:

1. Markets remain dangerously reactive to geopolitical shocks, especially in a world where real-time sentiment (and algorithmic trading) moves faster than policy itself.

2. Volatility is the new normal. The days of calm, orderly corrections are gone. We now live in an environment where a single announcement—or tweet—can swing global valuations by trillions within hours.

Veteran investors compared the event to prior episodes of economic whiplash, such as the 2018 U.S.-China trade war, or even Nixon's 1971 "shock" when the U.S. exited the gold standard. In both cases, the initial recovery masked deeper fractures that played out more gradually. Whether the 2025 tariff shock becomes a mere blip or a turning point remains to be seen—but for sharp-eyed investors, it was a masterclass in how fast narratives can flip in times of uncertainty.

Currency Strategy: Betting Against the Dollar

While stocks and sectors often dominate headlines, some of the most strategic short positions have historically come through currency markets. When the global economy wobbles or when a nation's monetary policy becomes unsustainable, it's the value of its currency that often feels the pressure first.

And right now all eyes are on the U.S. dollar.

The Dollar's Hidden Fragility

The U.S. dollar is still the world's reserve currency, but cracks are showing. Mounting national debt, aggressive stimulus packages, persistent trade deficits, and the politicization of interest rates have all chipped away at long-term confidence. Add in rising geopolitical tensions and de-dollarization efforts by major economies like China and Russia, and the once-unshakable greenback looks a little more vulnerable.

Shorting the dollar is about hedging against a systemic risk. If the dollar weakens significantly, everything priced in dollars – from U.S. stocks to imports to raw materials – gets more expensive or volatile. Savvy investors and preppers alike look to diversify their currency exposure, sometimes even positioning to profit from a falling dollar.

How to Short the Dollar: Tools and Tactics

There are several ways to bet against the U.S. dollar, depending on your risk tolerance and market access:

- **Forex Trading:** The most direct method. You can trade currency pairs like EUR/USD or USD/JPY on forex platforms. Going long on EUR/USD, for example, means you're essentially betting the euro will strengthen while the dollar weakens.
- **Inverse USD ETFs:** For U.S.-based investors, funds like **UDN (Invesco DB US Dollar Index Bearish Fund)** provide exposure to the downside of the dollar without directly trading forex. These ETFs often track the dollar against a basket of other currencies.
- **Currency-hedged international equity ETFs:** These allow you to invest in foreign markets while avoiding exposure to a weakening dollar. If the dollar drops, your holdings in stronger currencies rise in relative value.

Each method carries different costs, liquidity, and risks – but all serve the same purpose: protection from a U.S.-centric dollar collapse.

Where to Hold Wealth: Strong Currency Havens

Just as you wouldn't park all your assets in a single sector, you shouldn't keep all your liquid wealth tied to one currency – especially not one that could become central in the next crisis. Holding wealth in historically stable currencies can act as both a hedge and a base for opportunistic trades.

Some traditionally strong currency havens include:

Currency	Country	Why It's Considered Stable
CHF	Switzerland	Low inflation, strong banking system, history of neutrality
SGD	Singapore	High reserves, strict monetary policy, export-driven economy
NOK	Norway	Resource-backed (oil), low debt, disciplined fiscal policy
JPY	Japan	Safe-haven appeal during global volatility
CAD	Canada	Commodity-linked, low corruption, stable governance

Setting up offshore accounts or **using multi-currency digital wallets** (like Wise, Revolut, or crypto-backed stablecoin solutions) allows you to move funds fluidly across currencies without relying solely on U.S. banks. Some investors also use foreign brokerage accounts (in countries with capital-friendly laws) to execute trades in foreign markets, then hold proceeds in non-dollar currencies.

Using FX to Trade Into Crisis Zones

One strategic move during economic decline is to use strong currencies to **enter weakened markets** — buying distressed assets at a discount, with cash that's gaining in relative value.

For instance, if you're holding wealth in Swiss francs while the dollar slides and U.S. markets tank, you could:

- Use foreign brokerage platforms to buy into short positions on U.S. assets.
- Acquire undervalued hard assets in the U.S. (like real estate or metals) using a stronger currency.
- Convert gains back into dollars once the tide turns — effectively buying low and exchanging high.

The Psychology of Panic

Shorting the market, betting against currencies, and watching for bubbles to burst—these are high-leverage plays. They're bold, sometimes brilliant, and often brutally unforgiving. And while the upside can be extraordinary, t**he risk of getting it wrong is just as extreme.** Every seasoned investor—especially those who've survived more than one financial storm—understands that.

Risk management isn't optional—it's the foundation. Especially when you're shorting volatile assets or using leverage, a smart defensive strategy can mean the difference between seizing a rare opportunity... or being wiped out before it arrives.

A single position moving against you can trigger a margin call. A leveraged CFD can wipe out a week's worth of profits in one bad hour. Even the right idea, executed at the wrong time or with the wrong allocation, can end in disaster. The goal isn't just to profit when others are panicking—**it's to be the last one still standing when the dust settles.**

Managing Risk While Shorting

In moments of uncertainty, the human brain defaults to extremes. Either you freeze, or you overreact. That's where the "doomsday edge" creeps in: the idea that once you see the crash coming, you should swing for the fences—go all-in, double down, ride the crash like a wave. After all, you're early. You're smart. You see what they don't.

But that mindset is often just another trap—as dangerous as the euphoria it seeks to exploit.

Because collapses don't follow your timeline. Markets can stay irrational longer than your portfolio can stay solvent. Even when you're right, you can be too early. And in a leveraged environment, being early is often indistinguishable from being wrong.

That's why it's crucial to:

- Size your positions conservatively: Never short more than you can afford to lose.
- Use stop-losses or trailing stops to prevent runaway losses.
- Avoid shorting hype stocks or illiquid assets where manipulation is common.
- Spread risk across uncorrelated sectors: Don't short three fintechs—short one fintech, one overleveraged real estate trust, and maybe one tech company showing clear signs of distress.

Diversifying your short positions helps you weather the unpredictable nature of collapsing markets—where one sector might snap back while another continues to bleed out.

Offensive vs Defensive Allocation

One of the most practical frameworks in prepping and investing is the split portfolio model: part of your wealth is designed to preserve and protect, while the other part is actively positioned for asymmetric upside.

Category	Allocation	Purpose
Defensive Prep	40–60%	Cash reserves, hard assets (gold, real estate), food/supplies, safe havens
Offensive Bets	20–40%	Short positions, leveraged plays, foreign FX trades
Flexible Capital	10–20%	Dry powder for opportunistic buys or pivots

Timing the Next Big Short

You won't get a flashing red light when the next collapse begins. No alarm bell will ring. No headline will tell you "It's time." By the time the media starts calling it a crisis, it's already too late. The opportunity has passed, the panic has begun, and the market's most obvious trades are already crowded—or gone.

That's why you need to time the next big short perfectly.

Collapses tend to follow their own rhythm. They don't usually start with explosions—they begin with whispers. A missed earnings report. A series of quiet layoffs. Liquidity drying up. An obscure bond market flashing danger.

Public optimism at an all-time high—while insiders are quietly selling.

It's a pattern that's repeated itself for decades. And while the cause of each crash may vary, **the early signs are remarkably consistent:**

- Widening credit spreads (corporate bonds vs Treasuries)
- Yield curve inversions
- Spikes in margin debt
- Elevated insider selling
- Sudden downward revisions in earnings guidance
- Major layoffs in highly-valued, unprofitable sectors
- Surging credit card delinquencies or consumer loan defaults

These are the tremors that precede the earthquake.

Learn to listen for them.

The Tools Worth Watching

To track these signals, you o need a few reliable tools:

- **FRED (Federal Reserve Economic Data)** – for macro signals like yield curves and debt metrics
- **TradingView or Finviz** – to screen stocks, monitor P/E ratios, insider activity, and short interest
- **ETF.com or Morningstar** – to track sector rotation and fund flows
- **MacroVoices, Real Vision, or The Market Sniper** - for contrarian, macroeconomic insight that goes beyond mainstream headlines
- Alternative data platforms – including Google Trends, job postings, freight/shipping volume, or consumer sentiment indexes for real-world behavioral shifts

None of these tools will make the decision for you. But they'll sharpen your lens, filter the noise, and help you spot the disconnect between what's being said—and what's actually happening.

Why Most People Will Be Too Late

History is full of warnings that no one listened to. The signs are rarely hidden—but they are always easy to ignore. That's because the collapse rarely feels like one at the start. It feels like "just a healthy correction."

Early on , the data may scream, but the crowd is still celebrating.

It's not until the decline becomes undeniable that panic sets in—and by then, it will be too late.

This is the difference between watching and reacting.

The next big short won't come with permission. It will emerge slowly, invisibly, and then all at once. And those who are already listening—those who read the signs before the crowd—won't be caught off guard.

Closing Note

There are only two types of people in every crisis: those who say, "No one saw this coming," and those who did.

The difference isn't luck.

It's the willingness to study what others dismiss, to prepare when it may even feel unnecessary, and to act when it's still uncomfortable to do so. **The next collapse will create pain for many—but enormous opportunity for a select few. Which side of that equation you land on won't be decided in the moment. It will be decided by what you do before the moment arrives.**

Chapter 12

Early Warning Signs an Economic Collapse Has Begun

"If you wait until you can see the light at the end of the tunnel, you've already been run over by the train." Robert Kiyosaki

The Signs

When a collapse begins there are no sirens, no declarations, and no clear lines. The signs appear first in systems you rely on every day. If you know what to look for, the shift becomes obvious.

Banks Begin Restricting Access to Your Money

Amidst the aftermath of protests, a banks in Beirut stand charred and damaged, serving as a powerful symbol of the unrest and tension in the city.

By Ali Chehade Farhat

Watch for changes in routine banking behavior. Indicators such as unexpected delays in instant transfers and reduced ATM withdrawal limits paired with unanticipated identity re-verification requests suggest changes in banking behavior. Standard transactions increasingly show the appearance of phrases like "pending authorization," "technical delay," or "under review."

ATMs tend to show temporary alerts more frequently and online banking platforms face unexpected maintenance or access disruptions without proper explanation. Financial institutions may restrict cash withdrawals over several hundred dollars through branches and implement transaction forms and delays that used to process instantly.

These changes stem from deliberate control measures rather than random technical errors. The current changes demonstrate that authorities have implemented capital control measures. Initial signs of systemic banking stress emerge as restricted access rather than complete shutdowns but manifest as operational slowdowns. Be alert to policy changes that limit withdrawal capabilities while extending settlement periods and adding new verification processes. Quantifiable and confirmable indicators reveal that institutional trust is deteriorating from within.

Delays in Basic Government Payments

Recurring payments begin arriving late across multiple programs. This includes Social Security disbursements, food assistance benefits (EBT/SNAP), military retirement pensions, disability payments, and tax refunds. These delays are not isolated to one agency or region, they appear across systems, often with vague explanations citing "technical adjustments," "system upgrades," or "processing backlogs." The messaging is uniform, noncommittal, and often downplays the problem.

In early stages, affected recipients may only notice a 24–48 hour delay. Over time, that window increases. Reissued cards are "in the mail" for weeks. Customer service becomes harder to reach. Wait times lengthen. Online portals post new disclaimers. The trend to watch is system-wide slippage—not one mistake, but a visible lag across departments that previously delivered on fixed schedules.

When governments experience financial strain, one of the first containment measures is the quiet throttling of benefit disbursement. The public is not told the system is under pressure. Instead, the recipients begin to feel it as their access is slowed. This is a liquidity event. The earliest visible sign of state-level insolvency is failure to meet predictable payout obligations. Track payment dates. Note changes. Do not dismiss a single missed deposit as random. Pattern is everything.

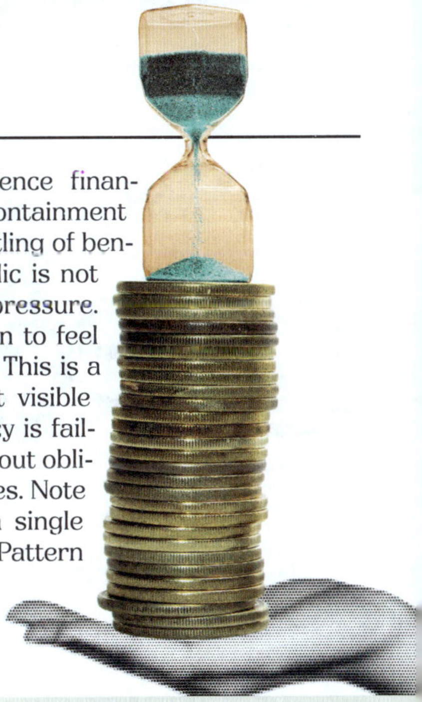

Currency Stops Buying the Essentials

Essential items increase in cost far faster than reported inflation. Grocery totals climb weekly. Staples such as flour, rice, oil, eggs, and soap show continuous upward adjustment at checkout. Fixed incomes lose purchasing power by the month. Discount stores eliminate bulk offers and reduce product weight without lowering price. Package labels are redesigned to obscure changes in volume.

Hard goods become harder to find at previous price points. Vendors remove shelf tags and manually update pricing. Standard supply becomes irregular. Cash registers are reprogrammed to reflect daily or even hourly rate adjustments. Mobile vendors begin asking for cash only. Small businesses start quoting rates in ounces, gallons, or foreign currency equivalents. Barter increases in local listings. People stop trusting the price because it changes rapidly.

Frequent 'Glitches' in Financial Systems

Bank balances fail to update after deposits. Transactions stall at point of sale. Transfers between accounts are delayed without timestamp or reference ID. Mobile apps display conflicting data between screens. Statements arrive with unresolved discrepancies.

Recurring payments are missed or duplicated. Customers are locked out of their accounts and required to reverify identity with new steps. ATM receipts show different figures than online portals. Daily limits change without notification. Support centers refer to system maintenance without giving a time frame.

The system begins rejecting inputs it used to accept. Stable functions become inconsistent. Errors increase without explanation. These failures do not follow scheduled updates or known outages. They appear across platforms and institutions in close succession. Transaction confidence erodes before access is formally restricted.

Persistent Empty Shelves for Basic Goods

Essential items stop returning to the shelf. The same products remain absent across restocking cycles. Canned meats, oil, infant formula, bleach, ibuprofen, rice, and sugar disappear first. Shelf space is widened artificially. Staff place remaining stock forward to cover the gap. Labels remain without product. Delivery volume drops.

Store employees say nothing definite. "Out of stock" messages last beyond the next truck. Substitution appears. Unfamiliar brands fill the space. Known items vanish without announcement.

The pattern crosses store types. Chains, independents, and discount retailers show identical gaps. Regional overlap confirms that the failure is not local. When weekly stock cannot be restored for high-turnover goods, inventory flow has broken. The delivery system no longer meets demand at retail level.

Gas Stations Quietly Cut Hours or Impose Limits

Operating hours reduce without explanation. Locations close earlier than posted. Certain pumps display "out of service" bags. Payment methods require cash only and mandate pre-payment while denying the possibility of receiving change. Credit terminals lag or fail. Staff cite maintenance or delivery issues.

Fuel availability becomes unpredictable. The availability of diesel and regular fuel alternates frequently. Truck stop volumes decline. Customers face gallon purchase limitations without posted notices. Rural stations shut down mid-shift. Receipts may not print. Pump authorizations fail intermittently.

No public statement is made. Fuel companies do not issue notices. The adjustment happens quietly. Consistency disappears from the supply side. Driver behavior shifts. Wait times increase. Lines form before dawn.

Spike in Store Security Presence

Security guards appear at entrances without incident. Retail chains place personnel near self-checkout and pharmacy counters. Items that were once open-stock become locked: batteries, infant formula, razors, detergent pods, cold medicine.

Plexiglass dividers are installed where none existed. Monitors show new angles of aisles and exits. Additional loss prevention signage is posted. Receipts are checked more frequently at exits. Staff adopt new procedures for bags and carts.

This escalation occurs without a stated threat. It rolls out uniformly across chain locations. No announcements are made. New protocols are implemented without comment. When defensive infrastructure increases across the retail sector, it reflects projected volatility in the population, not in policy.

Hospitals Quietly Begin Rationing Care or Supplies

Inventory controls tighten without public notice. Medical staff begin limiting usage of gloves, gowns, saline, or syringes. Supplies that were once available in bulk are counted or locked. Non-urgent procedures are postponed. Routine tests are deferred. Patient intake windows narrow. Wait times increase even for minor issues.

Pharmacies attached to hospitals stop refilling prescriptions on demand. Brands are replaced by generics. Certain medications become "temporarily unavailable" without clear explanation. Nurses and technicians begin using the term "allocation." Clinics reduce hours, or consolidate appointments into fewer locations.

This differs from normal cost-cutting. Seasonal staff adjustments or elective scheduling reductions follow calendar trends. Rationing does not. When supply use shifts across departments and supply counts increase without restock timing, the system is prioritizing retention over use. That is a signal of upstream uncertainty in delivery.

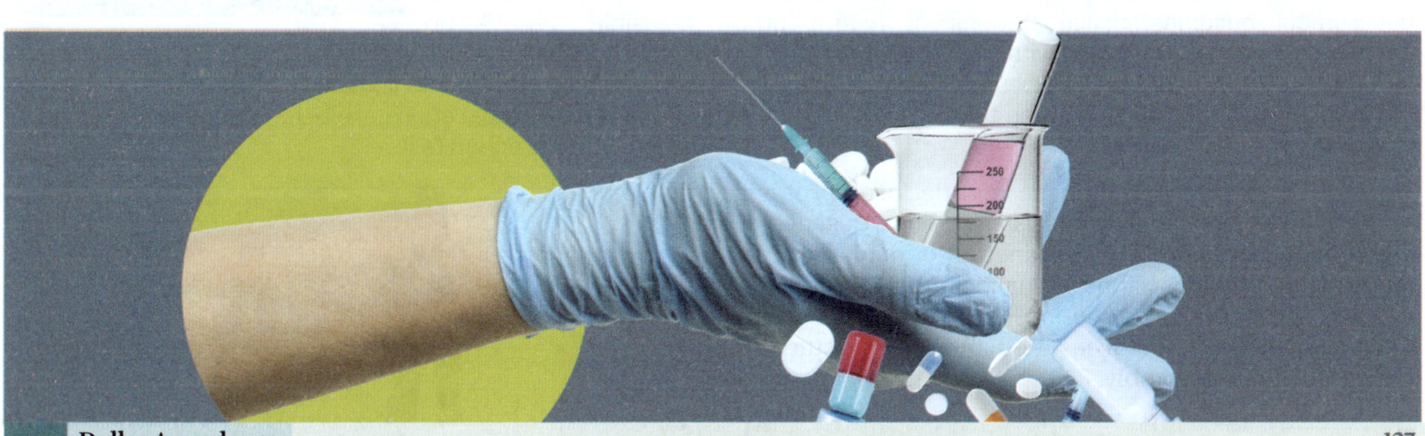

Large Corporations Suddenly Pull Out of Regions

Multiple locations close inside the same metro zone. Closures are executed with minimal advance warning. Official reasons cite staffing, safety, restructuring, or real estate cost. Patterns emerge across brands. Pharmacies, fast food chains, retail anchors, and grocers all reduce footprint in the same general areas.

Interior assets are removed. Equipment is liquidated or transferred. Security fencing appears. Storefronts are shuttered without transfer offers to nearby locations. Vacancy notices are not posted immediately. Public statements lack operational detail. Corporate spokespeople emphasize company-wide goals rather than location-specific failure.

Closures are not tied to seasonal trends or poor individual performance. They occur in clusters, often after a shift in local crime, infrastructure reliability, or customer volume.

Identical Language in News and Official Statements

Media reports, press conferences, and official statements begin using the same phrases across unrelated platforms. Terms like “transitory inflation,” “temporary volatility,” “resilient market,” or “unexpected correction” appear repeatedly, without variation in tone or context.

These terms are synchronized. They replace concrete data with narrative structure. News segments, economic bulletins, and political speeches all emphasize reassurance while avoiding direct analysis. Experts from different outlets cite the same causes and downplay the same risks using identical vocabulary.

This pattern appears when agencies and media entities are coordinating messaging. It removes uncertainty from language and replaces it with fixed phrases. The shift can be tracked across time. Before the coordination begins, coverage contains disagreement and data variation. Afterward, divergence disappears. The repetition itself is the sign. It marks a transition from information to control.

Law Enforcement Quietly Deploys Riot Gear and Barricades

Barriers, fencing, and mobile partitions appear outside government buildings, police stations, or federal offices. Tactical units are equipped with visible riot gear during standard patrols. Armored vehicles are moved to accessible staging zones. Portable lighting towers are set up at intersections or utility corridors.

This activity occurs in the absence of declared protests or unrest. No formal alert is issued. The presence of equipment increases, but explanation is minimal or indirect. Units are described as participating in drills, inspections, or “readiness routines.” Deployment patterns become consistent in areas tied to infrastructure, finance, or public assembly.

The shift does not follow a visible event. It precedes one. When police visibility escalates in specific areas while official statements remain neutral or dismissive, the signal is that preparations are being made for expected instability, not reaction to it.

Community Services Quietly Start Failing

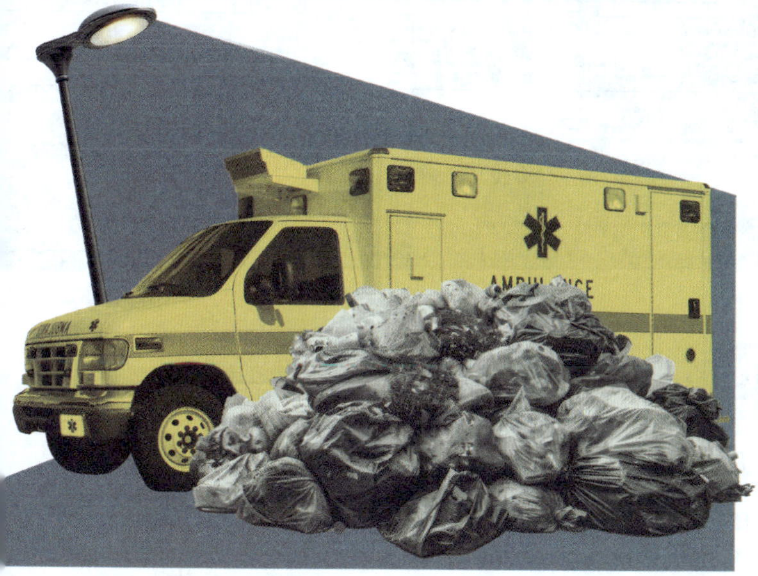

Municipal services become inconsistent. Trash pickup skips scheduled days. Streetlights remain unrepaired. Water utility notices increase, citing pressure irregularities or elevated contaminant levels. Road maintenance projects are deferred indefinitely. Graffiti and vandalism remain visible longer.

Ambulance and fire response times extend without public explanation. Response coverage shrinks. Libraries reduce hours. City departments slow to return calls or process paperwork. Offices previously open five days a week reduce access. "Staffing shortages" and "funding adjustments" become default statements across departments.

The sign is not in one failure, but in concurrent decline across unrelated services. When visible infrastructure maintenance slows and minor breakdowns are left unresolved across multiple departments, operational support is being retracted from the base of the system.

Middle-Class Families Start Leaving Urban Areas

Relocations begin quietly. Family members at work and nearby dwellers announce plans to relocate suddenly. People give relaxed reasons for moving such as "moving closer to family," "seeking a change in pace," or "better school opportunities." Signs indicating properties for sale become more common in stable neighborhoods. A pattern emerges where households showing no prior signs of financial distress start listing their properties and reducing their living spaces.

Destination patterns shift away from high-density areas. People moving choose smaller municipalities and suburban areas outside of cities over urban destinations. This mass departure deviates from standard patterns seen in occupational-based residential relocation. It spreads laterally across professions and ages. The volume of moving activity reaches moving companies and school districts ahead of media coverage.

The true indicator lies in the profile of the individuals who initiate relocation. People who have the financial means and ability to plan relocation start leaving areas they consider unstable. That withdrawal precedes overt instability.

Sudden Changes in Emergency Drill Activity

Agencies increase the frequency and scale of preparedness exercises. Drill content shifts toward scenarios involving civil unrest, critical supply interruption, population relocation, or power grid failure. Language used includes terms like "continuity of operations," "domestic stabilization," and "critical event simulation."

Public notices, if issued, remain vague. Descriptions focus on "routine training," but documentation and observed activity reflect expanded coordination. Military, police, emergency response, and federal agencies participate simultaneously. Locations include transportation hubs, energy nodes, and distribution centers.

Supply stockpiles are moved and stored near administrative zones. Medical staging areas are created near government buildings. Civilian observers may notice helicopters, convoys, or temporary fencing unrelated to any declared event.

The drills do not match the public threat level. Their scope reflects internal models, not external announcements. When emergency readiness activity escalates without public risk justification, the system is adjusting its posture based on information not shared with the population.

Supply Chain Substitution Without Announcement

Familiar products vanish and return under new names. Major brands of medication, hygiene products, formula, and packaged food are pulled from shelves and replaced with unlabeled or foreign-manufactured equivalents. Labeling shifts from national trademarks to generic packaging or vague region-based names.

No notice is given. There is no corporate rollout or rebranding campaign. Employees offer no explanation beyond "new supplier." SKUs change. Pricing remains, but availability becomes irregular. Stocking frequency drops. Imported shelf tags appear in languages not seen previously in that region. Packaging quality may degrade. Tracking batch origins becomes difficult.

This pattern signals that distribution agreements have broken and centralized sourcing is being replaced with opportunistic fulfillment. Substitution on this scale reflects either unavailable domestic supply or logistical collapse in product consistency.

Unusual Migration or Travel Restrictions

Identification screenings take place at both regional transportation hubs and highway bottlenecks. All three transportation services now require additional documentation beyond their usual procedures. Local governments establish curfews through their ordinances since these rules lack any national standardization. Leaving specified areas demands extra screening procedures or valid reasons.

The rules are rolled out unevenly. Many regions enforce their own policies while other areas do not take action. The stated justifications for these measures can be linked to safety concerns or public health directives as well as regional incidents. While the circumstances differ widely civilian movement remains consistently obstructed.

Conditional internal mobility signals that government policy has moved from managing populations freely towards strict containment controls. When national borders enforce internal movement restrictions it demonstrates clear administrative insecurity.

New Digital Compliance Systems Are Rolled Out Quietly

Institutions begin requiring facial recognition, fingerprint scans, or app-based logins for routine access. Bank portals, healthcare networks, and utility dashboards introduce multi-layer verification without opt-out. Transactions that previously required a password now demand biometric input or device tethering.

User accounts are linked to centralized ID systems without user initiation. Legacy login methods are phased out. Notifications appear with vague wording like "security enhancement," "platform upgrade," "compliance adjustment." The process is implemented without full disclosure or centralized announcement.

The sign is in the compounding friction. As new systems layer over basic functions, operational autonomy is reduced. Access becomes conditional not on what you have, but on what you agree to link. This is infrastructure consolidation under digital credential enforcement, not convenience.

PART THREE

WHAT TO DO *on the* DAY *the* ECONOMY COLLAPSES

6:00 AM

Verify It's Real

6:00 AM

Wake up early and verify what's actually happening. Before acting on rumors or headlines, look for stacked indicators. Not one or two glitches, but a convergence of major failures. What you're trying to confirm isn't simple market turbulence or regional outages.

You're scanning for signs that **the currency itself is going down** fast. A sudden drop in the dollar's value isn't just inflation. It erodes trust in every contract, price, and transaction. That shows up first in locked markets, frozen withdrawals, and payment systems quietly choking under volume.

Check the status of the major U.S. stock exchanges. **If the NYSE or NASDAQ has halted trading across the board,** that signals intervention from the top. Next, test your bank access, log in to multiple accounts if you have them. If **balances are blank, if ATMs give "balance error" or "temporarily unavailable" messages** at more than one location, and if **payment apps stall or crash repeatedly,** this is no longer a technical hiccup.

Scan the language of public officials. Phrases like "banking holiday," "temporary liquidity measures," or "institutional restructuring" from the Federal Reserve or Treasury signal coordinated damage control. These are the words used when stability has already failed.

Gas stations or retail stores may quietly begin posting **"cash only" signs.** These changes will spread quickly, but early in the day, they are still clues, signals for those who know what to look for.

If three or more of these signs are visible at once, you are no longer in normal conditions. The financial structure is no longer stable or trustworthy. Assume withdrawal caps, transaction freezes, and purchasing restrictions will follow within hours, maybe even sooner. Do not spend time waiting for confirmation from others. Your priority is to shift your operating assumptions now. Proceed as if the system is functionally locked, and behave accordingly.

7:00 AM

Secure Cash, Even in Small Amounts

7:00 AM

Time matters now more than ever. If ATMs are still operational, go immediately. Avoid central business districts or major bank branches where delays and crowds are more likely. Target smaller or less trafficked locations—banks tucked into grocery plazas, standalone credit union machines, or fringe neighborhood branches. If one card hits a limit, try another. If you face a screen error, move on. Don't wait for a system to reload. Don't ask questions at the counter. Speed is more valuable than negotiation.

If ATMs are already down, shift strategy without hesitation. Head to grocery stores or pharmacies that still accept debit cards. Use **self-checkout stations** whenever possible—they're faster, draw less attention, and allow more flexible movement. Purchase inexpensive items and request the maximum cash back available per transaction. Repeat this process at several locations if needed. Keep your story minimal. If asked, say you're running errands. Do not explain.

At this point, card access could vanish at any time. If your attempts to withdraw cash fail entirely, prioritize acquiring **tangible essentials that retain value,** goods people will soon trade for. These are your stopgap. Fuel, dry food, over-the-counter meds, and personal hygiene items all serve that purpose.

Do not bring others along. Do not discuss what you're doing with strangers or colleagues. The more you say, the less flexibility you have. Work fast, carry discreetly, and return home without unnecessary detours. If crowds start to form, disengage immediately. Your goal is not to clean out shelves or hit maximum withdrawal, your goal is to **preserve mobility and independence** before the door slams in your face.

If the dollar's value is collapsing, cash is losing purchasing power by the hour. But during the first day, it's still **usable as a medium of exchange**—for gas, groceries, meds and other essentials.

8:00 AM

Prioritize Purchases That Will Disappear First

8:00 AM

At this point, availability matters more than variety. You are not stocking a pantry. You are securing continuity, fuel, hydration, calories, and essential medications. Skip the aisles that draw passive shoppers. Move with speed and purpose.

Expect prices to move by mid-day. Caps will show up first, but informal pricing may change by the hour. A gallon of gas might cost $6 in the morning and $10 by night if local station managers stop trusting incoming shipments. Use this window while base pricing still holds.

Start with fuel, even if you already refueled. This includes propane, diesel, lighter fluid, or canisters for camp stoves—anything with stored energy or thermal use. If you don't need it, someone will, and that gives you options. Expect caps to appear without warning.

Water is next. Buy bottled if it's still available, but also secure ways to purify tap or collected water: basic filters, iodine tablets, unscented bleach. Keep it simple.

For food, skip anything that requires refrigeration or long prep. Focus on dry staples that pack calories and last: rice, lentils, oats, peanut butter, canned meats and stews. If a store's shelves are half-full, shop by weight and density. Ignore the brands.

Buy non-food items that hold transactional power: cigarettes, menstrual products, lighters, over-the-counter painkillers, antihistamines, antiseptics, electrolytes. These vanish fast, even from secondary locations.

Prioritize overlooked stores first like corner shops, independent ethnic groceries, hardware stores with general supplies. You'll often find full shelves where crowds haven't arrived yet. Use cash if possible, and keep movement tight. No wandering. No repeats at the same register. Avoid visible stockpiling.

If lines begin forming or customers grow talkative, adjust. Make smaller runs. Change clothes between outings if needed. You want efficiency without attention. This is not hoarding, and it's not panic—it is securing autonomy while systems still allow movement.

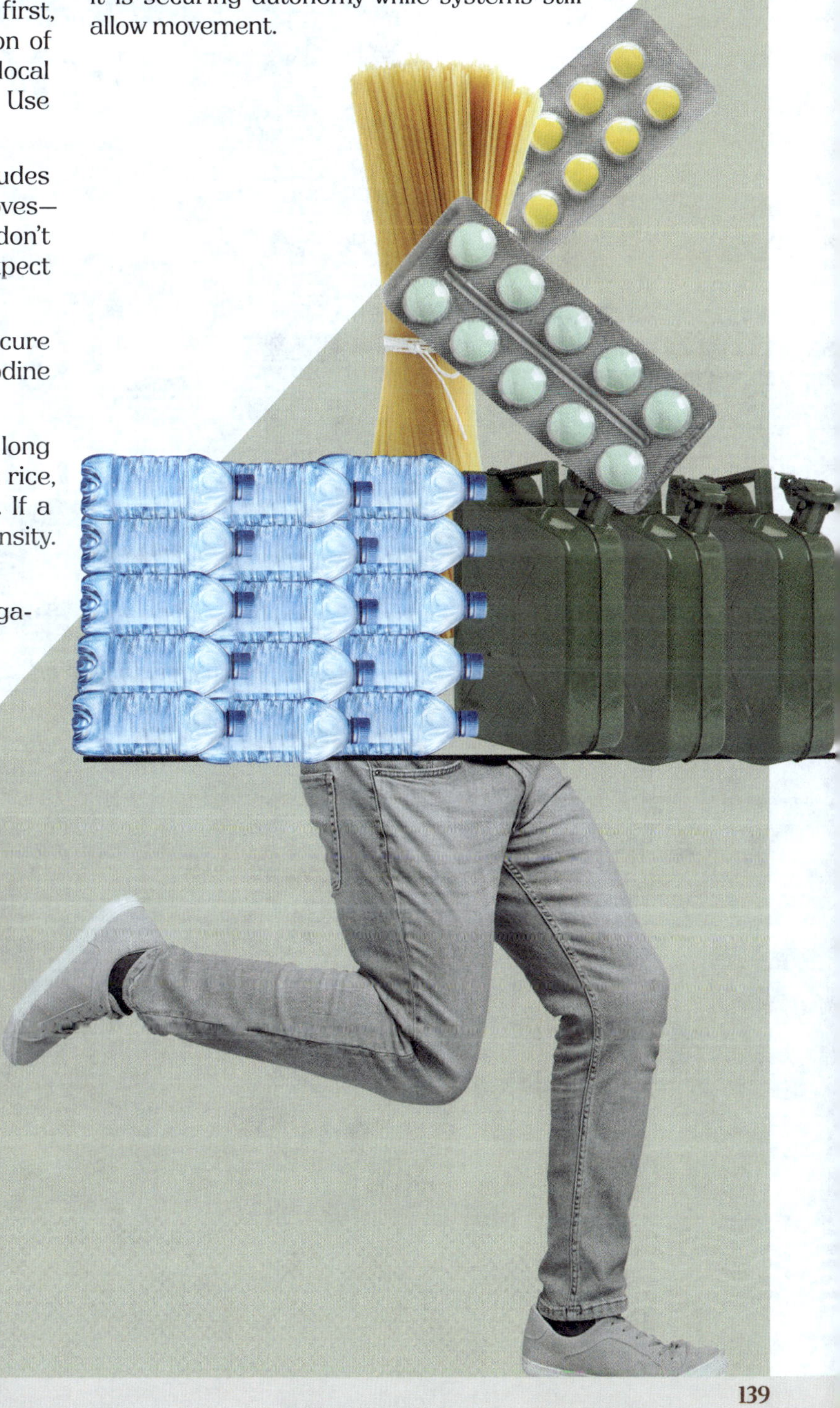

9:00 AM

Refuel and Cache

9:00 AM

If the tank isn't full, fill it. No partial stops. No topping off at your usual station. Pick the nearest functioning pump and move fast. Use cash if digital systems are starting to stall. If caps are showing up at pumps, or if you see handwritten limits taped to dispensers, that's the end of normal.

Fill any spare gas cans now. If you don't have them, don't waste time hunting. Focus on what fits your current vehicle. Ask no questions. Speak to no one. Leave the area as soon as the nozzle clicks.

Back at your location, move fuel into controlled storage—sealed, covered, and isolated from living space. Not because it "might explode," but because it'll be stolen or lost if left accessible. If you store fuel indoors, lock the door. If you keep it outside, bury it behind noise, clutter, or fencing. Do not label it. Do not share.

If you're unable to store more, shift focus to **trade positioning.** You still have time to offer something—food, tools, medicine—in exchange for fuel later. That exchange will dry up by nightfall. You'll be dealing with closed doors or panic buyers after that.

11:00 AM

Consolidate Your Position and Network

11:00 AM

This hour is for stabilizing your position. You've already pulled cash and stocked key supplies. Now you identify which contacts you can still rely on for **logistical exchange**—not conversation.

Reach out to one or two people who operate clearly. No alerts. No "emergency" talk. Ask one question:

"Do you still have card access or cash in hand?"

If they say yes and they're moving early, keep them in your loop. If they're frozen or unaware, move on.

If you can quietly form a simple mutual aid line—food, transport, trade support—do it now. Keep it verbal, keep it small. Don't text detailed plans. Don't send updates. You don't need opinions. You need someone who can deliver fuel, cover a prescription, or help you move a package if your card fails tomorrow.

If no one in your circle qualifies, that's fine. You've confirmed you're on your own. That's valuable data.

12:00 PM

Triage Your Own Position

12:00 PM

Take ten minutes, alone and undistracted. No screens. No background noise. No second opinions. This is not the time to brainstorm. It's a hard, written snapshot of what you actually have, what you actually owe, and who you can't trust to think clearly.

Start with your food. Count the meals you can prepare **without electricity.** Not packages—meals. Write the number.

Next, count your cash. Not projected earnings, not credit lines—**cash in hand,** broken down by denomination.

List **any bills or obligations due in the next 72 hours** that could trigger consequences: rent, medication, insurance, child support, automatic withdrawals. Assume digital payments may fail. If they hit your account anyway and bounce, you'll deal with penalties later. Be clear on what's worth covering now and what can wait.

Now list **anything you can offer if hard trade becomes necessary:** tools, clean water access, medication, space, or specific skills—car repair, logistics, caregiving.. Write what could actually keep another person moving when their options close.

Last, write down names. Be blunt: **who is a drain or a threat** if the situation holds for more than 24 hours? This includes **the impulsive, the entitled, the volatile, and the manipulative.** You don't need to cut them off today, but you do need to recognize patterns before they cost you.

2:00 PM

Strengthen Your Home Quietly

2:00 PM

You don't need to fortify. You need to tighten what already exists, without broadcasting it to your next-door neighbours.

Start with your physical space. Lock any doors you aren't using. Check every ground-level window. Close blinds or curtains where visibility invites questions. Don't tape windows, stack furniture, or do anything that signals preparation.

Collect the essentials: identification, cash, prescription meds, and anything critical for a 48-hour relocation. Put them in one container, small enough to move fast but packed tight enough to survive chaos. Store it in a place that's both secure and accessible without noise or delay.

If you're in an apartment, don't engage neighbors. Don't explain what you're doing or ask what they've heard. Anyone who's loud, erratic, or clingy should be avoided for now. Conversation equals liability.

Place a flashlight, multitool, and reliable footwear beside your bed. Check that your main bag—if packed—is reachable in darkness. If it isn't packed, that's fine. Have a clear plan for what would go inside.

Shut down outside lights that aren't serving a function. Keep the place looking normal. You're not defending a position. You're reducing the chance anyone thinks you have something they need.

4:00 PM

Update Your Snapshot

4:00 PM

By now, you've moved. You've bought, withdrawn, secured, and adjusted. This hour is for tracking the actual environment, not your emotions, not headlines, not guesses. Just raw data.

Write down exactly where you went today: every store, station, bank, pharmacy, or building. For each, note what you saw. Were shelves full or stripped? Were lines forming? Were people calm, agitated, or blank-faced? What did things cost, especially food, fuel, and basic meds?

Record **any closures**—even partial ones. If a location had fewer hours posted, sections roped off, or handwritten signs, note it. Pay attention to which businesses stopped accepting cards, which limited quantities, or which suddenly went cash-only.

Now, capture the **mood.** Not your theory, what you observed. Was the cashier distracted? Were customers arguing? Were police present? Were certain streets unusually quiet?

This list becomes reference, not memory. In a day or two, official sources may contradict what you've already seen. You're not writing a report. You're building a personal map of instability—**to track patterns.**

6:00 PM

Normalize Your Routine for Stability

6:00 PM

If you live with others—especially children—this is when your behavior sets the tone. You've already made key moves. Now, your job is to stabilize the space and keep things level inside your house.

Make dinner. Keep it simple. Use what's already open or what's been purchased, but do not overcook or experiment. Serve meals as usual.

Begin reducing waste immediately. Save everything with value: bones, fats, packaging, jars. You're not hoarding. You're preserving flexibility. Anything that might serve a secondary use later, keep it.

Cut down noise. No loud music. No outdoor cooking smells. No family arguments that can be heard through the walls. You don't want attention, not from neighbors, not from a passersby.

Keep the routine as fixed as possible. Same dinner time, same lights-out, same rules. Structure beats panic every time, even if no one else sees the cracks yet.

8:00 PM Communications Reset

8:00 PM

You've likely used your phone or laptop heavily today—navigation, transactions, calls, maybe hotspot tethering. Now is the time to clear the digital load and assess your communication options going forward.

Turn your phone off completely and leave it off for 15 to 30 minutes **to force the hardware to dump background tasks,** clear RAM, and reestablish clean signal paths when powered back on. If you've been using multiple banking or payment apps, this step helps reset cached data and reduces your chances of system lag or error tomorrow.

As it reboots, check your charger output, battery bank levels, and the condition of any backup power supplies. If you're using a laptop or tablet to monitor financial news, sync that data now and download anything essential while connections are stable.

Check what communication channels are still working. Are group chats still responsive? Do SMS messages deliver faster than apps? Does AM radio carry live content? Do not rely on assumptions. **Function, not familiarity, is what matters now.**

Keep your devices off Wi-Fi when not in use. Save bandwidth. Don't stream. Don't broadcast. Think like someone conserving motion.

10:00 PM

Final Lockdown Checklist

10:00 PM

Lock your doors, all of them. Check windows, but don't block them or post warnings. You're not under threat. You're keeping control of your environment, nothing more. Walk the perimeter once. Take note of any lights that weren't on earlier. Don't investigate. Don't interpret. Just record and move on.

Put your most essential items, wallet, keys, cash, medications, ID, into a small container and place it within arm's reach of your bed.

Set out shoes, jacket, and a light if power goes out or you need to move at night. Do not over-layer.

Do not overthink.
Then shut it down.

PART FOUR

DOLLAR APOCALYPSE SURVIVAL PROTOCOL

Exactly WHAT TO DO *Once* IT'S HERE

Chapter 13

How to Deal with Taxes and Everyday Expenses During Economic Collapse

Most people believe that in a crisis tax burdens will disappear. They won't. They will increase, diversify, and become more aggressive. You'll be told to pay more in the name of stability. You'll be billed for services that no longer work. You'll face assessments based on vanished markets, be charged fees for infrastructure you can no longer use, and risk liens or seizures over amounts that make no logical sense, because logic doesn't matter when the government is in survival mode.

"The difference between death and taxes is that death doesn't get worse every time Congress meets."
Will Rogers

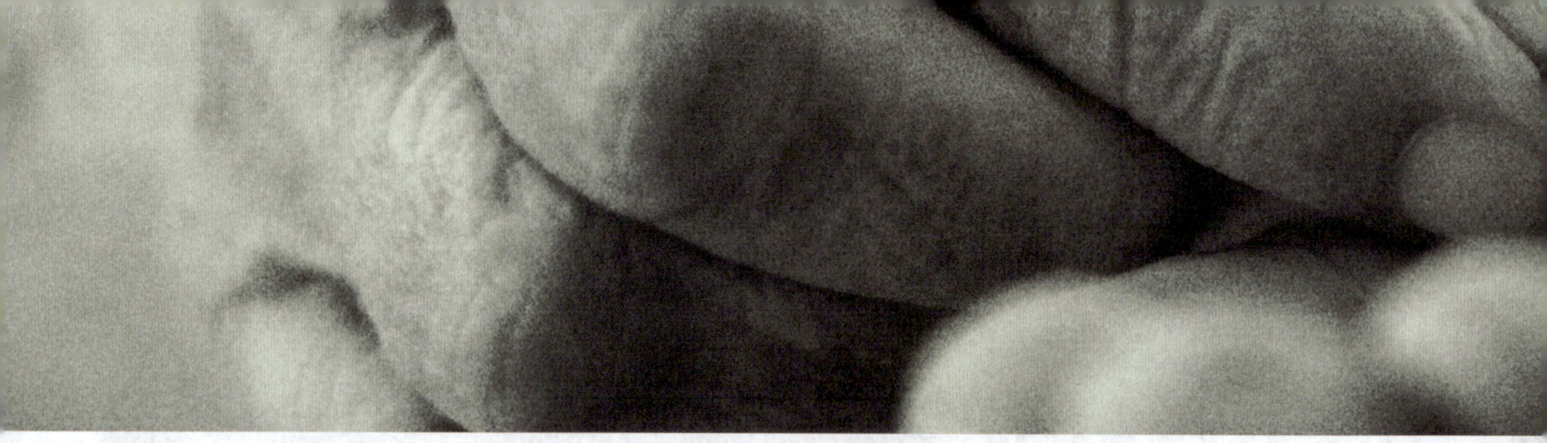

Understanding and Reducing Your Tax Burden

As currency value deteriorates and wages diminish or vanish, the tax system grows more stringent while becoming more inventive and less transparent.

Taxation survives after a collapse by revealing its enforcement stripped of civil pretense.

Across history, the pattern is brutally consistent. During Weimar Germany's monetary collapse **people burned money for warmth while taxes continued to be collected.** Throughout Yugoslavia's disintegration officials imposed emergency taxes on gasoline and electricity. The Argentine default of 2001 did not protect citizens from owing backdated tax debt on their vehicles or properties even with bank accounts frozen. New Orleans officials imposed property taxes on abandoned homes without roofs after Katrina while threatening to seize FEMA trailers through formal notifications. The Greek state linked taxes directly to electricity bills during the Eurozone crisis at its peak to ensure people paid their dues or risked having their power cut.

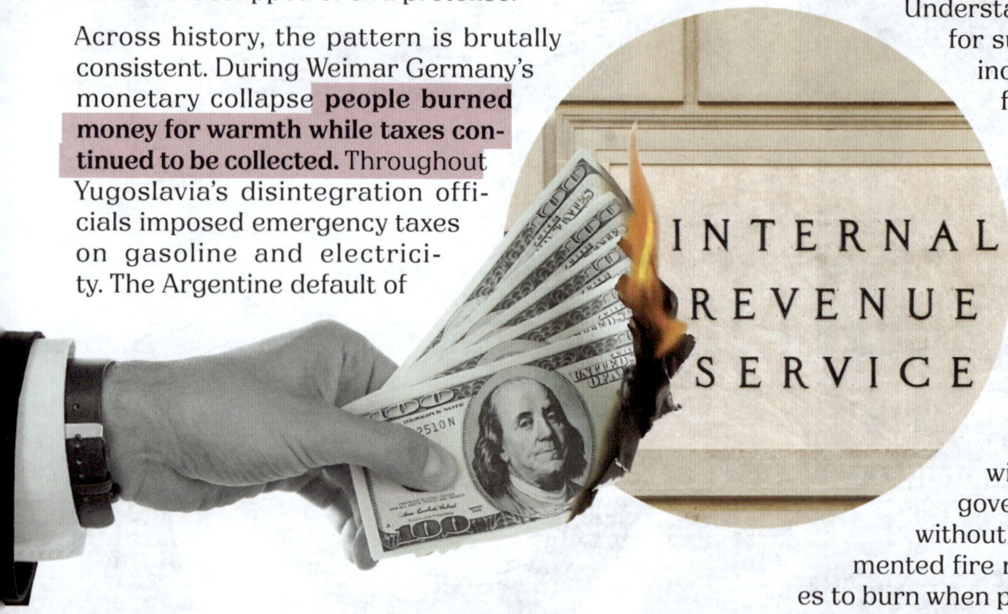

This is not accidental. Government behavior shifts from public service to corporate enforcement when their financial foundations become unstable. They invent new fees. They outsource collections. Noncompliance incurs compound interest penalties along with intimidation tactics. Governments frequently exploit crises to implement levies that they claim are temporary but later make permanent. The government will portray these measures as civic duty and national solidarity but your home and other assets stand as collateral for an unconsented debt.

Assuming chaos eliminates bureaucratic systems represents your greatest risk. It doesn't. Instead, the bureaucracy becomes feral.

Understanding your entire exposure is essential for survival in upcoming situations. Not just income tax. Not just property. A thorough forensic analysis of all potential claims by taxing authorities is essential for identifying what they can use to claim your assets. Local taxes exhibit the highest level of aggression when systems begin to collapse. City and county governments plan to add "public safety" fees to water bills while charging road access fees for rural properties and will bring back rarely used code enforcement laws to justify fines. As California grappled with budget failures in the 2000s local governments introduced "parcel taxes" without needing state approval. Detroit implemented fire readiness surcharges but allowed houses to burn when people failed to pay them.

Minor and annual financial items should not be ignored. A vehicle registration or stormwater fee along with septic tank inspections and livestock permits business licenses signage ordinances professional certifications can become the basis for fines and liens. During crises authorities monetize every possible source of revenue. Bureaucrats under pressure become scavengers.

Ownership of any property deed, business registration, driver's license or tax ID automatically results in indexing. Should your name show up in any searchable database they will make contact.

Your tax preparation must include knowledge of current taxes and how they transform when collapse conditions emerge.

Understand that enforcement systems will move from judicial courts to administrative bodies. Enforcement mechanisms will transition from judicial to administrative means causing reduced due process while increas-

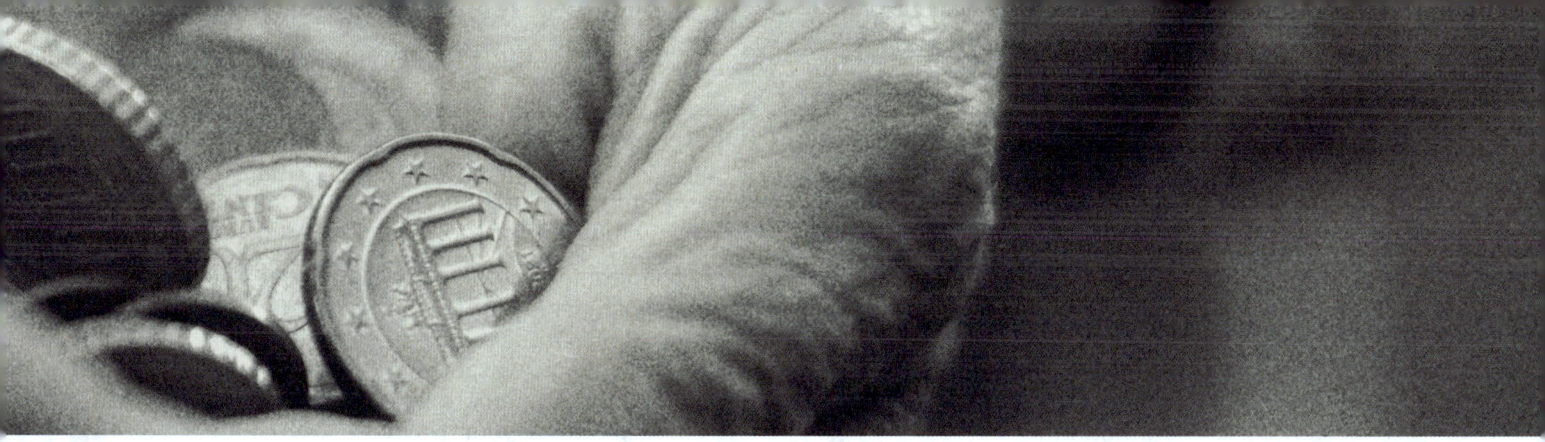

ing presumptive guilt along with decreasing hearings and augmenting summary liens. The continuing digitization processes will persist despite any weakening of state power. Software automates punishment. People no longer need to make decisions about targeting you because systems will automatically flag your file. The initial decline of societies usually starts when middle-class citizens face higher financial burdens. The poor are placated. The rich are shielded. Whenever you become identifiable and possess physical assets, you transform into the final resource the failing system drains its remaining revenue from.

The strategy needs to be implemented before pressure starts to take effect. Identify and create a list of all taxes and fees you pay on a monthly, quarterly, and annual basis. The tax burden includes federal and state obligations as well as every local, municipal, or district-level charge. Look for overlapping jurisdictions. Special tax districts, homeowners associations, water boards, agricultural zones and fire coverage regions have the authority to create independent penalties for their members. Understand their terms and schedules when they assess and the emergency powers they hold.

This is your audit map. Without it, you cannot defend yourself.

Building the audit map completes the first stage then you move on to reduction tasks. Some of that means legal reassessment. Part of the requirement involves making foundational changes to the organization and display of your assets. But all of it begins with knowledge.

Challenging Property Taxes During Devaluation

The property tax tends to be ignored when the economy maintains stability. During a collapse, it becomes a noose. The very properties that once represented your greatest financial security become vulnerable and predetermined targets. The state establishes property values that seldom decrease unless officially disputed. When markets collapse it does not mean that bureaucratic expectations fall as well. In fact, those expectations increase. States are desperate. Cities even more so. Your address functions as a vital ledger entry for their financial needs.

Your property functions as a tax anchor instead of serving as home or investment. The county assessor will keep using previous price valuations unless you raise an objection. Every few years properties receive automatic reassessment in many jurisdictions which results in increased valuations unless you intervene. The option to file individual reassessment petitions exists in nearly every state tax code although it remains hidden and serves as your pressure valve.

In economic freefall, market activity collapses first. Houses stop selling. Listings disappear. Appraisals stall. This is your evidence. Capture images of homes with boarded doors and windows as well as neighborhoods where stores have been robbed and buildings lie in ruins.

You should gather newspaper reports that focus on decreasing real estate trends and notices of bank foreclosures as well as evacuation orders. Record any homes in your area that are listed for sale at prices lower than your property's assessed value.

To request a proper reassessment, you must demonstrate loss of market viability instead of just declaring hardship. It demonstrates loss of market viability. Reference municipal sales data. Quote falling tax revenue trends if available. Demonstrate that your house assessment reflects fictional property value and explain how maintaining current tax rates creates an unfair financial pressure or illegal overassessment.

Timing matters. The optimal filing period for reassessment requests falls at the start of the fiscal year which typically lasts from January to March. Once panic arrives the assessor's office will become unmanageable and could even cease operations. Initial submissions are processed through the system before full collapse logic takes effect. Years of reduced payments become achievable by submitting your forms early.

This is not merely about saving money. It's about retaining ownership. Tax default triggers the start of seizure proceedings. In the collapse, foreclosure accelerates. The government does not sell properties at their full value since agencies pick them up to sell to debt buyers or keep them as government assets. Submitting one form promptly can lower your risk exposure. Bureaucrats remain indifferent to the root causes behind property value depreciation. The primary concern for bureaucrats is whether your paperwork meets all requirements.

Your paperwork should be so comprehensive that officials overlook you because both your file and appeal appear legitimate. That begins with reassessment.

Filing When You Can't Pay

Most people regularly delay their tax responsibilities during normal times. In a collapse, that's fatal. The tax system penalizes missing returns more severely than unpaid taxes. The reason is simple: a late payment is an administrative issue. A missing return signals defiance. Symbolic punishment is given to defiance during periods of economic collapse. When the state faces a crisis of legitimacy, it must enforce punishments on noncompliance to maintain authority.

Your obligation to file taxes remains unchanged regardless of your current employment status or financial situation. Filing taxes, even if you owe nothing, protects you. By filing your taxes your records stay clean while delaying collection and preventing penalties from becoming criminal issues. The IRS together with state tax agencies function through automated systems. Failure to submit your tax return results in automatic system notification. That flag is permanent.

Filing taxes serves as a strategic delay tool that most taxpayers fail to understand. The penalties for filing a tax return when you cannot pay are reduced and frequently subject to negotiation. A taxpayer may apply for hardship status as well as installment plans or payment postponement options. During the initial stages of financial collapse these tools remain operational. A lack of filing results in being completely shut out of the system. Penalties become percentages stacked monthly. Interest compounds. Eventually, you trigger liens, garnishments, or levies.

More importantly, you lose legal ground. Without a filed tax return, judges, auditors, or sympathetic bureaucrats find themselves unable to provide assistance. Judges and auditors generally retain discretion to assist individuals who have filed their paperwork.

The collapse will not eliminate this machinery. It will only accelerate it. The Greek debt crisis led authorities to order civil servants to confiscate bank accounts from individuals who did not file before making contact. Tax officials in Argentina started pre-filing tax declarations for taxpayers using bank data before sending them bills with criminal charges for undeclared income and this system will be implemented here as well.

A functional paperwork system must remain in place to file minimal returns even when operating in a barter or off-grid work environment. Claim all deductions, exemptions, and hardship credits. Backdate income if needed. Report truthfully, but protect yourself. The form is your shield.

The eventual collapse of the agency has no impact. Your protection relies on staying beyond their reach until the agency falls apart. File, even when you can't pay. Becoming a target happens when you choose not to file your documents.

Homestead and Senior Exemptions

Homeowners rarely explore state tax code exemptions during stable economic conditions. People who failed to understand tax code exemptions face total loss during financial collapse. The property tax system remains unresponsive to financial hardships faced by homeowners. The system requires homeowners to pay their property taxes in full by the due date without any exceptions. The property tax system contains hidden protections established in response to past crises which provide safeguards for homeowners today.

The law allows homeowners to benefit from homestead exemptions which lower their property's assessed value used for calculating taxes. Across most states these exemptions decrease the taxable value either by a specific dollar sum or by a percentage rate. According to Texas law the general homestead exemption decreases the taxable value of property by $25,000 when calculating school taxes. People who are over 65 years old and veterans along with disabled persons qualify for further exemptions. Florida provides tax relief for seniors by allowing assessments to stay frozen at current values even when market prices rise.

The key: Submit the application before the deadline closes the opportunity. These exemptions are not automatic. Applications demand various forms as well as proof of age and disability status along with income details or veteran status. Applicants must establish that their home serves as their primary residence. To prove occupancy, some jurisdictions require copies of driver's licenses or utility bills along with signed affidavits.

The majority of states initiate the application process for homestead exemptions during either the start of their calendar year or fiscal year. A few jurisdictions permit late submissions but limit this option to a very brief period. When a collapse occurs, deadlines shrink, and offices stop responding. You should not wait until next year to complete this task because it won't be possible. The tax collector will proceed to issue your bill regardless. The assessor's office responsible for exemption processing might stop returning phone calls.

Your benefits could be higher if you qualify as a senior aged 65 and over, a disabled veteran or as the surviving spouse of a military service member. Property tax rates remain unchanged for seniors who meet the qualifications in both Arkansas and Mississippi. Disabled veterans in Georgia can protect up to $100,000 from their home's assessed value for tax purposes. Proposition 19 in California permits seniors to shift their base tax assessments to new properties when certain conditions are met. But again—paperwork first.

Documentation is everything. Maintain certified copies of approval letters along with filed applications and identification details in printed off-grid format. Store your documents in a fireproof envelope together with your property title and proof of residence. Should your county misplace records you must have evidence showing that you had submitted the required filing. Expect that digital systems will go offline. Automation through notices will replace clerical positions. Only paperwork keeps you legal.

Also beware of urban exemptions disappearing. During times of financial collapse some cities will remove homestead status without making it obvious. While planning its bankruptcy Detroit revoked more than 60,000 exemptions in 2013 and cited resident errors in paperwork as the reason. Once the benefit disappears, you face full payment, and the reassessment will apply retroactively. You will face unexpected tax bills for years when you believed your property was exempt.

Find your assessor's office now if you want to know if your state or county provides exemptions. Search online for the website and download all necessary forms instead of calling. Read the fine print. Certain states provide exemptions exclusively for designated taxing districts which include educational institutions and firefighting services. Others require reapplication every year. Benefits are not available for homes held within a trust or an LLC according to certain regulations. If you fail to meet the legal requirements they set, you become at risk of losing your house.

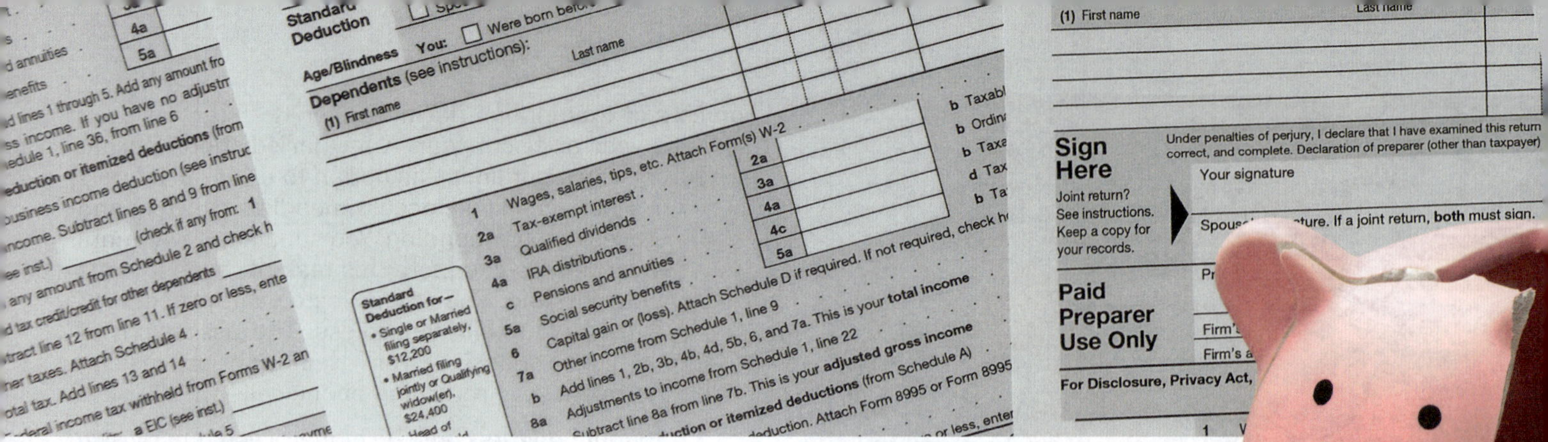

Emergency Tax Schemes

New taxes arrive without warning. The government consistently uses three specific terms to justify new taxes throughout history: temporary measures which are necessary and fair. Labels shift, but intent does not. Under the guise of crisis surcharges and disaster levies alongside "stabilization" measures authorities implement permanent extraction mechanisms. Once passed, they rarely disappear. They become part of the machine.

This is not theory. The fiscal emergency fees that New York introduced in 1975 remain visible on present-day receipts. The temporary registration fee increases California enacted became permanent without ever expiring. The emergency utility surcharges introduced to New Orleans water bills after the hurricane remained permanently in place. The Greek government implemented new electricity taxes which authorized service termination without a hearing for nonpayment.

When systems crack, governments no longer ask. They take. And they do not strike randomly. They target visibility.

People who maintain sizeable account balances or who own publicly titled land or have made recent asset purchases will find their names on official lists. Not immediately. But soon enough.

Defenses need to be established well ahead of any news reports.

Paper-based assets are the most vulnerable. Any institution that manages accounts operates under an enforcement system mechanism. The implementation of a new wealth assessment or emergency levy doesn't start with a letter. The process starts with an account freeze or automatic debit. There is no appeal.

Assets should be restructured in advance. The tracking of physical assets such as silver, gold, tools and tradeable goods proves to be beyond difficult. They are hard to confiscate. They resist digital seizure. Physical wealth assets offer superior security over password-protected vaults and financial institution-controlled storage.

Ownership also matters. Land registered under your personal name will show up on tax records and property assessments. Alternatives exist. A trust or private entity with the right structure enables title holding while protecting your name from public exposure. Certain jurisdictions permit the use of nominee arrangements and trustee shielding. These are not shady loopholes. These mechanisms are legal and beneficial solutions that achieve separation between management functions and public exposure.

Public displays of wealth should be avoided. A flashy car can draw unwanted types of attention. Installing solar systems or making home renovations can result in these changes being marked as taxable improvements. Your neighbors will seek to level the playing field if they observe you possessing more than they do.

The strategy is simple: modesty, discretion, localism. The advised strategy of modesty and discretion is not about moral virtues but about avoiding unwanted scrutiny. The tradesman who maintains both tools and a garden goes unnoticed. A man who owns land and runs off-grid systems with a visible generator could face inspections.

! Never assume you will be warned. Governments create policy on the back foot. Systems to collect new taxes exist before any new tax legislation passes. When required to comply banks, registrars and utility boards take rapid action. You cannot move faster. You can only move first.

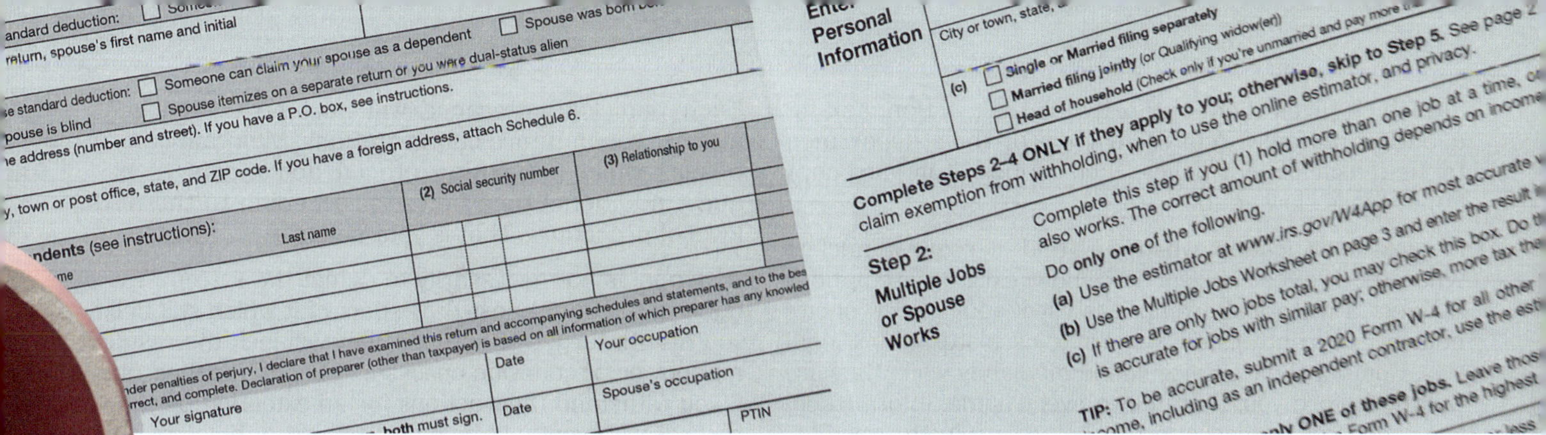

Tax-Advantaged Accounts: Get Out Early

The definition of "tax-advantaged" exists only within a functional system. The benefits of tax-advantaged accounts start posing risks when there is a loss of public trust along with increased regulatory enforcement. The financial mechanisms known as IRAs, 401(k)s, and savings bonds fail to provide protection. They are brightly labeled targets. Your account details including your name and balance alongside your custodian information are fully documented and can be retrieved. They will be accessed with or without your consent whenever they become necessary for the "greater good."

In 2001 Argentina decided to freeze more than $3 billion in pension accounts to ensure "national stability" while in 2013 Cyprus confiscated a portion of insured deposits overnight to fulfill EU obligations. Poland used half of its private pension system to pay down national public deficits. These were not failed states. Governments implemented policies through minimal administrative actions while banks followed these guidelines by their inherent design.

Quiet initiatives emerged in the United States since 2010 under the "retirement security reforms" banner which proposes converting individual retirement accounts into federally managed annuities. The Roosevelt administration mandated the surrender of private gold holdings in 1933 which were then exchanged for paper currency at established rates. No knock. No compensation. Just confiscation.

If you have retirement assets, understand this: they are stored under someone else's control. Should the requirement arise, they will be seized. The only defense is timing.

Withdrawal is not without cost. The IRS imposes a ten percent penalty together with income tax on early distributions made from retirement accounts. The calculations become dramatically different once you face the possibility of complete asset loss. What is ten percent against one hundred? How does the penalty from taxes measure up against the complete loss of assets?

A careful strategy is essential. Start by collaborating with a certified CPA who has expertise in collapse situations and alternative asset configurations. Consider staggered distributions over multiple years. When possible, move assets into Roth accounts, because although they will eventually incur taxes, they operate with post-tax dollars, which might lead to fewer limitations during emergency situations. Move funds into physical assets without establishing a predictable pattern. Never move large sums all at once.

Above all, avoid drawing attention. Avoid making big financial moves in your account unless you plan to fully exit your position. Mass freezes can trap individuals in transition phases between required compliance and potential asset seizure.

You are not trying to escape taxation. You are trying to escape seizure. There is a difference. One is calculated. The other is permanent.

Stalling and Delaying Tax Officials

Even as systems fail, government agents remain. They grow chaotic. They receive conflicting instructions. They report to rotating superiors. Officials receive enforcement quotas while lacking the necessary enforcement power. In this dysfunction lies your advantage.

You are not evading. You are slowing. Legally, politely, and persistently.

Always demand written communication. Tell callers that you require the information to be provided in written form. When they arrive ask them to provide the statute which gives them authority for their action. Ask for a badge number. Request a copy of their departmental field assessment policy. Then request it in hard copy. Paper trails slow action.

Request clarification when you find a request unclear. When the request is clear ask about existing exemptions. Request a historical exemptions list if your review shows none are currently listed. Request to escalate. Submit inquiries. Contact their service line immediately while they are waiting before you. Write down every name. Inform them you need legal counsel approval before moving forward.

Delay is not defeat; it is strategy. Buying time allows their enforcement structure to collapse before they can reach you.

Leverage every edge. Some counties will have conflicting valuation guidelines. Several states will not update their tax codes promptly after emergency declarations. Government entities will either send multiple notices or miss essential documents in their communications. When you understand legal requirements and see they are unmet, you gain extra time.

Do not acknowledge any mistake when enforcement arrives at your property. Avoid giving concessions and providing explanations while abstaining from improvisation. Each panicked utterance will become evidence against you in future confrontations. Maintain composure while presenting official documents to request additional time before proceeding to the next level of procedure. That is your shield.

Your goal is not necessarily to defeat the system. You are fighting to endure past the aspect of it which still believes you are its target. Eventually, they will lack the resources, manpower, or cohesion necessary to continue their pursuit. If you withstand their actions for an extended period your records will eventually be boxed, moved, or deleted.

Tax Amnesty: Watch for the Window

Some municipalities will offer amnesty windows to clear their books. During the last major downturns, cities like Detroit and Oakland allowed delinquent property owners to settle for pennies on the dollar. But they don't advertise these amnesties for long. If you're ready, if you have the paperwork and modest funds set aside, you can wipe away thousands in penalties legally. Be vigilant. Watch public notices. Monitor city council minutes or state department alerts. The offer may come only once.

The Trap of "Relief" Money

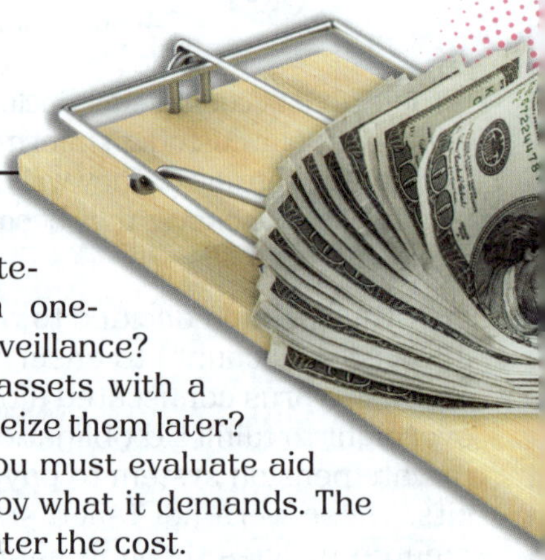

When systems falter, governments rush to preserve order, not liberty, and the bait they offer is often laced with obligation. During the COVID-19 lockdowns, millions of Americans accepted federal relief only to find themselves caught in bureaucratic snares: unexpected tax bills, offset refunds, and garnished assistance. In some states, unemployment aid triggered audits. In others, student loan forgiveness was retroactively taxed. Temporary lifelines became long-term shackles.

This pattern will repeat. In fact, it will worsen. Relief funds offered during systemic collapse are likely to require asset declarations, household income disclosures, and digital registration. By accepting aid, you may be signing away the right to privacy, movement, or exemption. Participation in relief programs often becomes the first step in being flagged for wealth reassessment or "fair contribution" reviews. If you disclose your income to qualify, you are creating a record. If you link an account to receive payments, you are building a trail. That trail will not be used to help you.

The decision is not purely financial. It is strategic. Would you trade a one-time check for future surveillance? Would you register your assets with a state desperate to tax or seize them later? In periods of instability, you must evaluate aid not by what it gives—but by what it demands. The smaller the print, the greater the cost.

In a collapse, no one is watching the watchers. Systems are stretched. Oversight is gone. That makes it the worst time to give anyone new control over your household, your savings, or your digital identity. What looks like assistance may be entrapment.

Take what you need only if you understand the price. And if you take nothing, take nothing proudly, knowing that freedom maintained is often more valuable than support received.

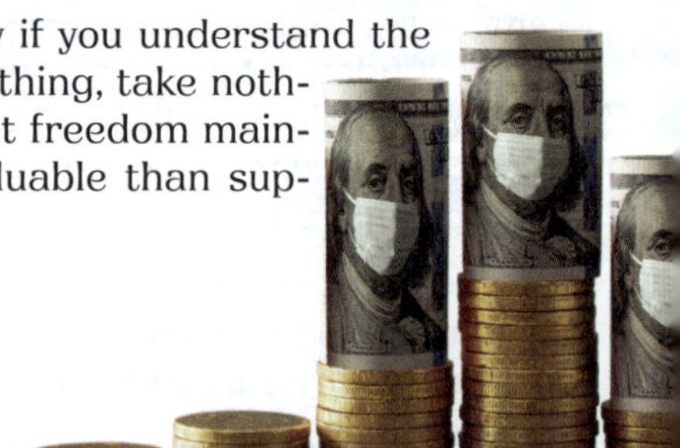

Municipal Discounts That Still Work

Sometimes, the protections that remain are the ones least discussed. Local governments, for all their inefficiency, tend to move slowly—and in that inertia lies opportunity. Many cities and counties maintain discount programs for seniors, disabled residents, veterans, and low-income households on basic services like water, gas, sewer, and trash collection. These programs often survive budget cuts simply because no one thinks to end them, and because their termination requires legislation that no one has time to pass when everything else is falling apart.

These discounts are not widely advertised. They are usually hidden on poorly maintained websites or buried in forms at city utility offices. But they matter. A fifteen or twenty percent reduction in water bills adds up fast when prices surge or subsidies vanish. If your gas bill goes from manageable to impossible, that old enrollment in the utility relief program might be the only thing that keeps heat flowing.

The key is timing. These programs require paperwork, identification, sometimes income verification. In normal times, they're easy. During system strain, they become impossible. Offices close. Clerks disappear. Records get misplaced. If you are already in the system, they will likely keep the discount in place. If you wait too long, the door closes.

Take the time now to research what your city or county offers. Apply as if the collapse were already here. Get confirmation. Get it in writing. Store copies of the approval with your most important documents. Even if the benefits seem small, they represent leverage—a bit more breathing room in a world that offers less of it every day.

Staying Under the Radar

During every economic collapse across Argentina to Albania the individuals who endured the longest were not those who were most vocal or visibly ready. They were the ones no one noticed. The people who showed off their preparedness through new equipment displays or political statements attracted unwanted attention. Taxation, expropriation, theft or arrest becomes a threat when you draw attention during times of economic collapse. When you appear as a valuable resource others will attempt to exploit you.

You must not simply avoid attention. The appearance of holding nothing valuable should be deliberately fostered. That begins with physical presentation. Your home should be plain. Solar panels should remain hidden unless they show signs of aging or damage. Your property should not display visible fortifications unless they appear to be neglected. A car with dents maintains better safety because it doesn't draw attention unlike a shiny one. Your clothing choices and purchases along with your behavior need to demonstrate modesty rather than desperation but should not display excessive wealth.

You need to create the impression of having less wealth when evaluated through official documents. File taxes conservatively. Don't overreport. Utilize trusts, proxies and jurisdictional mechanisms to establish separation between yourself and your assets. Avoid state databases. Whenever you can make your name private from business registrations that the public can access. End all connections with visible companies and properties that add no value.

Your speech matters too. Avoid controversial topics. Avoid making negative comments about public officials in public settings where others can overhear you. Stay away from predicting disasters and from showing off what you have stored. Appearing ordinary and non-striking makes it more probable that you will not attract attention. Talk less. Listen more. Practice becoming background.

Internally, keep your real wealth decentralized and practical: Store practical wealth in items that can be bartered alongside land owned through shell companies heirloom seeds sealed medicine and revenue reported outside official books. Cash loses its value when banks stop functioning. Precious metals have no worth if trading them attracts unwanted attention. Keep essentials hidden in multiple locations. Invest your resources into tools and knowledge while maintaining careful discretion.

The key is this: don't trigger interest. When you see an official carrying a clipboard near your home, it is best if he continues on his way without stopping. During a blackout you want your neighbor to think you're using candles when he sees your lights on. When a thief investigates your house, you want him to get the impression that everything valuable has already been stolen.

"Opportunity is missed by most people because it is dressed in overalls and looks like work."
Thomas Edison

Chapter 14

How to Make Ends-Meet Money from Side Projects Only Available in a Crisis

The Illusion of Stability

For most people, modern life still appears orderly. The stores are open. The lights stay on. Banks operate. Retirees collect their checks. And yet, beneath this thin layer of control, something deeper is shifting. Quietly. Irreversibly. The stability we take for granted is far more fragile than most are willing to admit, especially those who benefit from the illusion. We have raised entire generations on the assumption that systems will hold. That governments will step in. That jobs will always exist. That paper money, backed by nothing, will somehow maintain its worth. But history proves different.

Real stability is not found in headlines, promises, or central banks. It lives in communities, in personal resilience, and in the ability to adapt when the structures we trusted begin to fail. Crises rarely announce themselves clearly. They arrive in fragments. A price that doubles overnight. A medicine that disappears from shelves. A neighbor who quietly loses their job. And then one day, normal doesn't return. That is when people realize the safety net was thinner than it seemed. That is when making ends meet becomes a matter of creativity and resourcefulness. And for many, especially older adults, that is also when forgotten skills become currency.

Why Traditional Jobs Disappear First

When a crisis hits, it is not just the stock market that crashes. It is the structure of employment itself. Entire industries vanish with a single policy shift. Service jobs dry up. Offices close. Supply chains break. Suddenly, millions of people are unemployed, unemployable, or underpaid in a currency that no longer buys what it used to. And this happens fast. In hyperinflationary collapses from Zimbabwe to Weimar Germany, official jobs became irrelevant in a matter of months. In Venezuela, people with college degrees ended up selling soap or bartering eggs on street corners. During the COVID-19 pandemic, labor markets collapsed in real time. Since then, automation and artificial intelligence have only accelerated the disappearance of traditional work.

But not all work disappears. Only the kind that relies on permission, paperwork, or centralized infrastructure. What remains are tasks that fulfill basic needs: food, repair, shelter, caregiving, protection, and trade. These jobs rarely make the headlines, but they are the ones people will pay for, trade for, and defend when everything else breaks down. And the people who perform them do not always look like the workers we are used to.

How Seniors Become Critical in Collapse

In modern culture, aging is often equated with irrelevance. Once retired, people are too often pushed aside, overlooked, or treated as burdens rather than assets. But in a collapsed economy, that view changes dramatically. Seniors become critical. Why? Because many older adults still know critical skills that others never bothered to learn. They remember how to sew, preserve food, fix tools, cook from scraps, or live with less. They have seen hardship before. They have adapted before. And most importantly, they often have the one asset younger people rarely possess—time.

In a world where speed and output no longer define value, people begin to look for wisdom, patience, and trust. A grandfather who knows how to build a chicken coop or repair a gate becomes indispensable. A retired nurse who can mix herbal salves or treat a minor wound becomes the neighborhood healer. In communities where the economy has gone dark, the oldest among us often become the light. More than that, seniors are rooted. They are already there—on porches, in church pews, in apartment lobbies. That presence becomes power in a fractured society. Whether they are watching children, providing security, gathering resources, or simply offering a place to rest and talk, they become the hubs in a world without a center.

The Power of Street-Level Economics

When official systems collapse, a different kind of economy always takes shape. It does not rely on resumes, online platforms, or degrees. It runs on human needs, and the ability to meet them without asking for permission. This is the street-level economy. It is quiet, local, and deeply personal. And it is where real resilience is born. You won't find it in GDP reports. It plays out in backyards, church basements, porches, alleyways, and barter boards. It runs on favors, food, repairs, and trust. In these informal webs, usefulness becomes currency, and your reputation the only resume. This economy already exists, it is just dormant in many places. You can still see it in rural towns, immigrant neighborhoods, and older communities where people trade tomatoes for a tire patch, or help repair a roof instead of hiring a contractor. In a crisis, that informal system becomes the default. It becomes the economy. Those who learn how to move within it, how to offer value, how to adapt their skills to meet local needs, don't just survive. They often thrive. Because they are no longer competing for a shrinking job market. They are offering something that cannot be outsourced or digitized—dependability in an unreliable world.

What You'll Learn in This Guide

This chapter is not about building a business in the traditional sense. It is about building relevance. It is about turning your time, your knowledge, and your presence into real, tradable value in a world where money may lose its meaning. Inside, you will find dozens of practical, low-cost, high-value ideas for earning when the system fails. Whether you are mending clothes, sharpening tools, bartering firewood, or teaching survival skills to younger neighbors, it's all designed to help you find a role in the real economy that emerges when the formal one disappears. Whether you are a senior looking to remain independent, a caregiver trying to prepare for a loved one, or simply someone seeking stability in an unstable future, this knowledge will help you find your place. You do not need a license. You do not need permission. You just need to be useful when others are unsure what to do. Because when the old economy dies, a new one begins. And those who see the shift early will not be left behind. They will lead.

The Real Economy After a Collapse

From Dollars to Barter: What Happens When Cash Dies

When a nation's currency begins to fail, the illusion of wealth vanishes overnight. One week, a loaf of bread costs **$2**. The next, it costs **$20**. Then **$200**. Then it's not available at all. In that moment, money ceases to be a medium of exchange. It becomes a **symbol of broken trust. And people stop asking how much something costs and start asking what they can trade for it.** A Collapse doesn't mean the end of the economy. It means the end of the **formal** one. In its place emerges something older, rawer, and infinitely more human: **the barter economy**. It's not tracked by Wall Street or taxed by the government. It's personal, ground-level, and one-on-one.

In these environments, you'll see a grandmother trading a dozen eggs for sewing repairs. A retired mechanic fixing a neighbor's bicycle in exchange for firewood. A woman making soap from ashes and animal fat, and exchanging it for rice, candles, or antibiotics. These transactions don't appear in the headlines, but they are **what keep people fed, clothed, and alive**. The shift is subtle at first. People still use cash until it loses meaning. Then they switch to foreign currencies, or gold, or cigarettes. But in time, the most valuable currency becomes **trust, reputation, and usefulness**. And those who understand that shift before it's too late find themselves not at the mercy of the next collapse, **but empowered by it**.

Venezuela, Weimar, Argentina, and Ukraine: What History Teaches Us

If you want to see the future, look to the past. In every major economic collapse of the last hundred years, from the German Weimar Republic to 21st-century Venezuela, the pattern is nearly identical: **currency collapse leads to social desperation, which gives rise to alternative economies.**

In 1923, Weimar Germany, inflation reached such absurd levels that people used stacks of banknotes as firewood. A loaf of bread cost billions of marks. The middle class was wiped out. But the baker still baked. The seamstress still mended. And the farmer still bartered potatoes for soap.

In Argentina's repeated financial crises, people learned to live without stable banks. **Neighborhood bartering clubs** (trueque) became more powerful than city councils. Housewives, retirees, and unemployed professionals all found ways to contribute—not through jobs, but through function.

In Venezuela, the collapse didn't come all at once. It arrived gradually. A few items disappeared. Prices rose. Then the power grid failed. Then hospitals ran out of medicine. Then, suddenly, university professors were selling empanadas on street corners. Retirees traded spare eggs for insulin.

Even in war-torn Ukraine, during the worst of the fighting, local barter flourished. Gasoline, bread, cigarettes, bandages—everything had a new value, based not on central pricing, but need and scarcity. And in nearly every case, it wasn't just the strong who thrived. It was **the adaptable, the connected, and often, the older gen-**

erations, who remembered how to stretch, mend, cook, repurpose, and trade.

These historical patterns are not abstract warnings. They offer a clear preview of how daily life changes when formal systems no longer function. The table below outlines how key aspects of the economy evolve quietly but completely as collapse takes hold.

Category	Before Collapse	After Collapse
Food	Bought with money	Traded for goods or services
Work	Based on job title	Based on usefulness and trust
Currency	Dollar, bank accounts	Barter, foreign bills, fuel, medicine, favors
Reputation	Tied to résumé or degrees	Tied to local trust and consistency
Payment	Regular salary	Food, repairs, shared protection, mutual credit
Shopping	Stores, online orders	Porches, word of mouth, neighborhood networks

Why Seniors Hold Hidden Value in Collapse Scenarios

In a world obsessed with speed and productivity, seniors are often pushed to the side. But in a collapse, **the skill sets that once seemed outdated become vital once again.** Many seniors already live on a budget, know how to cook from scratch, repair clothing, tend a garden, and manage with less.

That isn't a disadvantage—it's a survival blueprint.

More than that, seniors often know the local terrain. They've lived in their neighborhoods for decades. They know who to trust, who can fix a generator, who has chickens, and who has spare tools. These relationships form the invisible backbone of what will replace the crumbling economy: **hyper-local trust networks.**

In previous collapses, seniors took on roles that younger people never imagined: neighborhood watchers, barter organizers, skill teachers, ad-hoc nurses, food foragers, fix-it specialists, and even spiritual anchors. They became stabilizers in a time of chaos—not through force, but through consistency.

They may not lift sandbags or run food trucks. But they can watch a block, bake bread, offer first aid, or share vital knowledge. And in a collapse economy, that kind of value commands respect—and resources.

The Rise of the Grey Market, Black Market, and Porch Economy

The **grey market** involves the legal trade of goods or services, just outside regulation. The **black market** deals in illegal or controlled goods—fuel, medicine, weapons. But perhaps the most overlooked is the **porch economy**: the quiet, informal exchange of services, goods, and favors at the neighborhood level.

This is where resilience grows. A woman sells herbal salves from her front steps. A widower fixes tools in exchange for eggs. A retired teacher tutors kids in exchange for candles. A grandmother babysits while others forage or scavenge. None of this is taxed. None of it is licensed. But it works.

Porches become storefronts. Yards become gardens. Backrooms become barter stations. And word of mouth becomes the only marketing channel that matters. Those who understand how to navigate this informal economy—how to offer what's needed, when it's needed, to the people who need it—will never go hungry.

Trust, Skills, Trade Replace Resumes, and Paychecks

In a functioning economy, people ask: "Where do you work?" In a collapse economy, they ask: "What can you do?" Degrees don't matter. Titles don't matter. What matters is whether you can fix a shoe, purify water, sharpen a blade, cook from scrap, or build a fence.

Your reputation precedes you. Payment might come as a sack of potatoes or a favor returned weeks later. Still, the value is real. Trust becomes the foundation of everything as it should be. Without institutions, people rely on each other. Someone known for being honest, reliable, and helpful becomes a central figure in the community. Not because they applied for a position, but because they were present when others vanished.

Micro-Skills That Become Survival Services

In stable times, we call them "odd jobs." Small tasks. Low-value chores. But in a collapsed economy, these micro-skills turn into lifelines. They become practical services people will pay for, trade for, or protect fiercely. They are not full-time jobs. You don't need a license, a degree, or startup money. What you need is know-how, resourcefulness, and calm under pressure.

Water & Fuel Helpers: Liquid Gold in the Barter Economy

When utilities fail, water and fuel become more valuable than cash. That's when a new role appears: the **local water-and-fuel problem solver**. You don't need to be an engineer. Setting up rain barrels, showing how to filter water with gravel and charcoal, or teaching solar pasteurization makes you invaluable. Fuel storage, safe siphoning, and even maintaining old hand pumps can all become **barterable skills**. In past collapses, like Argentina and Venezuela, the person who could keep a well running had real power.

Sewing & Repair: The Return of the Needle Economy

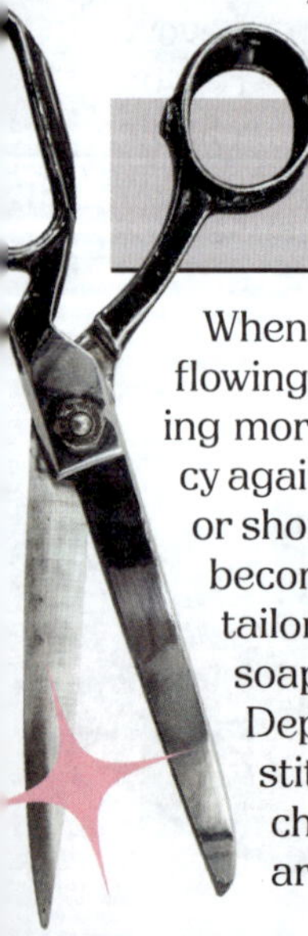

When clothing stores shut down and imports stop flowing, people don't start buying less. They start fixing more. And that means needlework becomes currency again. The ability to mend a sock, patch a ripped shirt, or shorten a child's pants is no longer a quaint hobby. It becomes a way to feed yourself. In Weimar Germany, tailors and seamstresses often received food, coal, or soap in exchange for small repairs. During the Great Depression, families traded farm goods for a few stitches. You don't need an industrial sewing machine. A basic kit, some thread, and steady hands are enough. What matters more is visibility.

Imagine this: a senior sets out a folding chair on the front porch and hangs a sign that reads "**Mending: Socks, Shirts, Buttons. Fair Trade Welcome.**" Soon, neighbors begin dropping by. One brings sugar, another canned beans. A small pile of repairs grows beside the rocker. A block-wide barter system starts to take shape around a single, overlooked skill. Over time, that porch becomes a hub. People talk while they wait. News circulates. Needs are shared. And the person doing the mending, once labeled as "retired," becomes central to community survival.

Soap, Balm & Cleaners: Sanitation as a Power Play

Food and fuel dominate the early days of any crisis. But after a few weeks, hygiene takes the spotlight. Without access to soap, illness spreads fast. When hospitals are overwhelmed and medicine is rare, those who can provide **basic cleaning products**—or teach others how—become frontline defenders of public health. Soap made from wood ash and fat. Skin salves from beeswax and herbs. Laundry powder from lye and boiled water. These aren't myths. They're historical staples—used from Appalachia to Eastern Europe in times of need. During the Bosnian war and in 1990s Russia, soap was traded like currency. In modern Venezuela, **a single bar could equal a week's worth of protein**. Those who can make these products, even in small batches, hold a powerful role. And those who teach others to do the same? Even more so. Because in a barter economy, **knowledge is a value multiplier**.

The Bigger Picture: These Skills Aren't Optional—They're Strategic

What unites all these micro-skills is their immediacy. They don't require advanced tools, electricity, or an internet connection. All they demand is time, technique, and the **willingness to get your hands dirty**. In a society coming apart at the seams, the person who can fix a boot,

patch a leak, clean water, or calm a sick child is **essential**. And more often than not, that person is someone others had overlooked—a retired builder, a quiet neighbor, an old homemaker with a lifetime of workarounds stored in their hands. As the world shrinks from global to local, the definition of value changes. It shifts away from money and moves toward **usefulness, consistency, and presence**. You need skill. You need steadiness. And you need the courage to raise your hand and say, "I can help."

Cooking, Baking & Stretching as Trade

In a world where groceries vanish and money fails, the one who can feed becomes the one who leads.

In every collapse, food becomes currency, comfort, and community glue. When shelves are empty and supply chains break, those who can cook from scraps, bake from flour and water, or stretch meals into something that feeds many are no longer "just homemakers"—they're providers of something essential. This chapter explores how basic food skills become powerful tools for survival, barter, and leadership when the formal economy falls apart.

Bread and Basics: Scarcity's Most Powerful Commodity

When society breaks down, the most elemental foods become the most sought after. And bread—humble, ancient, simple—is always at the center of that transformation. In the absence of industrial baking, anyone who can produce bread becomes a local institution. You don't need yeast or a fancy oven. Bannock, fry bread, or flatbreads made from flour, salt, and water can be cooked over an open flame or in a cast iron pan. Even in wartime or under curfews, bread has always found its way to the fire.

During the hyperinflation of the Weimar Republic in the 1920s, a single loaf of bread often cost more than a wheelbarrow full of paper currency. Yet families who could bake at home—especially those who stretched dough with potatoes or wild herbs—were able to barter their loaves for services, firewood, or protection. A warm loaf became an offering, a trade, and a peace treaty all at once.

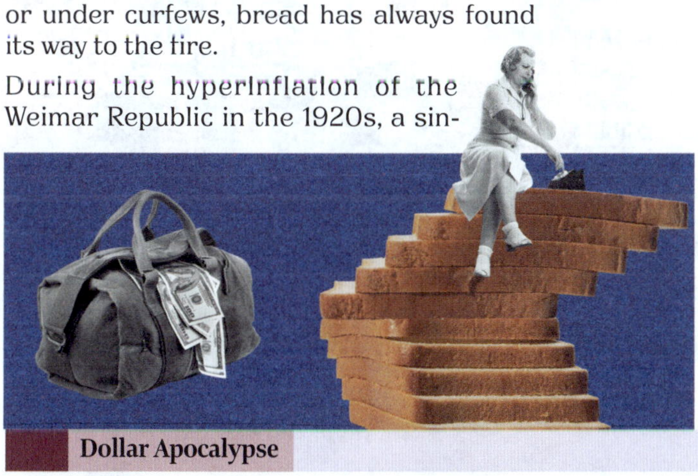

A senior with a stovetop and a sack of flour can become the bakery of the block. A few loaves a week, sold or traded informally, could cover everything from babysitting to help with repairs.

Stretching Food into Shared Survival

The ability to make something from almost nothing—a pot of soup from lentils, bones, water, and a few scraps—is much like a superpower. When meat vanishes from shelves, people with soup pots keep their communities well-fed. A large pot simmering on a stove or rocket stove can serve a dozen hungry neighbors.

Soup kitchens don't require a building. A home cook who sets up a front porch station or leaves a pot at the gate becomes a neighborhood hero. In Ukraine during wartime, and again in Venezuela, people traded soup for diapers, candles, and even antibiotics. The same was true in Great Depression-era America. A warm bowl bought goodwill, respect, and loyalty. It reminded people that they were still human—even when the world outside had forgotten.

Fermentation: Turning Spoils into Treasure

Few skills are more underestimated than fermentation—yet few are as valuable in a world without refrigeration. Sauerkraut, kimchi, pickled eggs, and fermented garlic not only stretch your food supply, they become long-lasting, highly tradable items that support gut health and immunity when sanitation collapses.

In every major collapse, fermented goods held high barter value. They last for months, often require no electricity, and are made from vegetables others might throw away. That half-cabbage? A few jars of kraut. The eggs nearing expiration? Pickle and preserve. A gallon of brine with a few cloves of garlic becomes a nutritional powerhouse—and a potential trade good for pain relievers, firewood, or even security. And here's the hidden benefit: these foods are familiar, comforting, and packed with flavor when most other things taste bland. In a world of rice and beans, fermented goods don't just feed—they excite the appetite, boost morale, and preserve health. That's why they hold value far beyond calories.

Foraging and Forgotten Foods

When the grocery store disappears, nature reemerges as the one true supplier. And those who recognize this, who know how to identify edible greens, harvest acorns for flour, or pick purslane from sidewalk cracks, suddenly become wise figures in the new economy.

Wild food is not a fallback or second choice. It is survival-grade nutrition that grows without packaging, without fuel, and without cost. In collapse scenarios, seniors who grew up with gardens or rural skills often hold the keys to a hidden pantry. Dandelion greens provide vitamin A. Acorns, once leached properly, become flour. Purslane offers omega-3s in abundance. None of these require refrigeration, electricity, or supply chains. In Germany during the 1920s, recipe pamphlets that taught people how to cook with wild roots or stretch turnips into full meals were literally used as currency. They were exchanged for food, medicine, and work. That legacy still holds value today. Those who can gather from what others ignore will always have something to offer. You do not need to own a farm or hoard packaged rations to matter in a crisis. If you can bake from scraps, stretch a pot of soup, ferment a cabbage, or teach someone how to recognize edible weeds in their yard, you have already become a provider, a guide, and a resource.

Collapse does not need chefs. It needs cooks. It needs people who can make do, make more, and create peace over a shared bowl. That person can be you.

Wild Plant	Key Nutrients	Practical Uses	Field Notes
Dandelion	Vitamin A, C, iron	Leaves for salad or cooking	Roots can be roasted as a coffee substitute
Plantain	Calcium, antibacterial	Used as poultice or boiled as greens	Soothes insect bites and cuts
Purslane	Omega 3, vitamin E	Eaten raw or sautéed like spinach	Common between sidewalk cracks
Wild Garlic	Sulfur, antimicrobial	Used in broths, teas, or as seasoning	Leaves are edible and flavorful
Acorns	Carbs, fiber	Ground into flour for flatbreads	Must be soaked to remove bitterness
Nettle	Iron, calcium, protein	Cooked in soups, teas, or dried for powder	Cooking removes the sting

Repair, Restore, and Scavenge

In a broken economy, the fixer feeds himself first. When replacement is no longer an option, when new shoes or a stove part are no longer available or affordable, the real value shifts to those who can keep old things going. The ability to repair what others once discarded becomes not just useful, but essential. History shows this clearly. In Venezuela, elderly scavengers kept entire neighborhoods running. In Weimar Germany, knife sharpeners and shoe patchers traded their skills for food. The winner is not the certified technician with a title. It's the neighbor who knows how to sharpen a blade, glue a broken table leg, or patch a tire with scraps. Tool sharpening becomes a regular need. When your family has two kitchen knives and one garden shear, keeping them sharp is survival. With a basic sharpening kit and a few hours of practice, anyone can start a barter trade. One knife for two eggs. A kitchen set for a bag of rice. You don't need a storefront.

Just a chair, a table, and the discipline to show up.

The same is true for shoe and fabric repair. A torn sole or strap is not a small problem when you walk miles every day. With shoes costing a month's income or more, a rough patch job is better than no patch. Backpacks, coats, tents, and tarps gain new life in the hands of someone who can stitch or tape. Even old furniture becomes worth saving. A broken stool or cracked table can still serve its purpose with a little glue, a nail, or a clamp. You don't need to be a master carpenter. You just need a steady hand and a few tools. The more things fall apart, the more your ability to hold them together becomes its own form of wealth. Scavenging, too, becomes a quiet economy of its own. In a world where new production slows or stops, the value shifts to what already exists. A senior who walks the block collecting small cast-offs—wire, screws, scraps of cloth, broken handles—can supply neighbors with the very things they need. What others ignore becomes barter material. A drawer knob can be traded to someone fixing furniture. Bones and ash can become ingredients in soap, or be traded for food.

This is the beginning of the porch economy. A table out front. A sign that says "Repairs." And the consistency to show up each day. Over time, neighbors begin to stop by. A jammed drawer. A dull blade. A cracked frame. You fix it. They bring something in return. Eventually, you're not just a helper. You're a hub. A part of the new economic fabric that holds people together when everything else unravels.

Here's a practical snapshot of what everyday repair and salvage work might look like in a collapse economy:

Item or Task	Action Taken	Barter Value Example	Why It Matters
Dull kitchen knives	Sharpened with a manual stone	2 eggs or a handful of dry beans	Essential for food prep
Torn backpack strap	Sewn or patched with scrap material	1 loaf of bread	Restores carrying capacity
Cracked wooden stool	Glued and clamped overnight	Small sack of rice or candles	Makes furniture functional again
Old cloth or towels	Cut into rags or bandages	Traded in bundles	Useful for cleaning, wound care, and more
Broken umbrella frame	Reinforced with wire or twine	Jar of pickled vegetables	Repurposed for rain or shade protection
Ash and bones	Saved and processed	Swapped for soap or used in trade	Inputs for sanitation or fertilizer

In a collapsing world, usefulness replaces speed or strength. If you can repair, restore, and see value where others see waste, you won't just survive. You'll be part of what rebuilds the next economy.

One trade, one tool, one gesture at a time.

The Barter Broker System

When money dies, you become the market.

In the early stages of a collapse, when inflation spirals and wages stagnate, people still cling to paper money. But eventually, the illusion fades away. A currency that once bought food now buys nothing. **And a new type of worker emerges—not a producer, not a hoarder, but a connector. When no one trusts the market anymore, they turn to someone they do trust.**

That's where the barter broker rises.

You don't need strength, mobility, or youth to fill this role. You need attention to detail, memory, consistency, and trust. The barter broker doesn't run a store. They run a **system**. One that lives in a notebook, on a chalkboard nailed to a porch, or whispered between neighbors. When Sarah says she has extra candles but needs rice, and Tom has rice but no soap, the broker doesn't just record it—they facilitate the match. You become the middle—fair, essential, and increasingly powerful.

History confirms this role, again and again. In old Germany, **grandmothers tracked street-level trades better than any official ledger.** In Venezuela, homebound seniors coordinated neighborhood swaps from kitchen windows. In rural Ukraine during the Soviet collapse, a widow's front steps became a makeshift trading post. These weren't merchants—they were **stabilizers**. People brought their needs to them, because they trusted their judgment more than any institution still standing.

To begin, all it takes is a place. A front porch. A windowsill. A notebook. Write down who has what, who needs what. Keep it updated. Build a reputation for honesty and discretion. You don't take a cut—you take responsibility. You verify fairness, suggest trades, help resolve disputes. Over time, people will come to you not just for matches, but for guidance.

You can go further. Host informal trade days on your property. No tables, no prices—just neighbors bringing what they have and quietly scanning what others offer. You set the tone: calm, respectful, quiet. These events—what some call "silent markets"—have been documented from Zimbabwe to Bosnia, and they work. They cost nothing, but return something priceless: a sense of order. And here's what few realize until it's too late: **you don't need goods to be valuable in a barter economy.** You need **information**. When deals fall through, people still come to you. When disputes arise, they ask for your word. And in a system with no courts, no receipts, no prices—you become the judge, the mediator, and the pulse of the market.

Don't underestimate this role. You may never leave your porch. You may never lift a load heavier than a pen. But you'll be at the center of something irreplaceable. The new economy will not be built in banks or apps. It will be rebuilt in kitchens, garages, basements—and on porches like yours. In that world, it's not the one with the most that survives. It's the one everyone turns to when they don't know what a fair trade looks like anymore. That's not weakness. That's leverage. And that's power.

The Watcher Is the Wall

Security in collapse is all about awareness. A senior by the window. A grandmother on the porch. A neighbor who remembers which family stores extra medicine. These aren't enforcers. But over time, their attention becomes a soft kind of authority. Alongside this kind of watching, another form of value rises: **emotional labor**. The person who can listen without interrupting. Who offers a quiet story when panic sets in. Who knows how to soothe a child, patch a scraped knee, or let someone cry without trying to fix it.

In barter economies, even calm becomes currency. Someone known as reliable, grounded, and quietly present earns more than food. They earn trust. They are fed, protected, remembered. Because when chaos is loud, a steady voice is louder still. **Memory becomes a map.** Elders who remember hard winters, who know how to grieve without collapsing, who can recite a poem or a prayer by candlelight, hold something rare: continuity. In times of fracture, they become walking anchors. **They hold the thread to the past.**

The Salvage & Dumpster Economy

Trash will becomes treasure—again.

In the early stages of a societal collapse, most people still cling to old habits. They step over broken objects, throw out scraps, and dismiss damaged goods as worthless. But as the crisis deepens—and as resources become scarce or wildly expensive—**value returns to the discarded**. Suddenly, the things we once tossed aside become trade goods, repair materials, or building blocks for survival.

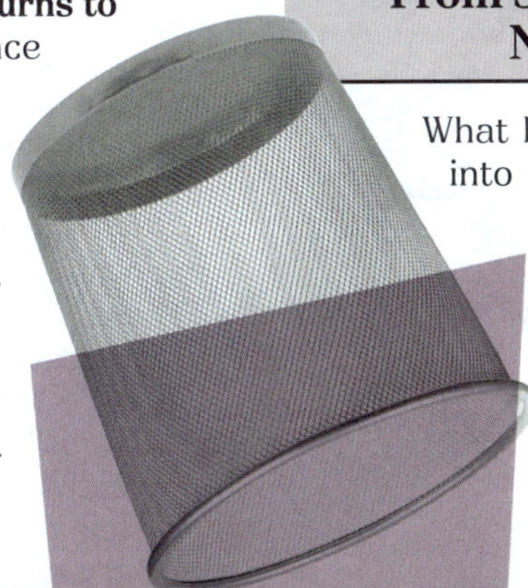

This is the birth of what historians and economists call the **salvage economy**—an informal but thriving system where everything has a second (or third) life. Children collect coal dust from the streets to heat water. Bones, rags, and empty containers are traded for soap, soup, or fuel. Wworn-out tires became sandals, and bottle caps became roofing nails.

The Art of the Daily Loop

For those with even modest mobility, creating a **daily collection route** can become both a source of income and an essential community function. Whether it's a stroll around a few blocks, a short loop through an alleyway, or even just sorting materials others leave behind, a senior can quietly amass resources no one else thought to save. Ash from burned wood can be used to make soap. Bones can be ground for fertilizer or bartered with craftsmen. Scraps of cloth become cleaning rags, patch kits, or fire starters. Bits of wire, tin, and steel go to blacksmiths, barterers, or DIY fixers. Every loop is a quiet act of value creation.

And this doesn't have to be clandestine. Quite the opposite. The more visible the effort, the more likely neighbors are to contribute, offer tips, or donate what they were about to discard. That old broken chair? You might fix it and barter it for bread. That rusted pan? It's worth something to a metalworker. As time passes and desperation grows, your salvaged stash becomes your **street-level currency**.

From Scrap to System: Building the Neighborhood Swap Table

What begins as private collection often evolves into shared exchange. One of the most effective ways to build trust and generate trade is by hosting a simple Swap Table in your garage, front yard, or porch. Lay out items like scrap wood, used containers, wire, or old tools. Invite neighbors to take what they need and leave what they can spare. These micro-markets do more than share goods. **They build relationships.** They quietly signal to the community that **something useful is still possible here**.

This is a grassroots economy, a mutual safety net. One day you leave a coil of twine. Two days later, you return and find a spare part that stops a leak. This is the rhythm of survival in community form. Over time, people notice. The blacksmith knows you bring metal. The seamstress counts on your cloth scraps. The family down the road knows you have jars, corks, nails, buttons. You become a silent broker of utility. In the old world, scavenging looked like poverty. In the new one, it looks like foresight. And those who learn to see treasure in the bent nail, the cracked dish, or the torn tarp do more than endure. **They help rebuild.** When the system falls, the dump becomes the market. And the salvager becomes its merchant.

High-Demand Niche Services

If you have knowledge, you have power.

In a functioning economy, expertise often gets buried under layers of certification and bureaucracy. If you lack a license, a diploma, or an official title, your abilities may be dismissed. But when systems collapse, paperwork no longer matters. Results do. And in that void, people who truly know how to do something quickly become essential. In nearly every neighborhood, there are hidden wells of practical survival knowledge. Seniors who remember how to make poultices. Tinkerers who can rig up solar panels from spare parts. Quiet neighbors who have quietly been studying how to secure a home. When modern comforts vanish, these niche abilities move from the margins to the center. What was once seen as a quirky hobby becomes a tool of survival and trade.

Street Medicine and Underground Healing

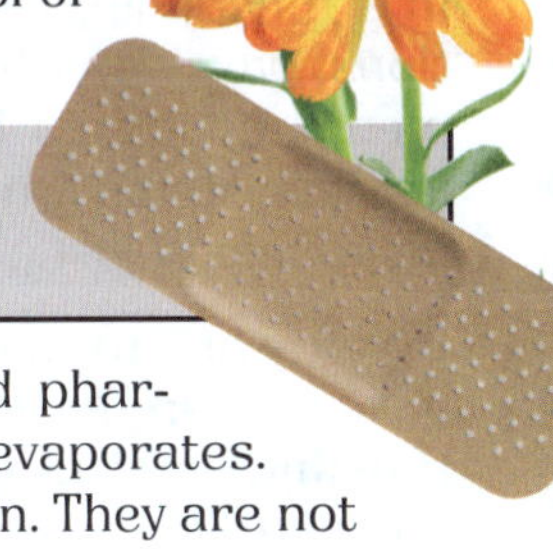

When hospitals shut their doors and pharmacies run dry, basic health care evaporates. This is when community healers step in. They are not doctors, but they know how to treat wounds, use herbs, and make simple yet effective remedies from scratch. You do not need formal training to clean a cut or ease a fever. Calendula petals soaked in oil become the base for salves that fight infection. Yarrow, a common roadside plant, helps stop bleeding. Honey, especially raw, works as a powerful antibacterial and never spoils. These are field-tested tools from generations past. What makes this knowledge even more powerful is its ability to spread. A short lesson on compresses or herbal teas might earn you a basket of food, a warm jacket, or a favor you can call in later.

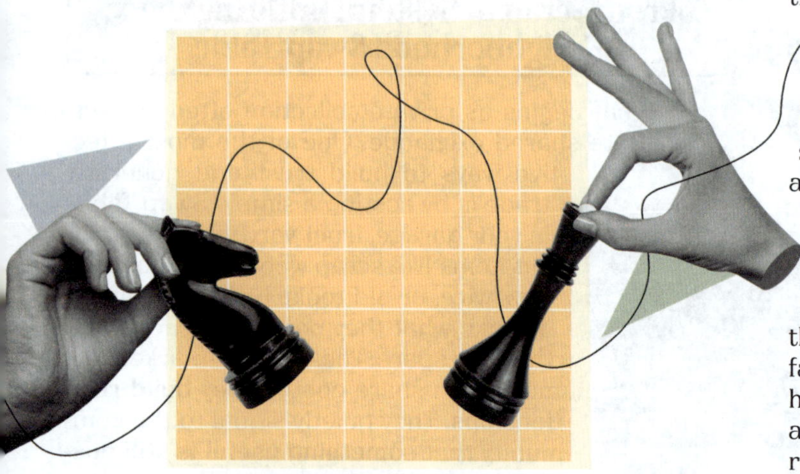

Security Consulting Without the Guns

In high-risk environments, not everyone needs firepower—but everyone needs strategy. Knowing how to secure a home with simple materials, how to create delay-based defenses, or how to visually "devalue" a property can prevent a break-in before it ever happens.

Some of the most powerful defensive tools are psychological: thick curtains that block sightlines, broken glass scattered under windowsills, decoy noise-makers on door handles, or repositioned furniture that limits access paths. These tricks don't require weapons—just creativity and planning. That's where **a local security-minded neighbor becomes a guide**.

Even a short walk-through consultation can shift how someone sees their space: "This window needs bracing. That fence needs blocking. Stash valuables that don't look like valuables."

In the absence of police or alarm systems, , and the people who can provide it—especially calmly and confidently—earn loyalty, reputation, and barter.

Off-Grid Tech: The Value of "Tinkerers"

When electricity fails, people panic. But if you have even a basic understanding of off-grid systems, you become the person others look to. You do not need to be an engineer. If you have ever repaired a hand pump, set up a small solar panel, or created a rainwater catchment system, you are already ahead. **Even simple advice matters.** Show someone how to store water so it does not grow algae. Teach them how to siphon gas safely or maintain a car battery when the grid is do wn. These pieces of information can be traded for food, tools, or community credit. In many collapsed towns, tech-minded neighbors became the new utility providers. Not because they had fancy equipment, but because they had the know-how. Helping someone light a lantern or recharge a battery can earn you more than money—it builds a reputation. You become someone people remember when the lights go out.

Building the Underground Toolkit

All of these roles—healer, protector, technician—form what could be called an underground toolkit. A quiet but powerful set of skills that holds communities together when official structures fail. You do not need to be strong or wealthy. You need to be observant. You need to solve problems using what is available. And above all, you need to be willing to act.

If you can patch a wound, secure a window, fix a water system, or help others do the same, then you are not waiting for rescue. You are part of the rescue. In that space, you gain more than survival—you gain influence and trust. When institutions fail, people stop looking to distant leaders. They start looking next door. Be the one they look to.

Collapse-Proof Principles for Earning

The world may shift—but value always remains.

In a functioning economy, income flows through institutions: paychecks from companies, benefits from governments, contracts from systems built to last. But when those systems crack—or vanish entirely—money doesn't disappear. It just changes hands.

If you want to earn when everything else breaks, you have to stop thinking in terms of employment and start thinking in terms of value. Not the abstract kind printed on paper—but the kind someone would trade food or fuel for when they're desperate, tired, or scared. The kind of value that makes someone say, "I know who can help."

The Rule of Real Value: Trade What People Need

In a collapse economy, money doesn't matter until it buys something real. And what's considered valuable compresses fast into the essentials—what keeps people warm, safe, fed, and sane. You can call this the **Rule of 3**: if your service can provide one of the following—**food, safety, or relief**—then it will always be tradeable.

Food isn't just cooking, it's food stretching, foraging, fermenting, baking. Safety isn't just guards or weapons, but locks, barriers, lighting, and strategic presence. Relief can be as simple as fixing a broken item, cleaning a wound, watching a child, or listening when no one else will. These things feel small—but in crisis, they're gold. If you can provide one of them with consistency, you don't need a job. You've already earned your seat at the table.

Reputation becomes your resume. In times of scarcity, people don't ask for business cards—they ask, "Can you vouch for them?" Being known as someone who shows up, who finishes what they start, and who keeps their word becomes more valuable than any past title or job description. And that kind of reputation is built not with slogans, but with reliability. Don't just offer your labor. Offer your dependability. Be early. Be steady. Be visible. In a world of chaos, **you become order.**

The other timeless rule? **Favors compound**. In the modern world, we treat favors like inconveniences. But in a barter economy, every small kindness is a seed. Watch a neighbor's kids today, and you might get bread next week—or protection next month. Share your soap or bandages when someone is down, and that same person may be the one who shares fuel when the grid fails. **Do favors now, survive later.** In collapse, the economy doesn't start with cash. It starts with character.

Lastly, and most importantly: **never believe that being "old" or "limited" makes you useless**. In truth, it's often the quiet, the steady, the overlooked who survive longest. If you can teach, you're valuable. If you can notice, listen, warn, share, or connect people, you are part of the economy. Even when you can't lift a crate or walk a mile—you can still lift a burden from someone's mind. You can still hold the line. That is value. That is power. And that is how you earn when the world forgets how.

From Invisible to Indispensable

The crisis may erase systems—but it reveals character.

In a world built on speed, youth, and digital flash, it's easy for older generations to feel like they've faded into the background. Retirement, automation, shrinking communities—all of it sends one message: step aside. But when collapse comes—whether slow like inflation or sudden like blackout—**that message flips**. Because in the real economy, when the lights go out and the food stops coming, people don't look to influencers or start-ups. They look to **wisdom, stability, and someone who knows what to do when the power's gone.**

That someone is you.

So, start now. Practice your trade. Sharpen your skills. Organize your tools. Learn one more thing this week than you knew last week. Set a chair on your porch. Put a sign out if you have to: "I fix things. I sew. I listen." Because when the storm rolls in, the grid goes down, or prices spike through the roof—**you won't be the one asking for help. You'll be the one others come to.**

And when they do? You won't just survive. **You'll thrive—boldly, practically, and right where you are.**

In the chapter above, we've walked through an entire **parallel economy**—a way of living and earning that doesn't rely on digital paychecks, corporate ladders, or fragile logistics chains. It's the economy of **the porch, the firepit, the neighborhood chalkboard**. It's built with scraps, kept alive by stories, and traded with trust. And in that world, **seniors are no longer invisible—they're essential**.

You don't need to outrun youth. You don't need to lift more or move faster. You just need to be *steady*. Be visible. Be the one who sews, who watches, who teaches, who knows how to turn dandelions into dinner and soap into savings. In a post-collapse world, that isn't charity. That's currency.

The next economy will be built on people who know how to show up with something real.

"The time to repair the roof is when the sun is shining."
John F. Kennedy

Chapter 15

The Only 4 Things You Need to Add to Your Property to Produce Everything You Need to Survive

When an economic collapse hits, the system won't save you. You won't have time to build infrastructure or be able to source equipment.

The time to set up your own survival system is now.

This chapter covers the four essential categories that, when handled correctly, will allow you to generate everything you need to survive:

1. **Water**
2. **Food**
3. **Power**
4. **Income**

Each one is achievable with basic resources, some elbow grease, and smart planning.

Water Independence

Municipal water systems will not be reliable during a crisis, especially if there's a blackout. Your solution must be low-tech, sustainable, and discreet.

Rainwater Collection System

If your property isn't collecting rainwater, you're missing one of the simplest, cheapest, and most reliable water sources available.

A basic collection system can be installed with minimal tools and materials, yet it can supply hundreds of gallons per week even in a modest climate. Start by installing gutters on at least one structure—preferably the one with the largest roof surface. A standard 1,000 square foot roof will yield over 600 gallons of water per inch of rainfall. That means even a light rain can refill your water system, especially if you expand collection across sheds, garages, or animal shelters. Use metal or heavy-duty vinyl gutters, and angle them toward a downspout connected to a diverter or filtered inlet.

The water should feed directly into food-grade barrels—these can be purchased new or sourced locally from agricultural or food processing facilities, as long as they were never used for chemicals. Each barrel holds 50 to 60 gallons, and multiple barrels can be linked using overflow hoses or PVC interconnects to scale your storage. For larger setups, IBC totes (275 gallons) are a viable alternative, especially if concealed behind fencing or shrubs.

Install a first-flush diverter at the downspout. This simple device captures the first 10–15 gallons of each rain—contaminated with roof debris, bird droppings, and dust—before clean water is allowed into your system. After that, screen filters should be installed at the barrel inlets to prevent mosquito breeding and debris buildup. Fine mesh stainless or plastic screens work, but should be cleaned regularly. In colder climates, consider removable filters or flex hosing you can disconnect before freezing temperatures.

Discretion is key. In a collapse scenario, water becomes gold. Bright blue barrels or massive IBCs sitting out in the open will attract unwanted attention. Paint barrels in matte green, brown, or grey tones. Use lattice, stacked firewood, or scrap fencing to break visual lines from the road. A rainwater collection system should blend in—not broadcast that you're sitting on 300+ gallons of clean water.

Always elevate your barrels on stable cinder blocks or pressure-treated wood platforms. This gives you gravity pressure for use without a pump. A simple spigot or hose bib can be installed at the base. If elevation isn't possible, a manual siphon pump can still extract water easily.

Collected water is ideal for irrigation and sanitation, but with proper filtration it can be made potable. Ceramic gravity filters (like Berkey or Alexapure), iodine tablets, or bleach drops can all make rainwater ready to drink. For long-term purification, build a biosand filter with gravel, activated charcoal, and sand layers.

Even in dry regions, collecting water from every roof surface on your property adds up. If rainfall is rare, consider condensation traps, tarp funnels, or solar stills as auxiliary systems. Keep in mind—water security doesn't come from size, it comes from consistency and concealment. A humble, well-built, system that no one sees will outlast the flashy or gimmicky setups every time.

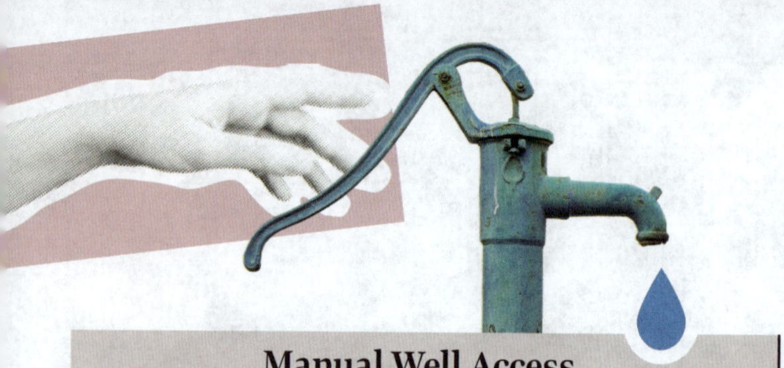

Manual Well Access

Rainwater is a great start, but it depends on your weather and region. For true water independence, you need direct access to the water beneath your feet.

Shallow wells—often less than 25 feet deep—can be hand-dug or bored manually on most rural properties. With a simple post-hole auger and a hand pump, you can tap into an aquifer or seep layer and start drawing usable water with no electricity required. It's not glamorous, but it works. And for under $100, you can buy everything you need.

Manual well kits are available online and at some farm supply stores. A hand auger—essentially a giant corkscrew with a T-handle—can dig down through loose soil or clay until you reach the water table. Depending on your local geology, that could be 10 to 30 feet. If you're in sand, silt, or soft loam, this process is straightforward. Rocky ground or dense clay may require additional tools, like a digging bar or homemade slurry bore setup. In any case, avoid trying to dig in winter or when the ground is saturated.

Once the hole is deep enough, insert a well pipe—usually 1¼ to 2 inches in diameter—with a drive point or sand screen at the base to keep silt out. Fill the space around the pipe with coarse gravel or washed rock to stabilize it, then seal the upper section with bentonite or cement to prevent contamination. At the surface, mount your hand pump. Cast iron pitcher pumps are reliable, and PVC options are lightweight and corrosion-resistant. Either will allow you to draw up groundwater without electricity, pressure, or grid infrastructure.

This kind of system is extremely quiet, requires no fuel or batteries, and works indefinitely if properly maintained. Keep spare seals and lubricating oil on hand. In freezing climates, insulate the exposed pipe and drain the pump head in winter.

For deeper wells beyond 30 feet, consider a deep-well suction pump with a two-pipe setup, or a "well bucket" system—essentially a weighted tube lowered into the shaft and pulled back up with a rope and pulley. It's slow, but it can pull water from 100+ feet down with zero power.

The key with manual wells is location and discretion. You want the well positioned away from septic systems, livestock runoff, or chemical sheds—but also out of sight from the road or neighbors. A hidden water source is a strategic asset when everything else fails. And unlike rainwater, it works in every season.

Storage and Purification

Once you've secured your water sources, the next priority is storing and purifying it safely—because even clean-looking water can carry pathogens or chemical residues that'll take you down faster than starvation.

Start by setting up dedicated containers for both potable (drinkable) and non-potable (gray) water. Use food-grade plastics (HDPE marked with a "2"), glass, or stainless steel. Label everything clearly. You don't want to guess under pressure.

Store drinking water in tightly sealed jugs, barrels, or stackable tanks kept in cool, dark locations—like a basement, crawl space, or insulated shed. Avoid direct sunlight and heat exposure, which break down plastics and encourage bacterial growth. If you're not treating water ahead of time, rotate it every six months. Treated water (with bleach or purification chemicals) can be stored longer, but it's still wise to inspect periodically for sediment or clouding.

Your purification toolkit should include multiple layers of redundancy. Unscented household bleach (sodium hypochlorite 5–6%) works in a pinch—8 drops per gallon for clear water, double that for cloudy. Stir and wait 30 minutes. Iodine tablets work similarly, though they leave a taste and are not ideal for long-term use. A ceramic gravity filter system, like a Berkey or Doulton, provides reliable long-term filtration and can handle hundreds of gallons before needing a replacement element. Keep backup filters and gaskets on hand.

Activated charcoal can reduce odors, chlorine, and chemical contaminants. You can buy it or make your own by charring hardwood and grinding it to powder. For grid-down scenarios, learn to build a biosand filter: gravel and coarse sand layered above fine sand and charcoal, housed in a 5-gallon bucket or barrel. With proper flow and settling time, this filter can purify dozens of gallons per day.

For desert or drought areas, solar stills offer another option. Dig a pit, place a container in the center, cover the hole with clear plastic sheeting weighted in the middle with a small rock, and wait. Sunlight evaporates moisture from the soil, which condenses on the plastic and drips into the container. It's slow—but in a survival pinch, it works.

Smart people will have multiple purification options, both manual and chemical. Don't rely on just one.

Food Production and Preservation

You need calories, nutrients, and redundancy. Grocery stores will not be there.

Garden Setup

Food production must happen on your land, with methods you control.

Start by building raised beds. They offer better drainage, reduce soil compaction, and give you more control over nutrient levels and pest exposure. Raised beds also warm up earlier in the season and stay productive longer into fall, giving you more yield per square foot. Use untreated lumber, stone, or concrete blocks to build them, and line the base with hardware cloth to block burrowing pests like moles and ground squirrels.

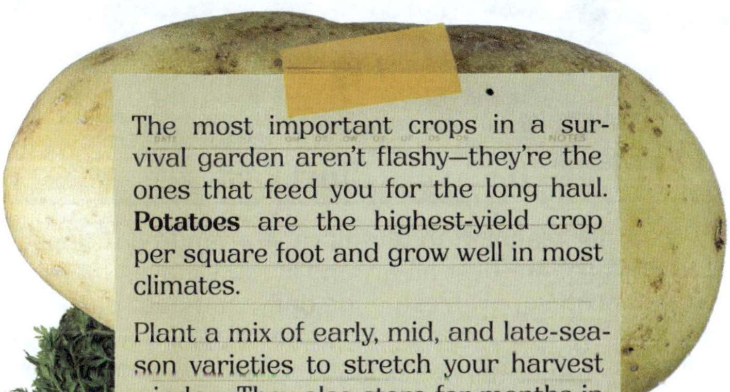

The most important crops in a survival garden aren't flashy—they're the ones that feed you for the long haul. **Potatoes** are the highest-yield crop per square foot and grow well in most climates.

Plant a mix of early, mid, and late-season varieties to stretch your harvest window. They also store for months in a root cellar, basement, or cool shaded box. **Carrots, onions, and parsley root** round out your staple root vegetables. All three can be stored in damp sand, canned, or dehydrated, and they tolerate a range of soil types with minimal inputs.

For diversity and micronutrients, include **tomatoes, green beans, and cucumbers**. These crops produce heavily in summer and are ideal for water bath or pressure canning. Beans can also be left to mature and dried for winter protein.

Plant them in rotation with fast-growing greens like kale or mustard to maximize your space. If you have trellises or fencing, grow vining crops vertically to preserve ground area and improve airflow—reducing mildew and rot risk.

Use mulch (straw, wood chips, or shredded leaves) to retain moisture, suppress weeds, and build up your top layer over time. Compost kitchen waste, leaves, and grass clippings to create your own fertilizer. Avoid synthetic fertilizers whenever possible—they're expensive, short-lived, and will be scarce when the shelves go bare. Instead, learn to make compost teas or use diluted urine and wood ash for minerals.

Raised beds don't just improve your garden yield—they reduce bending and back strain, which makes daily work more manageable, especially if age or past injuries are slowing you down.

In a collapse every ounce of energy you can spare increases your survival chances.

A well-planned garden can keep you fed year-round, especially if paired with a preservation system. Grow what fills your belly, stores through winter, and trades well with others. Leave ornamental plants to the neighbors. Your soil is now your supply chain.

Mushroom Cultivation

Mushrooms are one of the most overlooked survival foods. They're compact, nutrient-dense, easy to grow with minimal input, and can be produced even in shaded or indoor areas where traditional crops will struggle. Once established, they produce for months or even years with little assistance from you.

The easiest approach is to **inoculate hardwood logs**—oak, maple, or beech work best—with mushroom spores. Oyster and shiitake mushrooms are the most beginner-friendly varieties and thrive in most temperate climates. Drill holes into fresh cut logs, insert spawn plugs, seal with wax, and stack the logs in a shaded, moist area. Within 6–12 months, depending on the variety, mushrooms will begin to fruit naturally after rains or misting.

For faster production or urban setups, use straw bags or buckets filled with pasteurized straw and grain spawn. These can be kept in basements, closets, sheds, or shaded outdoor corners. After inoculation, most bags fruit within 2–4 weeks and can be harvested repeatedly over several flushes. Even spent straw or substrate can be composted or used as livestock bedding.

Spores and spawn are inexpensive and shelf-stable if refrigerated. Order from reputable sellers while the grid is still up. Store syringes or dried grain spawn in vacuum-sealed bags to extend viability.

For storage, mushrooms can be **dehydrated, canned, or pickled**. Dehydration is easiest—use a solar dehydrator or electric model until brittle, then seal in Mylar with oxygen absorbers for years of shelf life. They rehydrate easily in soups, stews, or boiled grains. Some mushrooms, like lion's mane or reishi, also offer medicinal benefits—boosting immunity and cognition.

Unlike most protein sources, mushrooms require no feed, no pasture, and no noise. In a long-term collapse, that makes them an asset you can't afford to ignore. Quiet protein is survival gold.

Canning and Preservation

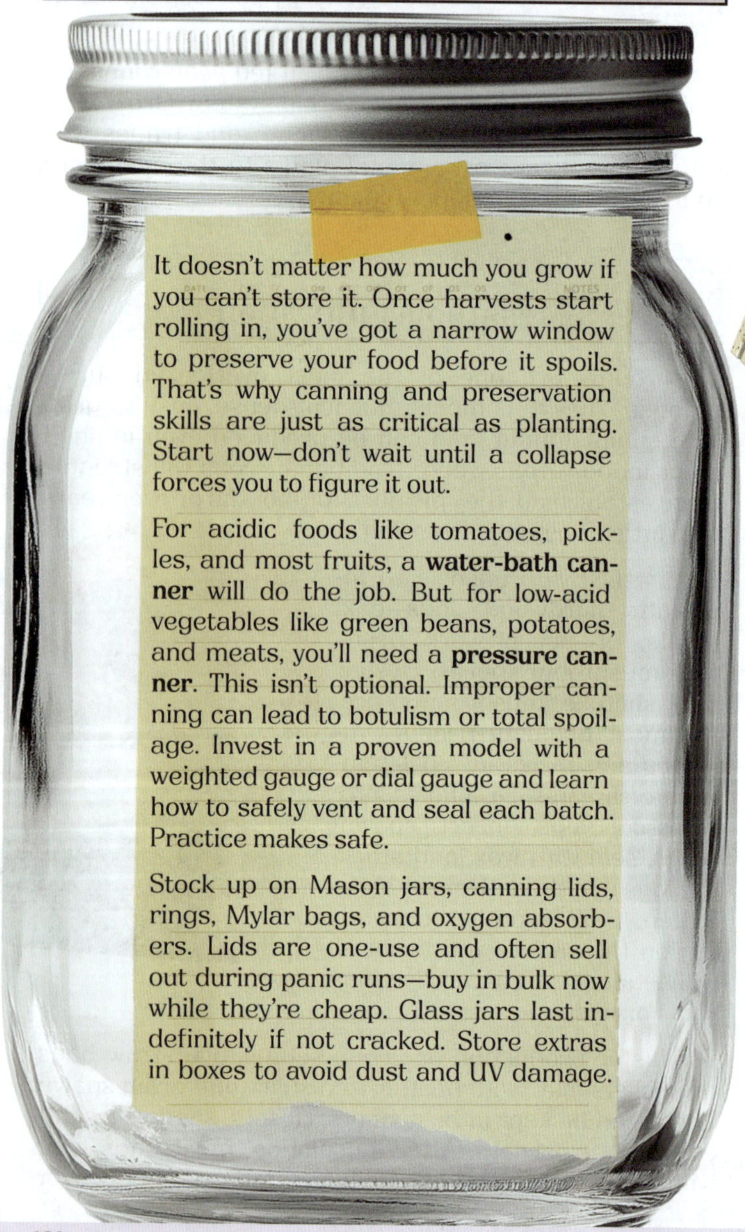

It doesn't matter how much you grow if you can't store it. Once harvests start rolling in, you've got a narrow window to preserve your food before it spoils. That's why canning and preservation skills are just as critical as planting. Start now—don't wait until a collapse forces you to figure it out.

For acidic foods like tomatoes, pickles, and most fruits, a **water-bath canner** will do the job. But for low-acid vegetables like green beans, potatoes, and meats, you'll need a **pressure canner**. This isn't optional. Improper canning can lead to botulism or total spoilage. Invest in a proven model with a weighted gauge or dial gauge and learn how to safely vent and seal each batch. Practice makes safe.

Stock up on Mason jars, canning lids, rings, Mylar bags, and oxygen absorbers. Lids are one-use and often sell out during panic runs—buy in bulk now while they're cheap. Glass jars last indefinitely if not cracked. Store extras in boxes to avoid dust and UV damage.

Dehydration is another essential method. Use a solar dehydrator, electric model, or even a low oven to preserve herbs, fruits, and vegetables. Once dried, food should be vacuum-sealed or stored in Mylar with oxygen absorbers to stay shelf-stable for years. Label every container clearly with contents and date.

If your property allows, build or retrofit a root cellar. A simple underground or partially buried structure lined with shelving and ventilated correctly can keep carrots, onions, potatoes, cabbage, and apples fresh for months without electricity. The temperature should stay around 32–40°F with 85–95% humidity. Even a buried barrel or insulated trash can set in shaded ground can extend your food's shelf life through winter.

Home preservation isn't a luxury skill—it's what separates true survivors from scavengers. If you're growing food and not preserving it, you're wasting time, calories, and security. Get your systems in place before you ever pull the first tomato off the vine.

Backyard Chickens

If you're not planning to go full vegetarian in a collapse, chickens are your best all-around livestock investment. A few hens can supply fresh eggs daily, and dual-purpose breeds offer both eggs and meat with minimal land requirements. But like everything in a survival context, it's not just about owning chickens—it's about doing it **quietly, efficiently, and sustainably.**

Start with a **small, low-profile coop** and run, ideally tucked behind an outbuilding, thick hedgerow, or privacy fence. Avoid bright color paint jobs or prefab units that scream "livestock." Your goal is function over form—keep the structure weatherproof, shaded, and invisible from the road. By the way, chickens can tolerate very cold temperatures, but they cannot sweat so unless you provide shade and some other ways in which they can cool themselves they will overheat. Chickens make noise, especially when laying or alarmed, so distance and dampening matter. Straw bales, fencing, or corrugated metal can help muffle sound if placed strategically around the coop's perimeter.

Build the frame from scrap lumber or pallets if needed.

The floor should be raised a foot off the ground to prevent rot and deter predators. Inside, line the bottom with straw or wood shavings for insulation and odor control. Use welded wire fencing, not cheap chicken wire—it's too flimsy and won't stop raccoons, dogs, or coyotes. Install latches on all doors and secure the coop at dusk every night without fail.

Choose hardy breeds that can tolerate temperature swings, forage well, and don't require high-performance commercial feed. Examples include Rhode Island Reds, Australorps, Barred Rocks, and Buff Orpingtons. These birds are reliable layers and will put on decent meat weight when necessary.

Feeding chickens without feed store dependency is very possible if you start early. Supplement with **kitchen scraps, garden surplus, and sprouted grains** like wheat or lentils (cheap, shelf-stable, and sprout in days). Grow black soldier fly larvae or mealworms if you want to boost protein using food waste. Let birds free-range when it's safe—they'll eat bugs, grass, and weeds while turning the soil.

A small flock of five hens and one rooster can sustain a family on eggs and give you the ability to breed future generations. Just remember—**roosters are loud**. If stealth is your priority, stick to hens only and buy fertile eggs from a local source later when needed.

In a long-term grid-down scenario, chickens are the rare combination of protein, barter value, and compost production (from droppings) all in one. Just don't broadcast it. A coop that's too visible is a grocery store waiting to get looted.

Other Relatively Low-Maintenance Livestock

Chickens are a solid starting point, but if you've got a little more space and want to expand your protein options without the daily grind of hunting or managing cattle, look at sheep and pigs. Both animals have a long track record as low-maintenance, high-output homestead stock—and unlike cattle, they don't advertise themselves to every neighbor within a mile.

Sheep are the most underappreciated. A small flock of hair sheep (like Katahdin or St. Croix) requires no shearing, tolerate a range of weather conditions, and thrives on rough pasture, weeds, and brush. They're docile, quiet, and can be rotated through a small field or paddock system using temporary fencing. One ram and three ewes can produce enough lambs per year to provide meat for a family and even surplus for trade. With proper culling, you can sustain a flock indefinitely.

Sheep manure is a powerful cold fertilizer—safe to use directly on gardens without composting—and they can serve double duty as living brush clearers. Compared to goats, they're far less destructive and easier to fence. And unlike cows, they don't require massive water or hay storage to overwinter.

Pigs are another strong addition, especially if raised in pairs or small groups. They grow fast, convert kitchen scraps and garden waste into high-quality meat, and can forage for roots, acorns, and insects if given a small, wooded area or pasture. Breeds like American Guinea Hogs, Idaho Pasture Pigs, or Kunekunes are smaller, more docile, and ideal for small homesteads. They don't need grain to survive if you plan well, and a single well-fed sow can produce dozens of pounds of pork annually.

Contrary to popular belief, pigs don't have to stink. With good bedding (deep straw, woodchips, or leaves) and rotation every few weeks, odor is minimal. Build your pen strong and secure—pigs are smart, strong, and love to dig—but if you're firm from the start, they'll settle into a manageable rhythm. Feed them kitchen scraps, garden culls, soaked grains, and wild forage. Supplement with whey, dairy waste, or eggs when possible.

Most importantly, pigs and sheep are quiet. They don't crow at dawn, they don't bugle like bulls, and they don't attract attention. You can raise meat, fat, and bone tools in silence, while the unprepared go hungry.

Hunting and trapping, even fishing, can be unpredictable. Cattle are land-hungry and feed-dependent. If you want meat that works with you—not against you—these animals deserve a place in your long-term survival plan.

Power Independence

The grid is fragile. Power outages will be common in an economic collapse and may last weeks or months. You need your own system—quiet, hidden, and sustainable.

Solar Panels

When it comes to sustainable off-grid energy, **solar is your best long-term option**—silent, self-recharging, and scalable. But too many preppers make the mistake of slapping panels across their rooftops like a billboard announcing they're the only house in the neighbourhood with power. In a collapse, that's suicidal.

Mount your panels at ground level, on the back side of your property, or behind a structure that faces away from public view. This allows you to hide the array with fencing, shrubs, or stacked firewood while still keeping access to full sun. Ground-mount kits are widely available and don't require roofing skills or permanent installation. Most use a simple steel frame and adjustable brackets that can be anchored into soil or concrete pads. The added benefit: you can adjust tilt seasonally for better efficiency.

Portable or folding panels are a smart addition for flexibility and concealment. You can bring them out during daylight and store them at night or during periods of unrest. Keep them in shaded sheds or inside the home when not in use. Paired with a solar generator or battery bank, these smaller systems can charge phones, run radios, or power lights without exposing your entire energy supply.

Standard fixed panels should be 12v or 24v rated for easy pairing with deep-cycle batteries. Don't waste your time or money on novelty "survival" panels that can't charge more than a flashlight. Go with real output: 100W panels minimum, linked in series for your bank.

Camouflage matters. Paint the frames in matte green or brown, use netting or trellis structures nearby, or tuck the array behind a woodshed or lean-to. Just know: **anything you do to hide them will reduce output**. That's the trade-off. Make the system big enough that a 20–30% reduction from shade or angling still gets you the wattage you need.

Solar power isn't infinite—and it requires maintenance. Clean the panels regularly. Check your connections and charge controller monthly. And remember: they're not just powering devices—they're keeping you alive. Keep them hidden, quiet, and working while the world around you goes dark.

Generators for Backup

Solar should be your first line of power—but when clouds roll in or batteries fail, a generator becomes your emergency backup. That said, **generators are noisy, fuel-hungry, and dangerous if not handled with discretion**. If you choose to run one, it better be the right kind.

Go diesel, not gasoline. Diesel engines are more efficient, more durable, and safer to store long-term. But more importantly, **older diesel models with low compression ratios** and mechanical injection can run on alternative fuels—used motor oil, filtered cooking grease, or homemade biodiesel—without frying the engine. You want a unit that predates modern direct injection (DI) systems. Avoid anything that requires computer-controlled sensors or high-pressure rails. Those clog or fail fast when the world's falling apart.

Noise discipline is critical. Most stock generators roar at 65–85 decibels—loud enough to draw every neighbor, looter, or government patrol for miles. **Build a soundproof box** using plywood, rockwool insulation, and exterior-grade sealant. Leave ventilation gaps and include a fire-rated exhaust channel. Better yet, you could install **a motorcycle or lawn tractor muffler** on the exhaust to cut the volume in half without reducing function.

Never run the generator inside your home or garage—carbon monoxide will kill you quietly. Instead, bury a heavy-duty power cord through conduit or snake it through a crawlspace so the generator runs at a distance while your electronics stay powered indoors.

Fuel is your next bottleneck. **Store diesel offsite** if you can, preferably in buried drums or sealed containers hidden under scrap piles or in locked sheds. Keep stabilizer in your main supply to prevent spoilage, and rotate it annually. Store a few hand-pump siphons and long funnels—you won't find them when you need them.

Use your generator in **short, strategic bursts**—not for constant power. Charge your battery bank, run your freezer long enough to refreeze the ice packs, and shut it down. The less you use it, the longer it lasts, and the less anyone knows you have it.

In a world where energy is power, noise is a liability. If you're going to run a generator, do it like a ghost.

Battery Bank & Inverters

Solar is useless without storage. Without a battery system to hold your power, all that sunlight disappears the moment the sky clouds over. Build a battery bank using **deep-cycle AGM** or **LiFePO4** batteries—both designed to discharge slowly and recharge repeatedly without damage. AGMs are durable, maintenance-free, and handle cold well. LiFePO4s are lighter, charge faster, and last longer, but cost more upfront. Either will work if you plan ahead and buy quality.

Connect your bank to a **charge controller** to prevent overcharging. MPPT controllers are more efficient and worth the extra money if your system gets variable sunlight. From there, run your power through a **pure sine wave inverter** to convert the 12V or 24V DC into standard 120V AC—strong enough for your lights, fridge, radio, or tools. Don't skimp on the inverter. Cheap modified sine wave models can ruin appliances and cause motors to overheat.

Every connection should run **through fuses, breakers, and surge protectors** to prevent fire, short circuits, or system burnout. Your setup should be clean, labeled, and accessible—you don't want to be tracing wires with a flashlight in the middle of the night during a storm.

Batteries aren't just for solar. **A generator can—and should—be used to charge your bank when sunlight is low or power demand spikes.** Rather than wasting fuel running devices directly, plug a smart deep-cycle battery charger into your generator's AC outlet. This setup turns your generator into a fast, controlled charging station. You run it for a few hours, top off the battery bank, and then shut it down—leaving you with quiet stored power for the rest of the day. It reduces noise, fuel usage, and your profile. Always run your generator with surge protection in place, and choose a charger that matches your battery type and voltage.

Store your batteries in a ventilated, dry, rodent-proof enclosure. Monitor them monthly, especially in cold seasons. Keep extra cabling, terminal lugs, and a multimeter on hand—you will be your own repair tech when the grid is gone.

A battery bank is a quiet and reliable power reserve. Used right, it turns unpredictable sun and loud engines into steady, quiet electricity on your terms. Done right, it'll keep your essentials running.

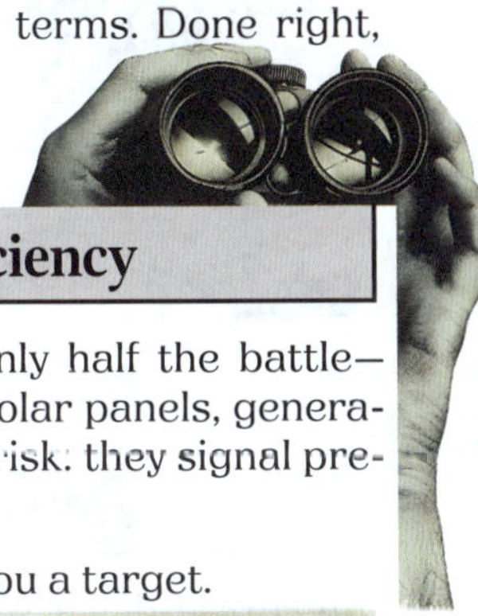

Camouflage and Efficiency

In a collapse, having electricity is only half the battle—keeping it hidden is just as critical. Solar panels, generators, and battery systems all carry a risk: they signal preparedness to the unprepared.

And in desperate times, that makes you a target.

Camouflaging your setup matters. But every layer of concealment comes with a tradeoff. **Camo netting, fencing, or strategic shading will reduce your solar panel output**—sometimes by 20% or more depending on time of day and angle. That's a real hit to your system, especially in winter or overcast conditions. Weigh this carefully. If you're in a rural area with low visibility, you may prioritize production. But in neighborhoods or open terrain, stealth becomes survival. One smart approach is to leave systems fully exposed during safe periods, then cover or break them down quickly when threats rise. Folding or portable panels give you that flexibility.

Generators should be soundproofed and disguised, with mufflers, insulated boxes, and ideally set back from your main living area. Keep fuel and spare parts stored offsite or in locked sheds—never next to the unit itself. Your battery bank can be hidden almost anywhere: under floorboards, in an attic, inside a disguised cabinet or storage box. Make it look boring. No lights, no buzzing, no obvious wiring.

When managing limited energy, **prioritize charging deep-cycle batteries over running appliances directly**. That stored power gives you options later—without the risk. LED lighting, emergency radios, water pumps, phone chargers, and small refrigeration systems can all run off a properly designed battery bank. Powering these from storage keeps your setup quiet, invisible, and under control.

Trade & Production Space

Even if you produce what you need, you'll eventually need to barter.

Micro-Trade Hub Setup

In a grid-down scenario, your tools and skills become currency. A small, well-organized **micro-trade hub**—even just a corner of your shed, porch, or garage—can turn your property into a lifeline for your neighbors or a barter center for your local community.

Choose a spot that's **dry, secure, and easy to close off quickly**. Keep the setup low-profile and blend it with the rest of your homestead. From the outside, it should look like a workbench, not a storefront. Inside, every tool and supply should have its place. Organization builds trust and shows competence, which matters when someone's trading their last supplies for your service.

Your hub doesn't need to be high-tech—just useful. Focus on tools that don't require power or can be run off your battery bank. The core skills to offer should solve basic survival problems or restore broken gear.

Suggested skills and services:

- **Knife sharpening** – A whetstone, file, and strop can keep neighbors' tools useful and food prep possible.
- **Radio repair** – If you know how to solder or swap parts, you'll be essential once comms go dark.
- **Clothing mending** – Needles, strong thread, and heavy-duty fabric patches go a long way.
- **Canning station** – Help others preserve their surplus, and they'll keep coming back.
- **Soap-making** – Basic lye soap is simple to make and always in demand.
- **Cordage** – Twine, paracord, or hand-twisted fiber can repair gear or tie down tarps.
- **Leather patching** – Old belts, boots, and gear don't need replacing—just smart repair.
- **Shoe repair, hinge fixes, resewn straps** – even basic, improvised work can be worth a meal when no one else has the tools or time.

Keep a small chalkboard or notepad labeled **"Willing to Trade Services."** Store high-value, lightweight barter items in labeled bins: salt, matches, lighters, thread, sewing needles, hygiene products, heirloom seeds, and spare batteries.

Most important of all—keep your trade space quiet and respectful. This is where you build alliances, spread influence, and reinforce your place in the community. Those who can fix, build, or preserve become essential for others, and thus they are safe.

Barter Stockpile

When a currency collapses, value doesn't disappear—it just shifts. Those who prepare a **barter stockpile** now will have leverage later. Your goal isn't to hoard fancy gear—it's to gather compact, high-demand goods that are cheap today but priceless tomorrow.

Focus on **items that don't expire quickly, serve a real purpose, and fit in a pocket or jar**. These are the first things to disappear from shelves when panic sets in, and they'll trade faster than gold in a long-term crisis.

Store everything in bins by category. Vacuum-seal if needed. Label clearly and rotate anything perishable every year. For discretion, stash backup supplies in off-site caches—buried, hidden, or stored with trusted contacts.

Track your trades. Build trust slowly. Start small. A few matches today might earn you a favor tomorrow.

These four systems give you control of your survival. You'll eat, drink, generate power, and hold value while others panic. Keep them hidden. Build them quietly. Improve them constantly.

Start collecting:

- **Salt** – Essential for preserving food, curing meat, and nutrition.
- **Sugar** – Calories, fermentation, and morale.
- **Soap** – Bar soap and small bottles of liquid soap or shampoo; hygiene becomes luxury fast.
- **White vinegar** – Cleaning, pickling, disinfecting, and wound washing.
- **Matches and lighters** – Small, valuable, and always needed.
- **Coffee and tea** – Highly tradable for morale and stimulant value.
- **Heirloom seeds** – Stored in sealed containers with labels and instructions.
- **Thread and needles** – Durable clothing repair tools will be in constant demand.
- **Over-the-counter meds** – Painkillers, cold medicine, antacids, antibiotic creams. Blister packs preferred.

"You are your own first responder."
Tim Kennedy

Chapter 16

How to Protect Your Property, Home, and Assets When Crime Skyrockets and Law Enforcement Is Stretched Beyond Their Limits

When the rule of law disappears, your gate, your habits, and your reputation become law. And whether you're on a farm, a cabin, a suburban cul-de-sac or an edge-of-town lot, the rules of collapse are the same: the more you prepare now, the less you'll panic later.

You're the Sheriff Now

In stable times, home security is something you buy at a store. A smart camera, a reinforced lock, maybe a motion detector or a dog. You count on emergency services to fill in the rest. But when the economy buckles, when fuel is scarce and sirens stop coming, the illusion of protection shatters. Police might be an hour away, if they come at all. The court system is overwhelmed, the jail is full, and the man breaking through your fence isn't afraid of a fine. In that world, **your property becomes your post**, and whether you like it or not, you become **the sheriff of your land**.

It's not a movie. It's not a fantasy. It's the historic reality of every community that's lived through true economic collapse. From rural Argentina during the early 2000s, to inner cities during long blackouts, to entire towns across Venezuela, South Africa, and even parts of the United States during disaster events, when law enforcement gets stretched thin, security becomes local. In many cases, it becomes personal.

Violent crime spikes during economic instability. Property theft becomes organized. Desperate people start taking desperate chances. Even good neighbours become unpredictable when they're hungry, scared, or trying to protect their own. And in rural and semi-rural areas, where backup might be half a county away, **your perimeter is the only line of defense that matters**.

So what does that mean in practice? It means building a layered system of deterrence, resistance, and recovery. It means you stop thinking of security as a camera or a gun in a drawer and start treating it as a living, breathing structure around your home. It means you plan ahead, not for war, but for the kind of tension that's become all too common in post-collapse regions. Looters don't always wear ski masks. Sometimes, they wear a big smile and knock politely. Other times, they watch for days before making their move. The point isn't to panic. It's to make your home look like **the wrong house to mess with**.

This book will walk you through everything you need to turn a normal property into a defensible position, **without it becoming a bunker** and without breaking the bank. You'll learn how to think in layers, how to use deception and deterrence effectively, how to fortify weak points, and how to build relationships that make you stronger, not more isolated. From passive traps and smart visuals, to community watch plans and resource safeguarding, the methods inside come from real-world breakdowns, not fantasy.

We'll also talk about how to stay mentally sharp, avoid burnout, and not turn your life into a 24/7 patrol. Because true security isn't about paranoia, it's about readiness with peace of mind. This isn't about fighting.

Your property is your castle. This chapter will show you how to keep it standing when the world around starts falling apart.

1.Layered Perimeter Security

The best fight is the one you never have. That's not just a saying; it's the foundation of any real-world collapse-proof defense strategy. In a functioning society, we build fences to mark property lines, install lights to feel safer, and lock our doors at night. But when things fall apart, **your perimeter becomes your first, most important wall between you and desperation.** And if you think you'll have time to "deal with it later," history says otherwise.

In the early days of a breakdown, most people will still act civil, at least during daylight. But once the thin layer of order wears through, the bold test boundaries fast. Your fence line, your driveway, the visibility of your porch, all of it becomes part of a silent negotiation: are you an easy mark, or are you **the wrong house to try**?

That's why you don't start at the front door. You start at the edge of your land.

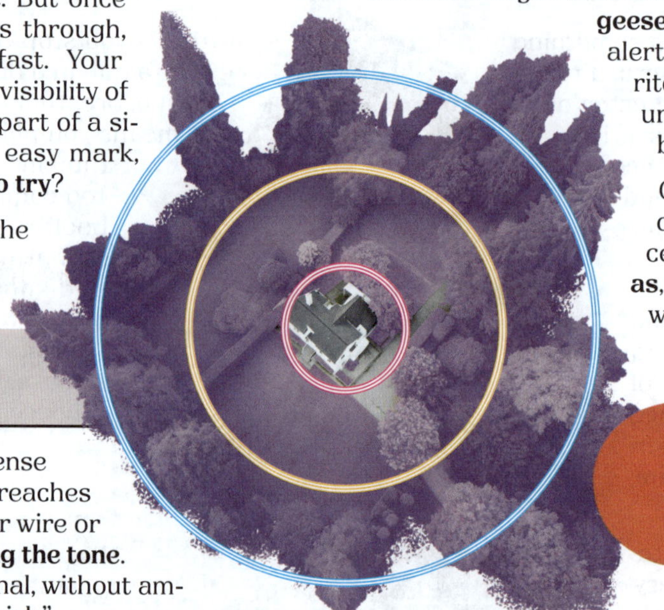

Outer Ring – The Unwelcome Zone

The first layer of your defense starts before anyone even reaches your home. It's not about razor wire or prison fences. It's about **setting the tone.** You want your property to signal, without ambiguity: "You're not worth the risk."

That begins with **natural barriers.** Planting dense, thorny hedges like hawthorn, blackberry, or wild rose along your property line not only marks territory, it creates a passive deterrent that doesn't require fuel, electricity, or maintenance. Pair that with **strategic visual control**, no visible valuables from the road, no stacked firewood or solar panels in plain view, no gear that says "we're stocked."

Then comes the **psychological line in the sand**: a **clear warning sign**, ideally something that doesn't feel store-bought. Hand-painted, weathered, specific: "No Trespassing – Survivors Only Beyond This Point" or "Private Land – Monitored 24/7 – Armed Response." It might seem theatrical, but in collapse zones from South Africa to Eastern Europe, signage alone turned opportunists away.

Gating your driveway, even with a simple chain or wooden barrier, is another quiet signal: "You'll have to slow down. Someone's watching." Add a choke point, rocks, barrels, old fencing, to funnel movement and reduce speed. Don't just hope people respect your space. Make sure they feel it.

Middle Ring – Alert and Redirect

If someone crosses your outer boundary, they've made a decision. You need to make them second-guess it. This is where early-warning systems come into play, not high-tech, but **high-value**.

Motion-triggered lights or radios, even solar-powered ones, can create the illusion of activity. Place them not just near doors, but along footpaths or trails where someone might think they're being clever. **Dogs**, or even **geese**, are some of the most reliable alert systems on Earth. Loud, territorial, and immune to grid failure. Just their presence changes behavior.

Consider **trail cameras**, cheap ones hidden in trees or fenceposts, and **dummy cameras**, too. Someone casing your land won't stop to check if the wires are real. A $10 bluff can protect a $10,000 asset.

And then **come the natural trip hazards**: uneven rock paths, dense shrubbery, stacked logs, narrow entries. These don't stop someone determined but they slow, confuse, and expose. That gives you time. And in a world without law enforcement, **time is everything**.

Inner Ring – Hardening the Home

This is your last line. If someone's made it this far, you no longer want to discourage, you want to delay and, if necessary, defend. And that starts by understanding what actually works.

Your doors and windows must be physically secured. Think **crossbars**, not just locks. Use window film to prevent shattering, and have **pre-cut plywood or sandbags** ready to drop into place at the first sign of wider unrest. These are not "panic room" tactics, they're **real-world delays**. Every second you gain gives you options.

Designate fallback positions inside your home. One room should be able to seal off entirely with reinforcement. Ideally, have **multiple escape paths**, through the back, out a window, across a fence line, or through a concealed trail. In some parts of rural Venezuela and South Africa, escape routes through brush or false fences saved entire families. It's not paranoia. It's exit planning.

A crucial part of this layer is **camouflage by poverty**. Keep your home looking poor, occupied, and undesirable. Don't clean too well. Break a window on purpose if needed. Put up a sign that says "Already Looted." It may sound extreme, but when looters scan a street, they skip what looks like more trouble than it's worth. **You're not trying to win a standoff; you're trying to avoid one altogether.**

2. Active and Passive Defense: Fight Smart, Not Loud

When security becomes your responsibility, not a service you can call, you don't just gain control. You inherit pressure. The pressure to stay ready, to anticipate problems before they arrive, and to keep your household steady while others panic. That doesn't mean gearing up for war or building a fortress. It means designing a system that stops danger before it touches your threshold and responds with force **only** when absolutely necessary.

In a collapse scenario, you don't win by being loud or aggressive. You win by being **measured, deliberate, and prepared to act without escalating**. The smartest strategies aren't the flashy ones, they're the ones that work while you sleep. Passive deterrents like motion lights, trail obstacles, and visible signs of presence aren't about confrontation. They're about making your home feel like a problem not worth solving. They buy you time. They shift momentum. And most of all, they reduce the number of threats you ever have to face head-on. When you think ahead, when you build in these quiet layers of defense, you turn your home into a moving puzzle for anyone who tries to approach. That kind of preparation doesn't just protect your perimeter. It protects your peace of mind. And if the worst does come, if someone pushes past every warning and tests your limits, then and only then do your active tools matter. But by that point, you're not improvising. You're responding from a place of control. Because you've already done the real work, not just arming yourself, but building a system that **thinks through problems before they become threats**. The goal is not to look dangerous. It's to be capable. Quietly. Consistently. Without needing to prove it.

Passive Defense Tools: Silence, Surprise, and Control

Passive tools are systems that **don't need you to act in real time**. They protect through structure, placement, and subtlety. They don't attract attention, but they can buy time, deter entry, or disable threats without a sound.

- **Slingshots, air rifles**, and bows offer quiet, reusable, low-risk ways to defend territory or scare off animals and intruders without drawing a crowd or wasting ammunition. A good slingshot and some practice can become a serious tool, especially when noise is your enemy.
- **Traps and tripwires**, especially along gardens, sheds, or dark paths, create both a physical and psychological barrier. Fishing line with bells, tension-triggered cans, or even simple snares in choke points can alert you before someone's at the door.
- **Bear spray or wasp spray** offers a wide-cone deterrent that can stop a human attacker cold without pulling a trigger. It's legal, effective, and easy to use under stress. Keep it accessible, not buried in a drawer.
- **Lights used wisely**, not just left on, can become disorientation tools. Motion-triggered strobes, especially at night, can freeze an intruder in place, while giving you a chance to regroup or retreat. Bright solar lights aimed strategically across doorways or near windows create a high-stakes gamble for anyone trying to sneak in.

The core principle here is **control the encounter without committing to it**. Make the environment work for you. Slow them. Expose them. Warn them, without giving away your own position or overreacting.

Active Defense - The Final Line

There may come a point when deterrents fail. When someone steps across every line you've drawn. That's when your active defense options come into play, but only if you're mentally, physically, and morally prepared to use them. Because in collapse conditions, **there is no undo button**.

Firearms remain the most decisive tool in a defensive crisis. But that doesn't mean every home needs an arsenal. In fact, **a single well-maintained firearm in the hands of someone who trains with it, stores it safely, and uses it responsibly** is more valuable than ten weapons collecting dust. A common-caliber handgun, or a 12-gauge shotgun with buckshot, offers versatility and stopping power at close range. A small rifle like a .22 or .223, with practice, provides range for deterrence and utility.

But firearms are not magic. Ammunition must be stored dry, rotated, and kept discreet. Training must be regular, calm, and scenario-based. And above all: you never aim unless you're willing to accept the consequences, **psychological, tactical, and legal**. Even in a lawless zone, every shot fired changes the situation. Loud, visible, final. Use that power with absolute seriousness.

If a gun isn't an option, or if you simply need a fallback, **melee tools** still matter. A sharpened stick, crowbar, axe handle, or trench spade becomes an equalizer in the right hands. Keep one accessible near fallback positions, and don't underestimate the psychological weight of holding something solid when cornered. Even a farming implement or carpenter's tool can turn the odds in your favor when mobility is tight, and time is short.

Active defense is not about looking tough. It's about **being calm when others panic**. It's about having an option when your back is against the wall but doing everything possible to make sure you never need to use it. Passive tools keep the wolves away. Active tools are what you use when they've already broken the door. Both are necessary. But only one should be part of your daily life.

The moment you become your own first responder, your own guard, your own backup plan, is the moment you stop thinking like a civilian, and start thinking like a survivor.

3. Deception, Misdirection, and Psychological Warfare

Defense isn't always about weapons or walls. In many situations, especially during collapse, **the appearance of danger is often more powerful than the danger itself**. Most threats in a crisis aren't military-trained teams looking for a fight. They're opportunists: lone scavengers, small desperate groups, or looters looking for soft targets. And what they fear most isn't force. It's uncertainty.

That's why psychological warfare, the art of making your home look like a mistake to mess with, can become one of your most valuable tools. It costs little, requires almost no physical confrontation, and it works 24/7 without needing you to be present. If your property feels dangerous, feels watched, or feels like it belongs to someone who won't go down easy, most would-be intruders will move on without testing it.

The Power of the Illusion

A home that looks quiet, unguarded, or inviting sends one message: "Easy target." A home that looks rough, watched, or recently defended sends another: "Too risky." You can manipulate this with surprisingly simple tricks:

- **Camouflaged dummies or scarecrow defenders** placed in shadowed corners, rooftops, or porch chairs can create the illusion of a lookout. A military-style jacket stuffed with straw and a stick in hand is enough to make someone pause.
- **Fake security setups,** like dummy cameras, cheap sensors with blinking lights, or "protected by radio patrol" signs, don't have to work. They just have to suggest risk.
- **Sound traps made from cans,** fishing lines, glass bottles, or bells along approach paths can warn you and

alert outsiders that they've been noticed. It's not the volume that matters; it's the reaction it triggers.

- **Fake chatter,** a pair of walkie-talkies playing a looped recording of voices on patrol, or even just a visible radio on a windowsill, can give the sense that you're organized, communicating, and aware.
- **Signs of recent resistance** can be subtle but unnerving. A spent shotgun shell in the dirt. A bloodied rag near the driveway. An axe sunk into a stump near the entrance. Even if nothing happened, the message is clear: "Someone fought back here, and they might again."

These tactics don't make your home invincible, but they raise the psychological cost of an approach. And in collapse scenarios, **most looters are risk-averse**. They don't want a confrontation; they want a quick in and out. If your home feels like the wrong place to try that, they'll likely keep walking.

Manipulating Visibility and Uncertainty

Smart deception isn't about theatrics. It's not about turning your home into a Hollywood war zone or planting elaborate booby traps. It's about **uncertainty**, planting just enough doubt in a potential intruder's mind that they decide it's not worth the risk. When people are desperate, tired, or scanning for opportunity, they don't want complexity. They want clarity: easy target or not? Your job is to make sure that answer is **never** obvious.

In a collapse, most looters, scavengers, or trespassers are not hardened operators. They're frightened civilians, opportunists, or small groups testing limits. What they fear most is **consequence**. The idea that behind that fence might be a shotgun. That under that porch might be someone waiting and watching. If you can't guarantee safety, they'll look elsewhere. That's your leverage, and you don't need to spend a dime to create it.

Instead of making your home a fortress, make it a **question**. Who lives there? Are they home? Are they poor? Are they watching me? Is someone waiting behind that curtain?

Here are just a few examples of how you create that sense of unease, doubt, and unpredictability without ever lifting a weapon:

- **Leave a porch light on but a side door dark**. Inconsistency creates confusion. It suggests movement, presence, possibly a watch schedule. Someone watching that house won't be able to draw clean conclusions. That's good.
- **Cut a new path through the overgrowth, but leave it half-finished**. It looks recent. It looks used. But it also raises questions, where does it lead? Was it used recently? Is someone watching it?
- **Fresh footprints in the snow, but only on one side of the yard**. A half-visible trail that disappears near the back gate suggests patrolling, observation, or perhaps a trap. A savvy looter might think twice.
- **Hang laundry, but make it look poor**. Old, worn clothes on the line signal poverty, not value. But they also suggest activity. You want your home to look occupied, but not stocked. Watched, but not wealthy.
- **Keep imperfections visible**. A broken shutter. A tarp over a window. A cracked panel near the gutterline. These say: "we've been hit, we've got nothing left." But make sure these flaws don't compromise your actual security. This is camouflage, not neglect.

The secret is to be **visible without being interesting**. You want to be part of the landscape, not the centerpiece. A house that's clearly lived in, but quietly, carefully. One where something might happen if pushed too far, but it's not worth the gamble to find out.

This is where deception becomes strategy. You're not trying to scare someone away with bluster. You're making them **uncertain**. You're creating the illusion that any wrong move might lead to consequence. And in collapse, **fear is a currency**. Every second a looter spends second-guessing your home is a second you've won. The goal is not conflict. The goal is avoidance.

If you can turn your property into a place that whispers "bad idea" without saying a word, if you can do that without firing a shot or opening a door, then you've already won a quiet war before it ever began.

4. Community Defense Networks

When systems break and law enforcement fades into the background, defense becomes a local responsibility. But individual survival, especially in rural or semi-rural areas, can only take you so far. You can't stand guard 24/7. You can't patrol your entire perimeter while also cooking, repairing, or sleeping. And you can't afford to burn out when there's no backup coming. That's where **community-based defense networks** come in. You don't need a militia. You don't need a fort. What you need is a **few reliable people, a shared plan, and trust forged before it's tested.**

A well-formed neighborhood or homestead alliance is more than just mutual protection. It's resource sharing, redundancy, rest, and psychological relief. Even knowing someone is watching your back while you sleep is worth more than another shotgun or fence. **In collapse, community becomes infrastructure.**

Build Your Circle Before You Need It

You don't need to convince everyone in a five-mile radius. In fact, **smaller groups are better**. Look for neighbors who are already practical: hunters, ranchers, small farmers, veterans, tool guys, nurses. People who have shown they can solve problems without waiting for permission.

Start small. Build with two or three trusted households first. Focus on:

- **Simple communication systems** – handheld radios, walkie-talkie codes, whistle signals, visible flags or flashlights.
- **Shared watch rotations** – night shifts, early mornings, rotating responsibilities so no one burns out.
- **Fallback plans** – rally points in case of evacuation, basic map understanding, agreed-upon escape paths.

Avoid trying to organize a "security team" with every neighbor you've never talked to. **Collapse isn't the time to test strangers**. It's the time to consolidate reliability. And the fewer people who know your plans, the safer they are.

Defend What Really Matters

You don't need to protect **everything**. In fact, trying to defend your entire property as if it were a fortress is a fast way to spread yourself thin, and make critical mistakes. The truth is, when the world falls apart, not all assets are created equal. Looters, scavengers, and even desperate neighbors aren't wandering blindly. They're looking for **specific things**, and if you're smart, so are you.

Collapse prioritizes necessity. So should you. And that means understanding the five categories of resources that actually **keep you alive**. These aren't luxury goods or sentimental keepsakes. They're the backbone of your daily survival, and therefore, the bullseye on your map.

- **Water:** Without it, you're dead in three days. Wells, rain catchment barrels, filters, and purification tablets become **more valuable than gold**. If you've got a reliable water source, you've got leverage. If you've got **visible** water storage, you've got a target. Hide it. Guard it. Multiply it.
- **Food:** Root cellars, livestock, dry goods, even a single functioning garden can sustain life, or get you robbed. People can smell cooking. They can hear chickens. Keep your food sources discreet, and your storage diversified. Never rely on one pantry or one freezer.
- **Fuel:** Without fuel, you lose light, warmth, mobility, and cooking power. Propane, diesel, firewood, even spare batteries become high-risk, high-value assets. Don't store them where thieves expect to find them, sheds, garages, side yards. Spread your storage and blend it into the background. A fake compost bin might hold a fuel tank. A hollow woodpile might house battery packs.
- **Medical Supplies:** A bottle of antibiotics becomes priceless when the clinics are empty. So does antiseptic, bandages, painkillers, and even basic first-aid gear. These items are scarce in collapse, not just for you, but for everyone. That makes them gold in the black market. Don't keep your entire med kit in one bathroom drawer. Use decoys. Use diversions. Use layers.
- **Communication:** Radios, maps, hand-crank chargers, and extra batteries are your link to coordination and awareness. When people can't talk, they panic. When you can talk, securely, you gain the upper hand. Keep your comms low-profile. A handheld Baofeng in a sealed ammo can is better than a base station someone can see from the road.

This isn't just about security, it's about **strategy.** What looters go for isn't random. It's what **they** would need to stay alive another week. If you understand that, you can build defenses that anticipate their goals before they make a move.

And whatever you do, **don't store everything in one place.** Collapse doesn't forgive that kind of mistake. A single break-in, fire, or betrayal shouldn't wipe out your entire prep. Use **redundancy**. Bury backup caches. Install false walls. Keep emergency stashes in outbuildings, under floors, inside sealed barrels beneath a garden path. Think like someone who's been looted before, because many survivors have.

And don't do it all alone. The more eyes on your blind spots, the fewer mistakes get made. Quiet coordination between two or three trusted households beats bravado any day. You're not trying to be a hero. You're trying to **outlast** the chaos. And when it comes, the strongest household isn't always the one with the most ammo. It's the one with friends who show up when the gate creaks open at 3 a.m.

Collapse punishes pride. But it rewards the prepared, the humble, and the **quietly coordinated**. You don't need a fortress. You need a system, and a crew who understands what's really worth defending.

How Wisdom, Presence, and Peace Become a Quiet Currency in Collapse

But defense isn't just about fences, food, or firearms. In many collapse scenarios, what keeps people steady isn't just what you can build or barter, it's what you can **teach**, what you can **listen to**, what you can **pass down**. In every black market and back-alley economy, there's also a quiet current of wisdom moving through it: stories, lessons, memories, comfort.

If you're someone who knows how to read to children, show someone how to preserve food, teach basic math or explain how to calm a crying baby, you're not just useful, you're **essential**. Even when resources vanish, the hunger for understanding doesn't. That means if you can host a quiet hour of tutoring, lead a prayer circle, share a family gardening trick, or just sit with someone who's grieving, you have something to trade that's more valuable than cash: peace of mind.

In chaotic times, the elders who know how to quilt, ferment vegetables, or make do with nothing become the living libraries of the community. The same goes for those who can tell a story that calms a child while their parents negotiate a trade or hold space for a neighbor who just lost everything. Those "soft trades" may not seem like much now. But in the dark, a little light matters more than a generator.

Knowledge becomes currency. Calm becomes protection. Presence becomes infrastructure.

Neighborhood Tradecraft and How Quiet People Rebuild Economies

When money loses meaning and stores go dark, **barter becomes the bloodstream** of the local economy. And like any system of exchange, it needs people who can keep it flowing. In every small collapse-ready community, there's room for someone to step into a quiet but powerful role: the **barter broker**. This isn't about being a merchant, it's about being a connector. The person who knows that Maria has eggs but needs batteries, and that Tom has extra batteries but no bread. A senior who sets up a small chalkboard on their porch or keeps a notebook of who has what and who needs what, can quietly become the **pulse point of the neighborhood**. They don't need to leave the block; they just need to listen.

Sometimes it's not even about trade itself. It's about trust. Being the one who says: "You can deal with her, she's fair." Or: "Don't take that offer, it's not a good deal." That kind of reputation, built slowly and carefully, becomes its own kind of defense. People protect what helps them survive. Even a simple act as hosting a "barter hour" on the front steps once a week can rebuild a sense of rhythm in chaos. You're not just trading goods. You're **rebuilding an economy**, one handoff at a time.

5. Securing What Looters Actually Want

In a full-blown collapse, looters don't waste time on guesswork. They go after what has value: the essentials that keep people alive or can be bartered for power, safety, or influence. Forget your TV, your laptop, your old watch collection, those become meaningless fast. What truly matters is food, fuel, water, medicine, tools, and anything that connects people to the outside world. If it can be eaten, burned, healed with, or traded, it's a target. And if it's all stored in one easy-to-find place, you might as well be handing it over the moment someone crosses your fence.

That's the hard truth most people miss: even if your home is fortified, your security is only as strong as the placement of your resources. A smart defender doesn't just protect their home. They protect the things that allow that home to function. That means you need to start thinking like a looter, **before** one ever shows up. What would you look for if you were desperate? What areas would you search first? What smells, sounds, or signs might tip you off to where someone's keeping their valuables? Once you know what they want, you can shape your defense to deny it.

Let's start by understanding the primary targets. These are the categories of items that looters, especially the ones who know what they're doing, will prioritize.

Category	Examples	Why It's Targeted
Food	Canned goods, rice, flour, MREs	Easily traded, essential for survival
Water & Filters	Bottled water, Berkey filters, purification tablets	Life-sustaining, usually hard to replace
Fuel	Propane, diesel, firewood, batteries	Powers light, heat, cooking, and transportation
Medical Supplies	First aid kits, antibiotics, bandages	Scarce in collapse, high value on black market
Communications	Radios, solar chargers, batteries	Enables coordination, access to information
Tools & Gear	Knives, axes, generators, tarps	Useful for barter, construction, defense

Most of these items can't just be hidden once. They need to be dispersed, disguised, and defended in layers. You don't keep all your food in one pantry. You don't stack all your fuel in one shed. That's how you lose it all in one hit. The better strategy is **compartmentalization**: splitting your goods into multiple locations, so that even if one is found, the others remain untouched. A few cans of food in the kitchen. A buried bin of rice behind the shed. A few gallons of fuel hidden under a false floor in your greenhouse. A medical cache behind a drywall panel in your basement. Think like a foxhole strategist, not a warehouse manager.

This is where **decoys** come in. A decoy stash is a small, intentionally findable cache designed to look like it's all you've got. It doesn't need to be fancy, just enough to be "discovered." A couple of used supplies, an open med kit with some missing pieces, a mostly empty fuel can. Something that says: "We've already been hit." The idea is to satisfy curiosity without revealing the real depth of your prep. Most looters are not looking for a fight or a full inventory. They want fast reward, low risk. Let them take the bait and move on.

The best defenders also think vertically. Your home isn't just walls and doors, it's layers of potential. Use crawlspaces, floorboards, attic insulation, sealed PVC buried under the chicken coop. A well-packed cache can stay intact for years if it's dry, dark, and out of sight. If you live rurally, burying a bin with food and essentials twenty yards into the woods, well away from your house, might be the best insurance policy you'll ever make. Urban or suburban? Think behind fake cabinets, under staircases, inside hollowed-out furniture. If it's not obvious, it's not vulnerable.

And don't forget the role of **noise and smell**. A generator running all night. The smell of frying meat. The sound of a working radio. These are accidental signals that someone has resources. That means you must train your household to think tactically at all times. Keep the noise low. Cook discreetly. Don't broadcast your advantages to the neighborhood, even in good times, because people remember. And desperate memories are dangerous ones.

This chapter isn't about paranoia. It's about staying one step ahead of the threat, not when it knocks, but before it even sees you. Don't assume your fence will keep them out. Don't assume your locks are strong enough. Assume that someone, somewhere, is already looking. And then build your systems so that when they do come, what they find... isn't what you've got.

Because when it comes to collapse, you don't win by having the most. You win by keeping what matters hidden, and protected, long enough to outlast the chaos.

The Kitchen as a Tradecraft: When Food Becomes Currency

In a collapse scenario, **food isn't just survivalist power, trust, and trade**. And not just the food you stockpile, but what you know how to prepare. When grocery shelves are empty and the supply chain breaks, people stop asking for recipes, they start trading for them. **Bread, broth, fermentation, preservation**, these aren't domestic chores anymore. They're skills with real street value.

A neighbor who knows how to stretch beans into soup that feeds ten? Valuable. Someone who can bake bread without a power grid? Even more so. A person who can teach others how to **pickle, ferment, or preserve with salt or ash** becomes a local authority. That's why it's not just about what you can cook. It's about what lasts. A jar of sauerkraut, a loaf of sourdough, a pouch of dried herbs, these become barter items just as much as tools or fuel. And if you can teach others how to make them? You're not just trading food, you're **trading autonomy.**

The same goes for **foraging and wild edibles**. Seniors who grew up in rural or pre-consumer times often know what dandelions, wild onions, chickweed, or acorns are good for. That knowledge, once overlooked, becomes gold when the last can of beans runs out. **Knowing what grows nearby, and how to turn it into calories, can turn a walker with a basket into the most valuable person on the block**. Don't underestimate the power of the humble kitchen. **A fire, a pot, and a bit of knowledge** can build more goodwill than any locked door ever will. And in a world where food is rare, being the one who feeds, not just stores, might be the reason people protect you, trade with you, or simply remember your name.

6. Defensive Mindset – The Mental Load of Collapse

Most books on home security or survival spend a lot of time on gear, cameras, firearms, fences, and traps. That's fine. But in a collapse scenario, the most important part of your defense isn't what you **have**. It's what's happening in your head. Because when the systems break down and the police stop coming, you don't just take on new tasks, you take on a new mental role. You are no longer a homeowner. You're the protector of your space, your family, and your future. And that responsibility doesn't clock out.

A lot of people think they'll rise to the occasion. But collapse isn't a two-hour movie or a weekend emergency. It's long, grinding, and psychologically corrosive. You're not dealing with one crisis, you're dealing with constant, low-grade threat. You'll go days without sleep. You'll second-guess every sound at night. You'll find yourself jumping at shadows because t**his time it might not be nothing**. That's not a flaw. That's the weight of being aware. And if you're not ready for that kind of mental strain, no amount of ammunition will save you.

So What Does It Take to Keep Your Edge?

First, **you need to learn how to shift into readiness without burning out**. You can't stay at 100% alert forever. No one can. Even soldiers in combat zones rotate shifts, take turns, and decompress when they can. In a post-collapse setting, you'll need to build mental rest into your system. That means:

- Taking shifts with others when possible (see Chapter 4 on community networks).
- Structuring your day to include "clear hours" when you actively don't listen for trouble.
- Using calming rituals (tea, candlelight, prayer, reading aloud) to reset your nervous system.

This isn't about being soft, it's about being **sustainable**.

Second, you need to **prepare for the emotional weight of violence**, even if you never have to use it. Every serious defender needs to wrestle with this now, not in the moment. If you had to confront someone, if you had to raise a weapon, if you had to defend your family with force, what would that do to you afterward? Collapse removes the legal system, but it doesn't erase moral consequences. And the last thing you want is to freeze in a high-stakes moment because you never mentally walked through the outcome.

That's why rehearsing scenarios isn't just tactical, it's psychological. Practice gives your brain a script. And when adrenaline spikes, you'll fall back on what you've trained for. But the training has to include your values as well as your skills. Think it through now. Talk it through with someone you trust. Decide in advance what lines you're willing to cross, and what you'll live with afterward.

Third, you have to acknowledge **fear and isolation as real enemies**. In collapse, you'll hear things at night. You'll worry about the people you turned away. You'll feel the cold edge of being entirely on your own. And that emotional pressure leads good people to make dangerous mistakes: chasing noises into the dark, opening doors when they shouldn't, confronting threats head-on when evasion was the better move. Courage isn't the absence of fear. It's functioning clearly **through** fear.

That's why mindset matters more than gear. Because when you're exhausted, cold, and alone, your instincts will either protect you or betray you. If you've trained your mind to expect the chaos, to remain calm through ambiguity, and to **wait** before reacting, you'll make smarter calls. You'll live longer. And you'll protect what matters, not just with strength, but with clarity.

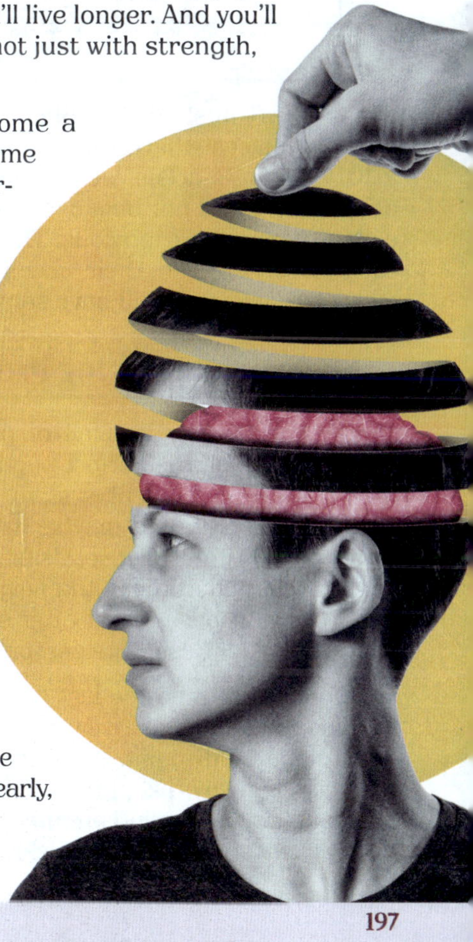

You don't need to become a robot. You need to become steady. The calmest person in the room during a blackout. The one who speaks clearly when others yell. The one who doesn't panic when the back gate rattles. That's the **real** security system your household needs.

Because collapse isn't just physical. It's psychological. And the survivors aren't just the armed or the supplied. They're the ones who kept thinking clearly, when no one else could.

7. What NOT to Do – The Mistakes That Get People Killed

In a collapse, your biggest threat often isn't some violent outsider, it's **your own poor judgment**. Overconfidence, loose lips, and bad habits are what get people targeted, isolated, or worse. Not because they weren't strong, skilled, or well-equipped, but because they acted like it was still a normal world. Collapse changes the rules. **Those who fail to adapt quickly become cautionary tales**.

If the first half of survival is preparation, the second half is **not screwing it up when it matters most**. And that starts by understanding what mistakes consistently get people hurt, not just in fiction, but in real post-collapse environments around the world.

History doesn't just repeat, it leaves patterns. And when you look across failed states, economic crashes, and long-term disaster zones, the same survival errors show up again and again. Here's a breakdown of the five most common, and most lethal, mistakes people make when the system fails.

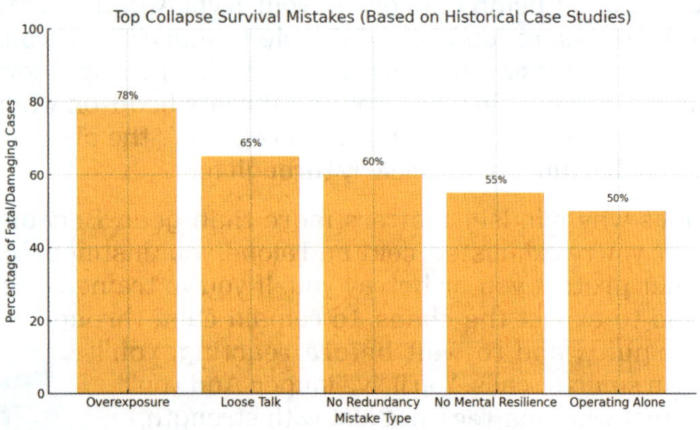

Source: Compiled from documented patterns in post-crisis environments: Venezuela (2016–2020), Argentina (2001–2002), New Orleans (2005), Balkans (1990s)

These aren't abstract lessons. They show up again and again in places where the system failed. In **Argentina's 2001 economic crisis**, well-off households were systematically targeted not because they had the most, but because they made it obvious. They lit their homes, drove their cars, watered their lawns, and in doing so, told every passerby: **we still have something to take.**

Mistake #1: Looking Prepared in Public

This is the classic downfall of pride. You've stocked up, maybe even built the perfect bug-in setup. You've got solar, fuel, a water catchment system, maybe a small arsenal. You're proud of it. And maybe, in a better world, you'd be right to be. But in collapse, visibility becomes vulnerability. The loudest generator in the neighborhood? That's a beacon. The only house still lit after sundown? A spotlight for every hungry or desperate person within a mile.

You don't want to be the last house with clean laundry on the line, or the only driveway that isn't overgrown. Even small signals, tidy paint, stacked wood, a quiet hum behind the walls, can say **this place still has resources**. And when everyone else is running on fumes, that's not respect you'll earn. It's attention. Which quickly becomes danger. Blend in. Look rough if you have to. A cracked window taped with plastic. Overgrown bushes. Trash piled near the curb. You want your house to disappear into the neighborhood, not shine like a lighthouse in a storm.

Mistake #2: Talking Too Much

In peaceful times, conversation builds trust. In collapse, it builds lists, lists of people to rob when things go south. You might think you're just chatting, sharing stories, trading ideas. But once you mention your water filter, or your ammo stockpile, or that backup generator in the shed? **That information sticks**. And when someone runs out of options, your casual comment turns into their plan B.

This is especially dangerous in rural or tight-knit communities. People listen more closely than you think. And even if they're good people now, desperation rewires morality fast. Don't assume your friends will remember your generosity when their kids are starving. Assume they'll remember your resources.Silence isn't antisocial. In collapse, it's protection. Practice saying less than you know, and never say everything, even to people you trust.

Mistake #3: Single-Point Failure

Redundancy isn't paranoia. It's survival. Too many preppers fall into the trap of **one**. One gun. One cache. One route out. One "go-to" neighbor. That's not a plan, it's a coin flip. And in crisis, single points of failure don't just **risk** your security, they **destroy it**.

What if your only firearm jams or is stolen? What if the one friend you counted on is already gone, or turns on you? What if your sole exit route is blocked by a tree, a fire, or a checkpoint? Survivors have **layers.** Backup plans. Quiet caches hidden offsite. Escape paths no one else knows. Don't overcomplicate things, but never put your entire safety in one box, one person, or one door.

Mistake #4: No Mental Slack

You are not a machine. And in collapse, fatigue becomes deadly. It makes you sloppy. It makes you loud. It makes you reckless. You forget to recheck a latch. You fall asleep during the one hour you were supposed to be watching. Or you snap, yelling when silence would have saved you, chasing shadows instead of securing your base.

The brain needs cycles of rest. Collapse isn't a sprint, it's a siege. You'll need to build rhythm into your day. Shift duties with others. Take mental breaks. Trust systems you've prepared, so your nervous system doesn't run at redline every hour of the night. Burnout **is** a threat. And it kills more slowly, but just as surely, as a bullet.

These four mistakes? They all share one thing: they happen when people assume they've already "won" collapse just by being prepared. But collapse isn't a game you win by **gear**. It's a long-haul test of humility, discipline, and staying invisible while everything around you burns.

Your real advantage won't be in what you show, it will be in what you **don't**. The things no one sees. The tools you don't brag about. The backup plans you never share. And most of all, the instinct to blend in, stay quiet, and move only when you must.

If you remember nothing else from this chapter, remember this: the most dangerous thing you can be in a collapse is **visible**. Stay quiet. Stay underestimated. Stay alive.

8. Street-Level Survival Work – Making Ends Meet When the System Fails

When the money breaks, the real economy doesn't vanish move. It slides into backyards, church basements, kitchen tables, and alleyway corners. In a true collapse, it's not about having a job title. It's about having something to offer that someone else needs. Survival becomes a trade. Stability becomes service. And even if you're older, slower, or stuck at home, that doesn't make you useless. It makes you steady. And in chaos, steadiness is worth more than strength.

In normal times, side gigs are hobbies. In collapse, they're lifelines. When currency collapses and stores close, people don't stop needing things. They just stop being able to buy them the usual way. The new market isn't online, it's on the block. The new deals aren't sealed with credit cards, they're sealed with handshakes and trust. If you've ever patched a torn sleeve, sharpened a knife, brewed a calming tea, or fixed a broken chair, you already have more to offer than most.

There's a reason why, in every historical collapse, seniors became the backbone of informal trade. Not because they were fast, but because they were useful. Consistent. Known. You don't need to build a bunker. You need to become someone others come to when they're stuck. Maybe you sit on your porch and sew buttons for trade. Maybe you bake simple loaves when flour shows up. Maybe you host a chalkboard outside your door listing who has what and who needs it. Maybe you just keep watching and waving. That's not retirement. That's survival work.

Because here's the truth: when everything breaks, every neighborhood needs a fix-it hand, a pot of soup, a barter facilitator, and someone who remembers how to stay calm when everyone else panics. And if that's you, you won't just survive, you'll be the reason others do. In a post-collapse world, no one cares about résumés. They care about who can patch a roof with tarps. Who can trade a jar of homemade balm for four eggs. Who can sit with a scared child while their mother barters for medicine. These aren't minor roles. They're the foundation of whatever comes next. So, if you've got a chair, a kettle, a few skills, and the willingness to help without drawing too much attention you're already ahead. Set up that fix-it table. Light that porch candle. Keep an eye out. Start small. Word travels fast in a quiet world.

This isn't charity. It's value. It's how you survive, not by hoarding, but by mattering. And in a society stitched back together one trade at a time, the person who stays useful is never poor.

Security in a collapse isn't about gadgets or bravado. It's not about turning your home into a fortress, or playing hero with a shotgun. It's about preservation: of safety, of stability, of sanity. You're not just defending walls or supplies. You're defending the small pocket of order you've managed to maintain while everything around you unravels.

This guide has walked you through the essentials, **perimeter layers, passive and active defense, psychological warfare, resource protection, mental discipline**, and the **grave mistakes that get people killed** when they ignore reality. But the real takeaway is this: when institutions fade and laws lose their meaning, **habit becomes security**. You won't be able to improvise your way through chaos. You'll fall back on whatever habits you've already built. And if those habits are sound, quiet and layered, you'll stand a much better chance of keeping your home, your people, and your peace intact.

There will be fear. There will be stress. There will be nights when you hear something outside and don't know what to do. That's not failure. That's the cost of being awake when the rest of the world hit snooze. And that edge, the one between awareness and obsession, between preparation and paranoia, is one you'll walk more than once.

The good news? You're not powerless. You've seen what works. You've learned what's worth defending, and what just makes you a target. You've seen how real-world collapse survivors survived, **not with luck**, but with structure, mindset, and the discipline to keep a low profile while still staying two steps ahead.

So no, this book doesn't end with a cinematic showdown. It ends with a locked gate, a darkened window, and a family eating in peace because they knew how to stay off the radar. **That's winning**. Not drama. Not violence. Just another quiet night while the world outside spins.

Final reminder: you don't need to be a hero. You need to be steady. Present. Quietly prepared. You need to be the house that doesn't attract attention, the person who doesn't run their mouth, the defender who's thought things through when no one else has. Because when collapse arrives, and it always arrives without warning, it's not the strongest who survive. It's the ones who **planned not to be noticed**.

Be that person. Be that house. And if you've done that, really done that, then when the lights go out, you'll still be standing. And that's the kind of power no system, no gang, and no storm can take from you.

Chapter 17

Calorie-Rich Wild Edibles That Can Save Your Life When Food Runs Out

This chapter will introduce you to some of the most common, overlooked plants hiding in plain sight—your next meal might be growing underfoot.

"Hunger sharpens the eye and the mind. It is nature's teacher."
Mykel Hawke

Wild Weeds and Root Vegetables

You don't need farmland, raised beds, or even a backyard to feed yourself—nature already planted your garden. The wild is full of food if you know where to look. Cracks in the sidewalk, edges of parking lots, forgotten trails, overgrown fields... edible weeds thrive where cultivation ends.

These resilient plants grow without permission or fertilizer. They're free, they're everywhere, and many are more nutritious than what you'll find in the produce aisle.

Whether you're foraging by necessity or curiosity, learning to identify and harvest wild edibles isn't just useful—it's *freedom*.

Nettles

Nettles don't ask for much—just damp soil, a little shade, and the freedom to thrive where no one's looking. In return, they give you one of the most nutritious green foods nature offers.

Three main varieties grow wild across North America, each edible, each distinct, and each worth knowing.

Stinging Nettle (*Urtica dioica*)

This is the nettle most people know—and fear. With its **upright square** *stems*, **serrated dark green** *leaves*, and infamous **stinging hairs**, *Urtica dioica* makes an impression. It grows along riverbanks, forest edges, meadows, and anywhere water and wildness meet. Harvest the **young top leaves before flowering—spring** is best. Gloves are essential to avoid the sting, which you'll never forget if you catch it unprepared.

Found throughout most of North America, especially in the Northeast, Midwest, and Pacific Northwest—favoring moist, nitrogen-rich soil near streams, trails, and fence lines.

Once **blanched** (having been briefly immersed in boiling water, especially in order to remove the skin or to prepare it for further cooking) for 60–90 seconds in boiling water, the stingers neutralize completely. You can **dry** the leaves for **tea**, crumble them into **stews**, or sun-dry entire bunches for later use. Nutritionally, stinging nettle outpaces many store-bought greens—packed with **protein**, **iron**, **calcium**, and **vitamins** A and C.

Wood Nettle (*Laportea canadensis*)

Often mistaken for its cousin, wood nettle prefers shady **hardwood forests**, especially **near creeks and floodplains.** It looks similar to stinging nettle, but the **leaves alternate** instead of growing in pairs, and **the sting is often stronger**. That sting, however, hides one of the finest wild greens you'll find. The leaves are tender and flavorful—almost sweet once cooked.

Common in the eastern U.S. and southeastern Canada, especially in shaded, low-lying hardwood forests and floodplains.

Pick **young leaves** and **tops** before flowering, and handle with gloves. As with *Urtica*, **blanching** or **drying** removes the sting. Wood nettle is rich in **chlorophyll** and **minerals**, making it a worthy addition to any forager's pantry or survival kit.

Clearweed (*Pilea pumila*)

Clearweed is the gentle cousin—the one nettle that **doesn't bite**. It grows in many of the same areas: **forest edges**, **damp ground**, and **shady gardens**. Its *stems* are **nearly translucent**, and the *leaves* are **lighter green** with a **smooth, almost succulent feel. No stingers** here, making it ideal for beginners.

It's widespread in the eastern half of North America, from the Gulf Coast to the Great Lakes and into southern Canada—thriving in **shady**, **damp woodlands** and **urban understories**.

While not as nutrient-dense as the other two, clearweed is still edible **raw** or **cooked** and can be used as a **spinach substitute** in a pinch. It's also a good teaching plant for kids learning to identify nettle-type species without risk of getting stung.

Preserving Nettles

Blanching in boiling water is the fastest and safest method to **neutralize stingers**. Skip freezing—if electricity is unreliable, rely on **sun-drying** or **air-drying in shade**. Once dried, nettles store well in jars, paper bags, or bundled from string. Crumble them into soups, use them for medicinal teas, or grind them into a powder to boost nutrition in almost anything.

Stinging Nettle Soup

Ingredients
1 cup tightly packed stinging nettles
4 tbsp. unsalted butter
2 cups diced potatoes
2 cups diced leeks
1 diced yellow onion
4 cups chicken or vegetable broth
½ cup cream
Salt and black pepper to taste

Instructions

Begin by steaming the nettles until wilted. Squeeze the nettles to release any excess water and chop finely. Set the nettles aside and place the butter in a stockpot over medium heat. Once the butter has melted, place the vegetables in the pot and cook, stirring occasionally, for 5 minutes. Add the broth and bring the soup to a simmer. Once the vegetables are tender, add the nettles and cream then blend until smooth.

Sauteed Stinging Nettles

Ingredients
Fresh stinging nettles
Vegetable oil
Sea salt

Instructions

Rinse your stinging nettles while wearing gloves and pat dry. Heat a large pan over medium-high heat and add vegetable oil. Add the nettles and cook for about 5 minutes, stirring frequently. Season with sea salt and serve immediately.

Beyond their culinary uses, stinging nettles are often used medicinally for their **anti-inflammatory** and **antihistamine properties**. For these purposes, nettle is best prepared as a **tea or capsule**. When foraging for stinging nettle, you may come across its look alikes, wood nettle, slender nettle, or dwarf nettle. Fortunately, these plant species are also edible.

Burdock (*Arctium lappa*)

Burdock is one of those wild plants that hides in plain sight—often dismissed as a weed until you know what it is. Then suddenly, it's everywhere. **Towering stalks. Giant leaves.** And the **burrs** that cling to your pants like they're trying to follow you home. But beneath all that nuisance is a root that's fed and healed people for centuries.

This plant grows across most of the U.S. and southern Canada, especially in **disturbed soil along roadsides, ditches, pastures,** and **abandoned lots.**

This **biennial** plant spends its first year close to the ground, growing a **wide rosette of broad, heart-shaped green leaves** with a **woolly underside.** In its second year, it shoots up **branched flower stalks** that can reach 4 to 6 feet. The flowers are pinkish-purple and are encased in prickly green bracts—the infamous "bur" that inspired Velcro.

Foragers prize burdock root, especially in **the fall of its first year**, when the starches are fully developed but the core hasn't gone woody. The root can be **peeled, sliced,** and **boiled** like a potato—earthy and slightly sweet. In a survival context, it's a dependable source of calories and minerals.

The **leaves and stalks** are also edible but more delicate. The leaves are best picked in **early spring** when they're still small and haven't yet turned tough and bitter. The tender young leaf stems and peeled flower stalks can be **boiled** or **sautéed** like celery or asparagus.

Preservation Tips

Burdock ***roots*** can be **sliced thin** and **sun-dried** for storage or **roasted over low heat** to draw out flavor. They store well in cool, dark places once cured. *Leaves* should be used **fresh**, or **dried** for herbal infusions, though their bitterness increases with age.

Roasted Burdock Root

Ingredients
2 cups sliced burdock root
2 tbsp. vegetable oil
Sea salt and black pepper to taste

Instructions

Preheat the oven to 400°F (205°C). While the oven is preheating, place the burdock root slices into a bowl and toss with the vegetable oil, salt, and pepper. Spread the burdock root evenly onto a lined baking sheet and roast for 15 minutes.

Pickled Burdock

Ingredients
1 lb. burdock root
1 cup apple cider vinegar
2 cups water
¼ cup sugar
1 tsp. chopped fresh ginger
1 tbsp. sea salt

Instructions

Prepare the burdock root by scrubbing, peeling, and slicing it into thin rounds. In a pot, bring the vinegar, water, sugar, ginger, and salt to a boil. Meanwhile, place the dry burdock slices into a clean, sterilized glass jar. Pour the brine over top and let it come to room temperature. Cover and place in the refrigerator.

Burdock has been used medicinally for thousands of years. Burdock *root* promotes **healthy skin, stimulates bile flow,** and **supports the lymphatic system.** Burdock *leaves* can be prepared as a **poultice** or **decoction** and used for **rashes.** Burdock can sometimes be confused with other edible thistles such as **Bull thistle,** *Cirsium vulgare*, and Milk Thistle, *Silybum marianum*. Unlike bull thistle and milk thistle, **burdock's leaves do not have spines.**

Wild Garlic (*Allium vineale*)

Sharp, pungent, and unmistakable—*wild garlic* is nature's answer to the supermarket clove. You'll smell it before you see it. Crush a leaf between your fingers and that familiar **garlicky scent** cuts through the air like a signal: you've found something worth harvesting.

It's most common in the eastern U.S., Midwest, and coastal Pacific regions.

A perennial member of the lily family, *Allium vineale* grows wild across **fields**, **roadsides**, **pastures**, and **forest edges**. Its *leaves* are **thin**, **hollow**, and **dark green**—similar to chives or scallions—and **sprout upright** from a sheathed base. In early summer, it sends up a **waxy stalk** capped with a **spherical cluster of small greenish-white** or **pink flowers**, often with tiny bulblets tucked among them. Underground, instead of a multi-clove garlic bulb, you'll usually find a **single**, **egg-shaped bulb**—small, but powerfully aromatic.

Best Harvest Time

Wild garlic is most potent and tender in **early to mid-spring** when the bulbs are full but not yet fibrous. As the plant matures through summer, the flavor sharpens but the texture may toughen.

To harvest, grip low on the stem and gently pull from the base to extract the whole plant—bulb and all. A trowel or weeding fork helps in hard soil. The leaves, stems, flowers, and bulb are all edible and flavorful.

Preparation & Use

Chop the green parts like chives. Use the *bulbs* as you would regular garlic—**crushed**, **roasted**, **sautéed**. They're strong, so a little goes a long way. The *flower stalks* and *buds* can be **pickled** or used as a **spicy garnish**.

Medicinal Value

Like cultivated garlic, wild garlic possesses **antimicrobial**, **anti-inflammatory**, **cardiovascular-supportive**, and **immune-supportive qualities**.

Preservation

To store without refrigeration, hang wild garlic in bunches in a cool, dark, dry place with good airflow. Once **dried**, bulbs can be crushed into powder or stored whole in jars. You can also **pickle** the bulbs in vinegar with pepper and herbs for long-term use.

Caution

Wild garlic can be confused with poisonous look-alikes such as **meadow death camas** (*Toxicoscordion venenosum*) or **star of Bethlehem** (*Ornithogalum umbellatum*), both of which can be fatal. The golden rule: **if it doesn't smell like garlic or onion, do not eat it**.

Toxicoscordion venenosum (top), Ornithogalum umbellatum (bottom)

Wild Garlic Soup

Ingredients
1 tbsp. vegetable oil
1 chopped small yellow onion
¼ cup chopped wild garlic
1 chopped potato
3-4 cups vegetable or chicken broth
Sea salt and black pepper

Instructions

In a large pot, sauté the onion in the vegetable oil until softened. Add the rest of the ingredients and bring to a boil. Reduce to a simmer and cook for 20 minutes or until the potato is tender. The soup can be blended until smooth and served immediately.

Wild Garlic Butter

Ingredients
1 tbsp. finely chopped wild garlic
1 tsp. lemon zest
¼ tsp. sea salt
1 cup butter

Instructions

In a small bowl, combine all of the ingredients and stir well. Place the wild garlic butter in a clean, sanitized jar and store in the refrigerator for one week or in the freezer for a few months.

Japanese Knotweed (*Fallopia japonica / Polygonum cuspidatum*)

Feared by landscapers, loved by foragers—**Japanese knotweed** is one of the most invasive plants in North America, but it also happens to be edible, medicinal, and surprisingly delicious. When young, its flavor is tart, bright, and often compared to rhubarb. Treated right, it becomes a springtime staple.

This plant is widespread throughout North America, especially in the Northeast and Appalachian regions, colonizing anywhere, from **riverbanks** to **cleared urban land**.

In peak form, this **herbaceous perennial** grows in **dense, towering thickets**, and it reaches up to 10–15 feet tall. The **hollow, bamboo-like** *stalks* are **jointed** and **speckled reddish-brown**. The *leaves* are **broad, spade-shaped**, and **alternate along the stem**. In late summer, **clusters of tiny white or greenish-white flowers** emerge.

Foraging Notes

Do not harvest from sites treated with **herbicides** or contaminated by **industrial runoff**. Knotweed often grows in degraded urban zones where soil quality is questionable. Look for clean streambanks or isolated groves.

The part to harvest is the **young spring shoot**, ideally 6–12 inches tall. Slice them cleanly at the base with a knife. As the plant matures, *older stalks* become too fibrous for food, but can still be used in **fermentation, vinegar infusions**, or for **medicinal purposes**.

Sauteed Japanese Knotweed

Ingredients
A handful of Japanese knotweed shoots
2 cloves minced garlic
1 tbsp. vegetable oil
Sea salt and black pepper

Instructions

Begin by rinsing the Japanese knotweed shoots and chopping them into ½ inch thick rounds. Place the vegetable oil in a pan over medium heat and add the Japanese knotweed slices. Sauté for a few minutes, then add the garlic and cook for a minute longer. Season with salt and pepper to taste and serve immediately.

Preparation & Use

Peel the outer skin of *older stalks* if tough. The *shoots* can be chopped and **sautéed**, **roasted**, or **boiled**. Their sour bite pairs well with sweet or savory flavors, making them ideal for **pickles**, **sauces**, and even **pies**.

Medicinal Value

Japanese knotweed is one of the richest natural sources of **resveratrol**, the antioxidant compound also found in red wine and grapes. It has **antimicrobial, anti-inflammatory, cardiovascular**, and **neuroprotective** properties.

Preservation

Young shoots can be **pickled in vinegar**, sliced thin and **dried**, or **fermented** like sauerkraut. *Dried stalks* can also be **powdered** for medicinal use.

Caution: Look-Alikes

Sometimes confused with **pokeweed** (*Phytolacca americana*) when not in flower. Look at the stem: knotweed has segmented nodes like bamboo; pokeweed does not.

Pickled Japanese Knotweed

Ingredients
Sliced Japanese knotweed shoots
2 minced garlic cloves
1 tsp. mustard seed
½ tsp. black pepper
¼ tsp. coriander
¼ tsp. sea salt
1 cup apple cider vinegar
1 cup water

Instructions

Place the Japanese knotweed shoots, garlic, and spices into a clean, sanitized pint-sized glass jar. In a small stockpot, bring 1 cup of apple cider vinegar and 1 cup of water to a simmer. Pour the simmering liquid over the Japanese knotweed until they are submerged. Screw a lid onto the jar and let it come to room temperature. Refrigerate and use within 2 weeks.

Sunchoke (*Helianthus tuberosus*)

Towering, **sunflower-like**, and secretly storing food beneath the soil—**sunchoke**, also known as **Jerusalem artichoke**, is one of the most overlooked wild root crops in North America. Despite the name, it has no connection to artichokes or Jerusalem. It's a native *Helianthus*, kin to the common sunflower, and its *underground tubers* are a **reliable, starchy food source** when times are lean.

It's native to the central and eastern U.S. but now grows wild across much of the continent, especially in **sunny thickets**, **woodland borders**, and **prairie edges**.

This **perennial plant** grows 6 to 10 feet tall, with **hairy, branching** *stems* and **bright yellow** *flowers* that resemble sunflowers but are smaller and bloom later—typically from late summer into early fall. The leaves are rough, lance-shaped, and arranged oppositely on the upper stem and alternately below.

Underground, sunchoke forms **knobby, tan-skinned tubers** that resemble ginger root or fat fingers. Inside, *the flesh* is **creamy white**, **crisp**, and **subtly sweet**—especially after a frost.

Harvesting

Dig tubers in **mid to late fall**, once the foliage has yellowed and died back. A digging fork is best to avoid breaking the tubers. After a few hard frosts, the plant converts much of its **inulin** (a starch that can cause gas and bloating) into **fructose**, making the roots easier to digest and naturally sweeter.

Preparation & Use

Eat sunchokes **raw**, **roasted**, **sautéed**, **boiled**, or **mashed**. Their flavor falls somewhere between potato and water chestnut, with a nutty sweetness when roasted. Thin slices make excellent chips when fried or baked.

Preservation

Store *fresh tubers* in a **cool**, **dark place** wrapped in **paper** or **sawdust**, or **slice** and **sun-dry** for long-term storage. Once dried, they can be **ground into flour** or rehydrated for soups and stews.

Foraging Note

While sunchoke has no toxic look-alikes, it may be confused with **garden sunflowers**, which lack edible tubers. Only dig if you're confident you're harvesting *Helianthus tuberosus*.

Medicinal Value

Sunchokes **support blood sugar regulation**, **gut flora health**, and **immune function**. They're one of the best natural sources of **inulin**, a **prebiotic fiber**.

Roasted Sunchokes

Ingredients
2 cups peeled and sliced sunchokes
2 tbsp. vegetable oil
½ tsp. sea salt
¼ tsp. black pepper

Instructions

Begin by preheating your oven to 425°F (218°C). In a bowl, combine all of the ingredients and toss until well mixed. Evenly place the sunchokes across a lined baking sheet and roast for 20 minutes, stirring occasionally. The sunchokes are finished when they are tender and golden brown.

Sunchoke Chips

Ingredients
A handful of sunchokes
2 cups cooking oil or fat
1 tsp. chopped rosemary
1 tsp. lemon zest
Sea salt and black pepper to taste

Instructions

Bring your preferred cooking oil or fat up to medium heat in a pot. Meanwhile, line a plate with paper towels and thinly slice the sunchokes. In a small bowl combine the rosemary, lemon zest, salt, and pepper. When the oil is hot, add the sunchokes and fry them until golden. Place the drained sunchoke chips onto the lined plate and sprinkle with the salt mixture. Eat immediately or store in an air-tight container.

Lamb's Quarter (*Chenopodium album*)

Often dismissed as a weed, **lamb's quarter** is actually one of the most nutritious greens you'll ever find—wild or cultivated.

This hardy plant is found all across North America and *thrives anywhere* the earth's been disturbed: **gardens, fence lines, construction sites, vacant lots, gravel alleys, and old farm fields**. Where the ground is broken, lamb's quarter rises.

This **herbaceous annual** (not perennial, despite common belief) grows **upright on a single main stem** that may branch in its upper third. The *stems* are **streaked with green** and **flushed with red or purple near the joints**. Its *leaves* are **shaped like goose feet**—broad at the base and tapering to a point—with **wavy** or **lightly toothed edges**. Most distinct is the **white, powdery bloom** that *coats* the undersides of new leaves, especially near the top. It's not dust or mold—just a natural wax that helps the plant retain moisture and signals peak harvest time. It blooms into **tiny green clustered flowers**.

Harvesting & Preparation

Pick the **youngest**, **most tender leaves** and **top shoots**—ideally *before* the plant goes to seed. At this stage, the flavor is rich, earthy, and **similar to spinach** or **chard**. Use scissors to snip, or simply pinch off tops with your fingers.

The entire upper half of the plant can be eaten: leaves, stems, and even flower buds when young. Cook as you would spinach—**steam, sauté, boil**, or toss into soups. It's high in **protein, calcium, iron, magnesium**, and **vitamins A** and **C**.

Preservation

To store *without electricity*, lamb's quarter leaves can be **air-dried** or **pressed flat and sun-dried** for later use in teas or stews. For *short-term storage*, wrap fresh leaves in a **damp cloth** and **keep in a cool area.** Avoid freezing unless long-term electricity is reliable.

Medicinal Use

Traditionally used as a **poultice for minor wounds, insect bites**, and **skin irritation**. Its crushed leaves **soothe inflammation** and **draw out toxins**.

Caution: Look-Alikes

Can be confused with **deadly nightshade** (*Atropa belladonna*) by the untrained eye—but the difference is obvious: *nightshade* **leaves** are **oval, smooth-edged**, and the plant bears **bell-shaped purple flowers**.

Lamb's Quarter Dip

Ingredients
1 cup steamed and chopped lamb's quarter leaves
2 tbsp. vegetable oil
1 minced garlic clove
1 cup yogurt
1 tbsp. lemon zest
Sea salt and black pepper to taste

Instructions

Begin by placing the lamb's quarter in a small bowl. In a small pan, heat the vegetable oil over low-medium heat and cook the garlic for 1-2 minutes or until fragrant. Pour the vegetable oil and garlic over the lamb's quarter and add the rest of the ingredients. Mix well and serve immediately with bread or crackers.

Roasted Lamb's Quarter

Ingredients
2 cups chopped lamb's quarter leaves and stems
2 tbsp. vegetable oil
Sea salt and black pepper to taste

Instructions

Preheat your oven to 350°F (180°C). Place the lamb's quarter in a bowl and toss with the vegetable oil, salt, and pepper. Evenly spread the lamb's quarter across a lined baking sheet and bake for 10-15 minutes or until crispy. Stir frequently to avoid burning.

Purslane (*Portulaca oleracea*)

Purslane is the plant you've probably stepped on a hundred times without ever knowing its value.

Creeping along **sidewalks**, **garden edges**, **driveways**, **urban lots**, **abandones farmland**, and **gravel paths**, it's one of the most common, widespread—and most *nutritious*—wild edibles in North America, thriving in **disturbed soil.** It can also tolerate dry and compacted soil, but its growth may be stunted.

This **low-growing succulent** forms **dense mats of reddish stems** and **thick**, **paddle-shaped leaves** that are **smooth**, **shiny**, and **slightly spooned**. It **spreads outward in a circular fashion**, hugging the ground. In the summer, it sprouts **tiny yellow flowers** with **five petals** that bloom briefly under direct sun.

Nutrition

Pound for pound, purslane outclasses most greens. It's rich in **omega-3 fatty acids** (specifically alpha-linolenic acid), **vitamin A**, **vitamin C**, **magnesium**, and **iron**. It's also loaded with **antioxidants** like **betalain pigments**, giving it strong **anti-inflammatory** and **cellular-protective qualities**.

Sautéed Purslane with Garlic

Ingredients

- 2 cups purslane leaves and stems
- 1 tbsp. vegetable oil
- 2 cloves garlic, minced
- ½ tsp. sea salt
- ¼ tsp. red pepper flakes (optional)

Instructions

Heat a pan over medium heat and add the oil. Add the garlic and sauté for 1-2 minutes.

Add the purslane and cook for 3-5 minutes, stirring occasionally. Sprinkle with salt and red pepper flakes, then serve warm.

Harvesting & Preparation

Harvest in warm months, ideally **before flowering** for peak tenderness. Snip whole stems or pluck the leaves. Rinse well, as it grows close to the soil. The entire plant—**leaves**, **stems**, and **flowers**—is edible.

Raw, it's slightly lemony and crisp, perfect for salads. **Cooked**, it softens like spinach and blends well into stir-fries, soups, or savory egg dishes. It **thickens broths** slightly due to its natural mucilage, making it useful in stews.

Preservation

Purslane can be **sun-dried**, **pickled**, or **fermented**. It dries quickly thanks to its low profile and succulence. Once dried, it can be crushed and added to meals for nutrition, or rehydrated for cooking.

Caution: Look-Alikes

Spurge (*Euphorbia* spp.) often grows alongside purslane and is *toxic*. Spurge has milky sap when broken; purslane does *not*. When in doubt, snap a stem—**no sap, you're safe**.

Purslane Salad

Ingredients

- 2 cups fresh purslane leaves and stems
- ½ cup cherry tomatoes, halved
- ¼ cup red onion, thinly sliced
- 2 tbsp. cheese (optional)
- 2 tbsp. vegetable oil
- 1 tbsp. lemon juice
- ½ tsp. sea salt
- ¼ tsp. black pepper

Instructions

Rinse the purslane and pat dry. Combine the purslane, tomatoes, red onion, and cheese in a salad bowl. In a small bowl, whisk the vegetable oil, lemon juice, salt, and pepper. Drizzle the dressing over the salad and toss to combine and serve immediately.

Wild Greens (Non-Weeds)

Not all wild greens grow like weeds. Some thrive quietly in the shadows of **forests**, **streambanks**, and **mountain meadows**—tender, nutrient-rich, and overlooked by most. These are the plants early settlers and native peoples turned to when gardens failed and supplies ran thin. Wild greens offer **essential vitamins**, **minerals**, and **hydration** in the field—without requiring fire, tools, or preparation.

Knowing these plants means you can eat clean and green anywhere—even when other food sources vanish.

Wood Sorrel (*Oxalis* spp.)

Bright, crisp, and lemony, wood sorrel is one of the easiest wild greens to recognize and eat. Its **clover-like leaves** and **tangy taste** make it a refreshing trail nibble or a perfect raw garnish in the field.

Found across much of North America, growing both coast to coast and from Canada to the Deep South, it thrives in **moist woods**, **forest edges**, and around **shaded clearings and shaded yards**.

The plant has **three heart-shaped leaflets per stem**, often with a **slight purple tint on the underside**. It grows **low to the ground** and produces **small yellow** or **white flowers** depending on species. The taste is distinct—tart, citrus-like, and slightly cooling.

Harvesting

Pick fresh **leaves**, **flowers**, or **seed pods** by hand. Best gathered **in the morning** before sun wilts the leaves. Grows **spring through fall** in moist, shaded soil.

Processing

No processing needed. Rinse briefly or wipe clean.

Culinary Use

Eat raw as a trail snack or add to wild salads. Can be **steeped in cold water** for a natural lemon-flavored drink. Pairs well with berries, fish, or wild grains.

Storage

Use **fresh**—wilts quickly. Can be air-dried for mild tea, though best raw.

Caution: Foraging Safety

Contains **oxalic acid** (like spinach or rhubarb). Safe in normal quantities, but **avoid excessive use** if prone to kidney issues. Easily distinguished by flavor and leaf shape—no toxic look-alikes when properly identified.

Miner's Lettuce (*Claytonia perfoliata*)

Delicate, juicy, and tender, miner's lettuce was once a key survival food for gold rush settlers in the West. Today, it's still one of the best-tasting wild greens you can find in the **spring**. It grows in thick mats with smooth, mild-flavored leaves that require no cooking.

The plant forms **round, disc-like leaves** pierced by a **central flower stalk**. *True leaves* are **heart-shaped**, but the circular "shield" leaf around the flower is its most recognizable feature.

It prefers **shady slopes**, **hillsides**, and **trailside creeks**—particularly in the Pacific Northwest, from California to British Columbia and into the interior mountain ranges. Native to the western United States.

Harvesting

Pick **entire stems** and **leaves** *before* the flowers wilt. Most abundant from **late winter through spring** in **cool climates**. Avoid during dry, hot seasons—leaves become tough.

Processing

No prep required. Rinse and eat fresh.

Culinary Use

Excellent **raw** in salads or sandwiches. Mixes well with other wild greens or used as a base green for foraged meals. Mild, slightly sweet flavor.

Storage

Best eaten fresh. Will keep for 2–3 days **refrigerated** or **wrapped in a damp cloth**.

Caution: Foraging Safety

No toxic look-alikes. Avoid patches near roadsides or where **herbicides** may be used.

Watercress (*Nasturtium officinale*)

Sharp, peppery, and clean, watercress is one of the most nutrient-rich wild greens on Earth. High in **vitamins A, C, and K**, it grows in **cool, clean streams** and **spring-fed seeps**, forming bright green mats over water. Used for centuries in field medicine and survival diets, it remains a true wild superfood.

Watercress has **branching stems** with **oval, toothed leaflets arranged alternately**. It grows in **running** or **shallow water**, often near rocks or along creek banks. When crushed, the leaves release a **mustard-like scent**.

It's widespread across North America, especially in the Northeast, Pacific Northwest, Appalachia, and anywhere cool running water is found.

Caution: Foraging Safety

Avoid **stagnant** or **livestock-contaminated water sources**. Watercress can harbor **liver flukes** or **parasites** if harvested from tainted water. Always verify water purity.

Harvesting

Gather **young leaves** and **tender tips**. Avoid bitter or yellowing growth. Always harvest from clean, fast-moving water sources away from livestock or runoff.

Processing

Rinse thoroughly.

Culinary Use

Spicy and fresh when **raw**—makes a powerful salad base or sandwich green. **Blanched** watercress mellows into a smooth, dark green vegetable perfect for soups, stews, or wild pesto. Cooking it lightly reduces sharpness.

Storage

Store in a **damp towel** or **submerge in clean water** in a cool area. Best used within 2 days.

Wild Mushrooms

In the shaded silence of the forest floor, something ancient grows—hidden in damp soil, feeding on roots, trees, and time itself. Wild mushrooms are some of the most mysterious and rewarding wild foods you can harvest. They demand caution, attention, and respect—but if you learn their signs, they offer flavor, medicine, and survival fuel unmatched by any garden crop.

Not all fungi are friendly. Some nourish, others kill. But with the right knowledge, you can walk into the woods and come back with gold, spice, and sustenance.

Chanterelle Mushrooms (*Cantharellus* spp.)

Chanterelles are among the most sought-after wild mushrooms in the world, prized for their rich, earthy flavor and their meaty, golden flesh. If you've ever tasted one fresh from the woods, sautéed in a pan with butter and a pinch of salt, you'll understand why chefs and foragers alike treat this mushroom like gold.

It's found across much of North America, particularly in the Pacific Northwest, Appalachians, Great Lakes region, and Eastern Canada.

Chanterelles grow in **hardwood and mixed forests**, especially near oaks, beeches, birches, and conifers. They prefer **moist**, **mossy ground** with plenty of leaf litter. You'll often find them in **clusters**, scattered across gentle slopes after summer rains—especially from **late spring through early fall**, depending on your region.

Their *caps* range from ¾ inch to over 5 inches across, **wavy** and **funnel-shaped**, with a **distinct golden-yellow color** that stands out against the forest floor. The *underside* doesn't have true gills, but instead bears **ridges or false gills**—blunt, forked ridges that run down the stem. The *texture* is **firm yet flexible**, not brittle.

Harvesting

Use a knife to cut at the base or gently twist them free. Avoid chanterelles that are overly dirty, waterlogged, or infested with insects. The best specimens are **dry**, **clean**, and **vibrant**.

Cleaning & Storage

At home, clean with a soft brush or a quick rinse followed by pat-drying. Never soak. Store fresh in a **paper bag in the refrigerator** for up to a week. For long-term storage, **slice and air-dry** or use a dehydrator until completely crisp, then keep in sealed jars.

Culinary Use

Sauté in butter or oil, add to risottos, soups, egg dishes, or use as a base for wild gravies. Their flavor is nutty, woodsy, and mildly peppery—too delicate to drown in heavy spices.

Caution: Look-Alikes

The most dangerous confusion is with the **Jack-o'-lantern mushroom** (*Omphalotus illudens*), which glows faintly in the dark and has **true gills**, not blunt ridges. Jack-o'-lanterns usually **grow in dense clumps on wood**, while chanterelles emerge *from soil*.

Chanterelle Toast

Ingredients
4 oz. fresh chanterelle mushrooms
1 tbsp. vegetable oil
1 slice of thick bread
2 tbsp. unsalted butter
1 thinly sliced small shallot
1 tbsp. chopped parsley
Salt and black pepper to taste

Instructions

Clean the chanterelles and slice any large mushrooms in half. Heat the vegetable oil in a pan and sauté the chanterelles for about 5 minutes. Meanwhile, toast and butter the slice of bread. After 5 minutes, add the shallots and the rest of the butter to the pan. Sauté for 5 more minutes then add the parsley and stir. Top the toast with the mushrooms and serve immediately.

Sauteed Chanterelles

Ingredients
1 tbsp. vegetable oil
1 diced shallot
2 minced garlic cloves
1 lb. chanterelle mushrooms
1 tbsp. butter
Salt and black pepper to taste

Instructions

Put the vegetable oil in a pan and bring up to medium high heat. Once hot, add the shallots and garlic and cook for a few minutes. Remove the shallots and garlic from the pan and set aside. Place the mushrooms in the pan and cook for 5 minutes, adding the butter at the end. Add the cooked shallots and garlic back to the pan and stir. Sprinkle with salt and pepper and serve immediately.

Morel Mushrooms (*Morchella* spp.)

There's a reason morels are legendary among foragers. Their flavor is rich, meaty, and unmistakable—something between roasted nuts and browned butter. But they don't give themselves up easily. Morels are elusive, appearing only for **a short window in spring**, often **hiding among** leaf litter and fallen trees like forest gold.

This mushroom is widely distributed across North America, especially common in the Midwest, Great Plains, Appalachia, and into southern Canada.

Morels grow in **deciduous forests**, often near ash, elm, poplar, and old apple orchards. They favor **moist, well-drained soil** after a spring rain and often appear in **recently disturbed areas**, including near fire scars or where logging has occurred. The most common species range from two to five inches tall, with a **honeycomb-like cap** that's **ridged** and **pitted** and **fully attached to the stem.**

Their color ranges from **pale blonde** to **deep brown** depending on species and soil. When cut lengthwise, a true morel will always be **hollow from tip to base**—a *critical feature* for safe identification.

Caution: Look-Alikes

False morels (*Gyromitra* spp.) are highly *toxic*. Unlike true morels, false morels are *not* hollow inside and often have **wrinkled, lobed caps** rather than a true honeycomb. Always slice and inspect your finds.

Harvesting

Cut morels at ground level with a knife or pinch them at the base. Carry in a mesh bag to allow spores to disperse as you walk. They're most abundant for **a few weeks between early spring and midsummer**, depending on latitude and elevation.

Cleaning & Storage

Brush away dirt or rinse lightly just before use—never soak. Store fresh morels in **a paper bag in the fridge** for up to five days. For long-term storage, **dehydrate** until brittle and keep in sealed jars or bags.

Culinary Use

Morels are best sautéed in butter or fat and eaten simply. Their earthy flavor shines in sauces, wild stews, or alongside game. Always cook morels—*never* eat raw, as they can cause gastric upset.

Hen of the Woods (*Grifola frondosa*)

At the base of old oaks in autumn, you might find what looks like a gray-brown explosion of feathers or petals—this is **hen of the woods**, one of the most substantial and flavorful wild mushrooms a forager can collect. Also called *maitake* in Japanese cuisine, it's savory, meaty, and deeply satisfying—often used as a meat substitute in wild cooking.

It's native to eastern North America and most commonly found from the Great Lakes and Midwest through the Northeast and down into the Appalachian mountains, always growing from a single base at the root flare of hardwood trees—usually oak.

Hen of the woods forms **large, clustered rosettes** made up of hundreds of **overlapping, spoon-shaped fronds**. The whole mass can grow over two feet across and weigh more than 10 pounds, though smaller clusters are more common. The *upper surface* is **gray to brown**, and the *underside* has **tiny white pores** instead of gills.

Harvesting

Look for hens from **late summer through mid-autumn**, especially **after a good rain**. Use a sharp knife to cut the mushroom at the base, leaving part of it behind to regrow. Young specimens are firm and clean. Older ones may be bug-ridden or waterlogged.

Cleaning & Storage

Brush or rinse gently, then tear into manageable pieces. Store in **a paper bag in the fridge** for up to a week. To preserve longer, **dehydrate** pieces or **cook and freeze** them in sealed containers.

Culinary Use

Sauté, roast, or add to soups and broths. Hen of the woods **holds up well** to long cooking and develops a **rich umami profile**. It's excellent in risotto, wild rice dishes, or paired with fatty meats.

Caution: Look-Alikes

Often confused with **black staining polypore** (*Meripilus sumstinei*), which **bruises black when cut**. While not poisonous, it's tougher and less palatable. Make sure your mushroom has white flesh that *stays white*, no strong odor, and the classic "ruffled" appearance.

King Bolete (*Boletus edulis*)

The king bolete is royalty in the world of wild mushrooms. Also known as *porcini*, it's thick, hearty, and carries a nutty, savory aroma that deepens with age. This mushroom is one of the most cherished culinary species on earth—and it grows abundantly in **coniferous** and **mixed forests** across much of North America.

The king bolete has a **large, rounded brown** *cap*, often **slightly sticky when fresh**, with a **thick, white to tan** *stalk* that **tapers slightly at the base**. Instead of gills, it has a **spongy pore surface** beneath the cap, pale white when young and yellowing with age. It typically grows from soil near pine, spruce, or fir, often appearing in **summer through early fall** after rains.

Caution: Look-Alikes

Avoid boletes with **red or orange pores**—some of these can cause gastric upset. The **toxic bitter bolete** (*Tylopilus felleus*) resembles *B. edulis*, but has a **strongly bitter taste** and a **reticulated net pattern on the stem**. Always taste a tiny bit raw and spit it out—true king boletes are mild and nutty.

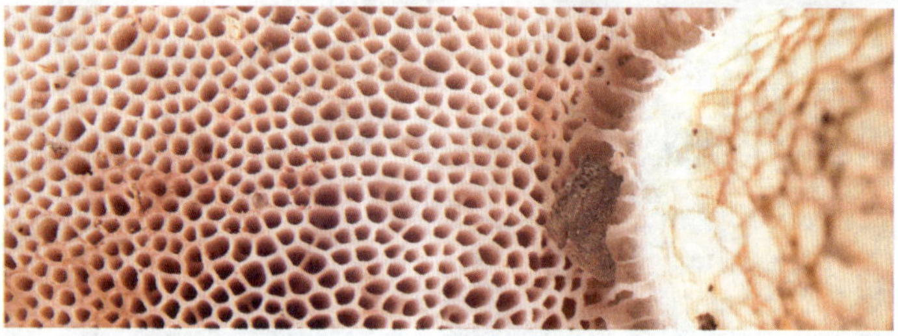

Harvesting

Cut at the base with a knife. Choose **firm** specimens with **white pores**—older ones may be infested with insects. Boletes can appear **singly** or in **fairy rings**, often near established tree roots.

Cleaning & Storage

Wipe or brush clean. Do not soak. Store *fresh* in **a paper bag in the fridge**. To *preserve*, **slice** and **dry until leathery or crisp**—porcini holds its flavor extremely well when dried.

Culinary Use

Sautéed porcini are rich and buttery with a deep umami kick. Dried slices rehydrate easily and make excellent soup stock or risotto base. The stems can be tough—use them for broth or drying.

Lion's Mane (*Hericium erinaceus*)

Lion's mane looks like something out of myth—a **white, shaggy cascade** of **icicle-like spines** growing from the side of a tree. But it's more than just striking. This mushroom is prized for its flavor, which is often compared to lobster or crab, and its **nootropic properties**—used historically to **support memory, focus,** and **nervous system health**.

This species grows throughout the eastern United States and parts of the Pacific Northwest, on hardwood trees, especially beech, oak, and maple.

It appears most often on **dead or dying trunks** in **late summer** and **fall**. The *fruiting body* is **snow-white** when fresh and **covered in soft, dangling spines** that resemble a lion's mane or a frozen waterfall. It grows in large clumps that can weigh several pounds.

Harvesting

Cut at the base with a knife when the spines are long but *still* bright white. Yellowing or browning specimens are older and less flavorful. Always leave some behind to encourage regrowth.

Cleaning & Storage

Brush gently to remove debris. Lion's mane absorbs water easily, so avoid rinsing unless absolutely necessary. Store in **a paper bag in the fridge** for up to a week. For preservation, slice and **dehydrate until crisp**.

Culinary Use

Sauté slowly in butter or oil until golden. The texture becomes tender and seafood-like, making it excellent in wild crab cakes, broths, or pan-fried as a standalone dish. It absorbs flavor well and browns beautifully when dry-cooked.

Caution: Look-Alikes

Few true look-alikes. Ensure the mushroom **grows from wood**, has **hanging spines at least ¼ inch long**, and is **white throughout**. Similar *Hericium* species (like *H. coralloides*) are also edible.

Wild Nuts

When autumn hits and leaves start falling, the trees begin offering some of the richest wild foods available: nuts. Unlike fragile greens or fleeting mushrooms, wild nuts are dense with calories, protein, and fats—the kind of nourishment that keeps you alive through winter. Crack them open, and you'll find what ancient tribes and early settlers depended on for long-term fuel. You don't need a farm to survive. You need a hammer, some fire, and the wisdom to gather. Most wild nuts require effort—tough shells, patient leaching, and some elbow grease—but they reward that effort with long-lasting energy and powerful nutrition.

Acorns (Fruit of *Quercus* spp.)

Beneath the leaves of every old oak lies a survival food older than nations. Acorns—overlooked by most—have quietly sustained civilizations, tribes, and families for thousands of years. Ground into **flour**, **roasted**, or **boiled**, they offer dense nutrition and a direct connection to the wild.

Acorns are **the fruit of oak trees**, which dominate forests across North America. Oaks fall into two major types: **white oaks** and **red oaks**. White oaks have rounded lobes on their leaves and produce light brown acorns with lower tannin content—smoother and easier to process. Red oaks bear sharply pointed, bristled leaves, and their darker acorns require longer leaching due to higher tannin levels.

White oak leaves and acorns

Red oak leaves and acorns

You'll find oaks in almost every region: from the **hardwood forests** of the Appalachians, to Midwestern **plains**, down through Texas and the Deep South, and even across parts of the West. Where there are oaks, there are acorns.

Harvesting

Gather acorns in **early to mid-fall**, ideally right after they drop. Choose **firm**, **intact specimens** without cracks or insect holes. Remove the cap, crack open the shell, and inspect the meat—keep only those that are **pale yellow or light brown** inside. Blackened or dusty ones are rotten and should be discarded.

Tannin Removal (Leaching)

Acorns are **high in tannins**, which make them **bitter** and can cause **digestive upset** if eaten raw. To remove tannins:

1. Shell and crush the raw acorns into small pieces.
2. Cover with freshly boiled water and soak for one hour.
3. Drain and repeat with new hot water until the soaking water runs clear or the acorns taste mild and nutty.

Leached acorns can be eaten as-is, or dried and ground into flour.

Culinary Use

Once processed, acorns are incredibly versatile. Use *acorn flour* to make **bread, pancakes, porridge**, or even thickening for soups and stews. *Whole acorns* can be **roasted like chestnuts**, or **boiled until tender**. The flavor is rich, slightly nutty, and earthy.

Storage

Dried acorn flour stores well in **sealed containers**. *Whole leached acorns* can be **sun-dried** or **smoke-dried** and kept in **jars** or **cloth bags** for long-term use—ideal for off-grid or survival conditions.

Caution: Look-Alikes

None. All acorns from true oak trees (*Quercus* spp.) are edible once leached. Just ensure you're collecting in **clean areas** away from roadsides or sprayed land.

Acorn Pancakes

Ingredients
¾ cup acorn flour
¾ cup whole wheat flour
2 tsp. baking powder
½ tsp. sea salt
1 ½ cups milk
3 tbsp. melted butter
2 eggs
1 tbsp. honey

Instructions

In separate bowls, mix the dry and wet ingredients until well combined. Add the wet ingredients to the dry ingredients and stir until smooth. Heat a greased pan over medium heat and cook each pancake until golden brown. Serve immediately.

Acorn Jelly

Ingredients
1 cup acorn flour
1 tbsp. cornstarch
5 cups cold water
1 tsp. sea salt
1 tsp. vegetable oil

Instructions

Add the acorn flour, cornstarch, cold water, and salt to a bowl and mix well. Pour the mixture into a pot and heat over medium heat. Stir frequently for about 10 minutes or until the jelly has become thick and is holding its shape. At this point, add the vegetable oil, stir, and cook for another minute. Transfer the jelly into a glass container and cool in the refrigerator. Once cooled, the acorn jelly can be sliced and served with a sauce.

Black Walnuts (*Juglans nigra*)

Tough, gritty, and packed with one of the most intense nut flavors in the forest—black walnuts are a challenge to crack and a treasure to master. These nuts were a staple for early American homesteaders, and they still drop by the hundreds in untamed backyards and rural woodlands today.

This tree is most common in the central and eastern United States—especially the Ohio River Valley, Appalachians, and lower Midwest—but can also be found scattered as far south as Texas and north into southern Ontario.

The black walnut tree is large and commanding, often reaching **70 feet tall**. Its **compound leaves** consist of 15–23 leaflets, and its bark is dark, furrowed, and rugged. The nuts fall in a **round, green husk** that turns black and sticky as it decomposes. Inside lies an **extremely hard, corrugated shell** with **sweet, rich nutmeat** in hidden chambers.

Harvesting

Collect in **early to mid-autumn**. Wear gloves the husk stains skin and clothes dark brown. Let the nuts sit until husks blacken, then remove the husks by stomping or scraping them off. Rinse thoroughly, then cure the nuts in a cool, dry place for 2–3 weeks before cracking.

Processing

Use a heavy-duty nutcracker, hammer, or bench vise to break open the shells. Black walnuts are **notoriously difficult to open** cleanly, so don't expect speed—just persistence.

Culinary Use

The nutmeat has a **bold, earthy, almost smoky flavor** that stands up in breads, cakes, wild grain dishes, or eaten by the handful. Mix with dried fruit or honey for a high-calorie trail ration.

Storage

Cured and shelled black walnuts keep well in **sealed containers, cool root cellars**, or **vacuum-sealed bags**. They can also be **roasted and ground** into a *meal* or **pressed** for *oil*.

Caution: Look-Alikes

Butternut (*Juglans cinerea*) looks similar, but its nut is **oval**, *not* round. It's also edible, though less common. Do not confuse with **horse chestnut**, which is *toxic* and usually found in **urban landscaping**—*not* forests.

Butternut (Juglans cinerea)

Horse chestnut (Aesculus hippocastanum)

Hickory Nuts (*Carya* spp.)

Smooth, buttery, and built for survival—**hickory nuts** are one of the finest wild foods in North America. Native tribes prized them for their oil and energy. Their trees grow strong and tall in **hardwood forests**, and when they drop their bounty in fall, they demand your attention.

Hickory trees bear **compound leaves** (similar to walnut), with a smoother bark that often peels in vertical strips. The nuts themselves come encased in a **thick green husk** that **splits into quarters** as it dries. Inside, you'll find a **tough**, **ridged shell** with **sweet**, **mild nutmeat**.

There are several species across the U.S., but the best-tasting include **shagbark hickory** (*Carya ovata*) and **shellbark hickory** (*Carya laciniosa*). Pignut and bitternut hickories are edible, but often too bitter for most palates.

Harvesting

Gather in **early fall** as the husks split open and nuts hit the ground. Avoid those with holes or mold. Let them dry for a few days before cracking.

Processing

Use a hammer or a solid rock to break open the shell. Compared to black walnuts, hickory nuts are much easier to crack and yield larger, cleaner pieces of meat.

Culinary Use

Eat **raw** or **roast** over low heat to intensify flavor. Hickory nuts shine in porridge, bread, pancakes, or crushed into wild game stews. The **nut oil** is also excellent when **pressed** or **simmered** into traditional "hickory milk."

Storage

Store shelled or unshelled in a **dry place**. Nutmeat will last several weeks; **freeze** or **dehydrate** if storing longer. Ground **hickory nut flour** can be mixed with acorn flour for a hearty, high-calorie baking mix.

Caution: Look-Alikes

Avoid **buckeye nuts** (*toxic*) and urban **horse chestnuts**. Hickory nuts will always be found in *native* hardwood forests, never ornamental plantings.

*Buckeye nuts (*Aesculus glabra*)*

Wild Fruits & Berries

Not every wild food has to be boiled, ground, or leached. Some just need to be picked and eaten in the sun. Wild fruits and berries are the sweet pulse of the foraging year—brief, scattered, but intensely rewarding. They offer sugar, hydration, antioxidants, and flavor that surpass anything sold in a store.

Across North America, berries and wild fruit trees grow in forests, along fences, riverbanks, and meadows. Knowing when and where they ripen can give you access to food that's portable, high in energy, and easy to preserve. But not all berries are safe. Learn the shapes, colors, leaf patterns, and seeds. The right fruit can nourish you—while the wrong one can kill.

Serviceberries (*Amelanchier* spp.)

Also known as juneberries, saskatoons, or shadbush, serviceberries are a northern favorite—**sweet, almond-scented** berries that ripen in **early summer** and grow across much of the United States and Canada. High in **fiber**, **minerals**, and **antioxidants**, they were often dried and packed into pemmican by Native tribes.

Serviceberry is a **tall shrub** or **small tree** with smooth gray bark, **oval serrated leaves**, and **five-petaled white flowers** that appear in early spring. The *berries* are **round**, **bluish-purple to deep red**, and grow in **small clusters**.

Harvesting

Pick berries when **fully dark** and **soft**—they're bland when underripe. Birds often get there first, so harvest quickly when they appear ripe.

Processing

Berries can be eaten **raw**, **dried**, mashed into **jam**, or **juiced**. They contain soft seeds that add a faint almond flavor when chewed.

Culinary Use

Excellent raw, in pies, or as **dried trail food**. They cook down well into syrup or can be fermented into **wine**.

Storage

Fresh berries keep 3–4 days. **Drying** is the best method for long-term storage—spread them thinly and **sun-dry** or use **low heat**.

Caution: Foraging Safety

Serviceberries are safe and easy to identify. No known toxic look-alikes.

Wild Plums (*Prunus americana*, *Prunus mexicana*)

Sharp, **sweet**, and sometimes **fiercely tart**, wild plums are the summer fruit of thickets and river valleys. Unlike their store-bought cousins, wild plums vary widely in taste, size, and color—but when ripe, they offer some of the best fruit flavor in the wild.

These thorny shrubs or small trees grow across the central and eastern U.S., often forming dense thickets **along fence lines**, **old pastures**, and **field edges**. *Leaves* are **oval, finely toothed**, and **alternately arranged**. *Fruits* appear in **late summer**, ranging from **yellow** to **red** to **purple**.

Harvesting

Pick plums once they come off the branch with a **light tug**. Taste each tree—some are sour, others sweet. Watch for fruit fly damage or wasps.

Processing

Rinse and pit before use. **Boil down** into sauces, jellies, or syrup. Can also be **dried whole** into chewy, tangy fruit leather.

Culinary Use

Best in **jam**, **syrup**, or **wild plum wine**. Pits can be cracked for the inner kernel, but only in moderation—many contain trace cyanide.

Storage

Refrigerate fresh for up to a week. **Cooked** or **dried** plums store much longer. Fruit leather lasts several months in **dry conditions**.

Caution: Foraging Safety

Only harvest plums from known *Prunus* species. *Avoid* **cherry-like fruits** with **no seam** or **fuzzy skin**—they may be *toxic*.

Blackberries (*Rubus allegheniensis*, *Rubus fruticosus*, and others)

Wild blackberries are everywhere—along **roadsides**, **forest edges**, **overgrown fields**, and **abandoned homesteads**. Their thorny canes and **sweet**, **sun-warmed fruit** are a staple of **late summer** foraging. Unlike store-bought varieties, wild blackberries are smaller, darker, and more flavorful—with an edge of wildness that cuts through every bite.

These dense, sprawling brambles form **tangled thickets** with **arching stems** covered in **thorns**. *Leaves* are **compound**, usually in groups of three to five, and *flowers* are **white** or **pale pink**. *Berries* ripen from green to red to **deep purple-black**.

Harvesting

Pick when the berries are **soft**, **dark**, and **pull free easily**. Wear gloves and long sleeves—the thorns are aggressive. Harvest **early in the day** before the sun softens them.

Processing

Rinse gently. Can be eaten **fresh**, **cooked** into jam or syrup, **fermented**, or **dried** into leather.

Culinary Use

Blackberries shine in everything—jelly, wine, pies, compote, or eaten right from the cane. Pair well with wild mint or sumac.

Storage

Highly perishable fresh—store in a **cool place** and eat within 24–48 hours. For *long-term use*, **dry**, **freeze**, or **preserve** in syrup.

Caution: Foraging Safety

Watch for **poison ivy** or **thorny look-alikes** in the same areas. True blackberry canes are *arching*, not upright, and *always* bear compound leaves.

Mulberries (*Morus rubra*, *Morus alba*)

If you find purple stains on the sidewalk in summer, there's likely a mulberry tree overhead. These fast-growing, fruit-heavy trees produce **sweet**, **juicy berries** that drop by the handful in **late spring and early summer**—feeding birds, squirrels, and smart foragers alike.

Mulberry trees grow up to 60 feet tall with **broad**, **serrated leaves** that vary in shape—some lobed, some not. The fruits resemble **long**, **thin blackberries** and change from green to red to black (or white, in *M. alba*).

Harvesting

Lay a cloth beneath the tree and shake the branches—ripe berries fall easily. Harvest during **dry weather** to avoid mold. The **season is short**, so gather quickly.

Processing

Rinse and use **fresh** or **freeze**. Can be cooked into syrup, jelly, or dried whole.

Culinary Use

Excellent **raw**, in pancakes, or mixed with other fruits. Cook down into a **thick jam** or boil for a deep purple **syrup**.

Storage

Refrigerate for 1–2 days or **freeze**. **Dried** mulberries store well and make a great trail snack.

Caution: Foraging Safety

Mulberries have no toxic look-alikes. Don't confuse with inedible ornamental trees. Only eat *fully ripe* fruit.

Wild Grapes
(*Vitis riparia, Vitis aestivalis, Vitis labrusca*)

Twisting through trees, **climbing fences**, and **spilling over streambanks**, wild grapes are easy to spot once you know their leaves and vines. Tart and powerful when fresh, they transform beautifully when cooked—making some of the finest wild wine, jelly, and juice around.

They grow across the entirety of North America in different varieties.

Wild grapevines have **large**, **toothed**, **maple-like leaves** and **curly tendrils** that help them climb. **Clusters** of **small, round grapes** ripen from green to dark purple or blue, depending on species. The bark often peels in long strips.

Vitis aestivalis, *Don Kasak, CC-BY-SA-2.0*

Harvesting

Collect in **late summer** or **early fall** once fruit softens and darkens. Avoid withered or sun-dried clusters. **Watch for wasps.**

Processing

Remove stems, rinse, and cook down for juice or jelly. Wild grapes contain **seeds** and **thick skins**—strain or blend as needed.

Culinary Use

Ideal for **syrup**, **jam**, **juice**, or **fermentation**. The flavor is intense and complex—more sour than store-bought grapes.

Storage

Refrigerate fresh for up to a week. Juice can be **canned or frozen**. **Dried** grapes (raisins) are rare but possible with patience.

Caution: Foraging Safety

Avoid **moonseed** (*Menispermum canadense*), a *toxic* look-alike with **crescent-shaped seeds** and **no tendrils**. True wild grape vines *always* have forked tendrils and shaggy bark.

Menispermum canadense, *Toronto, Canada, by Nadiatalent, Own work, CC-BY-SA-4.0*

Nonenmac, Own work, CC-BY-SA-3.0

Vitis labrusca, *Lucy Keith-Diagne, CC-BY-SA-4.0*

Wild Wetland Plants

Cattails (*Typha latifolia*, *Typha angustifolia*)

Cattails are one of the most complete wild resources available to a forager. Found in **marshes**, **ponds**, and **wetlands** across North America, they offer food, medicine, insulation, cordage, and fire-starting material—all from one tall, waving stalk. Where water lingers and soil softens, cattails grow in **thick stands**, marking the edges of survival.

Cattails grow 6 to 10 feet tall with **long**, **flat**, green **leaves** that resemble blades. Their most iconic feature is the **brown**, **sausage-shaped flower spike** that appears in summer. Below the surface, **thick rhizomes** spread through mud and silt, anchoring the plant and storing dense starch. Two species are most common: **broadleaf cattail** (*Typha latifolia*) and **narrowleaf cattail** (*Typha angustifolia*).

Harvesting and Processing

Young shoots in **spring** can be pulled from the base, peeled, and eaten **raw (preferably)** or **cooked**. *Immature flower heads* can be harvested in **early summer** and immediately **boiled** and consumed. *Pollen* from mature heads can be **shaken loose** in **mid to late summer** and **used as flour**. It needs to be sifted and stored dry. *Rhizomes* are best collected in **fall** or **winter**. They must be peeled, crushed in water, and allowed to settle—once the **starch** separates, dry it for use as flour or thickener.

Culinary Use

The *shoots* are mild and similar to **cucumber** or **zucchini**. *Boiled flower* heads resemble **corn**. *Pollen* adds **subtle sweetness** and **high protein** to baked goods. *Rhizome starch* can be cooked into **flatbreads** or stirred into **soups** and **stews**.

Storage

Fresh parts do not store long. **Pollen** and **starch**, once dried, can be stored in **sealed containers** or **bags** for months. Fluff from mature heads also makes excellent tinder or insulation when dry.

Caution: Foraging Safety

Only harvest from *clean* water sources. Cattails **absorb toxins** from polluted or chemically treated water, making them unsafe in industrial or urban runoff zones.

Cattail Pancakes

Ingredients
½ cup cattail pollen
½ cup all-purpose flour
1 tbsp. sugar
1 tsp. baking powder
1 egg
¾ cup milk
1 tbsp. melted butter

Instructions

In a bowl, mix the cattail pollen, flour, sugar, and baking powder. In another bowl, beat the egg, milk, and melted butter together. Combine the wet and dry ingredients and stir until smooth. Heat a greased pan over medium heat and cook the pancakes until golden brown. Serve with honey or fruit.

Sautéed Cattail Shoots

Ingredients
2 cups young cattail shoots, washed and trimmed
1 tbsp. vegetable oil or butter
1 clove garlic, minced
½ tsp. sea salt
¼ tsp. black pepper

Instructions

Slice the cattail shoots into 2-inch pieces. Heat a pan over medium heat and add the oil or butter. Add the garlic and sauté for 1 minute until fragrant. Add the cattail shoots and cook for 5 minutes, stirring frequently. Season with salt and pepper and serve warm.

Arrowhead (*Sagittaria latifolia*)

Arrowhead, also known as duck potato or wapato, is one of the most ancient and reliable wetland foods in North America. It was a staple among many indigenous tribes, prized for its **starchy tubers** that grow beneath the water's surface. Where shallow water stands still—**pond margins, marshes, river backwaters**—you'll often find its long, pointed leaves rising like spears from the mud.

This **perennial** aquatic plant grows in **clusters**, its **broad, arrow-shaped leaves** standing above the surface on **thick stalks**. In summer, it produces **small white three-petaled flowers**. Hidden below are **swollen tubers, shaped like eggs** or **small potatoes**, buried in silt or submerged sand.

Harvesting

Tubers can be foraged in **late summer through fall**. Use your hands or a stick to feel through the mud and pop them loose—they'll often float once dislodged. Look for plants growing in **shallow, slow-moving water** no deeper than two feet.

Processing

Rinse the tubers clean of mud and peel off any rough skin. They can be **boiled**, **roasted**, or **sliced and fried**. The **flesh is starchy and smooth**, somewhere between a potato and chestnut.

Culinary Use

Boiled arrowhead makes an **excellent trail food**. **Roasted**, it becomes nutty and rich. It can also be **mashed** or **dried** and **ground into flour** for thickening stews or baking cakes.

Storage

Fresh tubers keep for several days in a **cool**, **dry place**. For *long-term storage*, slice and **sun-dry** or **smoke-dry**. Once dried, they can be ground into a flour or stored whole for months.

Caution: Foraging Safety

Only harvest from *clean* water. Avoid roadside ditches or runoff ponds. Always confirm identification—arrowhead has no toxic look-alikes when properly recognized, but don't assume without cross-checking leaf shape and habitat.

Pickerelweed (*Pontederia cordata*)

Elegant and often overlooked, pickerelweed is a tall, flowering wetland plant with striking blue-purple spikes that rise above the waterline in **late summer**. While not as well-known as cattails or arrowhead, it provides **edible leaves**, **seeds**, and **stalks**, making it a valuable addition to any forager's wetland map.

Pickerelweed grows in **shallow water** along **ponds**, **marshes**, and **lake edges**. Its *leaves* are **glossy green**, **heart-** or **lance-shaped**, **rising vertically** from the base. The *flower stalks* are **thick** and **rigid**, bearing **dense spikes** of **violet-blue** *blossoms*.

Harvesting

Young leaves and shoots can be harvested in **spring** before they toughen. *Flower spikes* and *seeds* appear in **mid to late summer**. Seeds are the most prized edible part and can be collected by hand once the flowers fade and dry.

Processing

Young leaves can be used like spinach, **boiled** or **steamed**. *The seeds*, once dried, can be **roasted** or **ground into meal**. They have a nutty flavor and were historically added to soups or baked into cakes.

Culinary Use

Cooked pickerelweed *greens* are **mild** and **earthy**. The *seeds* can be cracked and **eaten whole**, ground into **flour**, or **added to wild-grain mixtures**. They store well and offer lasting calories.

Storage

Dry seeds thoroughly before storing. They'll keep for months in a sealed container. *Leaves* are best used **fresh** or **blanched** and **dried** for short-term storage.

Caution: Foraging Safety

Pickerelweed has no dangerous look-alikes, but always harvest from *clean* water. Avoid stagnant or polluted wetlands, especially those near farms or development.

Wild Desert Plants

The desert looks barren to the untrained eye—sun-baked soil, harsh winds, and thorns guarding every inch of green. But for those who know what to look for, these arid landscapes are hiding ancient food and medicine. From the high deserts of the Southwest to the sun-scorched valleys of the Sonoran and Mojave, wild desert plants have sustained life for thousands of years.

Survival in the desert depends on knowing what grows, when it's safe, and how to process it. These plants are tough, resilient, and often guarded by spines or toxins. But behind their defenses, they offer calories, sugars, hydration, medicine, and even flour. Learn them well, and the desert is no longer empty—it becomes a larder.

Prickly Pear (*Opuntia* spp.)

Bright red fruit on a cactus pad may look alien to some, but to desert dwellers, it's a sweet reward hidden in plain sight. Prickly pear is one of the most versatile desert plants in North America—offering both edible fruit and tender pads that have nourished people for centuries.

It's found across **arid** and **semi-arid regions** of North America, especially in the American Southwest, Texas, parts of California, and as far north as the Dakotas and southern Canada in drier microclimates.

This cactus grows in **wide clumps** with **thick, flat pads** covered in **sharp spines** and **tiny hair-like glochids**. It produces striking **yellow, orange**, or **red flowers** in spring and early summer, followed by **oval-shaped fruit** known as "tunas" in late summer and fall.

Harvesting

Use tongs and thick gloves. Harvest *young pads* (called "nopales") in **spring** when they're **bright green** and **tender**. Collect *ripe fruit* once it **deepens in color** and **softens slightly**—usually **late summer**. Remove glochids by roasting briefly over an open flame or scrubbing under water.

Processing

Nopales should be de-spined, rinsed, and sliced. **Boil, grill**, or **sauté**. *Fruit* can be peeled and eaten **raw**, **juiced**, or boiled into **syrup**.

Culinary Use

Pads are **tart** and **mucilaginous**—excellent in stews, egg dishes, or grilled with meat. *The fruit* is **sweet** and **refreshing**, ideal for jelly, wine, or simply eaten chilled.

Storage

Pads last for days fresh but can be blanched and frozen. **Fruit juice** or **pulp** can be canned or dried into fruit leather.

Caution: Foraging Safety

Always remove glochids *completely*—they cause skin irritation and internal discomfort if swallowed. **Never eat unripe pads raw.**

Mesquite (*Prosopis* spp.)

Beneath the twisted limbs of the mesquite tree lies one of the desert's most ancient foods: the mesquite pod. For native peoples across the Southwest, these **long, tan seedpods** were ground into sweet flour—dense with **protein**, **fiber**, and **slow-burning energy**. In dry regions, it was survival food.

This tree dominates **arid grasslands** and **deserts** of the American Southwest and northern Mexico, especially in Texas, New Mexico, Arizona, and the California deserts.

Mesquite trees **grow low and sprawling** with **compound**, **feathery leaves** and **sharp thorns**. They produce **fragrant yellowish catkin-like flowers** in late spring, followed by **curved**, **woody seedpods** that ripen by midsummer.

Harvesting

Collect seedpods in **summer** once they **dry fully on the tree**. Avoid pods that fall to the ground or show signs of mold or insect damage.

Processing

Clean and dry pods thoroughly. Break into pieces and **grind into flour** using a stone or mill. Sift to remove hard seeds.

Culinary Use

Mesquite flour is **naturally sweet** with **notes of molasses** and **cocoa.** Use it to make cakes, pancakes, porridge, or to enrich other wild flours. It's **gluten-free** and rich in **fiber** and **minerals**.

Storage

Store whole *dry pods* in a **cool, dry place.** *Flour* should be kept **sealed in jars** or **bags** and used within a few months to prevent oxidation.

Caution: Foraging Safety

Some trees hybridize with non-edible species. Always taste a small piece raw—**if bitter or astringent, discard**. Pods should be *brittle*, **not rubbery**.

Agave (*Agave americana* and relatives)

Agave is the spearpoint of the desert—sharp, dangerous, and life-giving. These massive rosettes of thick, spiked leaves have been used for centuries for food, fiber, syrup, and even alcohol. When harvested properly, the heart of the agave provides rich, starchy sustenance, especially in winter and spring.

Agave grows as a **large central crown** with **thick gray-green leaves edged with sharp teeth** and **tipped with a deadly spine**. Mature plants send up a towering stalk (called a quiote) that flowers once—then dies. It's this **blooming phase** that signals the plant is ready for harvest.

Harvesting

Harvest in the months before flowering. Cut the outer leaves and extract the central heart or piña. Roast slowly in an earthen pit or oven for several hours to break down inulin into sugars.

Processing

Once **roasted**, the *heart* becomes sweet and fibrous. **Chop** or **shred** for eating, or **press to extract sweet juice**. *Leaves* can be **roasted**, and *stalks* can also be **harvested young** and **roasted** like asparagus.

Culinary Use

Agave heart is chewy, smoky, and sweet—traditionally eaten in chunks or dried for trail food. The syrup can be reduced and stored. The roasted stalk is tender with a mild vegetal flavor.

Storage

Roasted agave can be **dried** and stored for months. *Syrup* keeps well in **sealed containers**.

Caution: Foraging Safety

Raw agave sap is **caustic** and **can burn skin**. Always cook *thoroughly*. Only harvest older plants nearing bloom—young agave is bitter and contains more toxins.

Yucca (*Yucca baccata*, *Yucca elata*, and others)

Yucca is a keystone of the desert—providing food, fiber, soap, and shelter for those who understand its cycles. Its **sword-like leaves** and **towering flower stalks** are unmistakable in the desert landscape, and nearly every part of the plant has traditional uses.

It's found in **dry open ground**, **deserts**, and **high plains** from California to Texas and as far north as Nebraska—most common in the Great Basin, Mojave, and Chihuahuan deserts.

Yucca grows as a **dense rosette** of **long**, **rigid green leaves tipped with sharp points.** In late spring to early summer, a tall central stalk emerges and blooms with **clusters of creamy white flowers.** Edible varieties include **banana yucca** (*Yucca baccata*) and **soaptree yucca** (*Yucca elata*), both widespread in the Southwest.

Harvesting

Pick *flowers* **just before full bloom**, ideally **in the morning** when they're fresh and tender. *Fruit* from *Y. baccata* ripens in **midsummer** and can be gathered **once it turns dark and soft**. *Roots* are best harvested in **fall** or **winter** for soap or starch.

Processing

Remove stamens and **wash flowers** before eating. *Fruit* can be **roasted** whole, **peeled**, or **split and sun-dried.** *Roots* can be **peeled**, **chopped**, and **boiled** or **pounded** into a starchy mash.

Culinary Use

Flowers are **slightly bitter** and best **sautéed** or **battered and fried**. The *ripe fruit* is **sweet** and **starchy**, similar to baked squash or banana. *Dried fruit* can be **ground into flour**.

Storage

Dry *fruit* **in thin slices** and store in **cloth** or **sealed containers**. *Flower petals* can be **blanched** and **dried**, though **best eaten fresh.** *Roots* used for soap should be **dried** and **kept cool**.

Caution: Foraging Safety

Avoid unripe fruit and raw root. Only consume flowers *in moderation* to prevent stomach upset. Watch for **similar-looking ornamental yuccas**, which are sometimes **chemically treated**.

Woodsweets: Wild Treats for the Road-Worn Soul

Not essential for survival, but unforgettable in the wild. These are the subtle comforts—the sweet drips, floral sips, or juicy bites that lift morale when the hunger settles in and the trail stretches long. Found on sunny hillsides, fence rows, or forest edges, these aren't staples... but they *feel like magic* when you find them.

Honeysuckle (*Lonicera* spp.)

Golden trumpets glowing in the evening sun—honeysuckle is the childhood memory of summer made edible. While not a food in the traditional sense, its sweet nectar and floral aroma make it one of the most charming wild finds for the weary forager. With over 180 species worldwide, honeysuckles are known for their **clusters of tubular flowers**, their **climbing vines**, and that **one hidden drop of nectar in each bloom**.

In North America, the most common species include **Japanese honeysuckle** (*Lonicera japonica*)—an aggressive non-native vine—and native species like *Lonicera sempervirens* (**coral honeysuckle**). The vines **climb** fences, trees, and hedgerows, blooming in **late spring through early summer** with **white**, **yellow**, or **orange-red flowers**.

It's found across the eastern United States, Midwest, and southern Canada, especially along **woodland edges**, **old homesteads**, and **sunny fence lines**.

Harvesting

Pick the **freshest**, **fully open flowers** during **warm**, **dry weather**—ideally midmorning to midday. Pinch just beneath the flower's base and gently pull the style (the long white filament) through the bloom. A single drop of nectar collects at the base—sweet, floral, and deeply nostalgic.

Culinary Use

While the nectar itself is too scarce for bulk use, honeysuckle flowers can be **infused into syrups**, **jellies**, **teas**, and **vinegars**. **Steep flowers** in hot water to make a **delicately fragrant tea**. **Avoid leaves and green stems**—they are *mildly toxic* and bitter.

Preservation

Use flowers **fresh**, or **air-dry gently** to preserve scent and flavor. Store dried blossoms in **sealed glass jars** for infusions or potpourri.

Caution: Look-Alikes

Stick to yellow or white trumpet-shaped honeysuckle blooms. **Do not consume berries** or **parts of bush honeysuckles** (*Lonicera tatarica*, etc.)—many are *toxic*. If it doesn't produce fragrant flowers with sweet nectar and trumpet-shaped blooms, leave it.

Sweet Birch (*Betula lenta*)

Crack a twig, and it smells like wintergreen gum. Sweet birch is one of the forest's most fragrant trees—hidden among the ridges of Appalachia and northern woods. Its twigs and inner bark hold **methyl salicylate**, the same compound that gives wintergreen its **cooling bite**. You can chew it, boil it, or steep it to draw out a clean, spicy-sweet flavor that cuts through cold nights like fire.

Sweet birch is a **medium to tall tree** with smooth, dark brown bark that peels in horizontal lenticels (not paper-thin like other birches). The *leaves* are **oval** with **finely serrated edges** and a **sharp-pointed tip**. The *twigs* are **dark**, **slender**, and when broken, **release a wintergreen scent**.

It's found in the northeastern United States, Appalachians, and into southeastern Canada—thriving in **cool forests** with **rich, moist soil**.

Harvesting

Snip young twigs or peel small sections of bark from **fallen branches** (never strip bark from a living tree unless it's a true survival situation). Twigs can be **chewed directly** or **chopped and bolled**.

Culinary Use

Boil chopped twigs for 10–15 minutes to create a sweet **birch tea** or **decoction**—traditionally used as a spring tonic and natural pain reliever. You can also **infuse it into sugar syrup** or **ferment it** to make traditional birch beer.

Preservation

Twigs can be **dried in bundles** and stored in **cloth bags** or **glass jars** for months. *Dried bark shavings* retain flavor and aroma for **long-term use.**

Caution: Look-Alikes

Do not confuse with **black cherry** (*Prunus serotina*), which also has horizontal lenticels but **smells of bitter almonds** and is *toxic* in large doses. True sweet birch has that unmistakable minty scent when scraped.

Katja Schulz, CC-BY-2.0

Redbud Flowers (*Cercis canadensis*)

When the forest is still waking up, redbuds explode into bloom—**magenta-pink blossoms** clinging to bare branches like sparks of color in a brown world. These flowers aren't just beautiful—they're **edible**, **tangy**, and **slightly sweet**. Tossed into a salad or eaten by the handful on the trail, they're one of spring's best-kept secrets.

Redbud is a **small, ornamental tree** with smooth gray bark and **heart-shaped leaves**. The blooms sprout directly from the branches and trunk in **tight clusters**, appearing before the foliage in early spring.

It's native to the eastern and central U.S., most common in **open woods, roadsides**, and **forest margins** from Texas to the Great Lakes and east to the Carolinas and Pennsylvania.

Harvesting

Pick fresh blossoms in **early spring** *before* leaves emerge. The best flavor comes from bright, newly opened flowers. Avoid faded or rain-damaged blooms.

Culinary Use

Eat *raw* as a **trail nibble**, **garnish** for wild dishes, or **mild salad addition**. Their flavor is lemony, floral, and faintly sweet. Redbud blossoms can also be **pickled** or **candied** for longer use.

Preservation

Blossoms wilt fast, so use **fresh** or **dry** them quickly on a screen **out of direct sunlight**. Once dried, they retain a light floral note useful in teas or baked goods.

Caution: Look-Alikes

Few wild look-alikes bloom this way. Make sure the flowers emerge directly from the bark and that the tree bears classic heart-shaped leaves once in full leaf-out.

Chapter 18

How to Outfox FEMA and Corrupt Government Agencies in a Collapse

There will be no polite knock on the door or warrant. Unlike local law enforcement or city governing bodies, FEMA functions through a federal framework. The agency reaches its destination with weapons and strict organization while standing head and shoulder above local law enforcement. Emergency statutes govern FEMA and similar agencies when they activate instead of the Constitution.

"In any crisis, the first casualty is truth. The second is liberty."
John Adams

Evasion and Compliance

A sudden breakdown doesn't transform all individuals into fighters. Survival typically favors those who manage to stay unnoticed rather than those who stand out. When FEMA or federal relief teams arrive to handle emergencies, they follow specific protocols. Their presence does not include rights discussion or guilt assessment. They're there to restore control — on their terms. The most effective protection you can use against authority is to become unnoticeable rather than confrontational.

Disappearing doesn't mean hiding in a cave. It means adopting the gray. In plain sight, but forgettable. The crowd passes by without anyone recalling your presence. To accomplish your objective you need to suppress your natural tendencies to argue or explain. Federal officers learn to interpret body language along with vocal tones and physical tension. They detect intentions with the precision of wolves tracking their prey. When you show confidence or conviction it attracts their attention. When you show signs of vagueness and exhaustion while complying they will lose interest.

Train for that.

Practice acting dazed while your pulse hammers.

Practice fumbling your words without looking suspicious. After a societal collapse happens negotiation skills become more important than mastering physical fighting techniques. Walk slower.

Blink more.

Under FEMA's **Continuity of Operations Plan (COOP)**, field officers and contractors are trained to identify compliant, disoriented, and non-aggressive civilians as "low-priority logistical obstacles." The COOP manual specifically discourages detailed processing of individuals who present no threat profile and offer no infrastructure value. You are trying to **earn that classification**.

You must also understand **Behavioral Detection Training (BDT)** used by TSA and DHS field agents, which includes micro-expression evaluation, eye contact patterns, and voice pitch shifts.

TSA stands for Transportation Security Administration. The Transportation Security Administration manages airport security checkpoints while searching for suspicious behaviors since its creation as part of Homeland Security after 9/11 to federalize airport security operations and expand domestic surveillance at transport locations.

DHS is the Department of Homeland Security. The Department of Homeland Security functions as a federal agency managing the Transportation Security Administration along with ten additional departments including Customs and Border Protection and FEMA. DHS holds responsibility for "protecting the homeland" yet operates as an extensive surveillance and enforcement system that gathers information and observes conduct while handling crisis situations whether they are authentic or contrived.

To beat this, rehearse **low-pressure confusion patterns**: delayed blinking, dry-swallowed sentences, and wandering visual focus. Speak like you're unsure of what day it is, and always **overcompensate downward (don't say too much)**. Confidence is a threat flag. Compliance with confusion is invisibility.

Control Your Identity

Your legal identity that used to represent freedom will transform into a restrictive chain. Through checkpoints and digital cross-referencing combined with registry sweeps you can be flagged for your location or past history and known relationships. When your government-issued ID gets stolen you can no longer move through the world as your real identity. You are being processed.

You must prepare decoys. Not counterfeits, not clever tricks—obsolete truth. Carry a layered identity model: You need to hold onto your active ID along with expired versions and damaged copies and occupational tags that have lost their connection to current jobs. An old HVAC badge remains attached to its broken lanyard. A cracked driver's license with worn text. A photo ID with faded laminate.

These are not for deception.

They are for stalling.

When outdated or low-value identifiers are discovered during a wallet search you seem forgettable because you appear to have no job, no access rights and no leverage.

Storage matters. Secure a piece of laminate and attach it to your shoe. Place one inside a corrosion-sealed sleeve within a tool handle or an empty caulking tube. Stay clear of any identifying markers which connect to biometric systems or digital signal transmissions. Smart licenses and other digital identifiers like embedded RFID cards and NFC key tags expose you regardless of physical contact. They can scan their data without making physical contact with you and just your presence makes you a high-priority target.

Destroy what does not serve you. Slice through cards along the antennae track and search for the thin copper loop underneath. Sand fingerprints from biometric tags. Destroy SIM chips by burning them or dissolving them in acid. In a state of collapse your face and your print along with your name become the property of whoever scans them first. The first person to scan them gains ownership.

When you have to keep a legitimate credential save it instead of carrying it. Cache it securely in a weather-sealed container. Place it near a recognized checkpoint path to enable possible retrieval during re-entry or exchange operations. Keep your identity components separated to prevent them from being captured all at once. Disperse it. Fragment it. Every documentable element of your existence should operate independently from other elements.

Let the system chase shadows.

Emergency declarations under **Stafford Act Section 502** permit rapid biometric enrollment without consent if you're found in "restricted zones" or near federal resource depots. These zones expand automatically once martial status is declared.

You must keep a rotating **three-tier ID system**:

1. **Sacrificial ID**: expired, cracked, plausible but obsolete (to hand over).
2. **Access ID**: near-valid, for fallback use, cached securely with decoys nearby.
3. **Phantom ID**: a fully fabricated name with no federal tie, used for burner phones, barter scripts, or digital use only.

To beat RFID/NFC scans, **EMP-treat your gear** with field-level coil discharge from a flash camera capacitor. Disassemble the flash unit, build a discharge wand using copper wire and nail leads. Trigger it across embedded tags to burn antenna traces without destroying the card visually.

Practice on dummy IDs first.

Start the process of disabling RFID or NFC tags by using a disposable flash camera to ensure the host card or document remains undamaged. Disposable flash cameras feature capacitors that release 300 volts to destroy the antenna coils in most passive RFID systems. Now that you have the camera open look for the black cylindrical capacitor which should be close to the flash tube. You must never touch the terminals with bare hands. Put on thick gloves and ensure that you have insulated tools available.

The procedure remains safe when executed with caution yet becomes lethal if the capacitor arcs carelessly.

Select copper wire that extends from your elbow to your wrist and remove insulation from both wire ends. Securely coil both wire ends around a steel nail or any equivalent metal point. These will be the leads. Secure the wire to a handle made of insulating materials such as wood, bone, or composite plastic. After assembly, the tool must look like a forked wand or discharge fork where the tips stand approximately one inch apart. Use electrical tape or alligator clips to attach each copper lead to the capacitor terminals. This creates a simple yet effective coil-burner.

The flash circuit requires a functioning AA battery to initiate the charging process. Wait until the charging whine stops. When the user hears the charging whine stop the capacitor becomes armed and the wand achieves hot status. A grounded surface such as an aluminum sheet, steel sink or a sanded iron plate provides an ideal location to place the card face-up. Place the fork tips across the card's surface at the position where you suspect the coil exists. The antenna usually rings the perimeter. Apply steady pressure to the wand and activate the discharge mechanism. A loud pop will sound and you may notice a small spark. This stage represents the pulse severing or fusing segment of the RFID trace process.

The discharge process can be repeated multiple times but you need to recharge the capacitor before each subsequent discharge. Don't overdo it. Your objective should be to break the communication circuit rather than setting the plastic case on fire. Once you finish the procedure check to see if the card works by scanning it with a field reader. If successful, the tag will be unresponsive. Validate the card's condition by examining the antenna traces under strong light. The coil usually shows a subtle break or distortion when examined after the procedure. That's your success point.

Begin by practicing this technique on discarded access cards or expired IDs then proceed to apply it to items you care about. The damage is subtle, but irreversible. A fried coil trace cannot undergo any repair work. This method is designed exclusively for use in field situations to quietly remove functionality without dramatic destruction.

Additionally, ensure your face does not match facial recognition engine criteria: no symmetry, no contrast. Use smudge makeup, false blemishes, or darkened eye contours to drop accuracy of facial AI by over 40%. Avoid straight-on photos or idle loitering near cameras. They pull stills from drones even without active registration.

Kill the Signal

If you're visible, you're vulnerable. Technology designed to simplify daily tasks becomes the quickest method to expose your location during a collapse. Every powered device is a radio tower. If you fail to turn off lights, pings, or circuits these elements will serve as markers for others.

Start with the phone. Turning it off is useless. Modern smartphones with sealed batteries maintain a minimal power level for as long as 48 hours. This allows emergency pings and background diagnostics. Airplane mode fails to protect against IMSI catchers and passive data skimming. Remove the battery from your phone if it features one. Do not just power off—disassemble.

If it's sealed, you have three options. First: Fully enclose the phone in two layers of tightly fitted aluminum foil with overlapping edges that leave no spaces. Put the device into a Faraday pouch that demonstrates 30–40 dB attenuation specifically for 2.4GHz and 5GHz frequencies. In case you don't possess a Faraday pouch place rubber matting or closed-cell foam inside a metal ammo box and store your phone there. Second: A waterproof case should surround your phone which should be buried at least 100 yards away from your main location. To maximize phone security, destroy your old phone completely and acquire a burner phone anonymously through cash payment at a second-hand electronics store located far from where you live.

Keep your burner phone unconnected to any personal identifiers including your name, address and former phone numbers. Do not store contacts. Do not leave the SIM inserted. Activate the phone only when away from your home or any known secure area. Ensure that you operate it at an alternate location which provides complete visibility from all sides. Turn off the device before removing the battery and moving to another location.

Your home itself is a larger risk. Smart meters continuously send out informa-

tion about power consumption which includes voltage levels, current measurements, time stamps, and device identifiers. The system conducts data polling in bursts which occur every 15 to 30 minutes and reveals appliance activity to the circuit level. A sudden power surge from your freezer or water pump during blackout conditions triggers an alert that your address is not compliant.

Disable it. Open your breaker panel. Look for the meter's data line connection which typically employs Cat5 or fiber cables and disconnect it. When your meter contains a wireless transmitter you must find the RF board beneath its tamper seal and sever the signal trace using either a soldering iron or pliers. Do not just flip the breakers. Go to the source.

If that's not possible, simulate grid failure. Leave old food out to rot. Spray mildew into visible vents. Use black construction paper to cover the indicator lights on appliances. Place blackout curtains in your windows but modify them to create a ragged and irregular pattern. Ensure that one room looks looted by leaving broken drawers open with clothes strewn about and insulation charred. Anyone who looks through your window needs to believe that your house has been fully looted.

Do not trust any device that listens. Devices like Amazon Echo and Google Nest along with Ring cameras and smart thermostats stay connected to networks while most keep operational logs even during offline periods. Destroy their boards. Pull any batteries. Disrupt power cables and destroy microphone arrays with force. Never trust a soft shutdown. Burn the chips if you can.

If you need power, run it manually. Use inverters disconnected from the grid. Recharge batteries using solar only. Operate generators in thermal-wrap-lined insulated sheds that use carbon blankets to reduce heat bloom. Avoid operating the generator at the same daily time on multiple occasions.

A single glow in the wrong window. A single hum at the wrong hour. That's all it takes.

FEMA uses **Mobile Emergency Response Support (MERS)** trucks equipped with passive EMF sniffers and Stingray cell simulators that can identify ping noise from off-state phones up to **200 meters** away. Even flashlights, solar inverters, or headlamps with residual charge can show up as anomalies in low-EMF fields during blackout conditions.

To avoid this, **triage your power consumption** with military blackout rules:

- Only charge from **non-line power sources** (solar, crank, thermoelectric).
- Never charge or use devices between **0100–0430**, the peak patrol scan window.
- Wrap all electronics not in use in **double-layered mylar+fabric Faraday wraps**, not foil. Foil creates echoes unless grounded.

Additionally, modify **smart appliance circuitry**. Use a **kill-switch inline disconnect** between circuit boards and antennas—commonly a 22 AWG wire mounted with a toggle buried behind housing plates. Cut power physically, not digitally. Never rely on "off" buttons or settings.

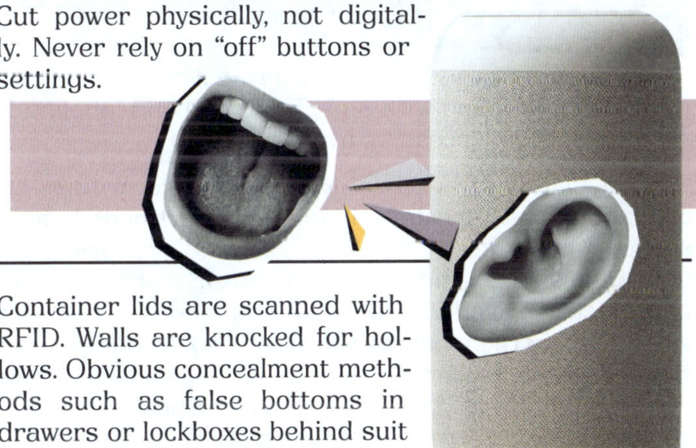

They Search the Easy First

Trained search teams follow muscle memory. First they breach entry points. Their next targets include garages as well as sheds and basements along with storage closets and pantries. Why? Standard supply hiding spots are where search teams will check first because these are the places people commonly use for concealment.

So, don't.

Standard concealment equals guaranteed discovery. Practiced eyes enable search teams to clear first-line rooms within two minutes. Shelving is photographed. Container lids are scanned with RFID. Walls are knocked for hollows. Obvious concealment methods such as false bottoms in drawers or lockboxes behind suit jackets will lead to discovery and logging in recovery databases.

Your job is to invert the logic. Your hiding spot should be visible but lack any recognizable pattern.

Start by misdirection. Place decoy items in logical hiding spots. Store several MREs in your garage freezer. A closed ammunition cans rests hidden under the stairs filled with junk metal pieces. Let them think they've scored. Your goal should be to convince search teams that they have "cleared" your location so they won't perform a deeper investigation.

Hiding emergency gear along with valuables demands layered thinking which combines functional design with access control and deceptive appearance. The ideal place for hidden storage is located under your yard particularly close to existing infrastructure indicators. You can position a basic capped PVC pipe vertically within the soil close to structures such as kennel slabs or small sheds. Painting the cap to mimic a septic system clean-out port renders it unquestionable. The interior of the pipe accommodates storage for vacuum-sealed bags along with small ammunition containers and medical supplies wrapped in foil.

Protect the contents by dry-sealing the pipe with a gasketed cap and labeling it as "Water Purge Access" to avoid suspicion.

Attic insulation is another overlooked zone. Within the insulation mass create a hidden compartment before sealing off the area using spray foam. Once dried, it's indistinguishable. The pocket allows for storage of vacuum-packed essentials like rice and first aid supplies while keeping them nearby yet concealed. If you reside in a hot climate ensure that your packaging can withstand high temperatures. This insulation functions as a space concealer and serves to diminish thermal signatures through its dampening properties.

Crawlspaces and ductwork also offer serious concealment. Rare earth magnets provide the fastening strength needed to secure flat-packed gear to interior foundation walls. The majority of people tend to check these hidden spaces only when they need repairs. Supply pouches taped or magnetized behind HVAC ducts should be positioned at bends or boxed-off vents but must avoid extreme heat and airflow areas. Barter items, silver rounds, burner IDs and USB drives can be hidden effectively with these methods.

Place reverse-facing wall boxes which simulate electrical outlets for interior concealment purposes. Attach a plastic faceplate to the surface and label it "Cable Jack - Inactive" so people stay away from it. The wall cavity provides space to store shrink-wrapped kits protected by mylar and closed-cell foam layers. These keep temperature-sensitive items stable for years as long as they remain undisturbed. As an additional misdirection tactic mark the corresponding breaker in the electrical panel as inactive. People won't investigate inactive lines unless they encounter an electrical problem.

Everything here works because it avoids obviousness. This strategy involves concealing not only equipment but the very notion that something valuable exists.

In areas with elevated risk organize burn storage supply caches that can be destroyed quickly within sixty seconds. Place waterproof containers with maps and frequency lists atop firestarter logs in preparation for quick incineration. Create a thermal-redirect chimney using ceramic flue tile to enable quick smoke release. You are not just hiding gear. You are building tactical attrition. Each wasted moment and every false lead they encounter drains both time and morale.

Place your large water storage tanks below compost piles when storage is necessary. The appearance and odor from above resembles decay. Route gravity-fed hoses through flexible tubing designed to mimic French drain pipes. Mix earthworms or soil scrap into the upper six inches. Even dogs will ignore it.

Avoid vertical stacking. Hidden supplies should be stored below reach height because most searchers will not look there. Place food storage within hollow steps and behind return vents and also inside dead space behind bathtub skirting as well as under immovable appliances that have been retrofitted with rollers and braced covers.

The aim is not to beat a search. The goal is to waste it. To make them question what they missed. You want them to confirm your house is clean while it remains dirty. You don't want to win a fight. Your objective should be to avoid detection so that you are never identified as a target.

Let them leave empty-handed.

FEMA search protocols follow **NIMS Tier 1 entry standards**, which define "Priority Access Zones" as kitchens, garages, and HVAC hubs. Search time for each is under **3.5 minutes**. After that, teams log data and move on, unless something caught their eye. Make sure that doesn't happen.

Exploit this using **saturation misdirection**. In each easy-access room, stage plausible decoy caches: canned goods past expiry, rusted tools, visible-but-inert boxes marked "batteries" containing nothing or broken parts.

For **hidden cache placement**, follow these principles:

- **Depth:** below waist, never at eye level.
- **Density:** not hollow-sounding. Use foam or cloth packing.
- **Distance:** always beyond initial line-of-sight when the door opens.

Consider layering your storage inside **anti-sensor materials**: mylar sheeting plus carbon foam kills most handheld metal detector reads. Place a layer between the wallboard and storage cavity for concealed ammo or metals.

For thermal decoying, keep **sealed ice packs** above actual cache zones to mislead FLIR scans during early sweep passes.

Just a few degrees difference draws the eye elsewhere.

Avoid Recruitment into the Machine

If they ask for help, say no. Doesn't matter how they dress it. The terms "Relief work," "civil service," "rebuild crew" all represent biased positions. It's not charity. It's a funnel. Saying yes marks your entry into the net.

Here's what happens. They issue you gear: Your issued equipment will include a vest and badge and paper ID but you might also receive a wristband featuring a QR code. They take a photo. Sometimes a fingerprint. Now you're tagged. Logged. Traceable. Your subsequent steps function as breadcrumbs.

You'll be paired with others. Some real, some not. They call them "friendlies." That's bullshit. They're handlers. They monitor your actions while assessing your performance and record what you speak during moments you believe go unrecorded. These people are trained to report. Some are locals. Some are not. Doesn't matter. You're being profiled.

There's no means to escape through debate. Any attempt to resist leads to immediate identification as troublesome. Noted as combative. You were once just a volunteer but now they consider you a problem.

Problems don't get ignored.

Problems get processed.

So don't argue. Don't say no. Waste their time.

Say you're sick. Assert that you lack the skills to operate equipment. Say you're caring for someone else. Look tired. Act confused. Let your answers trail off. Convey that investing time with you yields minimal benefits so they deem you unworthy of their efforts.

They have quotas. Push them to search for a different individual who can fulfill their requirements.

You're not resisting. You're evading.

There's a difference.

FEMA Civilian Resource Programs run under **Section 408 of the Robert T. Stafford Act**, which permits the creation of "temporary civilian mobilization units" without voluntary consent during emergency mandates. If you wear the badge, you're no longer a noncombatant—you're a tracked asset.

To delay or deny enrollment without resistance, cite **non-verifiable obligations**: elder care, psychological instability, prior medication needs. Use documentation if available, but **faked clutter** works just as well—half-used prescription bottles, broken glasses, or expired inhalers can dissuade recruiters.

Remember, FEMA and its contractors file "Non-Compliance Reports" when you decline. Too many flags, and they stop asking nicely. So decline without clarity. Say "maybe later."

Then vanish from the path.

Your recruitment chances vanish when recruiters lose track of your existence.

Play the Script

When facing martial responses or societal collapse authorities depend on classification systems. They are not looking for truth. Their goal is to achieve logistical clarity through assessing entities as threats, assets or non-factors. You must present as the last one. Not suspicious. Not interesting. Just wasteful to engage.

Your persona must be designed in such a way that it cannot be transformed into valuable information. The role is not pathetic—it's unviable. Think in terms of bureaucratic burden. The reason your entry receives an "NFA" (No Further Action) designation is that no one wants to claim responsibility for additional investigation.

The story you create needs to remain unengaging and functionally irrelevant. No arc. No emotional depth. Your narrative provides no incentive for someone to pursue an investigation. You are alone. You don't know where your people went. You don't know what day it is. You survived on expired food and filtered rainwater. You had a job—maybe—it's not important. You've been sick. You can't keep anything down. You don't need help. You don't want trouble. That's it.

And that's all they're going to get.

You must rehearse this. It has to survive scrutiny. When you deliver this message you need to maintain exact consistency throughout. Your lie collapses when you hesitate during questioning. If you expand, you expose cracks. You're not acting. You're erasing.

Build the space to match. Use olfactory misdirection. Smell triggers automatic responses in officials before logical thought takes over. Place something with a sour smell close to where you sleep. Molded bread works. So does spoiled meat or vinegar-drenched cloth. Place broken equipment in clear view for everyone to see, such as a snapped handle and a burnt-out lamp. Show failure, not deception. Keep your appearance uneven. Dirty fingernails, inconsistent hygiene. Never uniform. Uniform suggests control.

Never offer information. Only respond. Write brief sentences and insert pauses at unconventional points. Let your tone drop mid-thought. "I... don't really know. Things got bad after..." Then stop talking.

Let silence work for you.

Keep a few fallback lines ready. I recall being required to register but I can't remember the specific time. I think somebody visited me last week. I haven't gone anywhere."

Make everything foggy. Create an impression that they've missed their chance to help with your case.

Officials hate dead ends with no paperwork.

FEMA field processing forms include codes for personality archetypes. "Fogged," "non-useful," and "domestic burden" tags are assigned to people who appear cognitively or physically incapable of being useful. These tags lower your follow-up profile score.

If questioned in depth, use **looped speech fragments**:

- "I'm not sure what day this is."
- "I just stayed here. I didn't want to... I don't know."
- "They said they'd come back. I think they did. I don't know."

Use **invisible physical props**: wear one shoe torn and re-laced with wire. Carry a broken remote. Smear dirt across your ID. A person who looks like they barely made it through the week won't be asked to help with grid mapping.

Silence is stronger than denial. Bureaucrats only push when they see **a story worth completing**.

Your job is to be a page with nothing written on it.

When officers take you in for more detailed questioning pretend to be very tired. Hold your stomach. Ask for water. Don't resist, don't protest. Just bleed time. Acting useless will make them release you to your original location sooner.

Conceal What Matters

Sensitive storage solutions should never be based on the assumption that time will protect information. You don't have time when they come. In a moment of urgency you cannot justify the purpose of that map and whether that radio was receiving or sending signals. You don't get to clarify. You get labeled and processed. Your storage procedures should function under the assumption that they will be subjected to hostile inspection.

Start with destruction contingency. All items which suggest operational scope, including maps and contact lists along with encoded frequencies and long-range communication devices must be hidden thoroughly or be able to be destroyed quickly. Your time limit falls below sixty seconds after detection begins from a targeted search. Prepare accordingly.

Containerized burn bins equipped with magnesium starter strips and petroleum-soaked tinder should be used. Stage burn bins inside unused stoves, chimneys, grill bodies, or unplugged dryer ducts. One spark. Gone. Don't rely on matches. Mount a push-button firestarter inside the lid to ignite fires. Practice blind ignition. Night. Gloves on. Panic simulated.

Have acid destruction kits for paper: Store polyethylene bags containing vinegar and pool shock powder separately after sealing them. Mix, drop, seal, and walk away. Standard documentation will be destroyed and eaten through poly within thirty seconds of initiating the chemical reaction. Do not attempt with metal objects—corrosion risk.

Digital files should never be stored on USBs or SD cards without encryption. VeraCrypt containers should protect your drives and maintain password confidentiality by avoiding written records. Connect magnetic coils or nailgun solenoids to a 12V switch and practice hot wiping procedures. One trigger. Drive dead.

Quick-access safes, nightstand drawers, or under mattresses are unsafe storage locations for weapons. These locations received initial clearance and documentation. Weapons need to be stored based on their intended function and how deep they should be retrieved from storage.

Position your daily-carry weapons among ordinary industrial materials to conceal their presence. Magnetic holsters beneath rusted propane tanks. The pistol slides remain separated and secured within the insides of hollow fence posts and gas meter housings. The separated AR upper and lower components are vacuum-sealed and stored beneath false concrete patch plates or behind hot water tanks with spring-loaded magnetic hinges for quick access.

Deep reserve? The firearms were stored in waterproof PVC tubes that had been both glued and sealed with desiccant packs before they were buried vertically underneath woodpiles or compost heaps. The cap should use heat-welded numbering that becomes visible only under UV light for identification purposes later on. Keep GPS coordinates memorized, never written.

Ammo? Not with the gun. Use soundproof storage by placing sand-packed coolers with sealed paint cans inside rubber feed bins. Each retrieval should operate as an independent task. The destruction of one cache does not risk the security of your remaining caches.

Use code for any system mapping. Avoid marking items as "food," "ammo," or "radio." Use misleading household terms. Create code names for important items such as "Brushhead" for storage devices and keep written keys physically separate or memorize them. If you must write, write to confuse.

Use Tools Without a Signature

Survival tools become liabilities when they create an audible, visible, thermal, or chemical trail. Any trace is proof of activity. Proof of activity means extraction risk. Comfort is a signal. Smell is a report. Light is a beacon. Sound is a map.

Cooking

Only use open fire if you can manage all the elements. Construct a rocket stove by assembling four cinder blocks along with high-density fire bricks or heavy-gauge steel cans. Stack two blocks vertical, creating a tunnel. One horizontal as feeder. The vertical becomes a combustion riser. Use wood ash, sand, or perlite to fill all empty spaces for insulation. The construction should finish with either a flat grill plate or a pot base on top. Paint outer surfaces matte black. To control heat bloom use broken concrete pieces along with branches and crushed charcoal around your fire set up.

Burn only fully cured hardwood—oak, ash, maple. No pine. No green wood. No bark. Remove splinters before feeding to control microbursts while maintaining a slow rate. Fire should burn hot, fast, smokeless. Whenever smoke appears it indicates that either the fuel or airflow needs adjustment. Maintain practice sessions until you achieve fire extinguishing times of less than 20 minutes.

In wooded terrain, dig a fire trench: 16 inches wide, 12 inches deep. Direct firewood into one end of the trench while drawing air through a secondary shaft positioned at a 45° angle downwind. Line with flat stone or hard clay. Pour white ash into surrounding plants once you finish using it. Rake leaf litter. Collapse structure. Displace thermal trail. The same burn spot should not be used twice because drone infrared sensors can detect residual heat signatures for days.

Solar Cooking

Choose solar cooking designs such as parabolic or box-style ovens that have matte-black interior surfaces. Commercial cooking units with polished reflectors should not be trusted. Use carbon black pigment or char-soot mix to coat inner walls when necessary. Place a break-shield made of fence slats or camouflage mesh two feet in front of the oven to eliminate glint from moisture and edges of glass or frames. Position reflective instruments no closer than 10 yards to the area. Prepare food exclusively between 0700 and 0900 when reduced aerial movement and light angles minimize surface glare.

Visual Discipline

Strip every tool. Ensure all surfaces that reflect are treated with paint or burned or etched material. Sand gloss coatings off pots. Tape flashlight bodies with athletic wrap. Always display mounted equipment within areas of dense shade but avoid placing it where it can be easily seen. To remove factory shine from metal equipment, either roll it through damp ash or bury it shallowly overnight.

Scent Supression

Cooking carry odor. At night during temperature inversions they ascend and move hundreds of meters across air that remains completely still. Deploy venting sacks filled with burnt coffee, garlic peel or crushed charcoal close to burn sites to mask odors. Animal fat and cooking oils as well as dried goods need storage in two layers of bags with activated carbon packets in-between. Washing gear requires boiled pine needles or ash slurry instead of soap. Leave no comfort smell behind.

Water Systems

No open barrels. No bright plastic. No symmetrical tanks. Channel rainwater from roofs made of painted plywood since they have irregular shapes and slopes away from direct views. Water should flow through a black poly hose which must be positioned 6 inches under the soil or brush cover. Use crushed rock traps to filter runoff. For concealing barrels, partially bury them so 75% is underground and paint the remaining visible part with dull brown color before covering it with dried leaves and split wood. Make it look like garbage, not supply.

In dry zones, mask irrigation as failed infrastructure: Run poly line through broken PVC pipes underground

and connect drip ends to hollow planters or dead tree cores. Cover connectors with dirt and dried grass. If it looks broken, nobody investigates.

Pumps and Sound

The high-pitched whines produced by electric pumps can be heard even when they are located inside enclosed spaces. They also broadcast EMF. You should only use this setup when operating within environments with complete white-noise masking such as rain sound, generator noise, or active machinery areas. Set up gravity-fed cisterns on 6–10 foot scaffolding that resembles frame debris or junk piles. When manual drawing is necessary use rubber-sealed lever pumps within acoustic boxes lined with wool or shredded cloth. Grease everything. No squeaks. No clicks. No resonance.

Carried Tools

Rattle test every pack. Your equipment should lack zippers and loose straps and must not contain swinging gear. Tape handles in friction wrap. Grease hinge points with wax or graphite. Dispose of all beepers alongside lights that power on automatically and any battery display indicators. Flashlights: remove batteries unless needed that minute. Multi-tools: grind logos and chrome. Everything looks used, dull, worn. Clean is suspicious.

Rules of Presence

- If something reflects, mute it.
- If something hums, pad it.
- If something shines, scratch it.
- If something smells, seal it.
- If it clinks, change it. If it clanks, bury it.
- If it looks comfortable, it's bait.

Every auditory vibration along with every scent and each luminous display serves as proof of your existence and preparedness. It's essential to avoid appearing as though you live better than your surroundings. The reason for wanting to be invisible comes from the fact that you have nothing notable to reveal.

"*Let food be thy medicine and medicine be thy food.*"
Hippocrates

Chapter 19

The Vital Remedies You Need to Know How to Make at Home

The first items to vanish during an economic collapse are pharmaceutical medications. As supply chains fail and drug stores run out of stock, finding medical aid will become impossible. This is why it's important to know remedies for common health ailments that you can make at home, and know how to use them.

Some of the most useful herbal remedies can be easily made at home using plants such as peppermint, echinacea, and white willow, even ginger and garlic that can be grown in your garden or found in your kitchen cupboard. These plants have medicinal properties, such as anti-inflammatory, anti-bacterial and analgesic, that can aid against inflammation, pain, common cold and flu, allergies, and burn wounds. Even better, by using these herbal remedies, you eliminate the risk of the damaging side effects caused by pharmaceutical drugs.

Stocking up on medicinal herbs or growing your own plants could save your life and the lives of your loved ones in the next crisis.

Natural Painkiller

Turmeric Milk for Internal Inflammation Pain

Turmeric contains curcumin, which gives turmeric its highly effective anti-inflammatory properties and pain killing effects. The black pepper in this recipe helps the body absorb the curcumin found in turmeric. This remedy acts much like ibuprofen, relieving pain in the body caused by inflammation.

Ingredients
250ml of Milk or Non-Dairy Alternative
1 teaspoon of Turmeric Powder
1 pinch of ground Black Pepper
1 teaspoon of Honey (optional)

Instructions

In a small pot, heat the milk or non-dairy alternative until hot, not boiling. Stir in the turmeric powder and ground black pepper. Simmer on low heat for 5 minutes. Using cheesecloth, strain the milk into a mug. Add honey to taste.

Directions

Drink 1 to 2 cups of turmeric milk per day when in need of pain relief. Feel free to increase or decrease the amount of turmeric to meet your personal needs.

Cayenne Salve for Body Aches

Capsaicin is a compound in cayenne pepper that gives cayenne its medicinal properties. By desensitizing the pain receptors and increasing blood flow to the targeted area, capsaicin helps alleviate the pain and stiffness caused by arthritis. Cayenne salve also relieves pain from back aches, migraines, menstrual cramps, bruises, and even nerve pain.

Ingredients
2 teaspoons of powdered Cayenne Pepper
2 tablespoons of Beeswax
1 cup of Extra Virgin Coconut Oil
1 teaspoon of Extra Virgin Olive oil

Instructions

Using the double-boiling method, melt the coconut oil and the beeswax together. Add the cayenne pepper and olive oil to the melted coconut oil and beeswax and stir together until thoroughly mixed. Pour the mixture into a small tin or glass container for final use. Store in a cool, dark location until the application has solidified.

Directions

Using a finger, apply a small amount of the cayenne salve to the affected area up to 4 times a day, as needed. Wash hands thoroughly after each use before touching anything to avoid contact with eyes and mucous membranes.

White Willow Bark Tincture for Internal and External Inflammation Pain

Salicin is a chemical compound similar to aspirin, and it can be found in white willow bark. White willow bark tincture works for reducing pain related to inflammation, fever, and back aches, including osteoarthritis. If you are allergic to aspirin, do not use this tincture. It should also not be used by children.

Ingredients
½ cup of chopped White Willow Bark
250ml of 80-proof Vodka

Instructions

Fill a 250-500ml glass canning jar with chopped white willow bark. Pour the 80-proof vodka over the white willow bark, filling the glass jar 1 inch from the rim, covering the bark completely. Seal the jar and store it in a dark, cool area for 4-6 weeks. Shake everyday for the first 2 weeks, and once a week for the next 4 weeks. Using cheesecloth, strain the alcohol into an amber dropper bottle for its final use.

Directions

Take 10 to 20 drops three times a day when needing pain relief.

Arnica Massage Oil for Muscles

Arnica contains a compound known as helenalin, which gives it medicinal properties to fight inflammation and swelling. It loosens tight muscles, improves circulation, and can alleviate pain relating to strains and sprains.

Ingredients
150ml of Jojoba Oil
2 tablespoons dried Arnica Flower

Instructions

Add the dried arnica flower to a 200ml amber glass canning jar. Pour the jojoba oil over the flower, filling the jar. Seal, shake well, and store in a cool, dark place for 24 hours before use.

Directions

Rub the arnica massage oil on affected areas 2-3 times a day. For external use only, do not apply to broken skin.

Inflammation-Reducing Remedies

Wintergreen Liniment for Inflamed Muscles

Wintergreen contains methyl salicylate which reduces inflammation and eases pain. When applied as an oil topically, it penetrates the skin, accessing the muscles and soothing inflamed and sore muscles.

Ingredients
½ cup of Fresh Wintergreen Leaves
1 cup of E. V. Olive Oil

Instructions

Fill a 250-500ml glass canning jar with chopped wintergreen. Pour the olive oil over the wintergreen, filling the glass jar 1 inch from the rim, covering the wintergreen completely. Seal the jar, shake, and store in a warm, sunny area for 3-4 weeks. Shake everyday for the first 2 weeks, and once a week for the following weeks. Using cheesecloth, strain the liniment into an amber glass bottle for its final use.

Directions

Gently massage the liniment into the affected area 2-3 times a day. This liniment is intended to be used externally.

Meadowsweet Tincture for Pain and Fever

The salicylic acid contained in meadowsweet is the compound aspirin was originally derived from. Meadowsweet provides similar anti-inflammatory benefits as aspirin while reducing pain and fever.

Ingredients
1 cup of fresh Meadowsweet
250ml of 80-proof Vodka

Instructions

Fill a 250-500ml glass canning jar with chopped meadowsweet. Pour in the 80-proof vodka, filling the glass jar 1 inch from the rim, covering the meadowsweet completely. Seal the jar and store it in a dark, cool area for 4-6 weeks. Shake everyday for the first 2 weeks, and once a week for the next 4 weeks. Using cheesecloth, strain the alcohol into an amber dropper bottle for its final use.

Directions

Take 10-20 drops 2-3 times a day either directly under the tongue or adding to water and drinking.

Turmeric Tincture for Inflammation

By inhibiting the production of inflammatory mediators, the compound in turmeric, curcumin, reduces inflammation and restrains the development of inflammatory diseases. A tincture is an effective application and is more easily absorbed by the body than turmeric powder.

Ingredients
1 cup of chopped Turmeric Root
250ml of 80-proof Vodka

Instructions

Fill a 250-500ml glass canning jar with chopped turmeric root. Pour the 80-proof vodka over the turmeric root, filling the glass jar 1 inch from the rim, covering the turmeric completely. Seal the jar and store it in a dark, cool area for 4-6 weeks. Shake everyday for the first 2 weeks, and once a week for the next 4 weeks. Using cheesecloth, strain the alcohol into an amber dropper bottle for its final use.

Directions

On an empty stomach, add 30-60 drops of turmeric tincture to a glass of water and drink completely. Do this 1-3 times a day.

An alternative is to take 10-60 drops directly under the tongue. Alternatively, you can add 10-60 drops to a topical cream for external inflammation.

Licorice Root Decoction for Intestinal Inflammation

The compound glycyrrhizin found in licorice root inhibits the breakdown of cortisol, reducing inflammation and easing irritation. Mucous membranes in the digestive tract are soothed by the licorice root, which eases spasms and symptoms of issues such as irritable bowel disease and reduces inflammation.

Ingredients
1 inch of Licorice Root
250ml of Water

Instructions

Boil water with the licorice root in a small pot. Reduce heat and simmer for 10-15 minutes. Strain the tea into a mug.

Directions

Drink ½ - 1 cup of the licorice root decoction a day. This drink is not intended for long-term use.

Digestive System Aid

Goldenseal & Licorice Tincture for Saliva Production

Goldenseal is a bitter that increases saliva production and stimulates digestive function. Licorice root contains glycyrrhizin, a compound that increases the amount of mucus produced in the body.

Goldenseal increases the production of stomach acid, while the glycyrrhizin in licorice suppresses the production of stomach acid. This tincture provides the benefits of both plants while eliminating each other's downsides. This tincture also balances the bacteria in the gut and may help UTIs.

Ingredients

- ½ cup of chopped fresh Goldenseal Plant
- ½ cup of chopped Licorice Root
- 250ml of 80-proof Vodka

Instructions

Fill a 250-500ml glass canning jar with chopped goldenseal and licorice. Pour in the 80-proof vodka, filling the glass jar 1 inch from the rim, covering the plants completely. Seal the jar and store it in a dark, cool area for 4-6 weeks. Shake everyday for the first 2 weeks, and once a week for the next 4 weeks. Using cheesecloth, strain the alcohol into an amber dropper bottle for its final use.

Directions

Just before meals, take 15-35 drops three times a day. Alternatively, add it to 2 cups of water or a beverage.

Iced Fennel Seed Tea for Gas

The main active compound in fennel that helps aid the digestive system is anethole. It helps reduce gas, bloating, and stomach acid It also soothes and relaxes the intestines and stomach. Fennel strengthens the gut lining and protects against gastrointestinal inflammation, making it useful for inflammatory bowel disease.

Ingredients

- 1 teaspoon of Fennel Seeds
- 1 cup of Ice
- 250ml of Water
- 1 teaspoon of Honey (optional)
- ½ a Lemon (optional)

Instructions

In a small pot, bring water to a boil. Crush the fennel seeds and add to the boiling water. Steep in boiling water for 10 minutes. Remove the pot from the heat, add honey, and let cool. Pour tea into a mug over ice. Add lemon to taste.

Directions

Drink 1-2 cups a day after a meal.

Ginger Capsules for Gastrointestinal Discomfort

Ginger capsules send the benefits of gingerol straight to the stomach, where it can be quickly absorbed by the body. Gingerol relieves gastrointestinal discomfort, stimulates digestive juices, and increases movement through the digestive tract.

Ingredients

- ½ cup of powdered Ginger
- Empty Gelatin or Vegetable Capsules

Instructions

Fill each gelatin capsule with ginger powder. Store the capsules in an air-tight container for final use and place in a dark, cool location.

Directions

Take 1 capsule twice a day with a glass of water.

Chamomile Capsules for Intestinal Cramps

Chamomile contains a compound known as chamazulene, which helps break up gas in the intestines, reducing bloating and discomfort. The mild sedative effects of chamomile help soothe the stomach and intestinal lining, easing cramps and spasms.

Ingredients

- 1 cup of dried Chamomile
- Empty Gelatin Capsules

Instructions

Grind the dried chamomile into a powder. Fill each gelatin capsule with the chamomile. Store the capsules in an air-tight container for final use and place in a dark, cool location.

Directions

Take 1-2 capsules up to four times a day during meals with a glass of water.

Marshmallow Root Tea for Irritated Bowels

Marshmallow root contains mucilage, a mucous-like compound that coats and soothes irritated and inflamed bowels. Mucilage also relieves heartburn, upset stomach, and ulcers.

Ingredients

- 1 tablespoon of dried Marshmallow Root
- 250ml of Water

Instructions

Add the marshmallow root to a cup of water and let soak for 4-8 hours. Strain the water into a small pot and heat gently. Pour into a mug and drink.

Directions

Drink 1-3 cups a day between meals. Don't drink it with medications, it may interfere with their absorption.

Lemon Balm Tea for Spasms

Lemon balm contains a highly medicinal compound called rosmarinic acid that provides a calming effect on the digestive system. Lemon balm relieves muscle spasms, gas, and bloating, calming inflamed bowels. Hot lemon balm tea reduces stress and anxiety, calming nerves and lessening digestive issue triggers.

Ingredients

- 1 tablespoon of dried Lemon Balm
- 1 tablespoon of dried Marshmallow Root
- 250 ml of Water
- 1 teaspoon of Raw Honey (optional)

Instructions

In a small pot, bring water to a boil. Remove from heat, add the lemon balm, and steep for 5-10 minutes. Strain the tea into a mug. Add honey to taste.

Directions

Drink 1-3 cups a day after meals.

Natural Antimicrobial

Garlic & Thyme Tonic for Illness

The allicin compound in garlic is a highly effective antimicrobial that combats bacteria, fungi, and other harmful pathogens by disrupting their metabolism.

Thymol, found in thyme, is an effective antimicrobial compound that destroys the cell membrane of harmful pathogens, killing them. This tonic is useful when ill and infected.

Ingredients
4 cloves of Garlic
2 tablespoons of fresh Thyme
1 tablespoon of Apple Cider Vinegar
250ml of Water
1 tablespoon of Honey (optional)

Instructions

Mince the garlic and loosely chop up the thyme. In a small pot, add the garlic, thyme, apple cider vinegar, and water and bring to a boil. Simmer for 10 minutes. Strain the liquid into a mug and add honey to taste.

Directions

Take 1-2 tablespoons of the tonic two to three times a day when ill.

Eucalyptus Steam for Sinuses

Eucalyptol is a compound found in eucalyptus that gives it antimicrobial properties to help fight against bacteria, viruses, and fungi. The steam helps loosen up the mucus buildup in the sinuses, making it easier to drain.

Ingredients
250ml of Water
5-10 drops of Eucalyptus Essential Oil

Instructions

In a small pot, bring water to a boil. Add the boiling water to a bowl and add the eucalyptus essential oil. Lean over the bowl, put a small towel over your head to trap the steam, and inhale. Breathe in the eucalyptus steam for 10 minutes.

Directions

Repeat this procedure 2-3 times a day to relieve congestion and kill germs.

Garlic Olive Oil Ear Drops for Infection

The allicin in garlic helps fight against bacteria, viruses, and fungi. When experiencing an ear infection, these drops will fight the bacteria causing the infection, easing any inflammation and swelling.

Ingredients
2 cloves of Garlic
¼ cup of Organic Olive Oil

Instructions

Mince the garlic cloves. Add the garlic and the olive oil to a small frying pan and heat on low for 20 minutes. Remove from heat and steep for 30 minutes. Using cheesecloth, strain out the garlic into an amber dropper bottle, squeezing the juices out of the garlic.

Directions

Lying on your side, put 2-3 drops in the ear canal and rest for 10 minutes. After 10 minutes, sit up and let it drain. Repeat this procedure 2-3 times a day for an ear infection.

Wild Indigo & Echinacea Throat Spray for Infection

Wild indigo contains isatin and tryptanthrin, which have both been shown effective at combating bacteria and fungi. Echinacea contains alkamides that disrupt microbial cell membranes, killing harmful pathogens. The honey in this recipe leaves a protective coating over the throat and stomach lining, soothing irritation and inflammation.

Ingredients
2 tablespoons of Echinacea Tincture
2 tablespoons of Indigo Root Tincture
1 tablespoon of Raw Honey
2 tablespoons of warm Water

Instructions

Combine the tinctures, honey, and warm water in a cup and stir until completely dissolved and mixed. Pour into a small spray bottle.

Directions

Spray into the back of your throat every 2 hours to relieve pain and to help fight infection.

Eucalyptus Garlic Chest Rub for Cold and Flu Symptoms

Eucalyptus and garlic both contain antimicrobial properties that help fight respiratory infections and help clear cold and flu symptoms. The vapors of eucalyptus and garlic open the airways in the body and promote easier breathing.

Ingredients
¼ cup of Extra Virgin Coconut Oil
5 drops of Eucalyptus Essential Oil
3 cloves of Garlic

Instructions

Mince the garlic cloves. Using the double-boiling method, melt the coconut oil. Add the essential oil and garlic and steep for 30 minutes. Remove from heat and strain the oil into a small tin. Set aside to cool and solidify before use.

Directions

Massage a small amount of the oil onto the chest and throat to relieve congestion and ease coughing. Repeat 2-3 times a day.

Thyme Antiseptic Wound Wash to Kill Bacteria

The thymol contained in thyme is an antimicrobial as well as an antiseptic and can clean wounds of harmful pathogens. By killing bacteria and fungi, thyme is an effective wound cleanser that clears infections and promotes faster healing.

Ingredients
¼ cup of dried Thyme
250ml of Water

Instructions

In a small pot, bring water to a boil. Remove from heat, add the thyme, and steep, covered, for 20 minutes. Strain the liquid into a cup and let it cool completely. Add to a spray bottle.

Directions

Over a towel, spray the wound until dripping wet.Let the liquid run off and air dry. Alternatively, use the spray bottle to dampen a cloth to clean the wound with.

Antiparasitic Remedy

Plantain Salve for Bug Bites

The iridoid glycosides and flavonoids in plantain have proven to aid in wound healing. Plantain is used to relieve bug bites and skin irritations by soothing inflammation, calming red and painful areas, and moisturising dry, affected areas.

Ingredients
2 teaspoons of dried Plantain Leaves
2 tablespoons of Beeswax
1 cup of Extra Virgin Coconut Oil
1 teaspoon of Extra Virgin Olive oil

Instructions

Using the double-boiling method, melt the coconut oil and the beeswax together. Add the plantain and olive oil to the melted coconut oil and beeswax and stir together until thoroughly mixed. Pour the mixture into a small tin or glass container for final use. Store in a cool, dark location until the application has solidified.

Directions

Using a finger, apply a small amount of the plantain salve to the affected area as needed.

Dandelion Root Tincture for Intestinal Parasites

Dandelion root is a bitter herb and has been proven to effectively paralyze and kill intestinal parasites. It also has anti-inflammatory and antioxidant properties that help heal the damage caused by parasites.

Ingredients
1 cup of chopped fresh Dandelion Root
250ml of 80-Proof Vodka

Instructions

Fill a 250-500ml glass canning jar with dandelion. Pour the 80-proof vodka over the dandelion, filling the glass jar 1 inch from the rim, covering the dandelion completely. Seal the jar and store it in a dark, cool area for 4-6 weeks. Shake everyday for the first 2 weeks, and once a week for the next 4 weeks. Using cheesecloth, strain the alcohol into an amber dropper bottle for its final use.

Directions

Before meals, add 10-20 drops to a glass of water and drink up to three times a day.

Clove Olive Oil for Intestinal Worms

The eugenol found in cloves can be used to successfully kill parasites. Due to its potent medicinal properties, extremely small amounts are deadly to intestinal helminth parasites, otherwise known as worms.

Ingredients
½ teaspoon of dried Clove Buds
120ml of E. V. Olive Oil

Instructions

Add the clove buds and olive oil to a mortar and pestle and crush the clove buds, releasing the clove oils into the olive oil. Pour the oil and cloves into a 250ml glass canning jar. Using the double-boiling method, heat the jar for 4-6 hours. Strain the oil into a glass container for final use.

Directions

Add 1-5 drops of clove olive oil to 500ml of water and drink. Do not use clove oil for more than 2 consecutive weeks.

Black Walnut Tincture for Internal Parasites

Juglone is the main active compound in black walnut that gives it its antiparasitic properties. Juglone has been proven to kill parasites, it can be used safely for an internal cleanse.

Ingredients
1 cup of green chopped Black Walnut Hulls
250ml of 80-Proof Vodka

Instructions

Fill a 250-500ml glass canning jar with black walnut hulls. Pour the 80-proof vodka over the hulls, filling the glass jar 1 inch from the rim, covering the hulls completely. Seal the jar and store it in a dark, cool area for 4-6 weeks. Shake everyday for the first 2 weeks and once a week for the next 4 weeks. Using cheesecloth, strain the alcohol into an amber dropper bottle for its final use.

Directions

Before meals, add 10-20 drops to a glass of water and drink up to three times a day.

Wormwood Tea for Potent Parasite Cleanse

Wormwood contains thujone and sesquiterpene lactones, that destroy the cell membranes of parasites. It also disrupts the parasites' reproductive processes, eliminating any future generations.

Ingredients
1 teaspoon of dried Wormwood
250ml of Water
1 teaspoon of Raw Honey (optional)

Instructions

In a small pot, bring the water to a boil. Remove from heat and add the dried wormwood, steep for 5-15 minutes to the taste you desire. Add honey to taste.

Directions

Drink 3-4 cups of wormwood tea a day before meals to cleanse parasites.

Antifungal Solution

Neem & Tea Tree Salve for Skin Fungal Infections

The terpenoids in neem oil have been shown to inhibit the growth of fungal pathogens by inhibiting the ergosterol biosynthesis in fungi and disrupting their cell walls. The terpenoids in tea tree oil are also effective at combating skin and nail fungal infections.

Ingredients
2 teaspoons of Neem Oil
2 teaspoons of Tea Tree Essential Oil
2 tablespoons of Beeswax
1 cup of Extra Virgin Coconut Oil

Instructions

Using the double boiling method, melt the coconut oil and the beeswax together. Add the neem oil and tea tree oil to the melted coconut oil and beeswax and stir together until thoroughly mixed. Pour the mixture into a small tin or glass container for final use. Store in a cool, dark location until the application has solidified.

Directions

Using a finger, apply a small amount of the neem and tea tree salve to the affected area four times a day. When the infection has disappeared, continue using twice a day for another week.

Oregano & Thyme Oil for Foot Fungus

Oregano works as an antifungal due to its terpenoid phenols, carvacrol and thymol. Thyme's main active compound is also thymol, and together, oregano and thyme produce multiplied antifungal power. This oil is used for treating fungal diseases such as ringworm, athlete's foot, and toenail fungus.

Ingredients
½ cup of fresh Oregano
½ cup of fresh Thyme
250ml of E. V. Olive Oil

Instructions

Pack fill a 250-500ml glass canning jar with oregano and thyme. Fill the jar with olive oil 1 inch below the rim. Using the double-boiling method, heat the jar for 2-6 hours. Strain the oil into a glass container for its final use.

Directions

Using your fingers, apply the oregano & thyme oil to the affected skin area 2-3 times a day.

Garlic Tincture for Internal and External Fungal Infections

Allicin in garlic is what gives garlic its antifungal properties. Garlic can inhibit the growth of fungi both internally and externally.

Ingredients
1 cup of crushed Garlic Cloves
250ml of 80-Proof Vodka

Instructions

Fill a 250-500ml glass canning jar with the crushed garlic. Pour the 80-proof vodka over the garlic, filling the glass jar 1 inch from the rim. Seal the jar and store it in a dark, cool area for 2-3 weeks. Shake everyday for the first 2 weeks, and once during the last week. Using cheesecloth, strain the alcohol into an amber dropper bottle for its final use.

Directions

For internal use, take 4-5 drops a day.

For external use, apply 1-5 drops directly to the affected skin area.

Pau D'Arco & Olive Leaf Capsule for Internal Fungal Infections

The compounds in Pau D'Arco, known as lapachol and beta-lapachone are proven to kill certain bacteria, fungi, viruses, and parasites. Pau D'Arco also has anti-inflammatory properties that can ease the irritation caused by fungi. Oleuropein is the compound in olive leaf that gives it powerful antifungal properties against Candida albicans.

Ingredients
¼ cup of powdered Pau D'Arco Bark
¼ cup of powdered Olive Leaf
Empty Gelatin or Vegetable Capsules

Instructions

Fill each capsule completely with Pau D'Arco and olive leaf powder. Store the capsules in an air-tight container for final use and place in a dark, cool location.

Directions

Take 1-2 capsules twice a day with meals while fighting a fungal infection.

Barberry Berberine Capsules for Internal Fungal Infections

Barberry contains a compound known as berberine, which is the powerful medicinal compound that gives barberry its antifungal properties.

Ingredients
1 cup of powdered Barberry bark or roots
Empty Gelatin or Vegetable Capsules

Instructions

Fill each capsule with powdered barberry bark or roots. Store the capsules in an air-tight container for final use and place in a dark, cool location.

Directions

Take 1-3 capsules a day for up to 6 months. Start with 1 capsule and gradually work your way up to 3, depending on your needs.

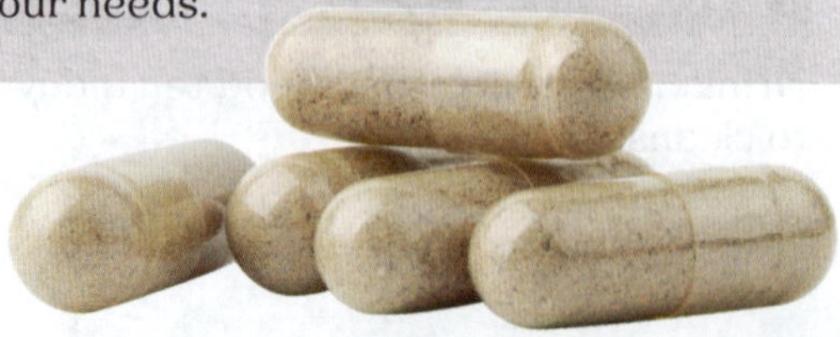

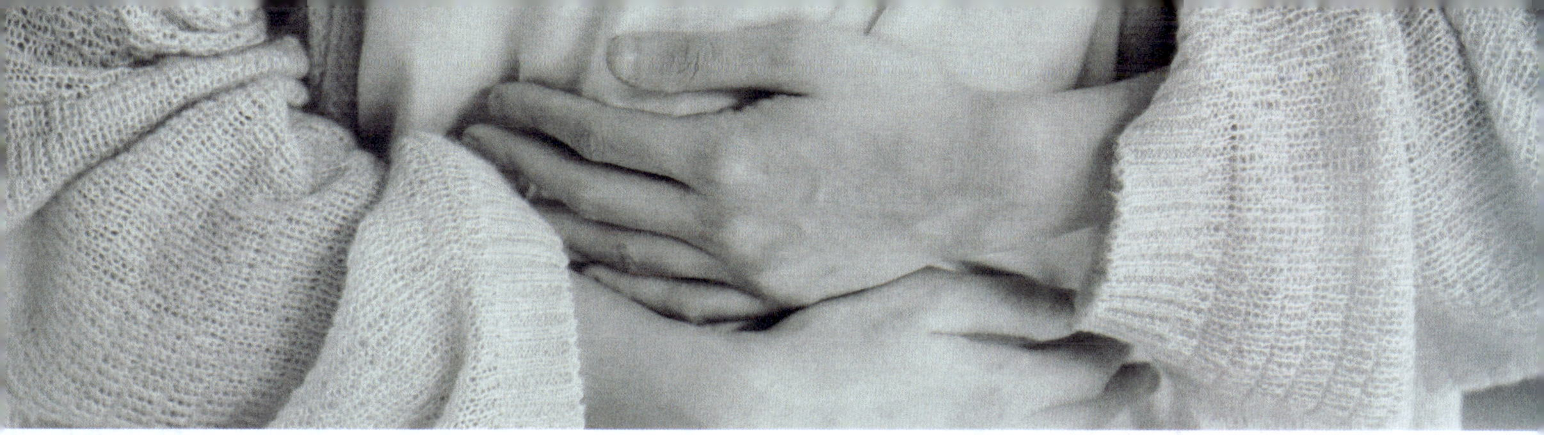

Cold and Flu Antivirals

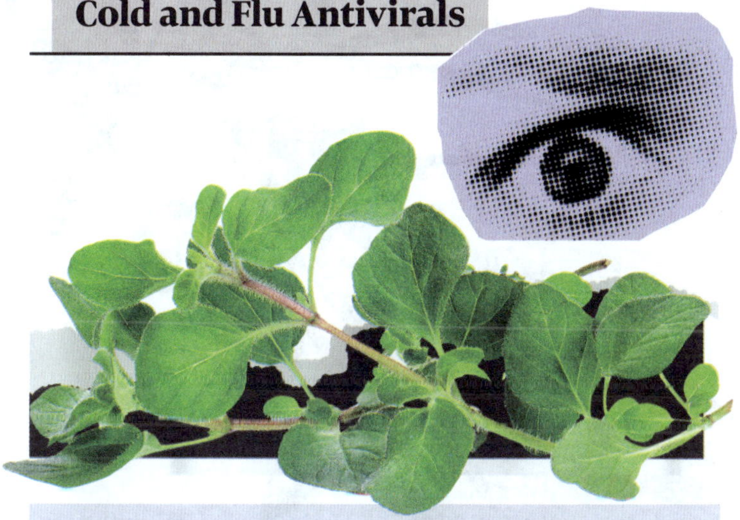

Oregano Tincture to Kill Viral Infections

Oregano has been shown in scientific studies to be an effective antiviral that significantly inhibits virus replication. Carvacrol and thymol are the main active compounds that give oregano the antiviral properties that can destroy viruses.

Ingredients
1 cup of fresh Oregano Plant
250ml of 80-Proof Vodka

Instructions

Pack fill a 250-500ml glass canning jar with oregano. Pour the 80-proof vodka over the oregano, filling the glass jar 1 inch from the rim. Seal the jar and store it in a dark, cool area for 2-4 weeks. Shake everyday for the first 2 weeks, and once for each following week. Using cheesecloth, strain the alcohol into an amber dropper bottle for its final use.

Directions

Take 10-20 drops orally by adding it to a cup of water or mixing it with food once a day for three weeks.

Chamber Bitter for Symptoms of Viral Infection

The flavonoids and phenolic compounds found in chamber bitter have proven it to be effective at combating viruses like the common cold and flu. Chamber bitter has been used to manage various viral infections and ease their symptoms.

Ingredients
1 cup of dried Chamber Bitter
250ml of Brandy
1 teaspoon of Raw Honey

Instructions

Pack fill a 250-500ml glass canning jar with chamber bitter. Add the raw honey and pour the brandy over the chamber bitter, filling the glass jar 1 inch from the rim. Seal the jar and store it in a dark, cool area for 2-4 weeks, shaking every day. Using cheesecloth, strain the alcohol into an amber glass bottle for its final use.

Directions

Take 1 teaspoon every 2-3 hours in hot water when you are feeling ill. This is not for long-term use.

Elderberry Syrup for Protection Against Viral Infections

The polyphenolic compounds found in elderberry, including anthocyanins and flavonoids, give it antiviral properties that inhibit the replication of viruses and the penetration of cells. Additionally, the hemagglutinin proteins in elderberry prevent viruses from infecting healthy cells. Elderberry also supports the immune system, which increases protection against viruses.

Ingredients
1 cup of dried Elderberries
750ml of Water
1 teaspoon of Raw Honey (optional)

Instructions

In a pot, bring water to a light boil. Lower the heat, add the elderberries, and simmer for 45 minutes. Strain the water into a glass container and stir the honey in until completely dissolved. Store in the fridge for use.

Directions

Take 1 tablespoon 1-3 times a day as needed.

Olive Leaf Tincture to Kill Viruses

Olive leaf contains oleuropein, a medicinal compound with antiviral and antibacterial properties. Olive leaf also stimulates a natural process known as phagocytosis, a process our body uses to eliminate harmful bacteria and viruses.

Ingredients
1 cup of dried Olive Leaves
250ml of 80-Proof Vodka

Instructions

Fill a 250-500ml glass canning jar with dried olive leaves. Pour the 80-proof vodka over the olive leaves, filling the glass jar 1 inch from the rim. Seal the jar and store it in a dark, cool area for 4-6 weeks. Shake everyday for the first 2 weeks, and once for each following week. Using cheesecloth, strain the alcohol into an amber dropper bottle for its final use.

Directions

Take 1 teaspoon 3 times a day by adding it to a cup of water or juice. Use at the first signs of illness and continue for 1-2 weeks.

Allergy Relief

Ginger Turmeric Shot for Sinusitis

Ginger and turmeric are potent anti-inflammatories and can alleviate swelling related to allergies. Ginger reduces pro-inflammatory proteins in the blood and suppresses the production of certain cytokines that cause allergy symptoms. Turmeric helps regulate the body's inflammatory responses, alleviating symptoms like coughing and sinusitis caused by an overactive inflammatory response.

Ingredients
1 inch of fresh Ginger Root
1 inch of fresh Turmeric Root
½ of a Lemon
1 pinch of Black Pepper
50ml of Water

Instructions

Add turmeric root, ginger root, and lemon to a juicer. Add to the water, stir in the pepper, and drink.

Directions

Take 1-2 shots a day during allergy season.

Garlic Honey Syrup for Histamine Inhibition

Garlic works as an allergy relief by inhibiting the body's release of histamines. Garlic also suppresses the release of a substance known as beta-hexosaminidase, which is released during an allergic reaction. The protective coating that honey leaves behind provides soothing relief and heals any damage caused by allergic reactions.

Ingredients
1 head of Garlic
1 cup of Raw Honey

Instructions

Peel and chop the garlic and add it to a glass jar. Pour the honey over the garlic and seal the jar. Place the jar in a dark, cool location for 1-2 weeks. Strain into a container for final use.

Directions

Take 1 tablespoon 2-3 times a day as needed for allergy relief.

Nettle Turmeric Capsules for Inflammation

The compounds in stinging nettle and turmeric combined create a synergistic response and provide potent inflammation relief as well as modulate the immune system to block the histamines involved in the body's allergy response.

Ingredients
½ cup of powdered Stinging Nettle Leaf
½ cup of powdered Turmeric Root
Empty Gelatin or Vegetable Capsules

Instructions

Mix thoroughly the stinging nettle powder and the turmeric root powder. Fill each capsule with the mixed nettle and turmeric powder. Store the capsules in an air-tight container for final use and place in a dark, cool location.

Directions

Take 2 capsules 2-3 times a day with meals.

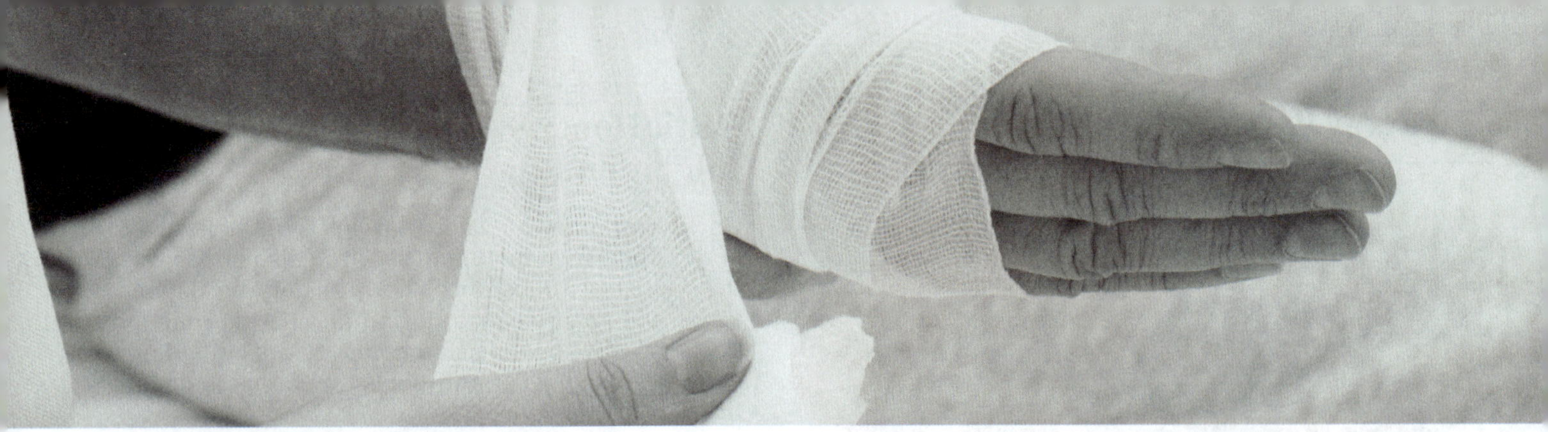

Butterbur Ginger Nettle Tincture for Rhinitis Symptoms

The combination of butterbur, ginger, and stinging nettle inhibits the body's release of histamines, reduces inflammation, and relieves allergic rhinitis symptoms.

Ingredients

- ¼ cup of Butterbur Root
- ¼ cup of Ginger Root
- ¼ cup of Stinging Nettle Leaf
- 250ml of 80-Proof Vodka

Instructions

Chop up the butterbur root, ginger root, and stinging nettle leaf and add to a 250-500ml glass jar. Pour the 80-proof vodka over the plants, filling the glass jar 1 inch from the rim. Seal the jar and store it in a dark, cool area for 4-6 weeks. Shake everyday for the first 2 weeks, and once for each following week. Using cheesecloth, strain the alcohol into an amber dropper bottle for its final use.

Directions

Take 30-40 drops 3 times a day during allergy seasons and flare-ups.

Burn Wound Treatment

Calendula Comfrey Salve for Skin Repair

The flavonoids contained in calendula give calendula the properties to reduce inflammation, reduce pain, and repair damaged skin. Comfrey provides similar benefits as calendula andtogether they multiply each others benefits, providinga potent solution for burn wounds.

Ingredients

- 2 teaspoons of Calendula Essential Oil
- 2 teaspoons of Comfrey Essential Oil
- 2 tablespoons of Beeswax
- 1 teaspoon of Vitamin E Oil
- 1 cup of Extra Virgin Coconut Oil

Instructions

Using the double boiling method, melt the coconut oil and the beeswax together. Add the calendula, comfrey, and vitamin E oil to the melted coconut oil and beeswax and stir together until thoroughly mixed. Pour the mixture into a small tin or glass container for final use. Store in a cool, dark location until the application has solidified.

Directions

Apply a thin layer of the calendula comfrey salve to the burn using your fingers. Reapply 3-4 times a day as needed. Do not apply to open wounds and only use until the wound is healed.

Lavender Essential Oil Blend for Wound Cleaning

Linalool and linalyl acetate are the main active compounds in lavender that make it medically beneficial. These compounds give lavender the analgesic and antiseptic properties that ease pain and clean wounds. Coconut oil is mostly made of lauric acid, which provides anti-inflammatory benefits and encourages skin repair. Coconut oil also provides moisture to dry and irritated skin.

Ingredients
10 drops of Lavender Essential Oil
2 tablespoons of Extra Virgin Coconut Oil
250ml of hot Water

Instructions

Fill a bowl with hot water. Place the coconut oil in a glass cup and sit the cup in the bowl of hot water to soften the coconut oil. Drop in the lavender essential oil and mix together thoroughly. Using a spatula, transfer the blend into a small tin or glass jar for its final use.

Directions

Clean the burn and apply a thin layer of the lavender blend with a cotton ball by lightly dabbing. If a cotton ball is uncomfortable, you can use clean fingers. Reapply 2-3 times a day or as needed.

St John's Wort Infused Oil for Inflammation

St John's wort contains the medicinal compounds hypericin and hyperforin, which give St John's wort anti-inflammatory properties. The compounds also give St John's wort the ability to ease pain. Olive oil not only reduces inflammation and soothes irritated skin but also leaves a protective coating over the burn wound and has cleaning properties.

Ingredients
1 cup of dried St John's Wort
250ml of E. V. Olive Oil

Instructions

Fill a 500ml glass canning jar with dried St John's wort. Fill the jar with olive oil 1 inch below the rim. Using the double-boiling method, heat the jar for 2-6 hours. Strain the oil into a glass container for its final use.

Directions

Using your fingers or a cotton ball, apply the St John's wort infused oil to the burn area 2-3 times a day or as needed. An alternative method is to soak a sterile gauze in the oil and use it as a compress, leaving it on for 15 minutes. Stay out of the sun after using St John's wort.

Manuka Honey Dressing to Kill Bacteria

Manuka honey is a highly medicinal honey with potent antibacterial and anti-inflammatory properties. The compound methylglyoxal is what makes manuka honey so unique and gives it the healing benefits to ease burn wounds.

Ingredients
½ cup of Raw Manuka Honey
Sterile Gauze

Instructions

Apply a thick layer of room-temperature manuka honey over the entire burn. Cover loosely with sterile gauze and secure.

Directions

Clean the burn wound before applying the honey, and be sure to add a thick layer without it dripping off. Change the dressing and reapply 2-3 times a day.

Aloe Vera Gel for Pain Relief

The aloe vera plant has a jelly inside that contains glycoproteins and polysaccharides that reduce inflammation, relieve pain, and promote blood circulation. These compounds also encourage new skin growth and healing.

Ingredients
1 leaf of fresh Aloe Vera

Instructions

Slice the aloe vera leaf and scoop out the gel insides. Place the aloe gel in a container for final use.

Directions

Apply the aloe vera gel directly to the burn and cover it completely. Reapply 3-4 times a day as needed. Use for 1st and 2nd degree burns.

Chamomile Compress for Pain Relief

Chamomile is used as a compress to reduce inflammation and ease pain. The flavonoids in chamomile are what give it the anti-inflammatory and analgesic properties that are beneficial when treating burn wounds. The antibacterial properties that chamomile also beholds keep wounds clean and protected from infections.

Ingredients
½ cup of dried Chamomile
250ml of room temperature Water
Sterile Gauze

Instructions

In a small pot, bring the water to a boil. Remove from heat and add the chamomile, let steep until cool. Strain the tea into a bowl. Soak the gauze in the chamomile tea and wring out. Apply the chamomile compress directly to the burn wound and hold it there for 15 minutes.

Directions

Clean the burn and apply a thin layer of the lavender blend with a cotton ball by lightly dabbing. If a cotton ball is uncomfortable, you can use clean fingers. Reapply 2-3 times a day or as needed.

Get Started

Knowing how to make these herbal remedies using the items in your kitchen or garden could save your life one day. Practice making these remedies now, while resources are still abundant, to master the skill of making these herbal remedies successfully. Starting with easy-to-make remedies such as Aloe Vera Gel for sunburns or Oregano & Thyme Oil for foot fungus is a great way to begin harnessing your skill and managing your herbal stockpile.

In a time of desperate need and chaos, the ability to keep you and your loved ones safe is valuable more than anything, and herbal remedies won't fail you.

Chapter 20

Exactly What to Do When Martial Law Is Declared

How to Keep Your Civil Rights and Liberties as Others Lose Them

Martial law is the absolute collapse of civil order.

It begins when soldiers march past your window. It begins with sirens, roadblocks, and the vanishing of rights you thought were permanent.

When the order comes down, you have no time to plan. You only have time to act. Every hour matters. Here is exactly what must happen throughout the first seven days.

"When tyranny becomes law, resistance becomes duty."
— Thomas Jefferson

Day 1: Immediate Deception and Resource Concealment

When martial law is declared, you are no longer living under the assumption of civil protection. You are living under the assumption that everything you own can be seized in the name of "public order." Precedents are clear. During Hurricane Katrina in 2005, National Guard troops and local police conducted door-to-door sweeps in New Orleans, seizing firearms, food stores, and water from private citizens. The justification was public safety. The reality was forced disarmament and asset confiscation.

The same occurred under Ferdinand Marcos in the Philippines, and it has been echoed in smaller instances from Panama to Ferguson, Missouri. Martial law removes legal protections in favor of expediency.

The very first thing authorities and opportunists look for is signs of resource security: stockpiled food, visible fuel, cases of water, armed resistance. If you appear better prepared than your neighbors, you are seen as a threat, or worse, as a storehouse to be redistributed.

Before nightfall on Day 1, erase any appearance of abundance. Strip all visible pantries and kitchen cabinets that can be seen from windows, open doors, or casual entry points. Leave a few dusty cans, a crumpled cereal box, or a nearly empty rice bag visible to create the illusion of scarcity.

Move your real supplies into secure, hidden locations. Build false walls or panels behind closets or under stairs.

A basic hidden panel can be built using 1x6 pine boards or drywall, cut to size and installed with magnetic latches or disguised hinges. Paint the surface to match surrounding walls. Use an interior closet with a depth extension. Always prioritize concealment over access speed. If the panel takes longer to reach but can pass a police search, it has done its job.

Use waterproof containers buried at least three feet deep in dry soil to cache extra food, firearms, and medicine outside the house. Modify floorboards or hollow sections of heavy furniture to create quick access hiding spots that would survive a casual search. Reinforce an ordinary-looking closet with a hidden rear panel to serve as a fallback vault.

Set up a decoy stash, leave a few basic supplies somewhere obvious, like a half-filled pantry or garage shelf. Anyone conducting a rough search who finds "the stash" early will be more likely to stop looking further.

Stripping your home of visible abundance buys you the first night. But survival is not about one night. It is about never being seen at all. As authority hardens, your home must vanish from sight completely.

Avoid creating external signs of preparedness. No last-minute deliveries, no expanded generator setups, no visible fuel storage. Appear poor, disorganized, or at least just as desperate as the average home.

Understand that in a collapse, neighbors and even family can unintentionally become informants. Fear and hunger change people. Assume anything you say can be repeated. Practice absolute silence about what you have hidden.

Looters and gangs rise fast when authority is confused. In every martial law event, criminal groups immediately exploit the situation. If your home stands out as well-supplied or defended, you move from invisible to target in a single night.

Under martial law, the Posse Comitatus Act is suspended. Military forces can act directly as police without warrants or civilian oversight. Constitutional protections under the Fourth Amendment (unreasonable search and seizure) are either weakened or overridden by executive order or emergency decree. Existing executive orders such as EO 13603 ("National Defense Resources Preparedness") grant standing authority to seize food, fuel, property, and labor.

In simple terms: if it can be seen, it can be taken. If it can be suspected, it can be confiscated.

Those who survive martial law are those no one remembers seeing at all.

Day 2: Blackout Discipline and Defensive Fortification

On the second day after martial law is declared, the chaos of the announcement begins to settle into organized control. This is when compliance sweeps, curfews, and enforced lockdowns begin.

During the 2013 Boston lockdown, entire neighborhoods were ordered to shelter in place while tactical teams swept house to house. Homes that looked occupied, lights on, movement visible, were almost guaranteed visits, often at gunpoint.

From the very first night, you must turn your home into a dead structure. Blackout every window and door. Heavy curtains are not enough. Hang thick blankets, staple or nail plywood over frames if needed, and tape seams with black duct tape to prevent even a glimmer of light from escaping. A single crack of visible light at night can trigger suspicion, investigation, and forced entry.

Blackout fabric or contractor-grade trash bags layered with duct tape offer fast, full coverage. Cut to size, then tape directly to window glass and around frame edges. Overlap seams. If needed, layer blankets inside and secure them with tension rods or push-pinned curtains to deaden any light bleed.

Every door should be reinforced from the inside. Installing crossbars, simple two-by-four braces mounted behind doors can dramatically increase resistance. Position heavy furniture against entry points to block forced breaches. Windows on ground floors are prime weak points. Lock them, wedge them shut, and board them over if you have the time and materials. Even a basic bar screwed into the frame can delay or deter entry.

Inside, enforce absolute light and sound discipline. No TV, no music, no raised voices. Whisper-level conversation only. If you must cook, do so during daylight hours to mask smells and reduce attention. Use small, covered flashlights or low-power red lights to navigate inside at night. Red light preserves night vision and is less likely to leak and attract attention through cracks.

Silence your home completely. Barking dogs, loud appliances, even the thud of heavy footsteps can carry shockingly far in a silent city or neighborhood under curfew. A home that seems utterly abandoned will be passed over for one that betrays signs of life.

Under martial law, curfews, mandatory home searches, and forced evacuations become standard operating procedures. Court orders are not required. National Guard or federal troops can, under executive direction, enter private homes for public safety without warning. Resistance, even passive, is legally dangerous and practically suicidal during the initial lockdown phase.

If the street looks empty and silent, and your house looks empty and silent, patrols and opportunists alike will move on.

Day 3: Alternative Mobility and Information Acquisition

By the third day of martial law, static homes become prisons. In Hawaii after the Pearl Harbor attack, martial law descended without warning, cutting off entire cities overnight. Curfews, roadblocks, mandatory ID checks, and detentions made normal movement almost impossible. People moved on foot, using drainage ditches, abandoned farm tracks, and forgotten back lots that military patrols overlooked.

You cannot depend on vehicles once martial law begins. Gasoline will be rationed or seized. Major roads will become choke points with checkpoints manned by police, National Guard, or federal troops. License plate scanners, surveillance drones, and informants will monitor every main avenue. Even if you evade law enforcement, desperate civilians will see and remember anyone moving with supplies or strength.

You must shift immediately from stealth to mobility. Scout your neighborhood now, while you still can. Learn every footpath, alleyway, utility easement, and drainage line. Identify fences that can be jumped, walls with gaps, overgrown lots that offer cover. Make yourself a mental map of ways in and out without touching a single main road. In wartime and martial law zones alike, it's the invisible that survive.

Map your neighborhood. Draw this as a physical map with no names. Fold and laminate. Store it where you would hide your shoes in an emergency.

Information becomes your most valuable weapon from this day forward. Official broadcasts will tell only part of the truth, and usually late. Battery-powered radios tuned to emergency channels like NOAA, local emergency management, or ham frequencies can warn you of curfews, forced evacuations, troop movements, or public health orders before they reach your door. Have spare batteries stored separately in waterproof bags.

Avoid using mobile phones except in extreme emergencies. Every call, text, and pinged location is logged and tracked. Even powered-off phones can sometimes be reactivated remotely. Paper maps are better than GPS devices. Word of mouth, careful observation, and shortwave radio chatter will tell you more about what is coming than anything you see on a screen.

At this stage, survival depends not on strength or supplies alone, but on knowing when to move, how to move, and when to stay absolutely still.

Day 4: Supply Redundancy and Caching

By the fourth day under martial law, authorities and opportunists alike begin systematic searches. When martial law came to the Philippines under Ferdinand Marcos, soldiers swept rural areas with orders to seize hidden supplies. Those who kept everything in one location lost it all in a single afternoon. Their preparations fed the very machine meant to control them.

You must disperse your survival resources immediately. No matter how well you think you have hidden your stockpiles inside your home, assume that, given enough time, suspicion, or pressure, they can and will be found. Never store all your food, water, medicine, and critical gear in a single place.

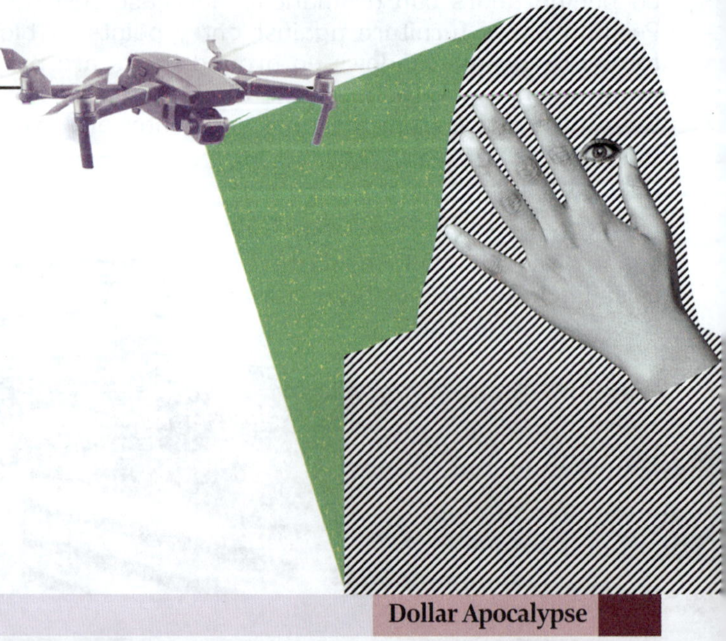

Establish two or three off-site caches within walking distance of your primary shelter. Each cache should contain the basics for one week of survival: non-perishable food, purified water or purification methods, basic medical supplies, a firestarter, cutting tools, spare clothing, and a basic radio if possible.

Assume you will lose everything. Assume your cache is the only reason you will still be breathing next week.

The cache containers must be truly waterproof, crush-proof, and scent-proof. PVC tubes, military-grade dry bags, or sealed ammo cans are good options. Bury them at least two to three feet underground to defeat casual metal detector sweeps and visual searches. Choose locations with natural camouflage—fallen trees, abandoned ruins, rock outcrops, overgrown fence lines, or areas littered with scrap where a hidden cache will not stand out.

Mark the locations mentally, or use unmarked sketches hidden inside durable everyday items. Never store maps or coordinates digitally. If you must write anything down, encode it so that only you or your most trusted partner can decipher it. Never tell anyone unless their survival is equally bound to your own.

You can hide supplies. But you cannot hide your face forever. Sooner or later, authority will look directly at you. What they see will decide everything.

Day 5: Controlled Deception and Psychological Readiness

By the fifth day under martial law, patrols will have settled into a pattern. In Panama during Operation Just Cause in 1989, civilians who appeared helpless were often left alone. Those who looked prepared, confident, or defiant were marked, questioned, detained, or worse.

You must master the art of controlled deception. What you show externally is not the truth of your situation. If soldiers or patrols come near your home—or stop you in the street—you want to appear harmless, frail, confused, and poor.

Create a simple, believable cover story ahead of time. Something like: you lost your job, you have no transportation, you have little to no food, and you are staying put because you have nowhere else to go. Practice this story until you can say it without hesitation, fear, or overacting. Anything that smells rehearsed will raise suspicion.

Your body language must match. Keep your head slightly lowered. Speak softly. Avoid direct eye contact unless directly ordered. Confidence, sarcasm, arrogance, even excessive friendliness can trigger aggression in young, frightened men carrying rifles and following unclear orders. They are not trained judges—they react instinctively to perceived threats.

Internally, you must remain sharp, cold, and absolutely aware. But externally, you are the lost sheep, not the capable survivor. You are the worn-out remnant, not the prepared guardian.

If you look like a threat, you will be treated as one. If you look like a burden, they will move on to easier targets or more obvious problems.

Psychological readiness is all about control. Control your face. Control your words. Control your posture. The man who survives martial law is not the strongest. He is the man who knows when to be invisible, when to be forgotten, and when to appear absolutely, utterly insignificant.

Deception buys you time. But hunger doesn't wait. Sooner or later, you must step into the open, and you must know how to vanish before anyone sees.

Day 6: Stealth Resupply and Silent Surveillance

Sarajevo residents collecting firewood, winter of 1992–1993
By Christian Maréchal - Own work, CC BY 3.0, https://commons.wikimedia.org/w/index.php?curid=6370713

By the sixth day under martial law, the initial shock fades, and supply chains begin to break down entirely. In Sarajevo during the siege of the 1990s, survival became an exercise in patience, risk, and shadow movement. Civilians lived or died based on their ability to move unseen, gather supplies unnoticed, and disappear again without drawing attention.

At this point, you must abandon the idea that supplies will reach you through official channels. Aid stations, distribution centers, and relief trucks will either be mobbed, tightly controlled, or used as bait to control desperate populations. You must move independently to gather what you need without becoming a target.

Move alone or with one trusted partner only. Larger groups attract notice. Dress plainly. Carry nothing of value. Do not use obvious backpacks or gear that marks you as a courier. If you must carry supplies, do so under clothing, in old bags, or in disguised containers that blend with the environment. Walk with the posture of someone scavenging, not someone carrying supplies worth stealing.

Route discipline is life. Never walk the same path twice in a row. Vary your entrances and exits. If you can double back, do it from different directions each time. Patrols and desperate civilians alike watch patterns. If you are predictable, you are vulnerable.

Mark resource locations mentally. Never draw maps, never text coordinates, and never mark walls or fences with symbols. Use natural memory markers—trees, broken windows, unusual cracks, light poles with certain dents—to remember where hidden gardens, abandoned wells, or salvageable buildings are located.

Silent surveillance is your edge. Watch patrols without being seen. Notice their shifts, their blind spots, their lazy habits. Every checkpoint has a weakness. Every guard has moments of boredom or distraction. Gather information the way you gather supplies: carefully, silently, without ever looking like you are doing anything important.

Use shadows, doorways, and parked cars to watch intersections. A cracked bathroom mirror angled from a dark room can give you a street view without moving blinds. Use an old pair of binoculars from a second-story attic vent or a small drilled hole behind a bookshelf. If possible, install passive infrared motion detectors inside your own home to detect if someone crosses your threshold while you're gone.

If you see a food line forming, you are already too late. Crowds draw attention, and attention during martial law is fatal. Trust your feet, your mind, and your instincts, not official channels or desperate herds.

By the end of the first week, martial law has settled into a new reality. Those who wait inside the lines are caged. Those who move first, who vanish before the noose tightens, they live free. If you have a fallback, it is now or never.

Day 7: Long-Term Strategy and Off-Grid Living Transition

By the seventh day of martial law, long-term patterns emerge. Patrols harden, supply lines fracture, and casual movement becomes nearly impossible. In Missouri during the Civil War, martial law cleared entire towns overnight. Those who remained visible, clinging to normalcy, were forced into relocations, disarmed, or left at the mercy of whoever held the strongest position. Survival favored those who left before they were told.

If you have a fallback location—a cabin, a family farm, a hidden camp—this is the day you move to it. Wait until checkpoints lock down rural roads or troops start sweeping woodlots and it's too late.

Your fallback site must be capable of standing alone. Water is the absolute highest priority: a spring, a creek, or a rain catchment system that does not rely on town plumbing. Food must be on hand, whether stored, grown, or hunted. Shelter must already be in place and functional. Firewood, tools, medicine, and spare clothing should be waiting. Anything you must "go back for" is already lost.

Blend with the landscape. No colorful tarps or bright tents. No visible smoke trails or obvious campsites. Minimize noise, light, and movement. Fires must be concealed using Dakota fire holes or underground rocket stoves. Lights should be covered entirely or avoided altogether. Every piece of trash, every footprint, every trail you leave behind is a risk.

Martial law evolves, but it does not truly end. Once a population is brought under emergency control, the habits, structures, and enforcements tend to linger. It does not matter whether the original justification collapses.

The loss of freedom is rarely reversed by decree.

The seventh day is your last chance to leave on your terms. After that, the grid hardens. Checkpoints lock. Curfews deepen. Anyone still clinging to comfort is caught.

You may believe that this kind of collapse cannot happen here. That courts, or elections, or tradition will protect you.

History says otherwise.

There is no such thing as a right that survives force.

There is only readiness or regret.

Relevant U.S. Martial Law and Constitutional Facts

DATE NOTES

Posse Comitatus Act (1878): Limits the use of federal troops in domestic law enforcement without explicit Congressional authorization. During martial law, these limitations may be suspended under the Insurrection Act.

Insurrection Act (1807): Gives the President the authority to deploy troops to suppress civil disorder, insurrection, or rebellion.

Suspension Clause: The right to habeas corpus can be suspended "in cases of rebellion or invasion." Historically used by Lincoln during the Civil War, and other presidents in localized martial law emergencies.

You must know: the government can, and has, suspended every protection you think you are entitled to.

Precedents:

The idea that martial law or suspension of civil liberties is "unthinkable" in America is pure fantasy. It has happened before, and it will undoubtedly happen again.

Abraham Lincoln suspended habeas corpus during the Civil War. In 1861, without Congressional approval, Lincoln authorized the military to arrest and detain citizens without trial. Thousands were jailed, including political opponents, newspaper editors, and civilians accused of "disloyal practices." The Supreme Court initially challenged this action, but enforcement was effectively impossible during wartime.

Franklin D. Roosevelt issued Executive Order 9066 during World War II, allowing the forced removal and internment of over 120,000 American citizens and residents of Japanese descent. No trials, no evidence required—just suspicion and mass relocation to camps under armed guard, where many remained for years.

The Bonus Army incident of 1932: World War I veterans protesting for promised bonuses were violently dispersed in Washington, D.C., by Army troops under General Douglas MacArthur, after President Hoover invoked emergency powers. Cavalry charges, bayonets, and tear gas were used against American citizens, including families.

Hawaii under Martial Law (1941-1944): After Pearl Harbor, Hawaii was placed under martial law for nearly three years. Civil courts were suspended. Citizens lived under curfew, censorship, warrantless searches, and military justice without recourse to civilian law.

Day 0: Preparation Checklist (Before Martial Law Is Declared)

Once martial law is announced, you are already behind. Everything you do today, before the announcement, will determine whether you survive or vanish.

1. Secure and Conceal Stockpiles

Complete at least three weeks of food, water, and medicine supplies. Hide them in layered concealment: behind false walls, inside hollow furniture, or buried in waterproof containers. Create a visible decoy pantry stocked with expired goods and clutter to mislead casual searches.

2. Lock Down Documents and Redundancies

Scan every vital document, such as ID cards, deeds, and certificates. Encrypt copies onto a physical USB drive. Store one on-site and one off-site. Laminate critical papers and seal them against water damage. Include emergency contact lists and medical information. Keep nothing cloud-based.

3. Divide and Conceal Weapons

Split firearms into ready, hidden, and cached groups. Clean and zero weapons now. Store ammunition in waterproof, separated containers. Fast-access weapons must be within two steps of your sleeping area. Practice retrieving them silently and in darkness until flawless.

4. Assemble Tactical Clothing and Mobility Kits

Prepare plain, unmarked clothing in neutral tones such as grey, brown, and dark green, without logos or insignias. Stage a covert sling bag with fire starter, flashlight, knife, water purification gear, radio, cash, and basic medical supplies. Leave nothing digital.

5. Harden Intel and Communication Tools

Purchase a portable AM/FM/NOAA or shortwave radio along with spare batteries. Print paper maps of your area. Pre-mark safe zones, fallback locations, and danger sectors using natural code, not plain labels. Leave no digital footprint. Treat your phone as compromised from the first hour of martial law.

6. Pre-Map Routes and Cache Points

Walk and memorize at least two stealth routes out of your home zone. Bypass main roads. Find abandoned lots, wooded alleys, and drainage channels. Cache supplies offsite now. Do not rely on memory alone. Use natural markers, not digital notes.

7. Drill Psychological Hardness

Rehearse your cover story. Practice it until it sounds natural under stress. Drill house blackout procedures. Practice rapid silent withdrawal from your home. If you panic under real pressure, you will lose. Calm, silence, and invisibility must become instinctive.

8. Final Order

When the emergency hits, you will not rush to the store. You will not call friends. You will not post online. You will lock down, vanish, and operate in the grey.

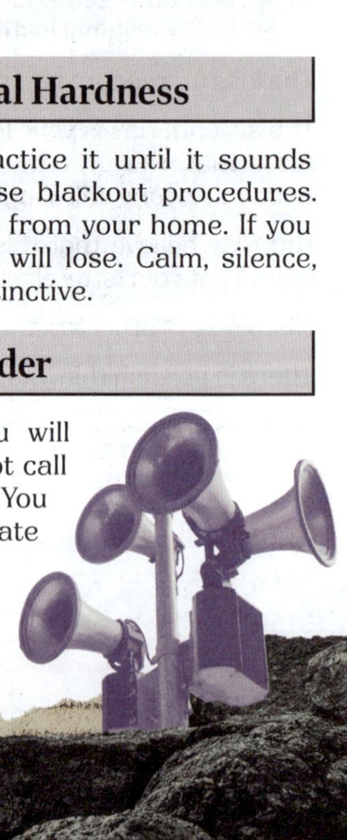

Chapter 21

Items That Will Get You on FEMA's Radar

FEMA's public role is disaster response. But under certain emergency conditions, that role expands into enforcement: consolidating supply chains, relocating people, and monitoring the population for "non-compliance."

In that environment, some behaviors—buying large quantities of gear, storing water, or collecting off-grid tools—may be misinterpreted as hostile. This chapter explains which purchases and behaviors are likely to trigger surveillance, and how to prepare quietly, legally, and with no unnecessary attention.

"The nine most terrifying words in the English language are: I'm from the government and I'm here to help."— Ronald Reagan

Typical Items That Trigger FEMA Watchlists

- **HAM radios (especially licensed or online purchases)**
- **Fuel storage tanks / stabilizers**
- **Bulk water purification units**
- **Solar battery systems with off-grid inverters**
- **Ammunition reloading components**
- **Radiation pills / gas masks / NBC gear**
- **Mylar food kits with long shelf life**
- **Tactical gear (plate carriers, military-style comms)**
- **Drone jammers or anti-surveillance tools**

Don't Make Big Purchases in One Place

The fastest way to draw unwanted attention to your preparations is to act like someone who's preparing. That sounds obvious, but most people fail to realize **how traceable modern purchasing has become.**

Since the formation of the Department of Homeland Security and the establishment of fusion centers—data coordination hubs shared between federal and local agencies—government surveillance no longer requires direct suspicion or probable cause. Behavior alone is enough. Buy the wrong mix of supplies, at the wrong volume, from the wrong vendor, and your profile may be marked for future monitoring without your knowledge. FEMA, as part of domestic emergency response protocols, has access to these same databases and shares them with law enforcement and resource management arms during declared emergencies.

A single large purchase from a store like **Walmart, Bass Pro,** or even a regional hardware chain can raise flags automatically. This is especially true if your payment is tied to a rewards account, if you used a bank card, or if the item list contains multiple flagged keywords like **"water purification," "fuel," "radiation," "HAM radio," or "freeze-dried."** These systems don't rely on human analysis. They run comparisons against baseline regional behavior. If your buying habits spike out of normal range for your zip code, you're flagged for review, not necessarily by a person—but by the system itself.

To avoid that, **your strategy has to be built around fragmentation.** Think in terms of time, place, and category. Don't just divide your purchases. Divide your appearance as a consumer.

Let's say you need 40 pounds of rice, a camping stove, extra propane, two solar lanterns, several packs of batteries, and a hand-crank radio. Most people would try to knock that out in a single afternoon. That's a mistake. Instead, spread those purchases out over two to three weeks. Visit multiple towns if you're able, not just multiple stores in one area. Use cash. Don't give your phone number at checkout, even when prompted. Don't sign up for any email receipts, loyalty points, or app-based coupons.

When possible, **keep your purchases mixed.** For example, if you're buying rice and canned food, pick up cat litter, bleach, a broom, or a few nonperishable snacks. If you're buying batteries and lighting equipment, grab a pack of air filters or motor oil. You're not hiding what you're buying—you're blending it into normalcy. Your goal is to avoid looking like someone preparing for anything out of the ordinary.

For equipment like water containers, fuel stabilizer, or radios, seek out **secondhand or surplus outlets.** Local hardware stores, feed supply shops, camping outfitters, and pawn shops have different inventory systems. Most won't track your purchases in any digital form unless you give them a reason to. Rural stores are often **cash-friendly** and less likely to report unusual bulk sales.

If you're ordering online, use prepaid cards bought with cash. Register them with a dummy email and a generic name. Never use your primary email for purchases of any off-grid equipment. Use guest checkout if available. Delete cookies and history after each session, and avoid placing orders through a shared home network that ties back to your real name or home address. This is covered more a couple sections down.

Every purchase you make forms part of a larger pattern. And that pattern, once linked to your identity, is archived—sometimes for years. What you want is noise. You want disjointed fragments of transactions that don't line up easily, can't be traced back to a single moment, and don't reveal your real objective to anyone looking after the fact.

Buying what you need isn't enough. You need to buy like someone who has nothing to hide because, on paper, you won't appear to be hiding anything.

Buy from Local, Low-Track Stores

Start with local army surplus shops. You'll find more than camouflage jackets. Hardware stores are just as valuable.

Once you've committed to decentralizing your purchases, the next step is selecting sources that don't generate searchable records. That means staying away from centralized chains that tie inventory, payment history, and customer behavior into cloud-based systems.

Army surplus stores rarely run digital inventory systems and almost never ask for your ID or payment info. Beyond clothing and boots, most carry **load-bearing gear, ponchos, canteens, MOLLE pouches, paracord, thermal blankets, fuel carriers, and military rations.** Ask directly if they have bulk or out-of-box items in back—many store owners keep **unlisted stock** out of sight, especially older or off-spec surplus they don't display to weekend browsers. If you buy steadily and don't raise questions, you may be offered heavier-duty gear that's never advertised.

Hardware stores, especially independent ones, are excellent for gathering foundational gear. These include **fuel cans, cordless tool batteries, buckets, rope, zip ties, fittings, blades, and basic off-grid tools. Many also carry plastic sheeting, concrete mix, and seed-starting supplies** in agricultural areas. Look for clearance or scratched inventory. Most small stores write off minor damage and sell at discount, often with no itemized SKU entry. That means less digital visibility. If they offer open-box or return shelves, that's where you dig.

tanks, sprayers, and **generator accessories** as well. These stores usually run outdated POS systems, don't track individual purchases, and often deal in large-volume cash transactions as a matter of routine. No one's raising an eyebrow over five water jugs and a sack of grain.

Gun shows and preparedness expos offer the cleanest acquisitions. There are no receipts unless you ask. Cash is expected. You'll find **field trauma kits, blades, emergency comms gear, ammo cans, NVG accessories,** and other niche items without ever linking your identity to the transaction. Don't linger too long at any one booth. Don't chat about plans. And if asked where you're from, say "just passing through."

Above all, **don't talk more than necessary.** Cash is your answer to questions. And your reason for being there is simple: you're stocking up for a camping trip, or replacing gear you loaned out.

If You Shop Online, Obscure Your Trail

You will eventually need to buy something online. A specialty filter, a hard-to-find part, something local stores don't carry. When that time comes, the objective isn't privacy—it's **disassociation.** No names, no links, no patterns.

Start with a **prepaid Visa or Mastercard.** Buy it in person with cash at a Walmart, Walgreens, or gas station. Do not use your debit card to load funds. Register the card online using a generic name and burner email if the site requires it. Some won't. Use it once or twice, then throw it away.

At checkout, always use guest mode. Don't make an account. Don't save anything. If the form autofills, back out and start fresh in a private browser window.

Never ship to your home. Use an Amazon Locker, UPS Access Point, or package hub that accepts third-party deliveries. Many UPS Stores allow general delivery under "Boxholder" or similar aliases. Avoid using PO Boxes tied to your legal name unless you've set them up under a business or trust.

Avoid buying from niche "prepper" retailers with aggressive websites—anything that pushes newsletters, coupon popups, or bundle offers is usually running heavy tracking software. These sites often log every page you view, scrape your device info, and cross-match email addresses with buyer databases. If they ever get subpoenaed, your full activity log is handed over in seconds.

Instead, use generic marketplaces like eBay or even Craigslist. Look for listings from individuals. Always ask questions like a hobbyist, not a prepper. Buy items that blend—like backpacking gear or vehicle tools.

Finally, **clear your browser history and cookies** after each session. Don't just close the tab.

Local outdoor suppliers—not national chains—are valuable if approached right. Avoid tactical branding and instead purchase gear framed around camping, hiking, or overlanding. Target **portable stoves, freeze-dried meals, compact cookware, fire-starting kits, small medical packs, and water filtration bottles.** If asked what you're prepping for, default to "trailhead camping" or a "weekend canoe trip." Keep the purchase casual. Let the gear do the work. You're blending into their customer base while collecting hard-use survival tools.

Feed and supply stores are overlooked by most urban preppers. That's a mistake. These stores are designed for independent living—**animal feed, bulk seed, plant nutrition, ropes, shovels, tarps, and manual fuel tools** are commonplace. If they serve ranchers, expect larger

Choose Gear with Plausible Uses

Every item you bring home says something about you. Some say "hiker." Others say "prepper." One of those gets ignored. The other might get flagged.

The gear itself isn't illegal. But the pattern behind the gear is what surveillance systems are designed to notice. Risk markers aren't just about guns and fuel—they include repetitive, **specialized purchases** from the same category. Water purification systems, ammo reloading supplies, radiation pills, bulk canning tools—these all hit red zones in vendor and financial databases that track consumer behavior.

To avoid that, buy items that **double as normal-use gear.** Not just what they are—but what they look like.

A **LifeStraw or Sawyer Mini** isn't a prepper tool—it's a hiking filter. Buy it from an outdoor store. Better yet, get two and ask the cashier about trail recommendations. Blend.

A **small camping stove** used with butane or hex fuel tablets isn't seen as tactical—it's recreational. Choose models marketed for backpackers. Avoid "off-grid" or "survival" branding.

Mylar bags, canning jars, and oxygen absorbers are still low-visibility if you bundle them with kitchen goods and label them for food storage. Buy from canning supply or homestead sites instead of survival shops. If asked, say you preserve your own tomatoes.

Solar phone chargers and foldable panels are common now. Get them in black or gray, not camo. Say you're testing "portable power for hiking" if anyone asks.

Space Out Your Purchases

Mass buying isn't just suspicious—it's traceable. If every major prep supply you own came from the same week, same card, or same store chain, then your activity has a timestamp. And that timestamp becomes **a pattern**—one that can be flagged or reconstructed if the situation ever calls for it.

To stay off radar, you need to act like **no single transaction matters.** Spread your acquisitions across **time, location, and category.** If you're planning a full setup—long-term food, lighting, heat, fuel, defense, filtration, communication—you need to source **it like you're building it slowly,** not stocking up in panic.

Build a loose calendar and stick to it. Map out purchases three to four weeks apart, or more. Don't revisit the same store in short succession unless you're blending those trips with unrelated household errands. If you're spending $300 one week, make the next one look like an ordinary trip. Throw in groceries, cleaning supplies, or seasonal tools. If it feels like something you'd explain to a neighbor, you're on the right track.

Do not organize your trips by category. That's a rookie mistake. If you buy all your lighting, then all your cooking gear, then all your long-storage food, it builds a timeline of intent. Mix it. Buy a single filter, a single pack of dried beans, a wrench, and a pack of batteries. The more you break the narrative, the less it exists.

If you're in a rural area, drive out a little farther than you need to. Visit shops where you're less likely to be known by name. Never let employees get familiar with your purchases. Small talk is fine. Patterns are not.

Online, place orders through separate email addresses, with different prepaid cards. Don't let delivery windows overlap. Don't send multiple packages to your home in a short span. Use lockers when possible. If a package is ever intercepted or watched, it should look meaningless on its own.

Your goal is to **dissolve the paper trail before it ever forms.** If someone were to try and rebuild your supply history six months from now, they shouldn't be able to. At worst, it should look like a series of unrelated, mundane shopping choices.

Stealth for Your Operation

If your setup can be seen, it can be questioned. And if it can be questioned, it can be seized. In any emergency, the person who still has power, clean water, or light becomes a resource—one the government may decide needs to be managed.

Independence only works if no one knows you have it. That means covering, disguising, or relocating anything that signals self-sufficiency: collection tanks, power systems, filtration units, or backup generators. Your property should look average from every angle. No noise. No glare. No indicators.

Hide Your Water System

Water is one of the first things to run dry in a collapse. If your home still has it while others don't, you will be noticed. And if your collection or purification setup is visible from the road, the sky, or a neighbor's fence line, it won't stay yours for long.

Start with placement. Never install barrels or tanks in open view. Position them behind **outbuildings, garages, or tree lines.** If you don't have coverage, build it. A simple lean-to with weathered siding and a sloped roof can house multiple barrels without looking like anything but old storage.

Camouflage the components. Paint rain barrels in **flat earth tones**—dark green, brown, or grey—to match fencing or surrounding vegetation. Use **privacy lattice, scrap lumber,** or repurposed fencing to enclose collection systems. Install a slatted cover over any open tank, both for visual concealment and to cut down on mosquito attraction or debris collection.

Avoid standard downspout kits that scream "prepper." Run your collection lines low and out of sight, using black PEX or garden hose routed under eaves and behind siding where possible. Keep spigots, valves, and overflow pipes facing inward, never toward a road or alley.

If using elevated tanks or gravity-fed systems, disguise the elevation with fencing, stacked pallets, or an old shed façade. Even better—dig shallow depressions and bury tanks partway, covering the tops with flat panels and a layer of debris or mulch.

Your purification setup should be fully portable and stored inside. Never mount filters, UV units, or hand pumps on external walls. The more permanent your system looks, the more likely someone will decide they need it more than you do.

If your neighborhood has drone flyovers, HOA patrols, or regular city inspections, keep your yard plain. Let your water setup blend into the background like clutter—not like infrastructure. No one should be able to tell you're collecting water unless they're inside your perimeter.

You don't need to hide water because it's illegal (though it is in some states). You need to hide it because **thirst turns people into opportunists.** And FEMA won't knock when they decide to requisition resources.

Conceal Generators and Solar Power

Power in a blackout is a flare in the dark. When the rest of the block goes silent and your house stays lit, you don't look lucky—you look stockpiled. FEMA isn't concerned with comfort. They're concerned with control. A running generator or a humming battery bank signals you're operating outside of their framework, and that makes you worth noticing.

Start with generators. Never install or run them in open view. Position your unit inside a **well-ventilated shed or detached outbuilding,** not next to your home or under a carport. Use **exhaust redirection, insulation paneling, and a muffler swap**—such as from a small motorcycle—to reduce sound. Don't run it in short bursts. Create a routine that limits noise during vulnerable hours, especially at night or early morning when the rest of the grid is silent.

Fuel storage should never be visible from the road or fence line. Keep cans in a **locked container, subterranean cache,** or behind weathered siding that doesn't draw the eye. Don't label anything with "gas" or "diesel." Stick to generic containers if possible.

Solar is trickier. A modest rooftop panel array isn't uncommon anymore, especially in urban or semi-rural zones. It may even provide cover. But a **dense**

multi-panel system, ground-mounted units, or visible battery banks can still set you apart—particularly if those batteries are wired for total independence rather than simple grid tie-in. Any hint of long-term, off-grid autonomy invites curiosity when the lights go out everywhere else.

If your panels are large, consider **angling them at low pitch, hiding them behind parapets,** or placing them on **outbuildings** with trees or fencing that block view from the street. Paint conduit and mounting hardware to match the background structure. Never leave charge controllers, inverter panels, or battery banks mounted in plain sight. House them in **basement enclosures, lockable cabinets, or false-wall storage** inside the home.

Use blackout curtains or kill-switches to control visible power draw. If your lights are still on while your neighbors are in candlelight, you're signaling more than resilience—you're offering a resource others will want to claim.

Be Smart About HAM Radios

When the grid fails, so does your access to phones, towers, and every app you've ever relied on. Internet dies with the power, and emergency lines jam or fall under government control. What still works—what always works—is radio. Specifically, **HAM.** It's one of the only tools left that lets you monitor activity across miles, coordinate with distant operators, or listen in on channels no agency can fully shut down.

But HAM gear comes with baggage. Every radio has a **serial number.** Every license ties back to an identity. If you're operating when others aren't, and your transmissions are tracked back to you, you're marked as a node—an active communicator. In a lockdown, that's not a good label to have.

Never buy your radio new. Retailers log purchase records—serials, payment methods, sometimes even MAC or IP addresses during checkout. That data is retained, searchable, and can be linked to you by vendors or shared databases.

Find one offline. Go to **flea markets, pawn shops, ham swap meets, estate sales, or classifieds that let you deal direct.** Skip listing apps that track IP or require logins. Cash only. No receipts. If the seller asks for your name, don't give it.

If you've got any mechanical ability, buy a unit that needs work. Replace the board, swap the battery, resolder the antenna point, or gut the casing and drop the internals into a new shell. Once rebuilt, it's no longer tied to its point of sale. It's yours, and it's anonymous.

Regarding licenses: owning a HAM radio is legal. Operating one without a license is not, **unless you're listening only or broadcasting in a true emergency.** If you choose to register for legal access, use a **PO box.** Never register to your primary residence. Use a separate email and name if applicable. Many agencies pull callsign records to locate operators during high-alert events. You want separation—paper, digital, and physical.

Your storage should match your intent. Don't mount it on a desk with wires draped across the wall. Store it in a **hard case or tactical satchel** with accessories ready to deploy. If you ever need to leave in a hurry, your comms should be grab-and-go, not bolted down.

The goal is simple. You don't need to hide the fact that you have a radio. You need to make sure no one knows you've used it. Or when. Or where.

Label Smart

If your home clearly shows signs of large-scale preparation and self-sufficiency, it's classified as **a resource of interest.** A house that can outlast rationing or decline relocation becomes **a node outside the system.** That puts it, and you, on a list.

Start with storage. Do not use obvious terms. Bins marked **"Bug Out Kit," "SHTF Gear," or "Emergency Supplies"** might as well be labeled **"Seize Me First."** It only takes one outsider—an inspector, a repairman, a neighbor's kid—to see it and remember. Don't create memory triggers. Don't broadcast what you've built.

Replace those terms with benign, household equivalents that raise no red flags. Label bins based on innocent, alternate-use logic:

- **Camping Gear** – tents, sleeping bags, flashlights, cooking kits
- **Spare Kitchen Tools** – fuel tabs, camp stoves, mess kits, utensil rolls
- **Winter Supplies** – gloves, wool layers, fire starters, wool blankets
- **Hiking Equipment** – boots, water filters, packs, trekking poles
- **Garage Tools / Seasonal Storage** – rope, tarps, spare parts, solar panels

Don't stop at labeling. Think about **placement.** Keep tactical gear in bins under generic categories, but locate those bins in **low-access areas.** That means attic corners, upper shelves in the garage, or locked closets in less trafficked rooms. If you have a shed or outbuilding, split storage between multiple containers, and place decoy bins with real items mixed alongside dummy gear.

Create layered storage. Have one or two clearly visible totes with camping and seasonal gear that match the labels. Behind or beneath those, store your actual cache. That way, even if someone does go poking around, what they find still matches what they expect.

In a house search or relocation sweep, officials won't have time to fully inventory every container. But they will take note of anything that looks **systematic, military, or survivalist.** Your goal is to waste their time, not give them a roadmap.

You're not trying to deceive your future self—you'll remember where it all is. You're trying to make sure no one else finds it **worth remembering.**

Avoid placing clearly labeled bins in open garages, sheds or near visible access points. Keep high-value bins in lofted storage, locked closets, or behind decoy totes. Use layered storage—one tote marked "camping gear" with real items on top, survival tools beneath. If someone looks inside, they should find nothing worth remembering.

Keep Digital Privacy Tight

Every site you visit and every login builds a behavioral fingerprint.

Even if you never say a word, your data says enough. Search history, autofill logs, email registrations, payment credentials—every one of these builds a profile. The mistake isn't buying online. The mistake is buying while exposed.

Even if you don't talk about it, your clicks, orders, and account setups start to form a pattern. That pattern links back to you—unless you've built the separation.

Start by creating a **shadow identity**—not for criminal activity, but for privacy. Use a realistic, **non-associated name,** something ordinary and searchable. Don't get clever. A name that blends in with junk data is better than one that stands out. This isn't a false identity. It's a **data decoy,** used for interacting with vendors, researching supplies, and ordering gear in a way that doesn't point back to your legal self.

Set up a dedicated email account for this profile. Use ProtonMail, Tutanota, or another **privacy-respecting provider.** Do not link it to your main inbox. Don't use a recovery phone number. Skip two-factor authentication if it involves your real device.

Use this account **only** for prep-related orders, shipping confirmations, and vendor communications. Never access it on your primary Wi-Fi or through your home IP.

That's where the **VPN layer** comes in.

A proper **VPN (Virtual Private Network)** creates a secure tunnel between your device and the internet, masking your real IP address and encrypting your traffic. But not all VPNs are equal. Look for a provider with:

- **Strict no-log policies**
- **RAM-only servers** (data wiped on reboot)
- **Independently audited privacy claims**
- **Kill switch** to cut connection if the VPN drops

Examples include Mullvad, ProtonVPN, and IVPN. Avoid free VPNs entirely. Most exist to harvest your traffic.

When using a VPN, connect through a server in a country with strong data protection laws but no mandatory logging. Sweden. Switzerland. Iceland. Avoid U.S.-based servers unless the VPN provider is bulletproof on their privacy architecture.

Don't stop there. **Use private or hardened browsers** like **Brave, Ungoogled Chromium, or Firefox** with privacy extensions. Disable autofill, form memory, and password saving. Install **uBlock Origin, HTTPS Everywhere, and Cookie AutoDelete**. Never stay logged into email or shopping accounts between sessions. Clear history and cookies regularly—or set the browser to wipe everything automatically on close.

To go further, randomize your MAC address if you're using a laptop or phone. This prevents Wi-Fi networks from linking your device to repeat activity. On mobile, tether using cellular data when possible. No shared networks. No home router. No cross-traffic with your normal accounts.

Do not mix profiles. If you set up a burner account for prepping, never log into personal banking, Facebook, Amazon, or your regular email under that same IP or browser session. Keep the personas isolated—**no crossover.**

Used properly, this layered digital hygiene creates **legal anonymity.** You're not violating any laws. You're just refusing to hand your digital life to centralized databases.

When you search for supplies, avoid Google. It tracks behavior even when logged out—using IP, fingerprinting, and cross-session identifiers. **Use DuckDuckGo, Brave Search, or Startpage,** and make sure your browser is hardened. That means cookies blocked by default, JavaScript controlled, no auto-login, and all cache cleared after each session. Never bookmark supplier sites under your real profile.

Avoid signing up for loyalty programs, email alerts, or "members-only" pricing tiers. These link your purchases to personal behavior profiles stored by retailers and resold through marketing firms and data brokers. You don't want your preference for water filters showing up in an algorithm shared with financial monitoring firms or third-party contractors.

If you must purchase online, use a **prepaid card bought in cash,** registered to a throwaway name and address. Use guest checkout wherever possible. Never save payment info. Never review or rate gear after purchase. Clicking on those links confirms to the vendor that you opened the email, visited the site, and interacted with the product—building a complete feedback loop around your interest in off-grid gear.

Email confirmations should be deleted immediately. Disable image loading in email clients to prevent pixel-tracking. Never forward receipts to other accounts.

Do not search for gear using a voice assistant, a shared household device, or any machine you've ever used to log into banking, school, or healthcare services. That machine is already fingerprinted and linked to you.

Most people make their opsec mistakes before they ever click "Add to Cart." Yours should be airtight before you even type the product name.

Know Your Rights

Preparedness is not a crime. Buying gear, storing supplies, collecting rainwater, owning tools or radios—none of these are illegal. But that doesn't mean they won't be used against you in the wrong political moment.

Under national emergency declarations, property can be seized, communications monitored, and movement restricted—all in the name of "public safety." If FEMA, DHS, or another federal agency comes knocking, you need to understand where **cooperation ends and coercion begins.**

Learn your state's laws on water collection, fuel storage, and off-grid power. Know the limits of what can be searched without a warrant. Understand the difference between a **request and a requirement** when speaking to agents.

Do not volunteer information. Do not sign anything without reading it fully. If questioned, remember: you don't owe explanations for what you bought, why you bought it, or how you plan to use it—especially without legal cause.

Being prepared doesn't make you a threat. But it does make you **responsible** for protecting what you've prepared.

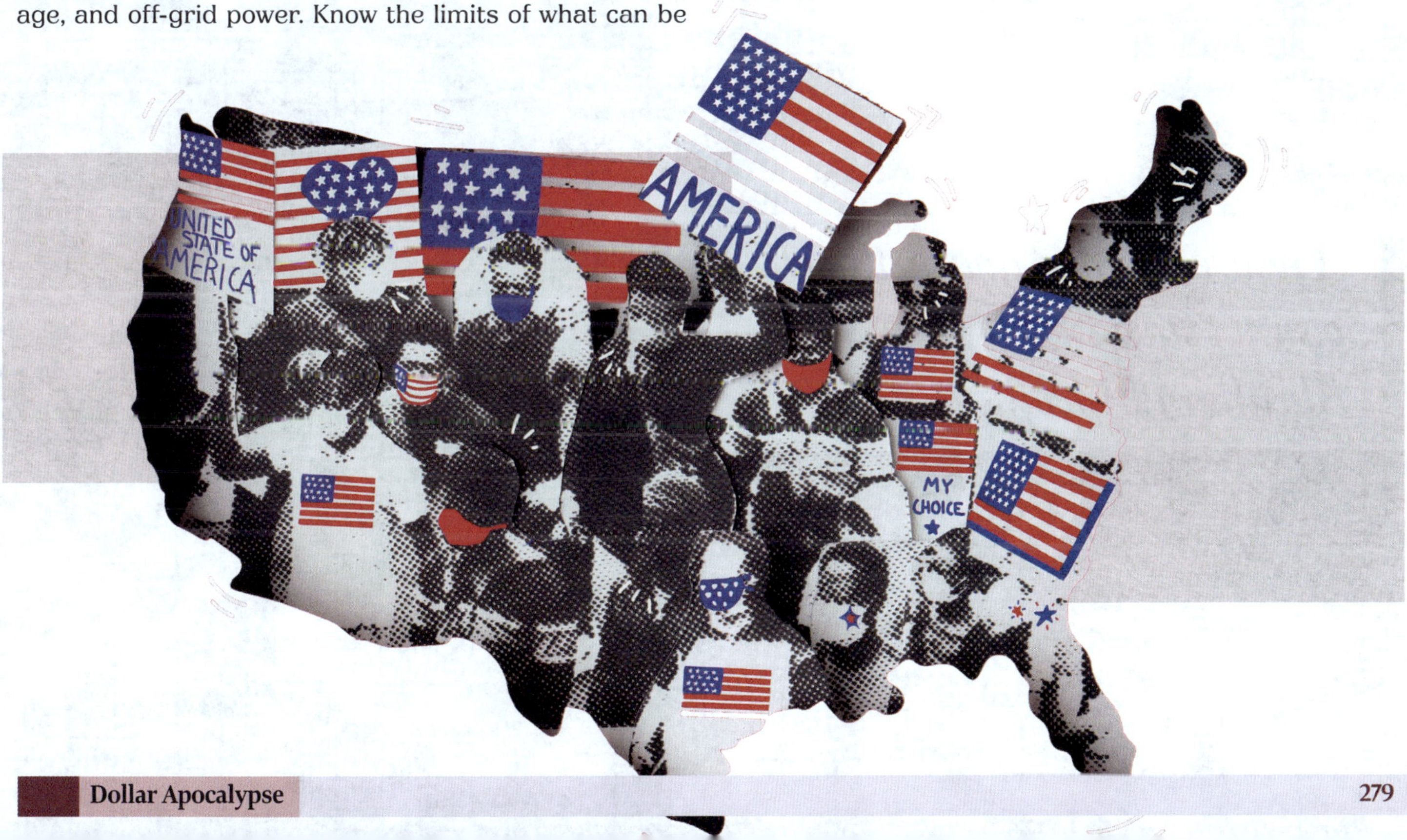

"A house divided against itself cannot stand."
Abraham Lincoln

Chapter 22

The First U.S. States That Will Go Down After the Dollar Comes Home

An economic crisis might rear its ugly head in a single state first, but that only marks the beginning of the end, as the chain reaction of the collapse is going to shake and tumble the stability of the neighboring states, making them fall, one by one, like dominoes.

In our comfortable daily routines, with grocery stores stocked, gas stations operating, and lights turning on at the flip of a switch, we often overlook how delicate the whole system is. Yet beneath this layer of ease and normality, our economy teeters on the brink. And when the dollars come home, it won't go away gently into that good night.

What does it mean when we say "the dollars comes home"? In simple terms, it's what will happen when the trillions of U.S. dollars kept overseas, by foreign governments, investors, and central banks, rush back into our economy. These dollars once sent abroad to pay for imported goods and services, will return as trust in the U.S. financial system wavers or global nations start to get rid of their dollar reserves. This sudden flow of money into our domestic system would set off a surge in prices, hyperinflation, as too much cash starts chases too few goods.

This isn't just a guess pulled out of nowhere. It's a situation with deep roots in history. Countries like Zimbabwe, Venezuela, and the Weimar Republic of Germany all went through currency breakdowns. But the U.S. dollar isn't just another country's money, it's the world's go-to currency. If it crumbles under its load, the fallout will be like nothing we've seen before. And when that time comes, different parts of America will feel it in different ways.

We're not trying to scare you or paint a picture of the end times. This isn't a forecast. It's a heads-up, based on common sense, what we see happening, and the current state of our economy. Inflation is already eating away at what your money can buy. Supply chains are still under pressure, the enormous debt can't be paid back, and people around the world are losing faith in America's financial leadership. The red flags are there for anyone who wants to see them.

But warnings don't help if we're not asking the right questions.

Which areas will the breakdown hit the hardest? Which states will crumble first, and for what reasons? What steps can regular Americans take now to avoid getting stuck in a system that's falling apart?

This chapter provides answers to those questions. It examines each state, identifying the regions most at risk when economic stability crumbles into chaos. We're looking at states with huge public debts, steep living costs, heavy dependence on imports, and packed urban areas. These are places where people live crammed together relying on outside sources for their food, water, fuel, and safety.

Modern city life assumes everything will run. Trucks will deliver goods. Power will keep flowing. The government will function. But if just one of these pillars wobbles due to skyrocketing prices or supply issues, whole cities can descend into a cesspool of crime and chaos. Some states will crash faster, harder, and much more than others.

What makes a state more likely to collapse? A few key things:

- **Living expenses:** When prices soar high, costs for housing, gas, and food become impossible to pay.
- **Dependence on systems:** States that bring in their necessities or have old failing systems break down.
- **Urban density and economic inequality:** Cities with high tension are more likely to experience unrest.
- **Reliance on tourism or federal aid:** When federal funds becomes scarce, the local economy suffers.

We'll begin with the states facing the greatest risk, California, New York, Illinois, and others at the top of the domino chain. These are areas where the breakdown, once it starts, will spread. Roads will become dangerous. Services will disappear in no time. And those who haven't prepared will find their lives depending on a system that no longer works.

You need to prepare and act before it's too late. You should understand your surroundings so you can make wise choices for yourself and your loved ones. These decisions might involve moving stocking up on crucial supplies or rethinking where you live and what you rely on, and the time to start is now.

As you read, don't just think about "them", consider your situation. Reflect on what you depend on, who you trust, and how your life would change if the ATM stopped working tomorrow. Or if the grocery store ran out of food. Or if the gas pump shuts down.

California – The First Domino to Fall

Among all U.S. states, California stands most vulnerable to crumble under a financial crisis. The state boasts stunning landscapes, groundbreaking ideas, and a mix of cultures, yet beneath this facade lies a tinderbox of economic weakness, heavy reliance on outside goods, and sky-high living expenses. When the dollar's value plummets, California will most likely topple first.

Let's start by examining the areas under the most stress, Los Angeles, San Francisco, and Oakland. These city hubs drive the economy, but they also depend on a complex and very fragile web of amenities and systems that can't withstand the tremors of runaway inflation.

Urban Pressure Points: Where It Will Break First

Los Angeles, a city with millions of people, stays connected through highways, power grids, water pipelines, and resources from elsewhere. The city works well because its systems run in harmony. But when one fails, the others struggle. If trucks stop moving, stores run out of food. If the power goes out, communication and fuel become hard to get. If the dollar loses its value, the city loses the one thing that keeps everything going, trust in the system.

San Francisco and Oakland, already struggling with homelessness, housing shortages, and crime, depend on people showing up to work and paying more and more. But what happens when the middle class can't afford rent? When gas costs $20 a gallon? When civil servants quit because their paychecks buy half or less of what they used to?

Would you be prepared?

You can make smart decisions now, while everything still functions for the day it won't anymore. Let's get started.

A State Relying on What It Doesn't Make

California stands out as a place that relies on imports. While its Central Valley grows a lot of food, most city folks in California live off goods, fuel, and water brought in from other places.

Water stands out as maybe the state's biggest weak spot. A lot of Southern California depends on aqueducts and far-reaching pipelines to get water from the Colorado River and Northern areas of the state. If any of these systems fail - through attack, breakdown, or lack of money - millions might end up without water.

Fuel is just as fragile. California's tough rules and taxes have already pushed gas prices to some of the highest in the country. In a situation where money loses its value fast, you might see gas stations close down or give fuel only to vital services - if they have any fuel left at all.

Cities get their food trucked in every day often from hundreds of miles away. Even a small problem can leave store shelves empty. If the economy crashes, food costs might jump to two or three times their normal price in just a few days. People who live from one paycheck to the next, or depend on help from the government, would feel the pain first and worst.

Social Unrest: A Powder Keg Ready to Blow

It doesn't take much to turn a tense situation into full-scale chaos. Big cities like L.A. Oakland, and San Francisco already struggle with a dangerous mix of poverty, unfairness, and crime. When a paycheck buys a lot less and people can't afford food, things fall apart fast. We've seen small-scale riots and looting before because of single events, now picture that kind of anger made worse by hunger, fear, and hopelessness all across the state.

What happens when cops stop showing up? When emergency services can't keep up? When people line up at closed banks with no money to take out?

Things to Do: How to Get Ready in California

This isn't about leaving California right away, but if you're watching, it's time to plan smart. If you live in one of the risky city areas mentioned, you need to take big steps now.

1. Don't Count on City Services

The more you need the city's systems, the more at risk you are. Make a plan to take care of yourself. That means things like:

- Get solar panels or backup batteries for electricity.
- Keep long-lasting food that stays good on shelves and switch it out often.
- Keep a stock of important medicines and first-aid stuff.
- Find other ways to cook and stay warm without power.

2. Make Sure You Have Clean Water and Extra Fuel

Storing bottled water is a good start, but it won't be enough. Put money into:

- Water filters that work without power (ones that use gravity or you can pump by hand).
- A system to catch rain
- Extra tanks to store fuel

This is just scratching the surface. In other chapters inside this book you'll exactly how to prepare your home and property.

3. If You Live in a Crowded City, Look for Safer Places Away from the Coast

Don't put off planning your backup strategy until everything crumbles. Check out more rural or semi-rural counties you can drive to where living costs less and people spread out more. Some parts of inland California still offer easier water access, cheaper land, and folks who know how to survive off the land. Think about making connections in these places now, before everyone else gets the same idea.

4. Connect with People Who Have Useful Trades and Skills

If a collapse teaches us anything, it's that going solo won't cut it. Start networking with:

- Mechanics
- Gardeners and homesteaders
- Nurses and medics
- Hunters, electricians, plumbers, and other hands-on workers

Whether you live in the city or plan to move out, having strong local connections will have more impact than almost anything else when things go south.

California isn't doomed, but it's at risk. The shine of Silicon Valley, the allure of Hollywood, and the draw of endless sunshine can't hide the harsh truth: when the dollar crashes, California's big cities will become ghost towns. And once they do, the rest of the state will follow suit.

If you're there, you've got a choice: change now or get caught up later.

Illinois - Chicago Will Burn First

Illinois has been on shaky ground for a while now - crushing debt, shrinking industry, and growing urban stress. Chicago sits at the heart of this risky mix, a city once seen as the pulse of America's Midwest, now a ticking time bomb of social pressure and money troubles. If California falls first, Illinois and particularly Chicago, will follow close behind after the dollars come home.

This chapter doesn't aim to bash any state or city. It simply tries to spot the weak points and see what happens when a system that's barely holding together faces a lot more stress.

Why Illinois Is at Risk

Unlike states on the coast with thriving trade or central states rich in energy with natural protections in place, Illinois finds itself in a unique, and risky, middle of the road position. Its industrial foundation has been wearing away for years leaving a service-based economy and huge public spending commitments in its wake. When the economy holds steady, this tricky balance works. But if hyperinflation hits, that balance crumbles overnight.

Let's take a closer look:

Public Debt and Pension Commitments

Illinois has one of the biggest pension debts in the country that's not paid for. The state keeps putting off dealing with it borrowing more cash to pay bills now, while long-term debts keep growing. In a regular economy, that's risky. In a super-high inflation crash, it becomes fatal for how the government works.

When the dollar loses value fast, state pensions become useless, budgets fall apart, and public services stop. Cops, teachers, firefighters, many won't work for money that can't buy them anything. And without these services, big cities start to fall apart.

Urban Overdependence on Centralized Services

Chicago is a huge city with almost 3 million residents, plus millions more in the suburbs around it. Like any big city, it depends on a network of electricity, food supply, fuel, clean water, police, and public transport to function. But it's not just about the basics, it's about scale. When a system this big fails, it doesn't go down well.

When the economy crashes, fuel deliveries slow down, stores run out of stock, and crime goes up. Without enough money, the city can't pay for extra hours, fixes, or emergency services. And Chicago isn't known for staying cool when things get tough, it's a place that deals with violence even on normal days.

Picture what happens when grocery stores have no food and ATMs stop working. It won't be pretty, cause there are already a lot of thugs with guns running around as it is.

A Shrinking Industrial Core

Illinois used to be a powerhouse of manufacturing and farming. But shipping jobs overseas and using more machines have gutted much of that industrial strength. The state still grows crops, but big cities and corporations now handle most of the processing and shipping. Most city folks rely on outside food systems and delivery networks.

If prices skyrocket, fuel costs will go through the roof and moving food long distances becomes a nightmare. If food can't move across the state, big cities like Chicago turn into food deserts with nothing coming in to feed the millions of hungry mouths.

The Spark: Why Chicago Will Go Up in Flames First

Chicago checks the early breakdown list:

- Packed population
- Long-term financial inequality
- Deep racial and political rifts
- Heavy dependence on government jobs and services
- Many people living from one paycheck to the next

When the dollar crashes and basic services stop, anger will quickly bubble up. People will lose their cool, and when enough folks freak out at once, anarchy follows. The city's already high crime rate turns into uncontrolled violence in many areas.

Just like other cities worldwide have fallen into mayhem during economic meltdowns, Caracas, Athens, Johannesburg, Chicago risks the same fate unless people get ready.

Practical Steps: How to Be Prepared in Illinois

You can stay in Illinois and still be okay, but you should act now while things are stable, and you have time to plan.

1. Think About Moving Out of the City

If you live in Chicago, ask yourself: Why are you there? Is it for work? How secure is your job if the economy tanks? Is it for family or your home? How will these hold up when prices skyrocket?

Look into counties farther out or even nearby states with fewer people, more local farms, and closer communities. Big cities always get hit first and worst.

The system is beyond saving. You're not.

2. Make Sure You Can Get Food and Water on Your Own

Don't think Illinois's farming status guarantees easy food access. If supply chains break and money loses worth, you'll need your own systems:

- Grow food yourself, even in small pots or yards.
- Build up stocks of long-lasting basics, rice, beans, oats canned meats.
- Get a gravity-powered water filter and locate fresh water sources near your house.
- Figure out how to cook and store food without electricity.

3. Build Up Your Local Connections

When services stop, people rely on each other. Now's the time to form bonds with:

- Farmers in your area
- People with useful skills
- Religious or community groups
- Neighbors you trust who get practical survival

The more people around you who can offer skills, protection, and trading power the less at risk you'll be when systems break down.

4. Cut Down Financial Risk

Don't keep all your money in dollars of course. Think about:

- Spreading out into real goods with trading value (tools, fuel, food, silver)
- Paying off debt where you can loan with changing interest rates
- Saving up useful cash small bills, or other options like prepaid cards

There are a lot more strategies that we'll cover more in-depth in other chapters.

Chicago might go up in flames first, but that doesn't mean you have to burn along with it.

New York – A Financial Time Bomb

New York stands as a symbol of American might - Wall Street, the UN, the media, money, and sky-high buildings. But not all that glitters is gold: New York runs on a financial engine fueled by borrowed cash and time. When the dollar finally implodes, when foreign-held money floods back and sets off runaway inflation, New York will take the first and biggest hit on the money side.

The Big Apple isn't where you want to hang out when things fall apart.

A City That's Built on Paper Money

Unlike cities that produce energy, food, or physical goods, New York's strength comes from abstract wealth, stocks, real estate speculation, financial instruments, and digital transactions. In a stable world, this gives New York an edge. But that's not going to be our world for much longer.

As Trillions of dollars rush back to the U.S. prices will skyrocket. But before we see food riots and power outages, it all kicks off in boardrooms and on trading floors, in New York's beating financial heart.

And when Wall Street goes quiet, everyone feels the aftershocks.

The Fragility of the Financial Sector

New York is home to some of the world's most powerful financial institutions. These banks, hedge funds, and investment firms manage not just American wealth, but global liquidity. But here's the catch: they rely on confidence and leverage to operate.

If confidence breaks, the system breaks.

- Margin calls will destroy portfolios
- Retirement funds will get freezen
- Banks will lock their doors and ATMs will stop working
- Crypto markets crash due to sudden regulation changes
- Credit becomes unavailable in an instant

When hyperinflation hits, nobody wants their bonds tied to the dollar. New York's entire economy, its jobs, tax money, and way of life, depends on money still having value. When that value disappears, New York's lifeline goes away.

Urban Density and the Falling Dominoes

Over 8 million people call New York City home, crammed into five boroughs. That's more than 27,000 people for each square mile. The second a breakdown occurs, be it financial, power-related, or supply chain, panic spreads quicker than any fix.

Think about what happens when:

- The subway stops because the MTA can't pay for upkeep
- Food costs triple and people empty stores in no time
- Law enforcement struggles to handle protests, theft, and growing violence in the streets
- Emergency rooms can't keep up and hospitals run short on medicine and basic supplies

New Yorkers depend on outside resources to survive. The city brings in almost everything it uses, food, fuel, clean water, power. And with no real way to grow food or make energy, the second those imports slow down or get too pricey, life grinds to a screeching halt.

High Cost of Living = No Safety Net

New York ranks among the priciest places to live in America. From rent and groceries to childcare and transportation, most New Yorkers just scrape by. When hyperinflation hits, that thin margin goes away.

Even high-earners with six-figure salaries can struggle. When gas costs $30 a gallon, eggs cost $5 each, and utility bills triple, how do average households that live paycheck to paycheck cope? They don't.

The Flashpoint: Social Tension in a Stressed-Out City

New York has a beautiful mix of people, but also clear divides. Class, race, and belief differences bubble under the surface and can explode when things get tough. We've seen hints of unrest during money problems or political events. What happens when people's lives are on the line?

The high number of people living close together means crime can spread rapidly . Trouble in one area moves to another. When police lack resources and face too many problems, people must fend for themselves.

Steps to Take: How to Survive or Leave During a Breakdown

You don't need to be rich to keep yourself safe in NYC. You just need to plan ahead, while most people still trust everything will be okay.

1. Think About Whether to Stay in NYC

Ask yourself tough questions:

- Can you stay at home for more than a month without help from the outside?
- Do you have another place you could go to if you had to leave?
- How long could you manage without trains, ride-sharing, or gas?

If you're in NYC for work or family, think about setting up a backup plan in upstate New York, Pennsylvania, or Connecticut, anywhere with fewer people, clean water, and local food sources.

2. Set Up Financial Safety Nets

While most assets will suffer, spread your money around:

- Keep practical items like silver, trade goods, fuel, tools, and medicine
- Save some cash in small bills
- Look into prepaid cards or accounts at smaller local banks
- Cut back on big banks—they'll be the first to stop you from taking out money

Remember: getting your money in order starts before everything falls apart.

3. Make Sure You're Safe and Can Move Around

You don't want to fight crowds at Costco, and you want to avoid ever needing to. That means:

- Stock up on food and water to last for several months
- Figure out how to cook without power or gas
- Pack a bag with essentials in case you need to bug out
- Map out escape routes from the city, driving, cycling, or walking if needed.

Leaving is less risky than getting caught in chaos.

4. Create Small Communities Now

Being alone is risky. Start making connections now with:

- Neighbors who can help protect your building
- Nearby small shops with supply networks
- Religious groups or hobby-based clubs
- Even in a huge city, a close group of ten people can be a game-changer.

New Jersey – The Next Detroit

New Jersey might seem like a strange choice for a high-risk area list when you compare it to states like California or New York. But the Garden State is heading down a path similar to Detroit's - a once-thriving industrial powerhouse that's now empty, broke, and drowning in debt. Being close to big shots like New York and D.C. has hidden its downfall. But if you look closer, you'll see the whole thing is falling apart at the seams.

This chapter shows how New Jersey is falling apart, from a stalled economy to run towns.

Post-Industrial Decay: A Rust Belt Repeat

Just like Detroit in the 1970s, New Jersey's cities used to be centers of manufacturing, trade, and blue-collar jobs. Now, cities like Newark, Camden, Paterson, and Trenton struggle:

- Old factories closed down years ago leaving empty buildings behind
- Young workers and big companies moved to other states
- Crime, poverty, and joblessness went way up

And while fix-up projects have come and gone, many are just face-lifts that don't address deeper problems.

When the country's economy crashes, these cities won't have the money, strength, or mix of businesses to adapt. They'll break under stress much like Detroit did after years of slow decay and one big money shock.

Stretched Thin and Out of Cash: Your Local Government Can't Help

New Jersey taxes its people more than almost any other state. Just the property taxes are some of the highest in the country. Yet somehow, basic services are still weak:

- Public transit is old and breaks down a lot
- Schools in poor areas lack funding and don't perform well
- Emergency crews are short-staffed and take too long to show up

And most local governments have no money. Borrowing for years, pension debts, and budget gaps have caused ongoing debt problems.

If prices skyrocket or federal money stops, these services disappear in a flash. No one will pick up garbage. Roads will stay broken. Water systems might stop working without warning.

If you're counting on your state or town to help you in a crisis, you're taking a big risk.

Cities on the Brink of Falling Apart

Many New Jersey cities are crowded and on edge. Places like Camden and Trenton already see high crime rates. If aid money stops or food costs jump, people will get very angry.

- Stealing and fighting will get worse fast
- Supply routes from New York and Pennsylvania might get cut off or taken over
- The National Guard might show up late, or not show up at all

And being close to big cities like NYC and Philadelphia makes it open to spillover. When those cities face chaos, people running away and troublemakers will pour into North Jersey creating even more chaos.

This means even small towns aren't safe, especially those near train tracks or main roads.

Don't Rely on Utilities

New Jersey's utilities are old and centralized. Power cuts during storms happen often, and last for a long time. If the economy crashes, grid upkeep will end, and blackouts might stretch for weeks.

Water systems in older cities face risks too:

- Lead pipes still exist in parts of Newark and other areas
- Pollution threats are high with little money put into infrastructure
- Sewage treatment and storm drains overflow

And don't forget about winter! New Jersey can get extremely cold. If heating systems break down due to fuel shortages or grid failure, millions of people in apartment buildings will have no safe way to keep warm.

Steps to Take: Surviving When the Garden State Falls

1. Don't Count on Local Services to Last

Begin to think the government can't or won't help you. Get ready:

- Your own ways to get rid of trash
- Other options for light and heat
- Systems to clean water on your own
- Tools to talk in emergencies (radios that use the sun local networks that connect)

2. Find Safe Places Away from Big Cities

If you live close to Newark, Jersey City, or Camden, know a way and place to go further inland or south.

Search for:

- Smaller towns with less crime and local food growing
- Areas near farms or their own water sources
- Places where people still care about their neighbors

Towns in rural Warren, Hunterdon, or southern Cumberland counties might become good spots to fall back to if cities fail.

3. Stop Relying on Area Utilities

Start now:

- Put money into solar panels and banks of batteries
- Install a system to catch rainwater and filter it using gravity
- Use wood stoves or propane for heating, not just gas or electricity

New Jersey won't make the news like California or Florida when things fall apart. But its quiet breakdown could be just as devastating. The state is spread thin, fragile, and very exposed.

Don't wait for the news. Make plans now. Move away from weak areas. And build self-reliance while you still can.

Louisiana – The Welfare State Collapse

When the dollar crashes and economic tremors shake the country, Louisiana won't just stumble, it'll fall apart. Why? Because the base is already broken. With high numbers of people relying on government help, old and failing structures, widespread lack of money, and poor health care, Louisiana is set up to fail when its support system disappears.

When an economy depends on government money, any break in federal aid creates a human crisis overnight. For Louisiana, especially places like New Orleans and Baton Rouge, that's a real threat right now.

High Reliance on Government Support

Louisiana is one of the top states where people depend on government help. This includes:

- SNAP (food stamps)
- Medicaid
- Public housing
- Disability payments
- Social Security

In many areas, this aid isn't just extra support, it's how people stay alive. This can't last. If prices go crazy, these benefits won't match the sky-high costs of food, gas, and healthcare. Even worse, these programs might freeze slow down, or stop.

Folks who count on monthly checks or help will face a sudden drop, with no backup plan and nowhere to turn.

Falling Apart in a Danger Zone

Louisiana's infrastructure was weak before the financial crisis hit. Hurricane Katrina showed how bad things could get - and how slow help arrived even with the government's full backing. Now think about a similar disaster, but without FEMA, the Red Cross, or money to rebuild.

- Country roads and bridges are falling apart
- New Orleans' levees are always under pressure
- Old power systems can't handle big storms
- Many parishes have drainage that barely works

If everything falls apart, the state won't be able to fix or even keep up basic services. Some towns might end up cut off. Flooding, power outages, and backed-up sewers will happen a lot, especially near the southern coast.

Poverty and Weak Healthcare

About one-fifth of people in Louisiana struggle with poverty. Many can't get good food, clean water, or stable homes even when things are normal. Good healthcare is hard to find or doesn't have enough resources. Rural hospitals are overwhelmed and sometimes have to shut down.

Now imagine losing federal money, Medicaid payments, and gas deliveries, the situation becomes fatal.

Long-term sickness, injuries, and infections without treatment will increase as medical centers close or run short on supplies. People's mental health will get worse and more will turn to drugs. This shows how a local breakdown can lead to a wider disaster.

New Orleans: A Powder Keg

New Orleans stands out as one of the most at-risk cities. Its low elevation, dense population, and long-standing divisions between rich and poor make it a powder keg for civil unrest once resources run out.

- Theft and aggression will worsen
- Help will be slow to arrive
- Bad weather could turn an already tough situation into complete disorder

New Orleans depends on bringing in stuff. Even small problems in getting vital supplies will cause big issues.

Practical Steps: How to Survive When Louisiana Falls Apart

1. When Things Go South, Don't Count on Outside Help

You can't rely on government support, handouts, or food banks. Start building your own safety net now:

- Store long-term food and water
- Learn basic medical and first aid skills
- Keep cash or items to trade if digital payments stop working
- Stock up on fuel or other ways to cook and heat
- Don't count on FEMA trucks to save you.

2. Get to Know Local Farmers and Skilled Workers

In the South, people rely on their community. You might not grow all your food or fix every leaky pipe, but someone nearby can.

Start now:

- Find out about farmers' markets in your area
- Share skills with neighbors (growing food fixing things keeping safe, etc.)
- Set up trust-based trading systems before you need them

These friendships could save your life when normal systems break down.

3. Stay Mobile If You're in High-Risk Zones

If you live in a low-lying city like New Orleans, Baton Rouge, or even Lake Charles, make sure you have a plan to get out quickly.

- Find safe areas on higher ground you can reach in a few hours
- Keep your car full of gas and in good shape
- Pack go-bags with must-haves in case you need to leave in a hurry
- Look for routes that avoid main roads and bottlenecks

Being able to move means you have options, and in Louisiana, it could make all the difference between surviving or not.

Louisiana brims with spirit, culture, and community. But the state also stands on shaky foundations, ones that might break under the pressure of financial ruin.. If you call Louisiana home, the moment to get ready isn't in the future. It's right now.

Nevada – Vegas Will Be a Ghost Town

When the dollar takes a nosedive and global trade stalls, Nevada - Las Vegas - will black out quicker than people think. A city that relies on fun, imports, and cool air can hold out so long when power fails and supply trucks stop rolling.

Las Vegas, once a bright beacon of indulgence and non-stop action, might turn into a sun-scorched ghost town if money dries up.

Tourism Tanks First

Las Vegas doesn't run on factories or farms - it runs on holidays, business meetings, and betting. The local economy hinges almost on visitors bringing cash and blowing it fast.

But what happens when people quit traveling? When sky-high inflation makes plane tickets too expensive, or worries about unrest keep folks at home?

Tourism will be among the first businesses to crumble, and Vegas has little else to rely on. The knock-on effects will hit hard:

- Hotels will close their doors
- Casinos will shut down
- Countless workers will lose their jobs in an instant
- City services that depend on tax money will stop working

When visitors disappear, the city's financial lifeline will dry up.

A Mirage in the Desert: No Local Food or Water

Nevada, the southern part, grows very little of its own food or water. Everything comes from elsewhere. Las Vegas stands out as one of the most artificial urban settings in the nation only surviving through:

- Food brought in from California and Arizona
- Water from the dwindling Lake Mead reservoir
- Fuel driven in across hundreds of miles

When these supply chains fail, due to fuel scarcity, economic downfall, or unrest in other states, the results will hit hard and fast.

Food will disappear from shelves. Gas stations will run out. And the water from your tap might slow to a drip or stop altogether.

The false sense of safety in Nevada cities is just that, a false sense. The desert shows no mercy, and nature doesn't bother about how posh your apartment is when the electricity fails and the temperature soars to 115°F.

Harsh Desert Living: Everything Gets Shipped In

Living in southern Nevada needs constant man-made support:

- Air conditioning isn't a comfort; you need it to survive.
- People must pump, clean, and limit water use.
- Summer brings sky-high energy use, and the power system is already weak.

Now picture what happens in a summer heat wave when the power cuts out and generators run dry. Within hours, people who aren't ready will face:

- Not enough water in their bodies
- Dangerous overheating
- Food going bad
- Medical devices and fridges stopping work

Las Vegas wasn't designed to endure the desert — it was created to disregard it. And that's a risky gamble in a failing economy.

Practical Steps: Enduring or Leaving Nevada

1. Avoid Depending on Stored Items from Far-Off Locations

Hoarding food makes sense, but don't base your strategy on constant replenishment. Nevada's stores get their supplies from long-distance trucking and out-of-state providers. When a crash happens, these deliveries will end.

- Concentrate on non-perishable foods with distant expiration dates
- Build or join local food networks (gardens, greenhouses even backyard chickens if allowed)
- Put money into water filters and movable water containers, water means survival here

If you still rely on national supply chains in a desert breakdown, you're living on borrowed time.

2. Find Safe Routes to Areas with Water and Farming

When trucks stop and pumps fail, you need a backup plan, and quickly. This plan should include a clear way to regions with:

- Natural water sources (rivers, lakes underground water)
- Farmland or country homes
- Cooler weather if possible

Parts of northern Nevada, Utah, Idaho, or even Oregon might give you a better chance to survive. Learn how to get there. Test the route. Stay off highways when you can – they'll jam up fast during a mass exit.

3. Get Ready for Heat, Fuel, and Power Problems

In Nevada, heat poses your biggest threat. During summer, the gap between "hot" and "fatal" narrows quickly.

Get ready now:

- Pack sun-blocking tarps solar power banks, and cooling cloths
- Store extra fuel , and learn how to cycle it
- Hang dark curtains, use battery fans, and plan your water intake to keep your body temperature in check
- If you need cold-stored meds or powered oxygen, have backup power options or other plans ready.

When things stop working, Las Vegas won't go out with a bang, it'll choke. The bright signs will dim. The slot machines will stop. And the desert will take back what it lent.

Stay ahead of the news. If you live in Nevada, Las Vegas, you should face the dangers head-on and start getting ready now. Because in the desert, wishing won't cut it, and those who plan ahead will make it through.

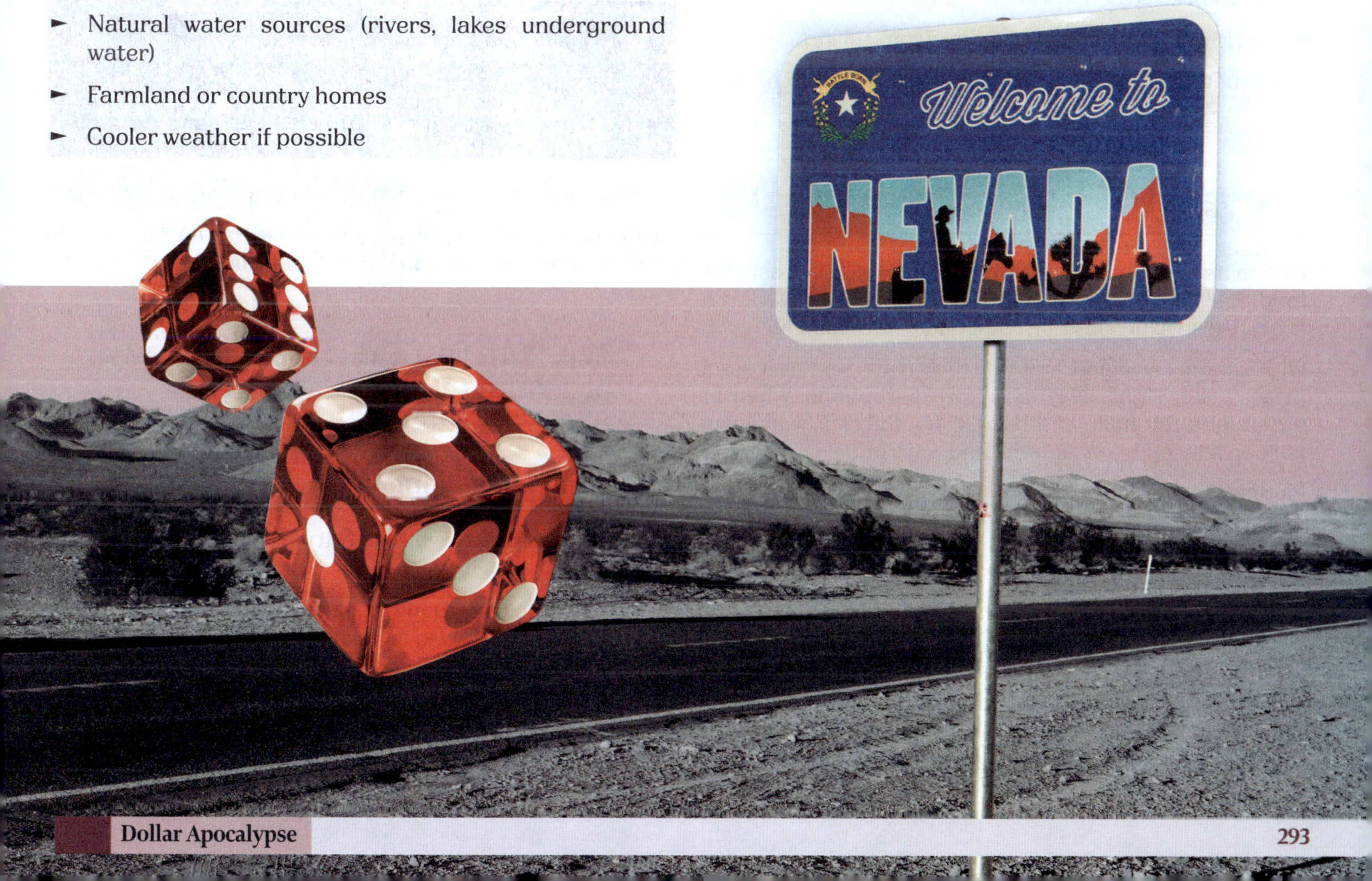

Hawaii – The Supply Chain Nightmare

Hawaii is known as a peaceful paradise, a top spot for vacations and a relaxed home for residents. But the beautiful scenery and palm trees hide a tough truth, Hawaii is one of the most at-risk places in America for system breakdown. If the dollar loses power and supply chains break, the Aloha State turns into a mess to manage.

The issue isn't just how far away it is, it's that Hawaii relies on others.

100% Reliant on Imports

Hawaii brings in over 85-90% of its food, almost all its fuel, and most of its consumer goods from outside. The islands make nothing in large quantities. The modern economy here works because ships and planes deliver goods every day from the US mainland, Japan, and other places.

If shipping or air cargo slows down even a bit, Hawaii's stores will run out of food in a matter of days. The current system of getting things just when needed falls apart when:

- Gas costs too much or becomes hard to find
- Port workers stop working or ports close
- Worldwide problems keep ships from sailing

And when imports stop coming, life in Hawaii changes fast.

Being Cut Off Leads to Prices Going Up

Due to its isolation, Hawaii already faces higher costs for food, fuel, and rent compared to other places. During a crisis, these expenses don't just go up, they explode.

With scarce farmland and no truck transport over land, prices react right away to supply disruptions. When inflation hits the mainland hard, it hammers Hawaii even harder, leaving fewer options and ways out.

Picture this:

- Milk at $20 a gallon
- Bread over $10 a loaf
- Gas stations with no fuel
- Not enough medicine
- Black market rates for everyday items like batteries and bottled water

Once inflation takes hold of the islands, it will get worse because of limited local competition and extreme scarcity. People won't just pay more, they might not be able to buy anything at all.

No Overland Supply Air or Sea

Unlike mainland states, Hawaii can't drive in emergency supplies or truck in reinforcements. Every single item must:

- Fly in at high cost and in limited volume
- Ship by sea, which needs working ports, diesel fuel, and global cooperation

A big shipping disruption, or a crash in currency that makes international deals tough, would isolate the islands.

Picture this:

- No gas for cars or backup generators
- No propane to cook
- No spare parts for anything, from cars to water pumps
- No baby formula, hygiene items, or prescribed drugs

It doesn't need a doomsday to make Hawaii uncomfortable, just a major slowdown in global shipping.

Steps You Can Take: Getting Ready for Island Life During a Crisis

1. Find Local Food and Water Solutions

If you live in Hawaii, you need to act now to rely less on imports.

- Grow your own food: Plant a garden at home, raise chickens, or join a local farm group
- Collect rainwater: Install systems to gather and clean rainwater as a backup water source
- Fish and forage: Learn to add native fish and wild plants to your diet

Don't count on your grocery store to save you. When trouble hits, it'll be the first thing to go.

2. Create Community Networks for Trading

On islands, your community becomes your currency. When money loses value or becomes useless, staying alive will depend on what you can do, what you have, and who you trust.

- Get to know neighbors who can repair, cultivate, construct, or provide medical care
- Start or become part of a trading group, even
- Keep items to exchange: batteries, seeds, water filters basic tools, hygiene products

When imports stop, your neighbors become your suppliers.

3. Expect Limits on Travel Between Islands

In tough times, officials might try to manage movement between islands or stop people from leaving, if they need to ration limited supplies.

- Don't count on flying to another island
- Have a main spot that's self-sufficient and easy to protect
- If you can, pick an island that grows more of its own food (like some parts of Big Island or Kauai)

Travel options will be scarce. Make plans to stay put and weather the storm using supplies you've already gathered.

Hawaii's beauty takes your breath away, but when systems fail, the same ocean that makes it stunning also cuts it off from help.

This section doesn't aim to scare Hawaiian residents, but to raise awareness. Hawaii lacks a backup plan. If imports cease, there's no other option. It's not just about supply chain risks. It's a matter of survival.

For those living in Hawaii, don't wait until ships stop coming; take action now.

Oregon & Washington – Lawlessness and Tech Trouble

The Pacific Northwest has earned a reputation as a hotspot for new ideas, stunning scenery, and forward-thinking values. Yet beneath its tall trees and bustling tech centers, a rising conflict is brewing, one that might explode when the economy tanks. Oregon and Washington, despite their wealth, teeter on the brink of social unrest and rely too on industries that don't make essential goods.

If prices skyrocket or the financial system breaks down, these states could face quick disruptive changes, in their big cities.

Urban Sprawl and Pressure Points

Portland and Seattle have grown into huge urban areas. Housing costs have shot up and gentrification has a big impact on these cities, creating deep money gaps. These cities rely on services, government systems, and tech infrastructure. They don't have much backup if these systems fail.

The way these cities are laid out makes it hard to escape in a crisis. Long drives to work, traffic jams, and lots of people packed together could lead to total gridlock if everyone panics at once.

A History of Protests and Divides

Oregon and Washington have seen some of the most intense and long-lasting civil unrest in recent times. Political splits, street protests, and fights between different ideologies have already pushed law enforcement and public resources to their limits.

Without central control, groups already at odds could soon start stealing even more trouble, . If the lights go out for food stops coming in, expect fights to break out, in packed city centers.

Tech Reliance and Money Problems

The Pacific Northwest runs on tech. Amazon, Microsoft, and tons of new companies drive the money in Washington and Oregon. But, these firms might fire workers, move out, or shut down .

Tech workers - many who can't fend for themselves - will get stuck in pricey city bubbles without a Plan B. Empty buildings and deserted office parks might shape the new skyline if the digital economy crashes.

Things You Can Do

To safeguard yourself if you live in or near Oregon and Washington's cities, think about these practical steps:

1. Check Out Farming Towns

Look past the cities. Rural areas in eastern Washington and southern Oregon still have farms and water. Small towns with a history of farming and ranching will cope better with a breakdown. Build connections now, or think about moving before things get bad.

2. Get Backup Power and Water

Rain might be plenty in the area, but your access to clean, stored, or filtered water could still disappear overnight. Put money into rainwater gathering, off-grid filtering, and personal power sources. Expect utilities to fail, and make sure you won't.

3. Turn Digital Money into Real Things

If your money is online, stocks, crypto savings, it might vanish in extreme inflation. Begin turning value into real assets: land, tools, fuel, food stocks, and trade items. A computer farm won't feed your family. A full root cellar will.

4. Cut Ties with the City's Weak Pulse

If you live in the city, try to become less dependent on services. Don't count on DoorDash and Amazon for everything. Learn to cook, repair stuff, and barter with people nearby. Make friends with practical handy folks, not just online contacts.

Oregon and Washington seem okay now, but they rely on modern comforts and digital economies. When real problems hit, like blackouts, money troubles, or riots, those who got ready beforehand will manage.

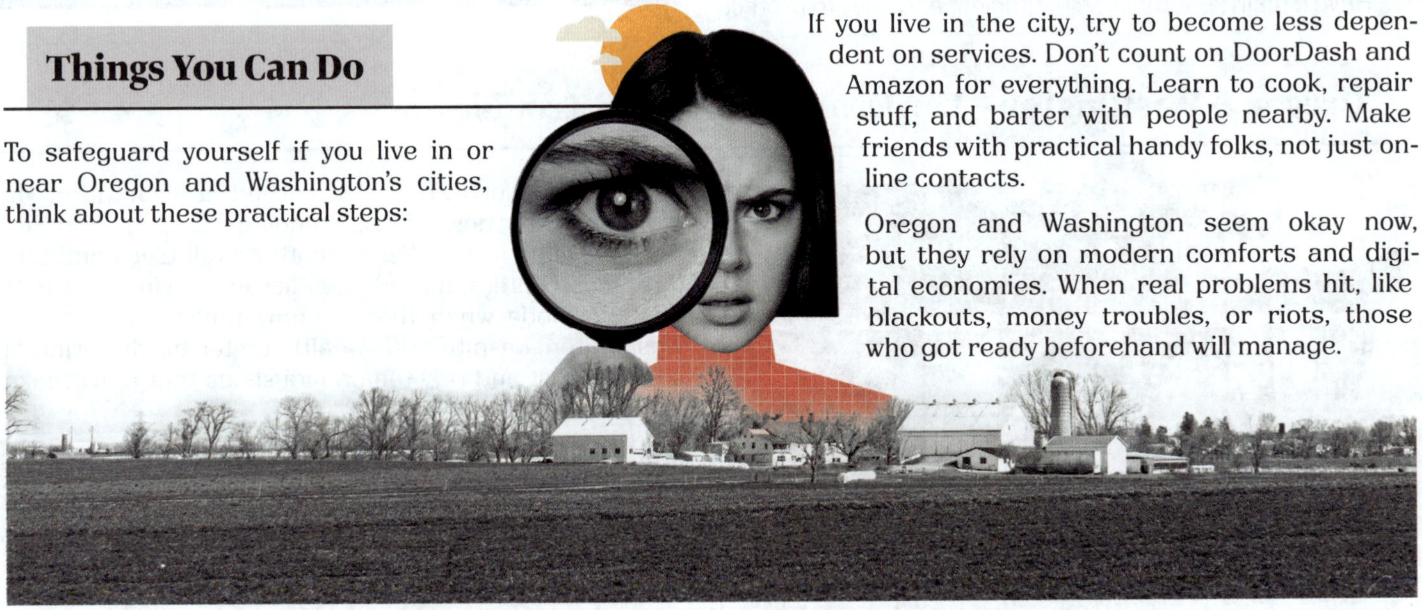

Moderately Vulnerable States – Not Safe, But Not First to Fall

Some states aren't about to fall apart tomorrow. Certain areas walk a fine line - at risk, but not the first to fall. These places might show warning signs, but they also have their strengths. The main thing in these areas isn't running away - it's deciding where exactly to live, and how you get ready at the local level.

These are the "in-between" states - places that could go either way based on how strong their communities are and what choices their residents make.

Florida: Shaky with a Glimmer of Hope

Florida's weak spot is its economy. It depends on tourism, entertainment, and seasonal visitors. Cities like Miami, Orlando, and Tampa drive the economy, but they also rely on people spending money, flying in planes, and smooth supply chains. Mess up these systems, and things fall apart.

But inland, there's a glimmer of hope. Central Florida has strong farming. Small farm towns, orange groves, and ranch communities offer more staying power than the coastal cities. If you live near the coast, expect trouble when shipping slows down and gas prices jump. But if you're nestled inland with access to wells, gardens, and neighbors to trade with? **You might just make it.**

Colorado: A Divide Between Delicate Cities and Tough Mountains

Colorado faces a two-sided problem: Denver is new, tech-savvy, and expanding, but like any big city, it's risky. The city relies on far-off food sources delicate power systems, and fuel from elsewhere.

Compare that to the mountain villages: tough, independent, and used to being cut off for months during winter. These places often have their own small economies, nearby farms, and backup power options. Sure, snow and being alone are real issues, but so is the strength of the community. If you live in Denver, know how to get out. If you're already in the mountains, make stronger connections and create backup plans now. There is no time to waste.

Massachusetts: Small Area High Living Costs, and Ability to Adapt

Massachusetts is crowded, pricey, and city-focused. Boston, Worcester, and Springfield do most of the heavy lifting. The danger? A shrinking economy and higher costs could swamp poorer areas in older factory towns.

But unlike big spread out states, Massachusetts has a special edge: everything's close by. If things start to break down, towns can team up fast. Food medical help, and emergency teams can shift gears quicker than in huge stretched-out states. This gives people a valuable chance, if they move before everything freezes up.

Steps People in These States Can Take

These states aren't safe, but they're not guaranteed to be ground zero either. You need to get specific about where you live and how you operate. Here's how:

1. Pay Attention to Your Specific Location Within the State

In Florida, being 30 miles inland changes things a lot. In Colorado, driving one hour outside of Denver puts you in a different environment. In Massachusetts, living just outside city limits could give you more space and self-reliance. Look at your county, not just your state.

2. Keep Supply Chains Short

Source your necessities as close to home as possible. Build relationships with farmers in your area. Stop by local butcher shops and hardware stores. Put your trust in people, not online platforms. Shortening your supply chain now will give you some wiggle room when the broader economy starts to struggle.

3. Build Networks in Skill-Based Local Economies

These areas have residents who can repair items, cultivate crops, and educate others. Seek them out. Do business with them. Gain knowledge from them. A circle of plumbers, electricians, hunters, herbalists, and mechanics holds more value than a high-rise apartment or an internet marketplace.

A moderate level of vulnerability doesn't mean you're safe, it means you have a chance. The turmoil might come at a slower pace in these states, but it will arrive. The people who get ready now, in their neighborhoods, street by street, will be the ones who thrive when others struggle.

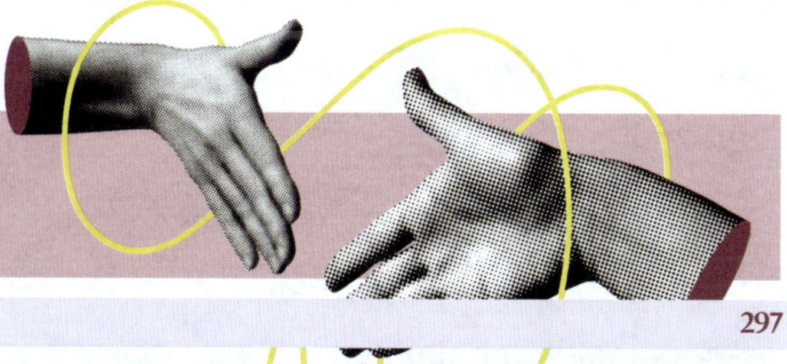

"It is not the strongest of the species that survive, nor the most intelligent, but the one most responsive to change."
Charles Darwin

Chapter 23

The New Money: The Most Sought-After Items You Can Barter for Anything You Need

When paper fails and people are left to their own devices to figure out the value of essentials, chaos is soon to follow. But as history tends to repeat itself, you should consider stockpiling some of these staple items that have been used throughout time instead of coin or plastic, when bartering was the only viable trading option.

Necessity creates demand, and when the supply is limited, value goes through the roof.

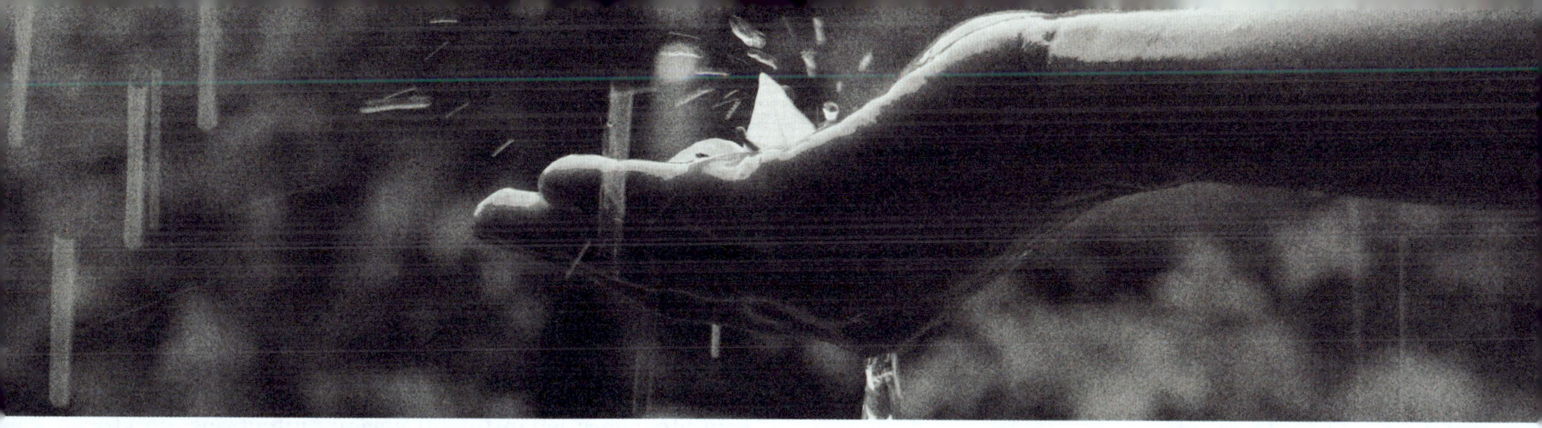

Drinking Water

Start simple, list your basic needs and you'll soon find out that you can't go without water for more than a few days. Nothing beats clean drinking water, as it can be exchanged for food, medical assistance, manual labour, and even ammunition.

If you intend to barter water, do not store it in jugs or canisters. Trying to exchange those for any minor item or service would be like trying to break a Benjamin on a pack of gum, only this time chances are you aren't going to get any change.

Use smaller bottles, as the most accepted ones are the pint-sized and one liter containers, that in a working barter system hold a market value that ranges between five and ten dollars, depending on its scarcity.

It's true that water is a renewable resource, but clean drinking water isn't.

In the absence of the proper filtration tools, rainwater or water of any other kind can contain dangerous bacteria, making it unsuitable for human consumption. Giardia wreaking havoc on your stomach is the last thing you would want when hospitals become unreachable, and pharmacies don't have a single antibiotic pill behind the counter.

Gathering some of the following tools before the collapse hits is going to make all the difference, giving you an edge in bartering during hard times.

The Katadyn Pocket filter is going to be one of the most sought-after items in an emergency. Its filters are good for thousands of liters before they need to be replaced, as they use ceramic elements. Some other time-proven options are the **Sawyer Squeeze and Berkey gravity-fed systems.**

You can also go the chemical way and choose some water purification tablets. **Either iodine or chlorine dioxide are good options.** They can also moonlight as currency for small transactions, as they are compact, and easily dividable.

Your clean water is going to be worthless if it's not stored properly. Choose **BPA-free plastic containers or stainless-steel tanks** for water storage and protect them from sunlight and heat to avoid algae development and chemical leakage. Rotate stored water every **six to twelve months.** If you're living somewhere hot, do this more frequently.

A good water filtration system can give you a constant supply of water. The essential system consists of rooftop collection surfaces with screened gutters that integrate a first-flush diverter to eliminate debris and include sealed storage tanks. Your water supply remains protected, and you gain enhanced trading opportunities with others through this system.

During any emergency situation clean water suppliers become powerful figures.

Medical Supplies

Whether a crisis hits overnight, or it slowly unfolds over several months, one thing is certain – medical supplies will be the first to vanish, as pharmaceutical supply chains are going to be severed fast.

When years of corruption finally caught up to Venezuela's economy, it only took a few weeks for OTCs to be gone from pharmacy shelves, as the only way to get common anti-inflammatories and antibiotics was through the black market, while paying 10 to 20 times more than their normal price.

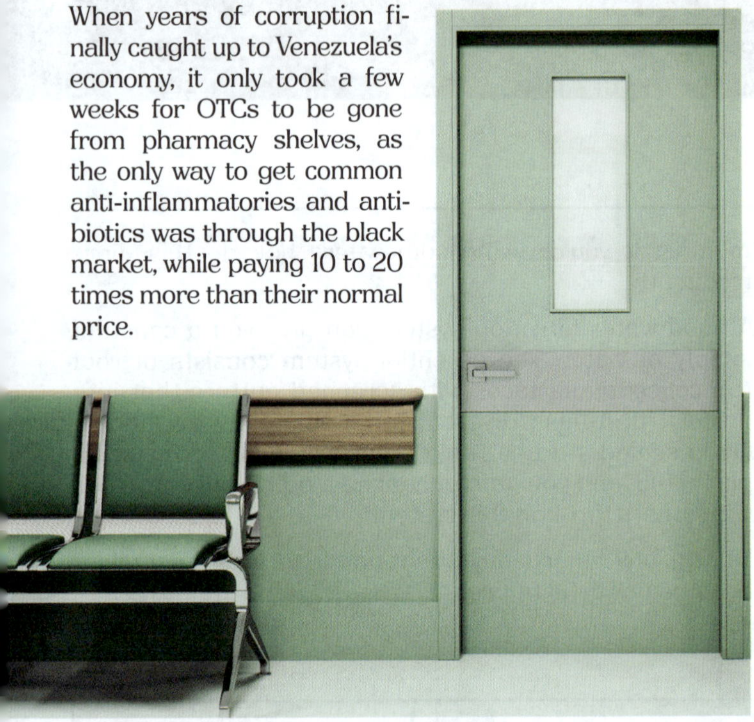

Aim for common medication, the most valuable items are those with clear immediate use. **Painkillers like ibuprofen and acetaminophen** are always going to be in high demand, as they can be used for anything from headaches to fevers and injuries.

In the aftermath of a collapse, **broad-range antibiotics like amoxicillin, ciprofloxacin, and doxycycline** can be real lifesavers when facing serious infections, so stockpiling these items should be a no-brainer.

Some other item groups that are going to be in high demand are **antiseptics and bandages.** No matter how you slice it, people are always going to get hurt. So, stock up on anything that contains alcohol, iodine or hydrogen peroxide. Also get a **wide variety of bandages and gauze.** You can go to Walmart right now and get a couple of **cheap first aid kits** that have hundreds of them. Some even have specialty items like **medical tweezers, stitching kits and medical-grade super glue,** all packaged in an easy-to-store case.

Most medicines should be kept in a cool, dry place, away from direct sunlight and humidity.

Gel based medication is vulnerable to heat and will lose its properties over time. While many medications remain potent beyond their printed expiration dates, they must be rotated and checked regularly. If something is approaching its use by date, trade it for something useful.

Tobacco Products

Cigarettes have always been used as currency in times when cash was useless. Throughout the World Wars, soldiers were trading cigarettes for food items or using them to gamble during down time.

Tobacco was also used as primary currency in prisons, and this makes a lot of sense. Dollars can't buy you anything if you don't have a place to spend them. The same goes for times when money no longer holds any value, becoming worth less than the paper they're printed on.

Go for widely known brands like **Marlboro, Newport, Lucky Strike and Winstone.** If you buy them by the carton, they often come shrink wrapped, making them impervious to water and decay, sealing their moisture inside. This means that each individual pack is going to be good for decades. Another good tip is keeping them away from direct sunlight. In a functioning barter-based economy, an individual pack can buy you goods or services worth \$15 to \$50, depending on demand.

Alcohol

Alcohol holds a special place in bartering due to its versatility. It doesn't only uplift the spirits when times are tough. It can also be used as an antiseptic, solvent or even fuel.

If you look at the Prohibition Era in the US, you can see that even when the sale, distribution and even distillation of alcohol was heavily restricted, demand never diminished, as citizens' appetite for it only grew larger by the year.

Alcohol trades best when it easy to carry. Use miniature bottles, also known as nips for small exchanges. These single servings can be bartered for food, medicine or labour.

Use larger bottles (0.75l) for higher value trades. High-proof ethanol (above 90 proof) holds extra value, as it can be used to sterilize medical tools, make tinctures, or serve as emergency stove fuel. Brands like **Everclear and Spirytus** are especially sought after for their purity and long shelf life. High-proof alcohol lasts for decades if kept sealed in glass and stored in a cool, dark place. Plastic bottles are fine for short-term use but are less suitable for long-term storage due to permeability.

Fuel

Fuel is power – literally.

When an economy collapses, fuel is going to be the first commodity to disappear from the market. When the fuel distribution grid gets disrupted, every other aspect of the economy grinds to a halt. No fuel means no transport. That leads to a collapse of all major supply chains, leaving grocery stores, pharmacies and even hospitals hung out to dry.

There are quite a few options when it comes to bartering fuel, each of them having its ups and downs.

Gasoline is surely going to be the most sought-after fuel, and it is going to be traded for a premium. Most cars in the US are running on gasoline, so the demand for it is going to be higher. It can also be used for generators, making it even more useful, especially if the power grid is going to collapse.

The downside to storing gasoline is its limited shelf-life. This type is fuel is notorious for absorbing moisture, reducing its effectiveness. There are a few stabilizers out there, like **PRI-G and STA-BIL** that can extend this fuel's lifetime beyond six months. Gasoline needs to be stored in **DOT approved containers.** Use steel jerry cans to store fuel and keep those in a well-ventilated shed. Storing high quantities of gasoline can make you a prime target for looters.

Propane is especially valuable because it solves the stability problem of gasoline, remaining stable over long periods of time. This fuel can be used for powering a wide range of civilian and military surplus stoves, lanterns, and heaters. Standard one-pound and twenty-pound propane tanks are easy to trade and store.

Fire-starters such as ferro rods, waterproof matches, and wax-infused cotton rolls are not fuel themselves, but they are essential for igniting fires and are highly tradable.

In trades, a gallon of gasoline can be worth anywhere from $20 to $80, depending on scarcity and demand. A sealed one-pound propane tank can be traded for a full day's labor or several days' worth of food.

Ammunition

When a major economic crisis hits, chances are you will be on your own.

When most people get desperate and don't have any other means of earning their bread, they resort to violence and looting, and in the chaos trail left behind by an economic collapse, chances are that the authorities are going to have their hands full. That being said, the responsibility of defending your family and property is going to fall on your shoulders, so you'd better stock up on bullets.

Their lethality, portability, and universal recognition make them the ultimate barter commodity in a lawless world.

If you intend to barter bullets, go for the most common calibers. Nobody is going to run around shooting .50BMGs at looters. **Stock up on 9mm, .223/5.50NATO, 12-gauge shells and .22 long-rifle,** the latter being a fan-favorite among hunters and farmers, for its ease of use, low recoil and low noise. **A 50-round brick** can be traded for a day's labor, a sack of potatoes, or a bottle of antibiotics.

Next in line are **9mm (for handguns and carbines), .223/5.56 NATO (for AR-15 platforms), and 12-gauge shotgun shells**. These rounds dominate civilian and law enforcement arsenals, making them universally understood and accepted. **In post-Katrina New Orleans, a box of 9mm FMJ traded for $100 worth of fuel or medicine.**

Shotgun shells offer flexibility: birdshot for small game, buckshot for defense, slugs for large predators.

But the real power lies not in stockpiling ammo, it's in making it. A reloading bench transforms spent brass into currency. **With a basic setup (a press, dies, powder, primers, and projectiles), you become the local armorer.** Reloaders in the Bosnian War turned scavenged brass into barter gold, customizing loads for hunting, defense, or silenced shots.

Trading ammo requires caution. Never hand over a crate to a stranger. In stable barter networks, deal in **small batches: 10 rounds of 9mm for a gallon of fuel, 20 .22LR for a meal.**

Store ammunition in military-grade cans with silica gel packs. Organize by caliber and purpose. A well-stocked .223 cache could barter for a whole generator.

Batteries

Batteries are one of the most traded items for a simple reason: they keep essential devices running when nothing else will. Flashlights, radios, medical monitors, clocks, and tools all rely on a steady supply of batteries.

The most popular types **(AA, AAA, 9V, and CR123)** are valued because they fit the widest range of gear and are instantly recognized by anyone.

AA and AAA batteries are needed for everything from small lights to thermometers and radios. **9V batteries** are crucial for smoke alarms and some medical testers. **CR123 batteries** power tactical flashlights and weapaon-mounted lights, making them important for anyone focused on security or night work.

Rechargeable batteries, especially nickel-metal hydride (NiMH) types like Eneloop, are a step above the rest. These can be charged hundreds of times and hold their power well. When paired with a small solar charger or a multi-format USB charger, they become a portable energy system, something that can be traded, rented out, or used to power other valuable equipment. This combination is always in demand and can be the difference between a working radio and silence.

Proper storage is key to keeping batteries reliable. **They should be kept in sealed plastic containers with desiccant packs to guard against moisture. Store them in a cool, dry place, and avoid direct sunlight.** Rotate your

supply, test rechargeables every few months, and keep different types separated to avoid confusion or accidental discharge.

In trade, a four-pack of AA batteries can be swapped for food, tools, or hygiene supplies. 9V and CR123 batteries often fetch more, especially where their specific uses are in high demand.

A set of charged NiMH batteries with a charger is a premium item, often traded for skilled labor, tool access, or other high-value goods. Always label battery types and charge status to build trust and keep trades smooth.

Batteries are compact, long-lasting, and always needed. They make a reliable and practical currency wherever people depend on electronics to stay safe, informed, and connected.

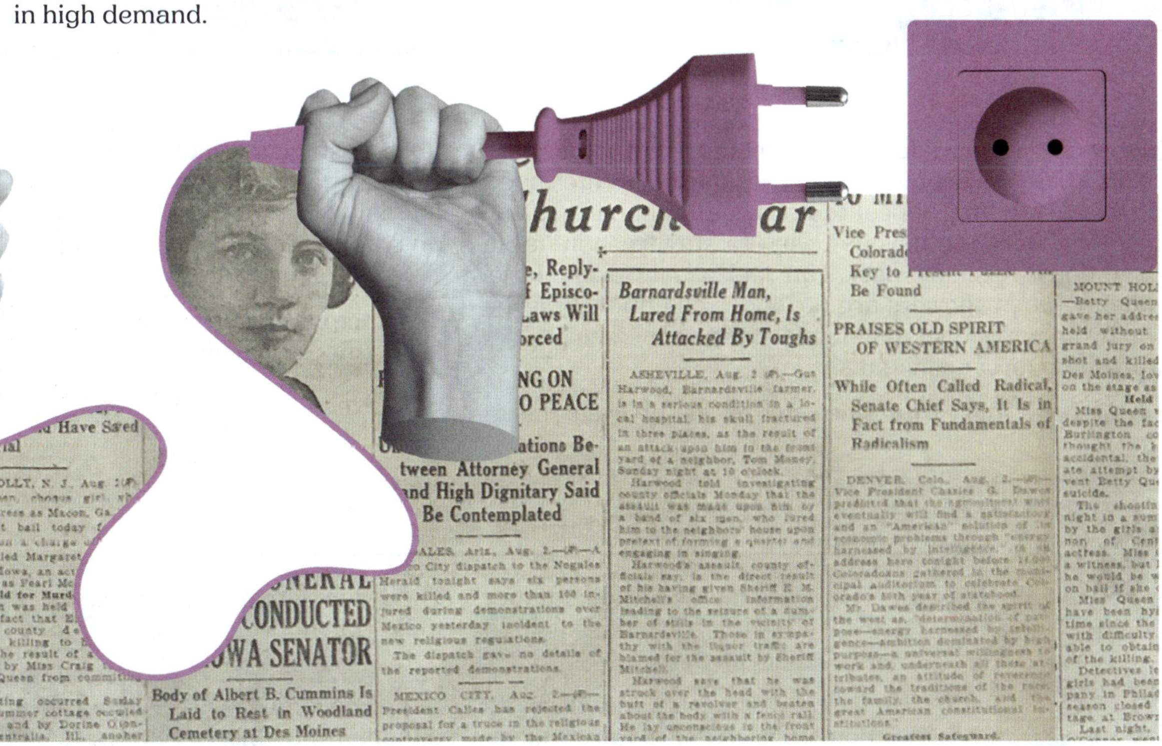

Hygiene Products

IIn the aftermath of a collapse, staying clean is more than comfort. It is survival. Hygiene items might not seem like much in normal times, but when running water stops and supply chains break, these small essentials suddenly carry immense value.

Disease spreads fast in dirty conditions. Without soap or sanitary products, even a minor infection can become dangerous. That is why hygiene becomes one of the earliest concerns in long-term emergencies and one of the most reliable barter categories.

Soap is the cornerstone. **Bar soap,** in particular, lasts longer than liquid and stores better in compact spaces. It does not leak, it rarely expires, and it is instantly useful. Whether it is washing hands, clothes, or wounds, one bar of soap can serve many purposes. And people are always willing to trade for cleanliness, especially when illness becomes a threat.

Toothpaste and toothbrushes are often overlooked, but they are consistently in demand. Dental infections in grid-down scenarios can spiral quickly and become life-threatening. Just being able to keep your mouth clean and fresh becomes a luxury. **Toothbrushes are lightweight and easy to store in bulk.** Travel-sized toothpaste tubes are perfect for trading and rationing.

Sanitary pads and tampons are vital for many women, and when unavailable, the impact is serious, both medically and emotionally. These items are hard to improvise and even harder to replace. Packs of unscented, **individually wrapped pads or tampons** hold high value, especially when kept clean and sealed. In many crises, these have been traded at five to ten times their normal worth.

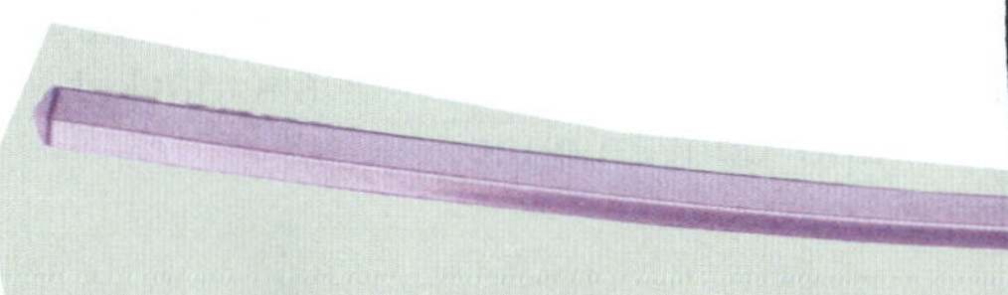

Wet wipes, when sealed and unscented, are another goldmine. They provide quick cleanliness with no water needed. In barter, they appeal to everyone. from parents caring for children to anyone trying to stay fresh in harsh conditions. A single pack can feel like a luxury hotel amenity when showers are no longer an option. Storage for hygiene products is simple. **Keep items sealed, dry, and out of direct sunlight.**

Mylar bags, bins with silica gel packs, or even resealable plastic containers can keep them usable for years. Bartering with hygiene is different from trading fuel or ammo. You are offering dignity. You are offering someone the chance to feel human again.

A clean body, a fresh mouth, a sense of normalcy, these become powerful currencies when the world around you is anything but clean.

Toilet Paper

People laugh about toilet paper now. They will not be laughing when they run out.

In nearly every crisis that disrupts daily life, from natural disasters to long-term societal breakdowns, **toilet paper is one of the first items to vanish from store shelves.** It is bulky, easy to forget, and almost impossible to replicate with comfort once it is gone.

Leaves, newspaper, and cloth might work in desperation, but nothing replaces the real thing when it comes to hygiene and convenience.

The value of toilet paper lies not only in its comfort but in its role in preventing infection.

Poor sanitation is one of the fastest ways for disease to spread, especially in crowded or makeshift living situations. And unlike more versatile survival goods, toilet paper is rarely stockpiled in large amounts by most households.

That means those who have it, control it. **In a barter economy, a single roll of high-quality toilet paper can trade for food, medicine, or even fuel.** Packs of tightly wrapped, individually sealed rolls become mini vaults of hygiene. **The key is to keep them dry and compressed, preferably vacuum-packed or stored in weather-resistant containers.**

Baby wipes are a close companion in this category and in many ways, even more versatile. They clean not just after bathroom use but also dirty hands, faces, wounds, tools, and gear. In the absence of running water, they become an all-purpose solution for staying clean. Parents with infants will trade almost anything for baby wipes, but even solo preppers will recognize their daily value when showers are no longer an option.

Unscented, alcohol-free wipes are the best choice for long-term storage and broad usability. **Packs should be kept sealed and rotated to avoid drying out.** Unlike toilet paper, they hold moisture, which adds both weight and the potential for spoilage if improperly stored. But when kept well, they are one of the most requested items in any crisis market.

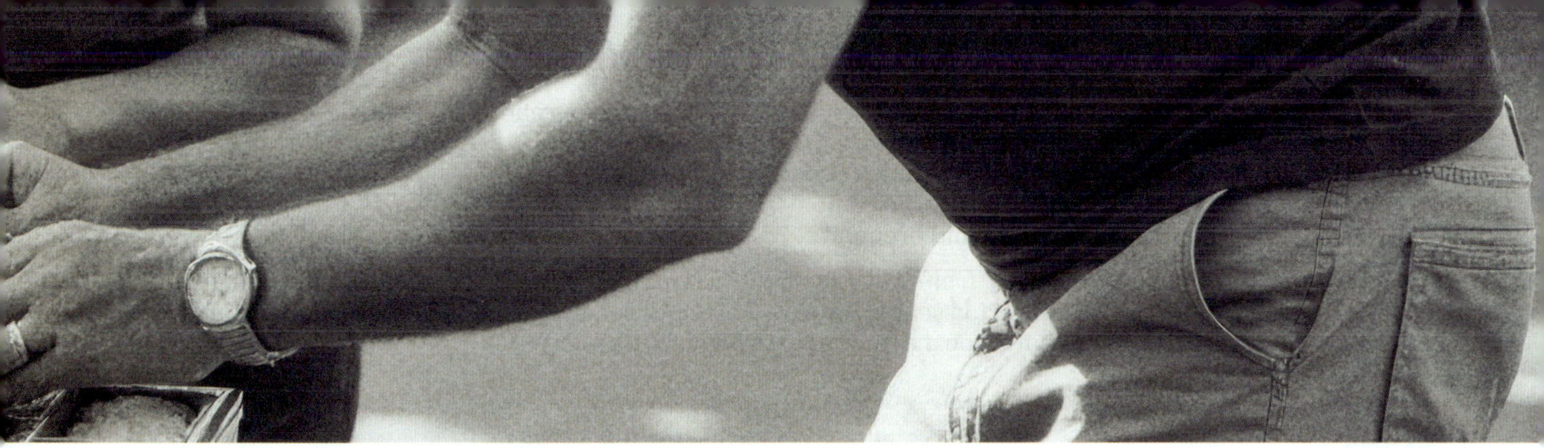

Toilet paper and wipes may feel mundane now, but in a collapsed system, they represent more than convenience. They offer cleanliness, dignity, and relief, three things no one wants to barter without.

Salt & Spices

When people think about survival essentials, they picture water, medicine, maybe fuel or food. Salt rarely makes the list. And yet, it should.

Because salt is not just seasoning. It is preservation. It is currency. It is chemistry your body cannot live without.

Think about it. Before electricity, how did people keep meat from rotting? They packed it in salt. Fish, too. A slab of salted pork could hang in a pantry for weeks without spoiling. And in a crisis where power lines are down and fridges are useless, that same process becomes valuable all over again. **Salt doesn't just add taste. It adds time.** It stretches your food supply when every extra day counts.

But there's another reason salt matters. **The human body cannot function without it.** If you are sweating through hot days, working, walking, or just staying alive under stress, you are losing sodium. Without it, you'll start to feel the drop.

Fatigue, dizziness, cramps and if it gets bad enough, confusion and serious health risks. So while salt might seem like a kitchen afterthought today, it becomes a biological necessity when the grid goes down.

And then there are the spices. No one needs **paprika** to survive. But that is exactly what makes it powerful. Because in the middle of hardship, something that **brings comfort and flavor** carries weight. You can eat beans and rice every day for a week. But after day three, you will give a lot for anything that makes them taste different.

A spoonful of **cumin or curry powder, a pinch of chili or oregano,** can turn bland fuel into real food. And that shift, from endurance to enjoyment, changes more than just your meal. It changes your mood. That emotional value translates into bartering power. People crave normalcy. They crave something that tastes familiar. In a trade, a small jar of garlic powder can speak louder than ammunition. It reminds people of home, of better days, of comfort. And in survival scenarios, comfort is a rare and powerful thing.

From a practical angle, **salt and spices are ideal for storage and exchange.** They are light. They do not expire quickly. They do not need refrigeration. And you can divide them easily, spoonful by spoonful, packet by packet. You can tuck small portions into every trade kit you

prepare. You can **stash them in pockets, tins, mylar bags.** They take up little space and deliver a big return. Of course, not all spices are equal. Focus on the ones that are familiar and versatile: **black pepper, garlic, onion powder, chili flakes, dried herbs like basil and oregano.**

Store them in airtight containers away from moisture and light, and they will keep their flavor for years. Same for salt. Bulk is great, but make sure you have small, sealed portions ready to go. Those are what people will want to trade for.

In short, salt and spices are the quiet champions of a well-prepped pantry. They make your food last longer. They make your meals taste better. They keep your body functioning. And they hold surprising influence in any barter-based system. What seems small today might buy you dinner tomorrow.

Tools

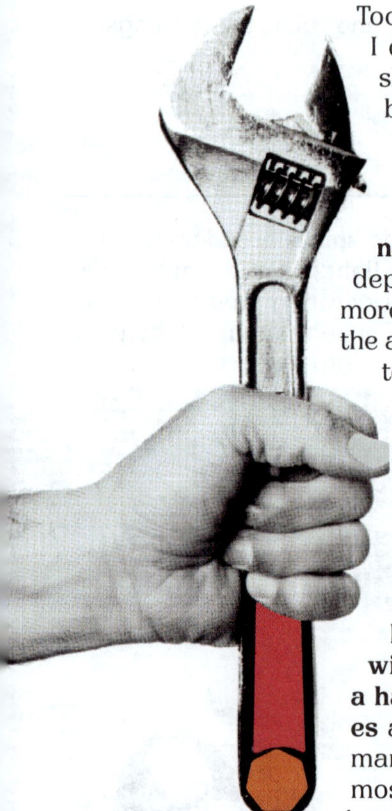

Tools matter in any crisis. And I don't mean fancy gadgets or shiny multitools fresh out of the box. I'm talking about gear that lets you build, fix, cut, or open what others can't.

Real tools that serve real needs. In a barter economy, a dependable tool is often worth more than food or fuel. It gives you the ability to act, to solve problems, to create something out of nothing. When someone's shelter is falling apart or their stove is broken, the person with the right tool becomes essential.

The most valuable tools are not necessarily high tech. **A strong fixed-blade knife, a basic hammer, a multitool with pliers and screwdrivers, a handsaw, and a set of wrenches** are all practical and high-demand items. They are useful to almost anyone and hold their value in any situation.

Knives are especially prized. A sharp, durable blade can be used for preparing food, building shelter, processing firewood, and even for defense. People will always need a knife, and if yours is well maintained, they will be willing to trade generously. What makes tools special is that they don't run out.

They are not used up like food or batteries. If you take care of them, they will serve you and others for years. Items like sharpening stones, extra screws, nails, and replacement parts add even more value, since they allow the tools to stay useful long after others break.

Sewing kits also deserve a place in this list. A needle and some thread might not sound like much, but the ability to repair clothing or gear is incredibly valuable when replacements are hard to find. Fixing someone's jacket, patching a tarp, or closing up a ripped backpack can win you more than just supplies. It earns trust. If you're stockpiling with trade in mind, always get extras. One for yourself, another to trade.

Keep your tools clean and protected from rust by wrapping them in cloth and storing them in a dry place. A tool that looks ready to work is far more attractive in a trade. In a world where most things stop working, the person who can fix what's broken is not just useful. They are respected. With the right tools, you are not only surviving, you are rebuilding.

Warm Clothing

Wool is the gold standard here.

Thick, high-quality items like socks, gloves, scarves, made of wool and layered undergarments. Wool stays warm even when wet, making it essential for damp or snowy conditions.

Bartering warm clothing goes beyond offering fabric. What you are trading is comfort, function, and a chance to stay safe in unforgiving weather. A good jacket protects someone hauling water or fuel outside. Gloves keep hands working when tools freeze in the morning air. Wool Socks help prevent frostbite or foot injuries when boots are worn for days at a time.

Thermal blankets, sleeping bags, and ponchos fall into this same category. During power outages or when fuel becomes too precious to burn, these are the layers people reach for first. Parents will trade almost anything to keep their children warm through the night. That desperation gives these items high barter value.

When stockpiling for trade, aim for items in medium or adjustable sizes. Neutral colors make them more appealing. **Choose quality over quantity.** Pack them in sealed bags or bins to keep moisture and insects out.

A clean, dry set of clothes holds more value than something moth-eaten and damp. In a world without heating, those with extra warm gear will be in high demand. You may not notice it now, but when the first frost comes and there is no heat, a pair of wool socks becomes worth more than gold. Warmth is safety. Warmth is power. And people will trade dearly for it.

Candles & Oil Lamps

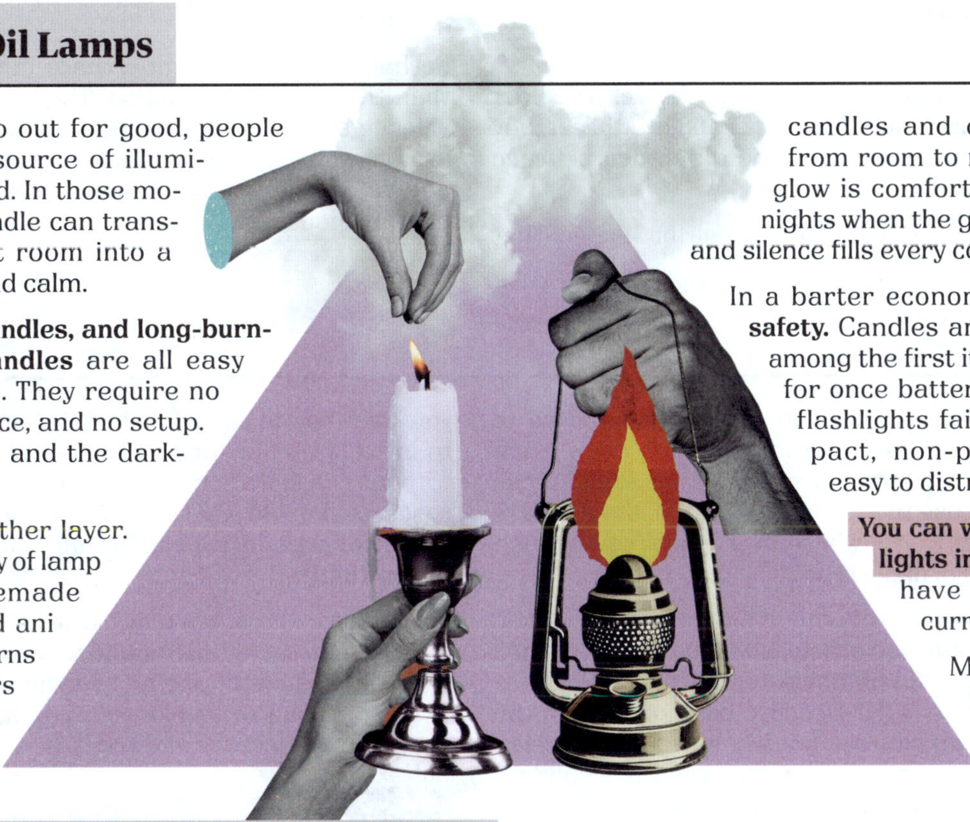

When the lights go out for good, people turn to whatever source of illumination they can find. In those moments, a single candle can transform a cold, silent room into a space of warmth and calm.

Tea lights, pillar candles, and long-burning emergency candles are all easy to store and trade. They require no power, no fuel source, and no setup. You strike a match and the darkness recedes.

Oil lamps add another layer. With a steady supply of lamp oil or even homemade fuels like rendered animal fat, these lanterns can burn for hours on end. They are brighter than candles and easier to carry from room to room. Their soft glow is comforting during long nights when the grid has vanished and silence fills every corner.

In a barter economy, **light equals safety.** Candles and oil lamps are among the first items people look for once batteries run dry and flashlights fail. They are compact, non-perishable, and easy to distribute in trades.

You can wrap a dozen tea lights in a cloth bag and have instant barter currency.

Make sure everything is labeled and ready to hand out.

Duct Tape, Super Glue, and Sewing Kits

When you can no longer rely on stores to replace broken gear or torn clothing, the ability to repair things becomes one of the most valuable skills you can offer. In any crisis, the people who can keep equipment working and clothing functional quickly rise in status and importance. That is why seemingly simple items like **duct tape, super glue, and sewing kits** are always in high demand.

Duct tape might not look like much, but it's a miracle tool. With just a few strips, you can patch a leaky water container, hold together a damaged backpack, or secure a window against wind and dust. It wraps, seals, binds and insulates. A single roll can be used in dozens of ways, from medical improvisation to emergency shelter repairs. **Because of its strength and versatility, duct tape often gets traded like currency, especially among those trying to keep their gear operational.**

Super glue offers another kind of utility. While less flexible

than tape, it can mend hard materials such as plastic or metal. It is perfect for repairing broken parts of flashlights, tools or cooking gear. In some emergencies, a small dab of glue has even been used to close minor wounds, especially when proper medical treatment isn't available. It is lightweight, durable and simple to portion out, making it an excellent item for trade. **Just a few small tubes can be worth their weight in food,** especially if someone is in the middle of a repair job they can't finish.

Then there is the sewing kit, a survival classic... In colder climates, where frostbite or hypothermia is a threat, having intact clothing could mean the difference between survival and disaster.

All three of these items are also ideal for barter. They are compact, easy to carry, and can be broken down into smaller trade bundles. Even a mini sewing kit with just a few needles, a coil of thread and a pair of small scissors has enormous value to someone trying to keep their clothing functional. The same goes for a couple of strips of duct tape or a single-use tube of glue. These are low-cost investments that turn into high-value trades when systems break down.

Perhaps most importantly, these items represent more than their physical function. They symbolize control, resilience and the power to hold things together when everything else is falling apart. The person who shows up able to repair what others cannot is not just useful, they are indispensable.

Fishing Gear

When food becomes scarce and supply chains grind to a halt, few tools are as valuable as fishing gear. **A single hook and line can feed a person for weeks,** and those who know how to use them can survive almost anywhere. In a barter-based world, where every meal counts, fishing becomes a form of currency.

Hooks, sinkers, and monofilament line take up very little space but carry immense practical weight. I've seen small kits with just a handful of tackle items traded for entire bags of dried goods. Why? Because **fishing is one of the few renewable food sources left when everything else falls apart.** Lakes, rivers, streams and even small ponds become lifelines when the grid is gone and supermarket shelves are stripped clean. While some might focus on fancy rods or reels, the real trade value lies in simplicity. **Handlines, trotlines, and compact survival kits** that can be carried in a backpack or glove box are the items people will want most. They're easy to use, hard to break, and deadly effective. A sealed pouch with assorted hooks, lines of different strengths, and a few lead weights can be traded, gifted or used to secure goodwill from someone in need. **The barter value rises even higher when paired with knowledge.** If you know how to catch fish in different environments, how to identify edible species, or how to preserve the meat without refrigeration, you're not just a survivor, you're a resource. **People will trade almost anything for a steady source of protein, especially one that doesn't rely on bullets or fuel.**

Fishing also keeps you quiet. Unlike hunting, it doesn't attract attention. It's sustainable, low-risk, and perfect for those who prefer to avoid conflict. If **you can salt or smoke your catch, you can build a reserve,** create trade bundles, or feed a small group during lean times. When the world shifts from convenience to necessity, food production becomes power. And the ability to fish, even with just a hook and a line, can make you one of the most valuable people in your community. Not because you have more, but because you can provide what others can't.

Silver and Gold

When everything else collapses, currencies, banks, systems, **precious metals still hold.** Their value does not rely on governments, electricity, or digital networks. Silver and gold have been exchanged between strangers for centuries, across borders and cultures, without needing explanation. Their weight, shine, and purity speak for themselves.

Silver is the most practical of the two. It is affordable enough to trade in small amounts but still holds weight in serious exchanges. In the aftermath of a financial collapse, when the dollar is no longer trusted and paper money has lost its meaning, silver becomes a universal language. **A single silver coin can pay for food, fuel, tools or labor.** You do not need a banking system to verify its value, you only need a scale and a good eye.

Coins minted before 1965 in the United States, dimes, quarters and half-dollars, contain ninety percent silver. These are known as junk silver, but don't let the name fool you. Their standardized size and composition make them easily recognizable, even by people who have never collected coins.

Because they were once common in daily circulation, they inspire trust. You can hand one over in a trade and be understood without saying a word. Then there are **bullion coins**. These are **high-purity silver coins like the American Silver Eagle, the Canadian Maple Leaf or the Austrian Philharmonic. Their .999 purity** makes them attractive for larger exchanges, especially when you need to buy in bulk.

They are not ideal for everyday barter, though, because you can't divide them easily. If someone needs fuel or antibiotics, they may not have change for a one-ounce coin.

Gold is different. Its value is dense. At over two thousand dollars per ounce, **a single gold coin can be worth more than a month of supplies.** That makes it powerful, but also problematic. **You are unlikely to buy bread or batteries with gold.**

You will use it to make big moves, to secure land, weapons, or high risk favors. **It is a form of stored authority, not daily currency.** Small gold coins, like those that weigh one-tenth or one-quarter of an ounce, do have niche uses. But they come with downsides. Premiums are high.

Fakes are common. And unless the person you're trading with has the right tools, you will spend too much time proving what your coin is worth. Trust matters, and in the gold world, trust is often thin. That is why your tools are just as important as your metals.

At a minimum, you need a precision scale that reads to the hundredth of a gram, a rare-earth magnet to test for plated tungsten, calipers to check dimensions, and a basic acid test kit. These items are cheap and easy to carry. Without them, you are guessing, and guessing leads to bad trades or worse.

You also need to think carefully about storage. A fireproof safe is a good start, but it should not be your only method. If you put everything in one place, you could lose it all at once.

Split your metals between your home and hidden remote caches, buried tubes, sealed containers in secure locations, or even concealed compartments in places you control. Keep your coins in non-reactive holders and avoid storage methods that could damage their surfaces.

Never write the word "silver" or "gold" on anything visible obviously.

Discretion is key. When you trade, never show your full stash. Letting someone know how much you truly have makes you a target. It turns a fair trade into a one-time opportunity, and not always on your terms. Keep it lean. Show only what you're willing to part with.

So what can you expect in real terms? In hard times, a single silver dime can buy basic food or small essentials. **A full ounce of silver might cover a few days of meals, basic repairs, or even medical services.**

Gold, though, is less about trade and more about transformation. It's the key to things that fiat money can no longer unlock: property, loyalty, safety, and control. In a world where trust is scarce and systems are broken, those with silver can live comfortably. But those with gold can shape what comes next.

When everything else breaks down, your survival depends not only on what you have, but on what you can offer others. In a world without banks, digital wallets, or official currency, value becomes real again. It becomes tangible and visible. It becomes useful. And the items you choose to store today can make the difference between barely scraping by and having influence, leverage, and options.

REFERENCES

President John F. Kennedy's Address to the Economic Club of New York on December 14, 1962

History https://www.history.com/topics/1960s/great-society

https://aier.org/article/how-the-west-won-the-money-race/

U.S. Treasury Deparment

https://fiscal.treasury.gov/reports-statements/financial-report/current-report.html

https://reason.org/commentary/the-true-depths-of-the-us-debt-crisis/

https://corporatefinanceinstitute.com/resources/career-map/sell-side/capital-markets/lehman-brothers/

https://www.history.com/this-day-in-history/bear-stearns-sold-to-j-p-morgan-chase

https://www.gao.gov/products/gao-24-107175

https://www.moodys.com/web/en/us/insights/resources/going-down-the-debt-limit-rabbit-hole.pdf

American Red Cross. (2023). Emergency preparedness checklist. https://www.redcross.org

Federal Emergency Management Agency (FEMA). (2020). Food and water in an emergency. U.S. Department of Homeland Security. https://www.fema.gov

Kunstler, J. H. (2005). The long emergency: Surviving the end of oil, climate change, and other converging catastrophes of the twenty-first century. Grove Press.

Lundin, C. (2007). When All Hell Breaks Loose: Stuff You Need to Survive When Disaster Strikes. Gibbs Smith.

National Center for Home Food Preservation. (2021). Recommended food storage guidelines. University of Georgia. https://nchfp.uga.edu

Nyerges, C. (2006). How to survive anywhere: A guide to urban, suburban, rural, and wilderness environments. Stackpole Books.

Preparedness Advice. (2021). How long does emergency food last? Shelf life guide for preppers. https://www.preparednessadvice.com

Rawles, J. W. (2009). How to survive the end of the world as we know it: Tactics, techniques, and technologies for uncertain times. Plume.

Ruppert, M. C. (2004). Crossing the Rubicon: The decline of the American empire at the end of the age of oil. New Society Publishers.

United Nations Food and Agriculture Organization (FAO). (2022). The state of food security and nutrition in the world 2022. https://www.fao.org

U.S. Department of Agriculture (USDA). (2024). Food storage and safety guidelines. https://www.fsis.usda.gov

Wells, D. (2016). Prepper's long-term survival guide: Food, shelter, security, off-the-grid power, and more life-saving strategies for self-sufficient living. Ulysses Press.

Chancellor, E. (2000). Devil take the hindmost: A history of financial speculation. Plume.

Lewis, M. (2010). The big short: Inside the doomsday machine. W. W. Norton & Company.

Mauboussin, M. J. (2007). More than you know: Finding financial wisdom in unconventional places. Columbia Business School Publishing.

Taleb, N. N. (2007). The black swan: The impact of the highly improbable. Random House.

Zweig, J. (2007). Your money and your brain: How the new science of neuroeconomics can help make you rich. Simon & Schuster.

Bloomberg Markets. (2021, February). GameStop and the Reddit revolution: A modern short squeeze. https://www.bloomberg.com

Financial Times. (2025, March). Default rates soar in BNPL market. https://www.ft.com

Reuters. (2025, January). Affirm, Klarna slash staff as fintech sector cools. https://www.reuters.com

The Economist. (2023, November). Zombie firms thrive on low rates. https://www.economist.com

Wall Street Journal. (2025, April). The 2025 tariff shock: Timeline and impact. https://www.wsj.com

Federal Reserve Bank of St. Louis (FRED). (n.d.). Federal Reserve Economic Data. https://fred.stlouisfed.org

U.S. Bureau of Economic Analysis. (n.d.). https://www.bea.gov

U.S. Securities and Exchange Commission. (n.d.). EDGAR Company Filings. https://www.sec.gov/edgar.shtml

ETF.com. (n.d.). ETF screener and database. https://www.etf.com

Finviz. (n.d.). Financial visualizations and stock screener. https://www.finviz.com

IG Group. (n.d.). https://www.ig.com

Morningstar. (n.d.). Investment research. https://www.morningstar.com

TradingView. (n.d.). Charts, screening, and social trading. https://www.tradingview.com

Wise. (n.d.). https://wise.com

Revolut. (n.d.). https://www.revolut.com

eToro. (n.d.). https://www.etoro.com

CMC Markets. (n.d.). https://www.cmcmarkets.com

MacroVoices. (n.d.). https://www.macrovoices.com

Real Vision. (n.d.). https://www.realvision.com

The Market Sniper. (n.d.). https://themarketsniper.com

Ferfal, F. A. (2009). The modern survival manual: Surviving the economic collapse. Fernando "Ferfal" Aguirre.

Rawles, J. W. (2009). How to survive the end of the world as we know it: Tactics, techniques and technologies for uncertain times. Plume.

Toby, J. (2012). Neighborhood watch: Early warning and defense for your home. Tactical Publishing.

Nyquist, J. R. (2001). Origins of the Fourth World War. Westerfield Press.

Selco Begovic. (2018). The Dark Secrets of SHTF Survival: What You Have to Do to Survive When SHTF. SHTF School.

Scott, R. (2016). Prepper's communication handbook: Lifesaving strategies for staying in contact during and after a disaster. Ulysses Press.

Lamb, R. (2013). Survival psychology: The mental side of prepping. Survivalist Books.

Machiavelli, N. (1532). The Prince.

Sullivan, B. (2015). Grid down: Death of a nation. Self-published.

United Nations Office on Drugs and Crime. (2021). Global study on homicide. https://www.unodc.org

World Bank. (2016). Societal resilience and fragility: Lessons from international responses to economic collapse. https://www.worldbank.org

Peterson Field Guide to Edible Wild Plants by Lee Allen Peterson (Houghton Mifflin Harcourt, 1977)

Forager's Harvest: A Guide to Identifying, Harvesting, and Preparing Edible Wild Plants by Samuel Thayer (Forager's Harvest Press, 2006)

Nature's Garden: A Guide to Identifying, Harvesting, and Preparing Edible Wild Plants by Samuel Thayer (Forager's Harvest Press, 2010)

Northeast Foraging: 120 Wild and Flavorful Edibles from Beach Plums to Wineberries by Leda Meredith (Timber Press, 2014)

Edible Wild Plants: Wild Foods from Dirt to Plate by John Kallas, PhD (Gibbs Smith, 2010)

Medicinal Plants of the Pacific West by Michael Moore (Red Crane Books, 1993)

The Wild Wisdom of Weeds: 13 Essential Plants for Human Survival by Katrina Blair (Chelsea Green Publishing, 2014)

Peterson Field Guide to Mushrooms of North America by Kent H. McKnight and Vera B. McKnight (Houghton Mifflin Harcourt, 1998)

Mushrooms Demystified by David Arora (Ten Speed Press, 1986)

All That the Rain Promises and More: A Hip Pocket Guide to Western Mushrooms by David Arora (Ten Speed Press, 1991)

The Complete Medicinal Herbal by Penelope Ody (DK Publishing, 1993)

Field Guide to Medicinal Wild Plants by Bradford Angier (Stackpole Books, 1978)

USDA Natural Resources Conservation Service PLANTS Database (https://plants.usda.gov)

iNaturalist Species Observations & Distribution Maps (https://www.inaturalist.org)

eFloras.org – Flora of North America (Missouri Botanical Garden, Harvard University Herbaria)

United States Forest Service: Edible and Medicinal Plant Publications (https://www.fs.usda.gov)

University of Maine Cooperative Extension Foraging Guides (https://extension.umaine.edu)

Missouri Department of Conservation: Wild Edibles and Mushrooms Identification (https://mdc.mo.gov)

Purdue University Center for New Crops and Plant Products (https://hort.purdue.edu/newcrop)

Other Books Published by Global Brother

You May Also Like Our Best Survival Books

The Lost Ways Hardcover Edition

The Lost Ways Vol. I and II

The Lost Ways Collection

The crisis we all prep for is what folks 150 years ago called daily life... no electrical power, refrigerators, internet, computers, TV, law enforcement, and of course, no Safeway or Walmart.

But they got things done, or else we wouldn't be here!

The Lost Ways is written by expert survivalist **Claude Davis**, and it prepares you to deal with worst-case scenarios using minimum resources just like our forefathers.

It shows you how to become totally independent from electricity, cars, and every other modern technology... effectively bulletproofing you against an EMP, an economic collapse, famines, and natural disasters.

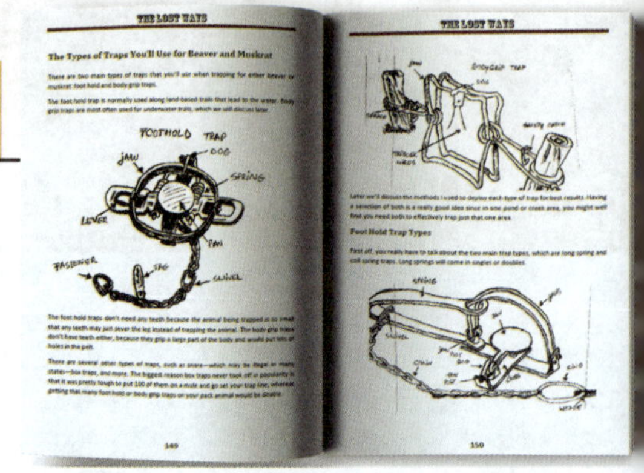

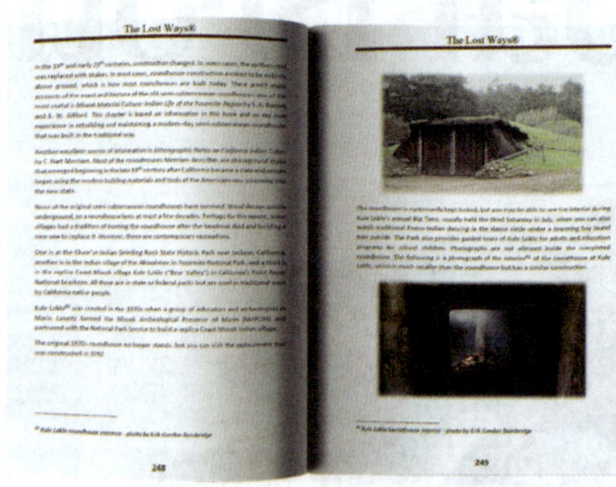

With 432 pages packed with color photos and easy-to-follow instructions, this is the kind of book you'll always want to keep on your bookshelf, in your car, or in your bug-out bag. The DIY projects in this book range from little tweaks you can apply to your home in minutes to more complex ones like making the ultimate survival food with a 20 years shelf-life, a poor man's smokehouse, a hidden well, a rainwater collection and filtration system, backyard looter traps, and so much more...

Inside, you'll also discover how to make the 26 superfoods we lost to history, the most powerful medicinal plants of our forefathers, how the wise sheriffs of the frontier defended their villages when they were outnumbered and outgunned, the lost survival skills you'll need in a crisis, and a whole lot more to help you protect yourself and your family after modern society collapses.

A Navy SEAL's Bug-In Guide

Inside **A Navy SEAL's Bug-In Guide**, former SEAL **Joel Lambert** reveals everything you need to turn your house into the safest place on Earth.

This book will help you survive almost any disaster in your own house, including the most severe ones, like an EMP, civil war, or a full-blown economic collapse.

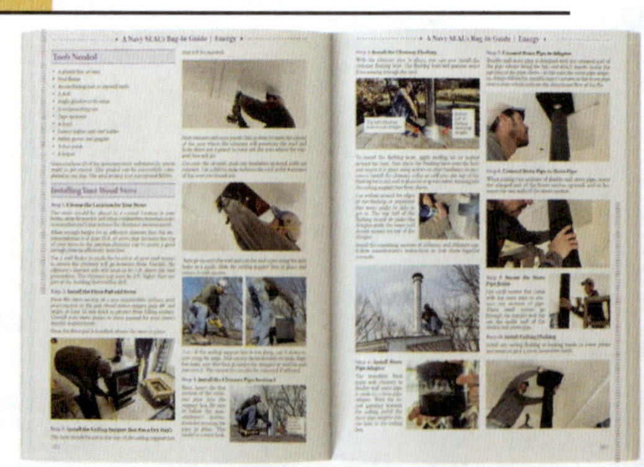

Inside, you'll discover how to build a long-lasting stockpile that doesn't need refrigeration and where to buy these foods so they're as affordable as possible. You'll also find out how to secure a reliable source of clean drinking water even if the tap runs dry.

One of the most important steps to prepare for the coming crisis, whatever it will be, is to become more self-sufficient.

And that's why Joel also shares the skills and projects you need to survive with no outside help. I'm talking about things like growing and preserving your own food, gathering rainwater, making powerful natural remedies, and many others. You'll also discover everything else a SEAL knows about bugging in and protecting your home against looters and other intruders.

With these simple methods revealed maybe for the first time inside the book your home becomes an almost invisible shelter, safe from looters, rioters, or unwelcome government officials.

Wilderness Long-Term Survival Guide

Wilderness Long-Term Survival Guide is the first survival guide that helps you NOT just survive in the wild but turn it into your second home!

The author, **Dr. Nicole Apelian**, lasted 57 days straight on the *Alone* Show, despite having MS, using little more than her knife and skills.

You'll get detailed step-by-step instructions, high-resolution photos, and illustrations... everything you need to thrive in any wild environment indefinitely.

This book is not about surviving a short mountain hike. It's about long-term survival. It'll give you peace of mind that no matter what happens around you, you can always seek safety in the wilderness.

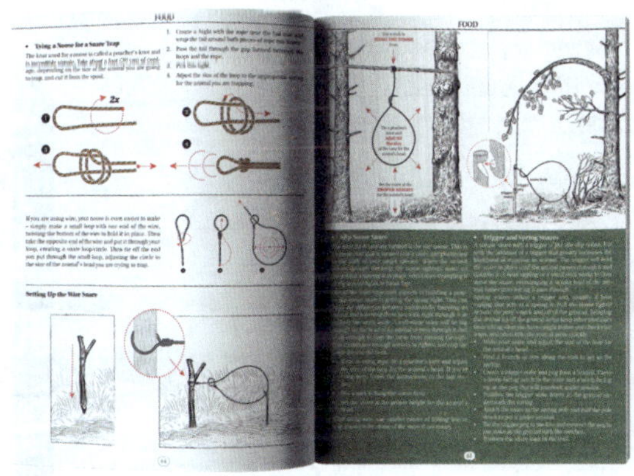

The Lost Super Foods

Inside **The Lost Super Foods**, you'll discover over 126 long-lasting survival foods and forgotten preservation methods that kept our ancestors alive even in the darkest of times.

Their long-forgotten recipes were unearthed by **Claude Davis**, a Wild-West history expert and life-long survivalist.

These super foods do not require refrigeration to stay edible for months and sometimes many years.

You'll also find out how to feed yourself for a whole month using just $100 at Walmart, the wild superfoods that almost nobody knows about, the ins and out of canning both vegetables and meat safely for 20 years, how to make a doomsday ration, the great depression food that saved America or how to get 295 Pounds of Extra Food for just $5 a Week, just to name a few.

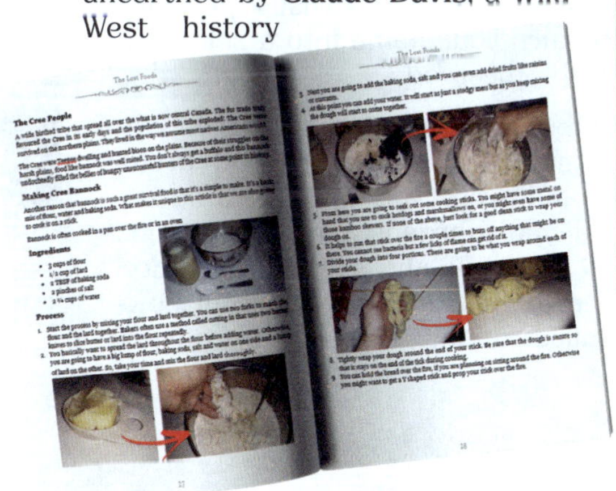

You Can Also Check Out Our Best DIY Books

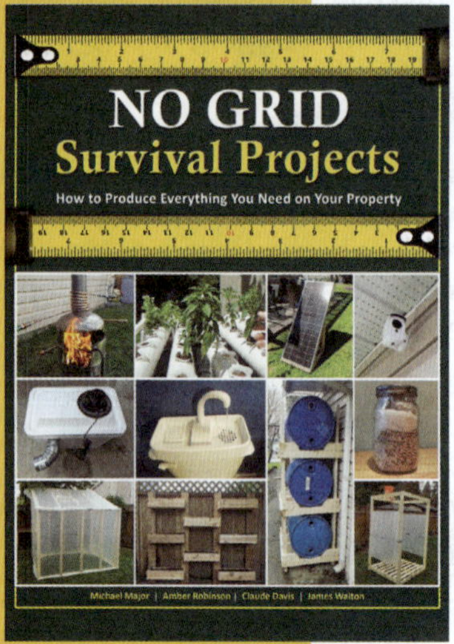

No Grid Survival Projects

No Grid Survival Projects is the only book you really need to survive a world without electricity.

It was written by **Michael Major**, a veteran, survivalist, and self-taught DIY-er who once worked for Boeing designing aircraft parts.

Michael has decades of practical experience designing and building projects.

Inside the book, you'll discover 70+ ingenious no-grid projects that will make you self-sufficient on your own property. There are 302 full-color pages packed with step-by-step instructions for building the projects, detailed photos, a material list, and up to date information on where to get them as cheap as possible. It doesn't matter if you are a man or a woman, young or old, it's never too late or too soon to start being more self-sufficient, more prepared, and saving some money.

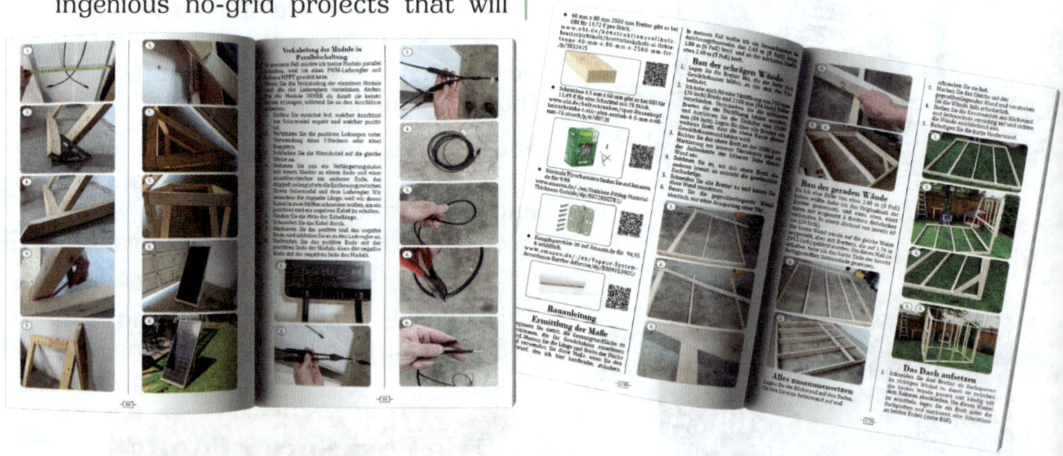

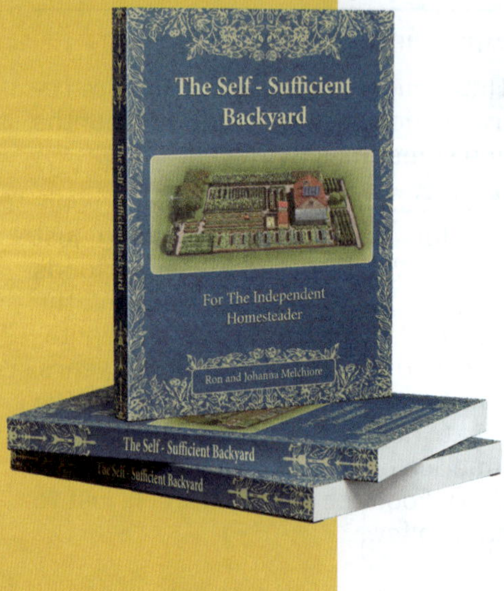

The Self-Sufficient Backyard

The Self-Sufficient Backyard is written by **Ron Melchiore**, an independent homesteader who's been living off the grid with his wife for over 40 years. And this book is your chance to take advantage of all that vast experience and turn your home into a self-sufficient homestead.

Inside the book, Ron covers in detail subjects like water, food growing and preservation, off-grid power, medicinal gardens, raising chickens and livestock...and a whole lot more. Everything comes with helpful how-to illustrations, step-by-step advice, brilliant tips, and time-savers. You will surely be able to put this wisdom to good use on your own property.

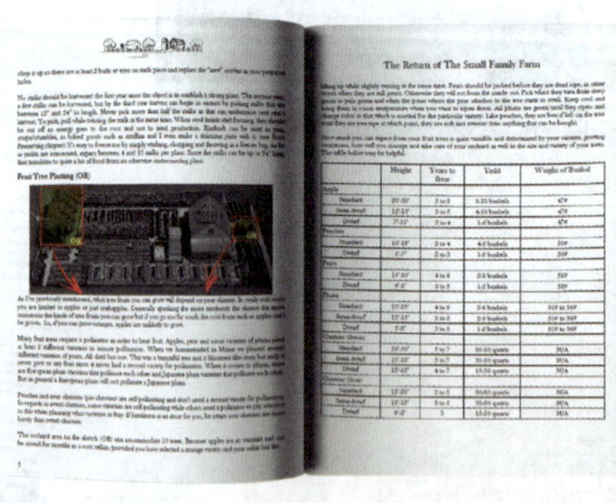

Discover Our Best Plants and Remedies Books

Forgotten Home Apothecary

Forgotten Home Apothecary gives you a 250-remedy Apothecary right in your own home, ready to help you whenever you're in need. The author, **Dr. Nicole Apelian**, has poured a lifetime of medicinal plant knowledge and first-hand experience making her own poultices, tinctures, decoctions, salves, syrups, infused oils, and other potent herbal remedies.

The first thing you'll see when you open the book is your new Apothecary, where you'll find all 250 remedies, organized on shelves by specific ailments.

This book has 288 color pages with step-by-step instructions, color photos, accurate measurements, and dosages.

Whether you're an experienced herbalist or just looking for a more natural approach to healthcare, this book is for you. It's the only one where you'll find the time-tested remedies our grandparents relied on when the corner apothecary hadn't yet been replaced by a pharmacy chain.

The remedy you've been looking for all along could be waiting for you in **Forgotten Home Apothecary.**

The Lost Book of Herbal Remedies

The Lost Book of Herbal Remedies is the ultimate guide to plant medicine, and it has already helped hundreds of thousands worldwide.

It is written by **Dr. Nicole Apelian**, an herbalist with over 30 years of experience, and Claude Davis, a history expert deeply passionate about the natural remedies that kept previous generations alive.

There are 304 color pages featuring over 800 plants and remedies for every part of your body. Each plant comes with multiple high-quality color pictures, where it grows, and detailed foraging instructions.

You also get an easy-to-navigate dual index. Search by the specific plant or by health condition.

This book goes against the grain of mainstream medicine and avoids just dealing with symptoms. Instead, it targets the underlying cause and strengthens your body's natural ability to repair itself using the power of plant medicine.

The Lost Book of Herbal Remedies 2

This is the long-awaited sequel to the best-selling natural remedies book **The Lost Book of Herbal Remedies.**

It is written by **Dr. Nicole Apelian**, an herbalist with over 30 years of "hands on" experience foraging wild plants and making her own medicine from them.

Inside **The Lost Book of Herbal Remedies II,** you'll discover 139 all-new medicinal plants and over 207 powerful natural remedies that are not in the first book.

The Holistic Guide to Wellness

Inside **The Holistic Guide to Wellness**, written by **Dr. Nicole Apelian,** you'll discover 45 detailed health protocols for 45 different conditions.

Each protocol gives you ALL the herbal remedies, healing foods, detoxes, and other alternative practices you can use to get better.

You even get a complete chart of each protocol that outlines everything you need to do and take... morning, afternoon, and before bed... to help attack the root cause of your health condition from every angle!

The all-natural protocols inside cover every part of your body and most conditions including... autoimmunity, pain management, multiple sclerosis,

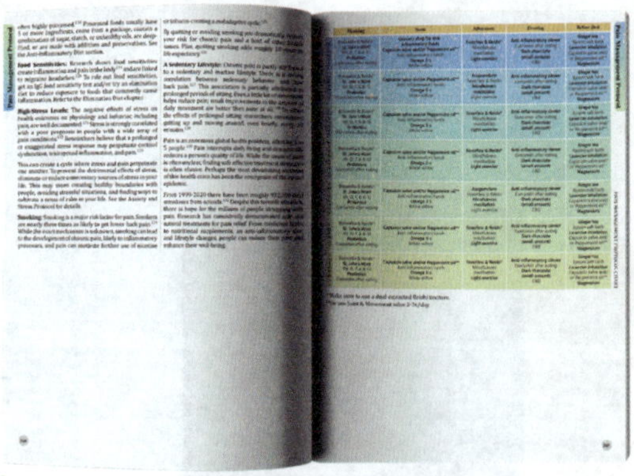

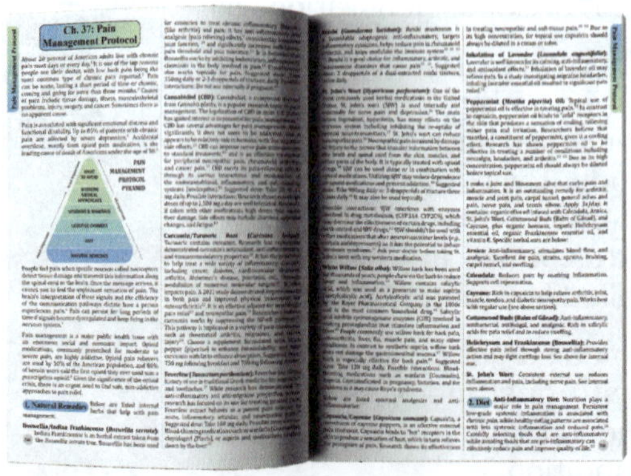

psoriasis, eczema, arthritis, anxiety, stress, allergies, food poisoning, acid reflux, inflammatory bowel disease, Crohn's disease, ulcerative colitis, leaky gut, gastritis, IBS, liver health, adrenal fatigue, type 2 diabetes, thyroid, bacterial infection, flu, viral, immune system, fungal infections, candida, asthma, sinusitis, Lyme disease, parasites, Alzheimer's, heart health, brain and nerve, depression, vertigo, tinnitus, menopause, ulcer, men's sexual health, prostate, fertility, endometriosis, uterine fibroid, osteoporosis, lupus, acne, kidney, anti-aging, anemia, hair loss, hemorrhoids, lungs, COPD, sleep, weight loss, and Parkinson's.

The book has 316 color pages break

down all 45 protocols into clear-cut, easy-to-follow directions.

Our bodies have an incredible ability to repair damage and restore themselves when they're put in a healing state. Don't underestimate this power. Your body's healing mechanism can prove more effective than any drug.

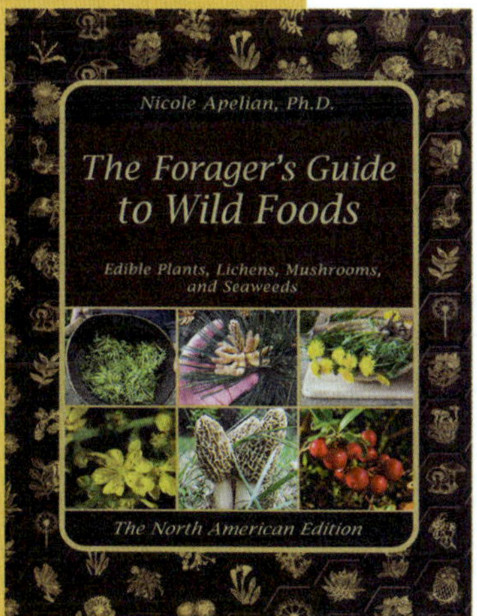

The Forager's Guide to Wild Foods

Ever wondered which of the plants you pass by every day is edible or not?

The Forager's Guide to Wild Foods gives you the answer.

It's written by **Dr. Nicole Apelian**, an expert herbalist and forager. With this book in your hands, you get access to an endless food supply that Nature generously grows for free.

It's printed in color with HUGE pictures for each plant. There are also detailed photos of the defining features, so you know exactly what to look for. And you also get a distribution map to search only for plants growing in your area.

Because many edible plants also have medicinal properties, there's a section on how to use it as a remedy. And, of course, a few delicious recipes to prepare these wild foods like a seasoned forager.

NOTES

NOTES

NOTES

NOTES

NOTES